Y0-BVN-652

SOCIOLOGY IN CENTRAL AND EASTERN EUROPE

Recent Titles in Contributions in Sociology

Stalking the Sociological Imagination: J. Edgar Hoover's FBI Surveillance of American Sociology
Mike Forrest Keen

Korean Immigrants and the Challenge of Adjustment
Moon H. Jo

Citizenship and Ethnicity: The Growth and Development of a Democratic Multiethnic Institution
Feliks Gross

Making a Life in Yorkville: Experience and Meaning in the Life-Course Narrative of an Urban Working-Class Man
Gerald Handel

Movies, Masculinity, and Modernity: An Ethnography of Men's Filmgoing in India
Steve Derné

Ideology and the Social Sciences
Graham C. Kinloch and Raj P. Mohan, editors

Sociocybernetics: Complexity, Autopoiesis, and Observation of Social Systems
Felix Geyer and Johannes van der Zouwen, editors

Voluntary Action and NGOs: A Cross-Sectional Study of NGOs in India
Radhamonyamma Sooryamoorthy and Kesharichand Dasharathasa Gangrade

Exchange, Action, and Social Structure: Elements of Economic Sociology
Milan Zafirovski

The Chinese Triangle of Mainland China, Taiwan, and Hong Kong: Comparative Institutional Analyses
Alvin Y. So, Nan Lin, and Dudley Poston, editors

International Perspectives on Homelessness
Valerie Polakow and Cindy Guillean, editors

Al-Anon Narratives: Women, Self-Stories, and Mutual Aid
Grazyna Zajdow

HM
578
·E82
S63
2003
West

SOCIOLOGY IN CENTRAL AND EASTERN EUROPE

Transformation at the Dawn of a New Millennium

Edited by Mike Forrest Keen and Janusz L. Mucha

Contributions in Sociology, Number 139

Westport, Connecticut
London

Library of Congress Cataloging-in-Publication Data

Sociology in Central and Eastern Europe : transformation at the dawn of a new millennium / edited by Mike Forrest Keen and Janusz L. Mucha.
  p. cm. (Contributions in sociology, ISSN 0084–9278 ; no. 139)
Includes bibliographical references and index.
ISBN 0–313–31802–6 (alk. paper)
1. Sociology—Study and teaching—Europe, Eastern. 2. Sociology—Study and teaching—Europe, Central. 3. Sociology—Europe, Eastern—History.
4. Sociology—Europe, Central—History. I. Keen, Mike Forrest.
II. Mucha, Janusz. III. Series.
HM578.E82 S63   2003
301′.071′047—dc21   2002193042

British Library Cataloguing in Publication Data is available.

Copyright © 2003 by Mike Forrest Keen and Janusz L. Mucha

All rights reserved. No portion of this book may be reproduced, by any process or technique, without the express written consent of the publisher.

Library of Congress Catalog Card Number: 2002193042
ISBN: 0–313–31802–6
ISSN: 0084–9278

First published in 2003

Praeger Publishers, 88 Post Road West, Westport, CT 06881
An imprint of Greenwood Publishing Group, Inc.
www.praeger.com

Printed in the United States of America

The paper used in this book complies with the Permanent Paper Standard issued by the National Information Standards Organization (Z39.48–1984).

10 9 8 7 6 5 4 3 2 1

*To the sociologists of Central and Eastern Europe for courage
in times past and present*

Contents

Preface   ix

1. Central and Eastern Europe and Its Sociology at the Beginning
   of the Post-Communist Era   1
   Mike Forrest Keen and Janusz L. Mucha

2. Unhandy Sociology: The Case of Belarus   19
   Wanda Rusetskaya and Olga Tereschenko

3. Bulgarian Sociology: Lights and Shadows at the Dawn of the
   21st Century   29
   Vyara Gancheva

4. Croatian Sociology after 1990: Toward New Institutionalization?   41
   Ognjen Caldarovic

5. Sociology in the Czech Republic after 1989   49
   Miloslav Petrusek

6. Estonian Sociology of the 1990s: In Search of an Identity   61
   Mikko Lagerspetz and Iris Pettai

7. More Evolution than Revolution: Sociology in Hungary,
   1990–2000   73
   Denes Nemedi and Peter Robert

8. Sociology in Latvia after 1990   87
   Aivars Tabuns

9. Lithuanian Sociology, 1990–2000   97
   Anele Vosyliute

10. Macedonian Sociology in the 1990s: Between the Old
    Conceptions and New Challenges   107
    Petre Georgievski and Mileva Gurovska

11. Polish Sociology, 1990–2000: Society after a
    Breakthrough, Sociology in Evolution   117
    Janusz L. Mucha

12. Sociology in Romania since 1989   133
    Ilie Badescu and Radu Baltasiu

13. The Return of Russian Sociology   141
    Valery Mansurov and Mikhail Chernysh

14. In Search of Its Own Identity: A Decade of Slovak Sociology   153
    Bohumil Buzik and Eva Laiferova

15. Sociology in Slovenia: The Challenge of Transition   165
    Franc Mali

16. Sociology in Ukraine, 1990–2000: A Decade of Firsts   175
    Nataliya Pohorila

17. Sociology without Society?: Yugolav Sociology after 1990   187
    Karel Turza

    References   199

    Index   235

    About the Editors and Contributors   251

Preface

This is the second book in what we hope will eventually be a trilogy chronicling the history of sociology in Central and Eastern Europe during the period leading up to and immediately following the great transformation symbolized most powerfully and poignantly, in 1989, first by the political debate at the Round Table in Warsaw, and then by the staccato of jackhammers dismantling the Berlin Wall, as if dancing to the beat of the rock music blaring in the background. As with our first book, *Eastern Europe in Transformation: The Impact on Sociology* (Greenwood, 1994), this book is as much a part of this history as it is an account of it.

For example, in our first book, recruiting and communicating with our contributors was a slow and often arduous process. Email and the Internet were in their infancy and few scholars in the region had access. We still remember quite vividly our own wonder at the ability to communicate back and forth without the necessity of an expensive long distance call, or the wait for a letter or package to cross the ocean. Sometimes, when we were both at our computers at the same time, much to our amazement, we were almost in conversation with one another. Today, this regular and virtually instantaneous communication has become old hat, and like us, all of our contributors take their access to the Internet for granted. As a result, the logistical nightmare of exchanging and editing drafts that plagued our collaborative efforts in our first book was no longer an issue. The biggest challenge we faced with this book was editing each of the chapters without significantly altering or misrepresenting the intent of their authors.

Since our first book, Central and Eastern Europe has continued its devolution. When we began the first book, there were only nine countries, now there are twenty and more may be on the horizon. Sociology has been freed from the ideological restrictions and orthodoxy under which it had previously labored, and independent sociological associations now exist in every country. For our last book, we recruited our contributors in a largely idiosyncratic manner, primarily on the basis of accessibility and our own happenstance networks of contacts. This time, we were able to contact the Presidents of each national sociological association and request recommendations of scholars who had backgrounds in the history of sociology, and who were often already doing research into the history of sociology in their own countries. While we have been able to include sixteen countries in this project, because of communication problems due to social and political upheaval, we were unable to recruit contributors from Albania, Moldova, and those Caucasus countries that are culturally European, Armenia and Georgia.

In our previous book, we noted the influence the orthodoxy of Marxism-Leninism still exerted on Central and Eastern European social scientific discourse. One of the more remarkable developments that have occurred during the last decade has been how quickly this has almost completely evaporated, with little or no formal "decommunization," in most of the nations of the region. This gives further credence to one of the conclusions of our earlier project, that during the period of Communist domination, many, if not most, Central and Eastern European sociologists found ways to maintain a significant intellectual independence and to continue to conduct good sociology throughout the duration. That tradition appears to have blossomed with the new openness afforded by the transformation, as evidenced by the very robust body of sociological research identified and discussed in this volume. During the last decade, Central and Eastern European sociologists, even though often beset by severe economic hardship, and in some cases devastating social upheaval, including war, have courageously struggled to pass the sociological imagination on to new generations of scholars, and to apply it to the most pressing problems facing their societies in the midst of unprecedented transformation.

As with our previous project, this work was made possible by the generous support and assistance of several institutions. Research for this book was supported by a grant from the International Research & Exchange Board (IREX), with funds provided by the U.S. Department of State (Title VIII program) and the National Endowment for the Humanities. Grants from Nicolas Copernicus University allowed us to bring our contributors together in Torun, Poland, for a working conference at the beginning of the project. An Indiana University South Bend (IUSB) Research and Development Grant supported Professor Keen's work on the project. Finally, a Council for International Exchange of Scholars Fulbright Scholar-in-Residence Award allowed Professor Mucha to join Professor Keen at IUSB for final completion of the manuscript. None of these organizations is responsible for the views expressed herein.

Once again, our greatest thanks must go to our Central and Eastern European colleagues for the generous contribution of their time and efforts to this project. We regret we were unable to offer them any significant compensation for their efforts. As is the case with scholars across the region, many must hold two, and sometimes even more positions, just to get by. It sometimes boggles the imagination as to how they are able to continue to carry on their scholarly efforts in the face of such circumstances. World sociology owes them and their colleagues a special admiration and gratitude for the heroic example they set for all of us.

Mike Forrest Keen
Janusz L. Mucha

1

Central and Eastern Europe and Its Sociology at the Beginning of the Post-Communist Era

Mike Forrest Keen and Janusz L. Mucha

With the collapse of the Soviet Union, the independence of Central and Eastern Europe, and the disappearance of the great polarity that separated East and West, the climate for sociology has changed radically. Throughout the region sociologists find themselves with a new independence, free of the ideological and intellectual restrictions that had been imposed by state and Party authorities. In the post-Communist era, sociology has begun to take on a new role, helping to understand the transformations that have occurred, as well as to facilitate the social change they have brought. As a result, sociology in Central and Eastern Europe has found itself facing a whole series of new challenges, many of which it shares with its sociological counterparts throughout the world.

A RECENT HISTORY OF CENTRAL AND EASTERN EUROPE

Though beyond the scope of this present work, it is not possible to fully understand the sociology of the nations of Central and Eastern Europe without at least some appreciation of their history (Keen and Mucha 1994a, 1–2). This includes careful attention to the differences between the disparate paths of economic, political, and cultural development in Western Europe and Central and Eastern Europe, from the late Middle Ages to the decline of Communism (for such detailed historical analyses of the region, see, e.g., Davies 1996; Johnson 2000). These different paths of development contributed to the specific economic, political, and cultural structure of Central and Eastern European societies, and to a sociology that emerged out of a synthesis of philosophical and scholarly influences from the West as well as the particularities of the local social situation.

Toward the end of the 1980s, societies of Central and Eastern Europe began the most recent chapter in their history, the uncertain and complex transformation from predominantly centralized planning and management economies to a form of market economies, from Communist dictatorship to democracy, from a general subordination to the Soviet Union to political sovereignty. After more than ten years of the post-Communist transformation, many Central and Eastern European countries appear to have established stable democratic political systems, relatively steady and high levels of economic growth, and a realistic chance to become members of the European Union. Others, however, continue to face serious (catastrophic in the case of the former Yugoslavia), social, political, and economic problems.

Several common characteristics of the current situation are exerting a regional and external influence on the internal transformations each nation is experiencing. First and foremost, the new geopolitical situation of the region is very important. Several new nation-states emerged in the aftermath of the dissolution of the Soviet Union, the former Yugoslav Federation, and Czechoslovakia. And, it is not clear that this process of national devolution is finished. While most of the new nation-states celebrate their sovereignty with great pride, for many this independence, having no or nearly no precedence in history, has not been entirely welcome. For example, in Belarus a large part of the political elite, as well as much of the general population, particularly in the rural areas of this predominantly agricultural country, are very much Russified. They support President Alexander Lukashenko's intention to unify the country with Russia, and several common institutions have already been established. Another example is the Ukraine, where ethnic Russians constitute about 22 percent of the country's population. While the Ukrainian political elite is proud of the country's sovereignty, in the eastern, Russian-speaking part of the nation, popular sentiment maintained a preference to belong to the Russian Federation, at least until the financial crisis in Russia in the late 1990s.

As in the case of the Ukraine, many of the other newly independent successor nations to the Soviet Union contain relatively large immigrant populations from Russia. For example, ethnic Russians constitute about 13 percent of Moldova's population, 30 percent of Estonia's population, and 34 percent of Latvia's population. Not surprisingly, these concentrations of Russians have had a significant effect on the relations between the successor states and the Russian Federation. And, this problem is not limited to the former Soviet

Union. In the former Yugoslavia, Serbs constitute about 10 percent of Croatia's population, and in some regions nearly 70 percent. Because of past shifts in borders, Hungarians (concentrated in the region of Transylvania) constitute about 7 percent of the population of Romania. Hungarians also make up about 10 percent of the population of Slovakia.

This intermixture and overlapping of ethnicity has not only had an effect on international relations, but has also complicated the attempts to create new senses of national identity and consensus, particularly within the context of newly emerging democratic freedoms and political institutions following the independence and decommunization of 1989. Not surprisingly, this new situation has often resulted in ethnic tensions, conflict, and, occasionally, war.

The nations of Central and Eastern Europe have also been faced with a series of political, economic, social, and cultural problems. As one may have expected, it was a relatively straightforward and quick process to provide for the formal organization of new political parties, to introduce parliamentary and local elections, and to institutionalize them on a more or less regular basis. It has been much more difficult, and will probably take many more years, to establish a post-Communist civil society and to change the mentality of the people, which has been shaped by decades of Communist rule.

More than forty years of Communism devastated the economic infrastructures and slowed economic growth in all Central and Eastern European countries. The Czech region, Croatia, and Slovenia have fared relatively well, thanks to higher stages of economic development already achieved in the first half of the twentieth century, and to a more developed industrial culture. Hungary, which began to transform a socialist economy toward a market direction soon after 1956, is also doing relatively well. Post-Soviet republics that were independent capitalist countries before World War II, such as the Baltic States, are in a better shape than countries such as Belarus, Russia, and the Ukraine, which suffered Communism for seventy years.

Geopolitical problems, as well as difficulties in catching up with Western European stages of economic development, have pushed the Central and Eastern European countries in the direction of the Western security alliance, NATO, and the economic and political arrangements of the European Union. The political elite and most of the populations of the Central and Eastern European countries believe that their transformations will occur much faster within these organizations. Preparations for access to the European Union require an effort to radically transform the economy, legal systems, and ecological practices, as well as the overall mentality.

It is impossible to overestimate the impact that the emergence of so many newly independent nations, realignment in security arrangements and international relations, and fundamental economic restructuring has had in the region. In March 1991, the military structures of the Warsaw Pact were dissolved, and in the following July, the Pact itself ceased to exist. Soviet troops had already begun to withdraw from Czechoslovakia as early as February

1990, from Hungary in March of the same year, and from Poland in September 1993. The last Russian troops left Germany (unified in October 1990) in September 1994. The Soviet-dominated regional economic organization, the Council of Mutual Economic Aid (COMECON), was dissolved in July 1991.

The process of dismemberment of the Soviet Union itself was more complicated and, one could say, had already begun in 1985, when Mikhail Gorbachev was elected the Secretary General of the Communist Party of the Soviet Union. In 1987, Estonians put forward a program for economic independence of their republic. In 1988, "popular fronts" were created in Estonia, then in Latvia and Lithuania. In March 1990, the right-wing, pro-independence electoral block *Sajudis* won the national elections in Lithuania (at that time still a part of the Soviet Union), and shortly thereafter the Lithuanian parliament declared the restoration of the nation's sovereignty. However, this declaration of independence was not recognized by the central Soviet authorities.

Similar processes took place in Latvia. In January 1991, Soviet troops invaded Riga (in Latvia) and Vilnius (in Lithuania), but the two cities and countries were defended by their national militias and ordinary citizens. In August, Lithuania, Estonia, Latvia, the Ukraine, and Belarus (Moldova waited until September) also declared full sovereignty. Lithuania, Latvia, and Estonia were formally recognized by the United Nations in September, after the State Council of the Soviet Union signaled its agreement. In December 1991, the Soviet Union itself ceased to exist.

In the summer of 1992, the Russian Federation signed an agreement with Moldova on the status of the Dniestr river region, inhabited by Russians and Ukrainians. Earlier, in 1991, Chechnya had declared that it was leaving the Russian Federation (at that time still within the Soviet Union), but this secession was never recognized by Russia. The war in this tiny Caucasus republic lasted from the end of 1994 throughout the rest of the decade, and it resulted in thousands of casualties and the complete devastation of Chechnya's economy. The last act of drama in Russia proper, in the 1990s, occurred in October 1993, when the Russian vice president and Russian parliament attempted a short-lived putsch, quickly suppressed by President Boris Yeltsin.

In Czechoslovakia, political debates on division began officially in June 1992. In comparison with other countries of the region, the divorce was really of a velvet character. Since January 1993, there have been two separate nation-states, Czech and Slovak. Both were quickly recognized by the international community and joined the United Nations.

The process of dismemberment of the Yugoslav Federation lasted for the entire decade, and even now it is unclear if it is entirely completed. Beginning in the late 1980s, Slovenian leaders were the first to publicly debate the issue of sovereignty. In February 1990, the Supreme Court of Yugoslavia warned them that any withdrawal from the Federation was against its law. Nevertheless, in July 1990, Slovenia declared independence "within the Federation." The Yugoslav People's Army intervened in the republic in June 1991, following the formal declaration of sovereignty by the Slovenes. The war lasted less than two weeks and was followed by international recognition of Slovenia, along with Croatia, in January 1992.

In May and June 1991, the first armed conflicts occurred between the Serbs and Croats in the then Yugoslav Republic of Croatia. In August, a real war between the Croats and the Serb-dominated Yugoslav army began. The United Nations (UN) sent its troops there (and to Bosnia Herzegovina) in February 1992, but the Yugoslav military offensive continued. Many Croat cities, including the architecturally rich Dalmatian Dubrovnik, were heavily bombed. Despite UN sanctions against Yugoslavia, the war continued with offensives and counteroffensives from both parties until the Dayton Agreement in November 1995. In August 1996, an agreement on the normalization of mutual relations was finally signed between a liberated and fully sovereign Croatia and the new Yugoslav Federation.

In August 1991, Bosnia Herzegovina's leaders declared that they wished to withdraw their republic, an ethnic mixture of Muslims, Roman Catholic Croats, and Eastern Orthodox Serbs, from the Federation. In December, Bosnia Herzegovina announced full sovereignty and requested international recognition. When, at the beginning of 1992, a new small Yugoslav Federation was in the process of creation, there were only two candidates who wanted to become its members: Serbia and tiny Montenegro. This new Federation was eventually formally established in May 1992.

In March 1992, in a referendum, a majority of the Bosnia Herzegovinian population expressed its wish to become an independent state. Yugoslavia intervened and yet another war began. When the first of very many cease-fires was announced in April 1992, about twenty countries recognized Bosnia. The war continued until an agreement, on the normalization of mutual relations between the "new Yugoslavia" and Bosnia Herzegovina, was signed in Paris in 1996. Nonetheless, it would be unrealistic to say that the situation is stable, even with the military and political involvement of the UN and NATO.

Macedonia did not agree to join the new federation of Serbia and Montenegro, but rather announced its independence. This was not recognized immediately by the international community, which seemed to share the conviction of the Greek political leaders that the very term "Macedonia" denotes solely a historic Greek province. Only when the Macedonians, who had no other name for themselves, decided in April 1993 that for the time being they would take as the country's name the term "Former Yugoslav Republic of Macedonia," did the UN Security Council recognize its sovereignty. In December 1993, the European Union recognized the newly independent republic. This led to internal tensions within the Union, and, in 1994, an economic blockade of Macedonia by Greece. In October 1995, Macedonia decided to change its national flag, which had also been a bone of contention, and Greece promised to end the blockade. Macedonia's name remains tentative, but the international tensions have been calmed, at least temporarily. The country received international attention once more during that decade when it accepted hundreds of thousands of ethnic Albanian refugees during the war in Kosovo.

At the beginning of the 1990s, Kosovo, a historic Serbian province and a shrine of the Serbian Orthodox church, was largely inhabited by ethnic Muslim Albanians. Strong tensions between Serbs and the Albanian population surfaced in 1990. Albanians organized a so-called alternative public system, with their own taxation, education and health services, and underground administrative and judicial system, all contrary to official Serbian (Yugoslav) arrangements. In 1998, the federal army and police, as well as the Serbian population, started an anti-Albanian policy of ethnic cleansing. Tensions turned into a civil war. Hundreds of thousands of refugees escaped to Albania, Macedonia (radically changing its demographic composition), Montenegro, and Italy. Had it not been for the strong economic support by the European Union, all three of these Balkan nations would have collapsed.

In 1999, the United Nations and NATO became politically and militarily involved in the Kosovo conflict. NATO first bombarded Serbian military targets in Kosovo, and later in Serbia proper. Eventually, in June 1999, the Serbs had to withdraw from Kosovo, but they refused to guarantee independence to the province. Albanians then took revenge and began to drive out the remaining Serbs. The superficial peace that followed has been possible only due to the presence of thousands of troops from the international peacekeeping forces.

Dismemberment of the (new) Yugoslav Federation may continue if Montenegro, which did not support Serbian policy in Kosovo in the late 1990s, makes good on its warnings during the last few years and declares independence. In actuality, the republic's leadership has been running the country as if it were independent from Belgrade. Since the beginning of 2002, the euro and not the Yugoslav dinar has been the official currency, and the Yugoslav visa system is not observed. However, with new, democratically elected Yugoslav authorities, the next and final secession will likely occur without fear of a new war.

During the entire decade of the 1990s, the Yugoslav Federation was ruled by the authoritarian, post-Communist and nationalistic forces of President Slobodan Milosevic. Political opposition, although legal, was always disunified and very weak. When the opposition won local elections, the results were never recognized by the central authorities. It wasn't until October 2000, that a liberal, mildly nationalistic leader of a unified opposition, Vojislav Kostunica, was elected president. Even then, it took several days of massive political demonstrations by the Serbian population and protests by the international community before Slobodan Milosevic accepted Kostunica's victory. Finally, in December 2000, in parliamentary elections, the democratic opposition led by Zoran Djindjic won. Only then did the international community decide to lift anti-Serbian sanctions and to begin discussions on a stabilization plan that could help rebuild the country ruined in the aftermath of four wars.

Following the dissolution of the Warsaw Pact, the leaders of the post-Communist countries of Central and Eastern Europe became strongly interested in a new international security arrangement, to be based upon democratic principles. The ongoing tensions and wars throughout the decade indicated the necessity of such an arrangement. Poland expressed its interest in joining NATO from the very beginning of the decade, and so did the Czech Republic, and later Slovakia (formerly Czechoslovakia) and Hungary. However, Russia strongly opposed these moves, fearing especially that with Poland's membership, NATO would sit on its immediate borders. In February 1993, NATO began negotiations with the four countries. NATO's project Partnership for Peace was declared in the same year, and Russia was invited as well. In 1994, NATO and the Partnership became deeply involved in the Yugoslav wars. Poles, Czechs, Slovaks, Hungarians, Russians and even Ukrainians collaborated with NATO troops in the restoration of peace and the peacekeeping forces. Eventually, in May 1997, an official agreement between Russia and NATO was signed, and at the Madrid NATO summit in June 1997, Poland, the Czech Republic, and Hungary were officially invited to become member states. In March 1999, the three countries formally joined NATO. It is not yet clear if, or when, which other Central and Eastern European countries will be admitted and on what conditions.

With democratic political transformations and the transition toward a market economy, many Central and Eastern European countries became potentially eligible as candidates for the European Union. In actuality, their economies were not advanced enough, but both their leaders and those of the Western European countries recognized that the process of preparation and later membership would contribute to the stabilization of peace, democracy, and the further and faster transformations of these economies. As early as December 1990, the European Commission had begun negotiations with Poland, Hungary, and Czechoslovakia on their future access to the European Economic Community (known as the European Union after 1993).

In September 1991, at the extraordinary meeting of the ministers of foreign affairs of the European Community member states, which was called after the putsch in the Soviet Union, the agreements on formal association with these countries were officially confirmed. Similar documents were signed with Romania and Bulgaria in 1993, with Lithuania, Latvia, and Estonia in 1995, and with Slovenia in 1996. Due to the dismemberment of Czechoslovakia, new agreements with the Czech Republic and Slovakia were signed independently in 1993. In December 1997, the European Council decided that negotiations for accession, a long formal process that requires the candidate nations to transform their social, legal, political, and economic policies to match those of the Union, would begin only with five associated Central and Eastern European countries, Poland, the Czech Republic, Hungary, Estonia, and Slovenia, along with Cyprus. In March 1998, bilateral negotiations were initiated with these six countries. However, also in 1998, accession negotiations began with Bulgaria, Latvia, Lithuania, and Slovakia. It is quite possible that by 2005, several of these Central and Eastern European countries will have formally joined the Western security structures and political and economic organizations.

Other countries of the region will have to wait in the line, to catch up only if and when they have met the economic, political, and legal requirements for membership. Until they are fully accepted, a new division will probably occur in Europe, between an enlarged NATO and an enlarged European Union on the one hand, and the rest of Eastern and South-Eastern Europe on the other. This division is already on the immediate horizon and its borders can be drawn quite precisely. For example, visa requirements will soon be necessary between Poland and the Ukraine, between Hungary and Romania, and they will be strictly enforced. It will take decades until the strong historic divisions of Europe into Western and Eastern regions will cease to be as significant as they have been until now.

SOCIOLOGY IN CENTRAL AND EASTERN EUROPE UNDER COMMUNIST RULE

The development of sociology in any given country not only reflects some general trends within the discipline as a whole, but is significantly influenced by local social, economic, and historical factors as well. Certainly, this has been the case with sociology in Central and Eastern Europe. Following World War II, and under Communist domination, sociology was generally denounced as a bourgeois pseudoscience throughout the region. However, the particular impact this had on the discipline in each country varied.[1] Not surprisingly, the Soviet Union was the first place where sociology came under attack, as early as the 1930s. But, it was only after World War II that it was largely removed from the institutional structures of the scientific and academic establishments in Russia and replaced by historical materialism. Even then, it was never officially and totally banned.

In Poland, whose sociological tradition was one of the most developed and firmly rooted in Eastern Europe, sociology was tolerated in the immediate postwar period until the Stalinization of 1948. In 1952, it was condemned as a bourgeois science and it disappeared, until 1956, from academic institutions. Its adherents were forced to adopt Marxism-Leninism in its place. In Hungary, sociology was a regular university subject until the Communist takeover in 1947–48, when all open teaching of the discipline ceased. By the end of World War I, Romania had a well-established tradition in sociology, one heavily influenced by French sociology. However, in August of 1948, hopes for continuing this tradition were dashed when a law was passed prohibiting sociological research and the teaching of sociology. Nonetheless, even though the institutional structures of the discipline were dismantled, research ordered by the state continued, but without any theoretical analysis. Similar processes took place in what are now the Czech Republic and Slovakia.

Yugoslavia had nearly no developed and institutionalized sociological tradition until after World War II, and it was soon banned and replaced by historical materialism. Slovenia, a part of Yugoslavia from 1919 to the early 1990s, had an indigenous, pre-Yugoslav tradition of Catholic sociology, which was influential even in the interwar period, but it, too, disappeared after the war as a bourgeois science. Sociology was first taught as early as 1913 in Croatia (at that time in Austria-Hungary), and, as in its sister countries within Yugoslavia, was regarded as a bourgeois science and therefore unacceptable following World War II.

Bulgaria had not established a national tradition in sociology until after World War II, and it was short-lived since the discipline was declared an ideological weapon of capitalism in the late 1940s. In the Ukraine, and in the postwar Latvia and Estonia, no systematic sociological research was even carried out until the late 1950s and early 1960s. Lithuania had a somewhat more developed tradition, but during the Stalinist period it was denounced and isolated from the West and only a Marxist tradition was allowed to continue. Perhaps East Germany represents the most unique case, since its particular sociological tradition, separate from that of its Western counterpart, was not established until 1964. Its was a completely Marxist-Leninist tradition and was wholly contained within the twenty-five years of the German Democratic Republic's existence until reunification in 1990, after which it was dissolved.

For all practical purposes, sociology as an autonomous discipline with an institutionalized structure of university positions, departments, research institutes, and a set of concomitant professional organizations and associations ceased to exist in Central and Eastern Europe from 1948 to 1956 (due to its specific development, in Yugoslavia, the year 1956 was not as important as it was in other parts of the region). During this period it was in dispute with, or replaced and dominated by, officially sanctioned versions of a Marxist-Leninist historical materialism. Sociology departments were dismembered and degrees canceled, research institutes were closed and professional associations disbanded. In many countries new courses on scientific Communism appeared in sociology's place. Nonetheless, the extent to which all sociological activity actually ceased to exist varied from nation to nation depending on the severity of the authority of the state and Party, as well as the strength of the national tradition already in place and the strategies adopted by sociologists themselves.

In response to the crackdown and purges by state and Party officials, sociologists in Central and Eastern Europe adopted several different strategies. After 1948, given the ideologically charged climate, they found themselves challenged with the dilemma of resolving the contradictions between the desire for intellectual independence and academic legitimacy on the one hand, and political survival on the other, especially when the results of their research contradicted official orthodoxies. No doubt some were sympathetic with the new regimes. Some simply went along with them. Others went underground, hiding their intellectual loyalties to maintain their positions. Some sociologists were allowed to do library research but not to do any empirical research nor to teach. Some Hungarian scholars and many Polish scholars emigrated to Western countries. One means by which the discipline continued to survive was through the "sociologization" of other disciplines as sociologists migrated to other faculties such as history, law, and pedagogy, or as these disciplines took up traditionally sociological questions and problems in sociology's absence.

With the beginning of the period of de-Stalinization in 1956, known as Khrushchev's thaw, the climate for sociology changed considerably and the discipline began to reemerge and rebuild throughout the region, though unevenly and still firmly under the watchful eye and control of the Party and state. In Russia, sociology was recognized as having an important potential in the building of Communist society and was itself allowed to begin rebuilding. This led to the emergence in the 1960s of concrete sociology, an applied and policy-oriented development of the discipline. Throughout the 1970s and 1980s, sociology slowly became more grounded in the institutional structures of the scientific and academic establishments, though still firmly harnessed to the agenda of the state and Party. Outside the Soviet Union, Poland was the first to resurrect its sociological community and served as a leader and resource for many of the other satellite nations, including Bulgaria and Croatia.

Following the thaw, sociology gradually recovered but then began to suffer in the face of an increasingly stagnant economy and tightening resources. In the 1970s, the authorities recognized the potential of sociology and encouraged its continued development, but with certain topics, such as inequality, race, and ethnicity, off limits. With the loosening of the Marxist-Leninist monopoly, the discipline that reemerged in the 1970s and 1980s was increasingly pluralistic but also increasingly empirical and applied. This trend was strengthened as state firms began hiring sociologists.

In Hungary, as reformers began to enter the government and recognize the need to understand the emerging consumer society and growing individualism, sociology was reborn. In the 1960s it was partly liberated from Marxist philosophy, and in the 1970s and 1980s graduate and undergraduate programs were reestablished. The discipline that developed was a highly empirical and quantitative one, reflecting the emerging technocratic ideology of the authorities, and it was strongly tied to the interests of the state. However, this did not keep Gyorgy Konrad and Ivan Szelenyi (1979a) from making an important theoretical contribution on the role of the intelligentsia in socialist society in their widely discussed book published during this same period.

The thaw also led to a profound change in the intellectual milieu in Bulgaria. Authorities traded intellectual autonomy for political submission and practical assistance as sociology's rebirth was carried out by Party-affiliated scholars. Throughout the 1960s, teaching and research developed, though some areas, such as ethnic relations, social movements, and the environment, were not allowed. International contacts increased but were still officially controlled. In Romania, the turning point did not occur until 1965, when Nicolai Ceausescu, the Communist Party's General Secretary, declared that sociology and its import had been underappreciated. New institutional structures were established, though still part of an academic network of centrally controlled authority and without any academic freedom. As in other countries, the attempts to avoid theoretical controversy led to a separation of theoretical and empirical research, and some topics were forbidden. Sociologists had to pursue topics determined by their State beneficiaries, for example, industrial development and urban and rural growth. However, in 1977, sociology was once again abolished in Romania and remained in obscurity until 1989.

In the Czech Republic and Slovakia (at that time Czechoslovakia) sociology was restored in the early 1960s, drawing on Poland for assistance. Many Czech and Slovak students majored in sociology at the universities in Krakow and Warsaw, eventually getting their master's or even doctoral degrees. Many Polish sociological books were translated into the Czech and Slovak languages. In a similar manner, Polish sociology also influenced young sociologists of that period coming from Hungary and Bulgaria, though to a lesser extent. From 1965 to 1969, there was a great upsurge in the discipline in Czechoslovakia, part and parcel of the general cultural ferment and growing opposition in Czech and Slovak society that culminated in the revolt of the Prague Spring of 1968. However, the Soviet supported counterrevolution and period of so-called normalization which followed had a devastating impact on the discipline. Sociology was once again repudiated as revisionist and subversive since many sociologists had acted on the side of the opposition. There was a new wave of purges, and institutes and departments were once again abolished, though not as completely as in 1948. The sociology that did remain was controlled by Party sociologists and directed to serving the needs of the authorities, mainly helping to manage social change. Between 1975 and 1985 this led to the development of an increasingly sociotechnical and empirical discipline with an applied focus.

At the end of the 1950s, greater academic freedom was also allowed in Yugoslavia, particularly in Slovenia and Croatia. In 1958, the Yugoslav Sociological Association was established, and the process of reinstitutionalization was begun. A relatively autonomous and vibrant attempt was made to develop an indigenous and independent tradition in sociology, which paralleled, and no doubt was facilitated by, the Yugoslavian attempt to find its own road to socialism. However, as in the case of the Czechs and Slovaks, in the late 1960s and early 1970s, there was a reversal in the wake of political crackdowns on student demonstrations in which many sociologists had participated. Until the end of the 1980s, sociology remained closely tied to and controlled by the state.

In the Baltic States, national traditions in sociology began to develop in the early 1960s. This new sociology, influenced by Parsonian structural functionalism, though disguised in the Marxist-Leninist vocabulary, tended to focus on socially problematic areas such as education, youth, family, work, urbanization, and social change. It was developed as an empirical and positivist discipline, opposed to the dogmatic tenets of Marxism-Leninism. The discipline was held in high regard as it was seen as being able to help the existing regime, though there were thematic restrictions on areas such as religion, politics, interethnic relations, and stratification. In 1975, the Baltic Branch of the Soviet Sociological Association was established (it closed its activities after 1989). And, while sociologists did not publicly contradict official stances, there was a healthy underground of informal discourse.

The situation in the German Democratic Republic was somewhat unique. Virtually abolished in the 1950s following the raising of the Berlin Wall, sociology was not officially reintroduced until 1964, rather late in the post-Stalinist period, when the East German Politburo recognized the importance of the discipline. They established the discipline without significant theoretical foundations, and it served largely as an auxiliary science in the planning and management of the Party and state. Politically questionable research was not allowed, and the research that was carried out was closely tied to social policy and performativity.

The intermittent purges, lack of academic freedom, and close scrutiny and control by state and Party officials notwithstanding, during this period, a significant amount of good sociology was carried out by sociologists committed to their disciplines and to understanding the developments and problems of their societies. As in the case of their Western counterparts, this work tended to address the most pressing issues facing each national community. In the case of Central and Eastern Europe, the transition from agricultural to industrial societies, youth, family, education, work, and eventually even inequality were all crucial questions, and a body of research was produced that should not be ignored.[2]

CENTRAL AND EASTERN EUROPEAN SOCIOLOGY IN THE EUROPEAN AND INTERNATIONAL CONTEXT

Even though sociology has had a quite long history in Central and Eastern Europe, and it has been undergoing a fascinating process of transformation during the last several decades, its institutional position has been lower on the international market than one would have expected during the last decade, 1990–2000. Indications of this circumstance are the levels of participation of Central and Eastern European scholars in the International Sociological Association (ISA) and the European Sociological Association (ESA) and their respective conferences and ruling bodies, and the number of articles on the region in major sociological periodicals as well as the number of authors from Central and Eastern Europe in major Western and international sociological journals.

During the Twelfth World Congress of Sociology, held in Madrid in 1990, among seventeen newly elected members of ISA's Executive Committee (including the President and Vice Presidents), there were three scholars from Central and Eastern Europe: Vladimir Yadov (Russia), Rudolf Andorka (Hungary), and Ivan Kuvacic (Croatia). Though the ISA itself appears to have been quite taken with the events of 1989 and 1990, this number of representatives has never been elected since. At the next Congress, in Bielefeld in 1994, among the twenty-one newly elected members of the Executive Committee, only Piotr Sztompka (Poland) came from Central Europe. None of the nine plenary lectures was given by a scholar from the region. Among fifty-four program coordinators and co-chairs of the six symposiums, there were three Russians and nobody else from Central and Eastern Europe. The Fourteenth World Congress of Sociology was held in Montreal in 1998. Again, twenty-one members of the Executive Committee were elected, and again only one, Sztompka, was chosen from Central Europe, this time as Vice President. None of thirteen plenary lectures was given by a Central or Eastern European. Among thirty-eight program coordinators and session organizers of the Symposia, only Sztompka came from the region. In 2002, at the Congress in Brisbane, Australia, Sztompka was elected the ISA's President.

During the decade of the 1990s, four European Conferences of Sociology were held. At the first conference, in Vienna in 1993, a Steering Committee of the European Sociological Association *in statu nascendi* was formed. Among the fifteen members of this, there were five scholars from Central and Eastern Europe: Elena Bashkirova (Russia), Maca Jogan (Slovenia), Wladyslaw Kwasniewicz (from Poland and soon replaced by Janusz L. Mucha from the same country), Katrin Paadam (Estonia), and Martin Potucek (the Czech Republic).[3] The Second Conference took place in Budapest, Hungary, in 1995. The ESA was already officially registered, and formal elections of the Executive Committee were organized. Among sixteen members, only four Central or Eastern European sociologists were elected, Rudolf Andorka (Hungary), Maca Jogan, Katrin Paadam and Janusz L. Mucha. Among twelve plenary lectures, only three were given by sociologists from Central and Eastern Europe, Ivan Szelenyi (Hungary and the United States), Gyorgy Csepeli (Hungary) and Piotr Sztompka (Poland). Four out of fourteen semiplenary lectures were presented by Central and Eastern Europeans.

At the Third Conference, held in Colchester, England, in 1997, among sixteen newly elected members of the Executive Committee, once again only three, Maca Jogan, Elena Zdravomyslova (Russia) and Maria Adamik (Hungary) were elected from the region. None of six plenary lectures was given by a person from Central and Eastern Europe, but three (out of twelve) semiplenary lectures were. None of nine meet-the-author sessions was devoted to a book from the region.

The Fourth Conference was held in Amsterdam, the Netherlands, in 1999. Sociologists from the region began to fare a bit better, perhaps a harbinger of things to come. Nearly one third of the newly elected Executive Committee members came from Central and Eastern Europe, Mojca Novak (Slovenia),

Elena Zdravomyslova and Vadim Radaev (both from Russia), Gyorgy Lengyel (Hungary), Elzbieta Halas (Poland) and Jiri Musil (the Czech Republic), who became the President of the Association. One of the six plenary lectures was delivered by Vadim Volkov, a Russian. However, none of eight semiplenary lectures was presented by a person from the region. And, at the meet-the-author sessions, while nine books were debated, only one had a connection to the region, published in Germany but coedited by Victor Voronkov from Russia.

Judging from this first indicator, it is clear that Central and Eastern European sociology was underrepresented in both of the international sociological associations, particularly in the ESA. The fact that this part of Europe has been undergoing dramatic transformations during the 1990s does not seem to have affected the interest of Western scholars very much. Interestingly, two large countries were named here: Poland and Russia, and five small countries: Hungary, Slovenia, Estonia, the Czech Republic and Croatia. Hungary and Slovenia seem to be particularly successful, if we take the size of the countries into account.

A similar picture results from an analysis of several major, front-line sociological periodicals published in the Western countries between 1990 and 2000.[4] In the *American Sociological Review*, ten articles on Central and Eastern Europe were published, but seven of them were based on the pre-1989 situation (Krymkowski 1991; Burawoy and Krotov 1992; Evans, Kelley and Kolosi 1992; Opp and Gern 1993; Botev 1994; Sekulic, Massey and Hodson 1994; Sorensen and Trappe 1995; Szelenyi, Szelenyi and Poster 1996; Mueller 1997, Kohn et al. 1997). In three of these articles, at least one author comes from the region (one from Russia, one from Hungary, two from the Ukraine, and two from Poland). In the *American Journal of Sociology*, among the ten articles (at least in part) on the region, seven are also historical (Collins 1995; Gerber and Hout 1995, 1998; Hodson, Sekulic, and Massey 1994; Kohn et al. 1990; Mueller 1999; Oberschall 1996; Rena-Tas 1994; Schuman and Corning 2000; Stark 1996). In one, a coauthor comes from Central Europe (Slomczynski listed here as a Polish scholar). In the *British Journal of Sociology*, among eleven articles, five are of a historical character (Duke 1990; Hall 1994; Headey, Krause, and Habich 1995; Joppke 1994; Kolarska-Bobinska 1994; Marshall 1996; Misztal 1992; Ray 1997; Weinberg 1992; Weitman 1992). Only one of these eleven is authored by a Central European (Polish) scholar (Kolarska-Bobinska). In *Sociology*, four articles were published on the region, all by the Western scholars (Cole 1998; Evans and Mills 1999; Misztal 1993; Watson 1993).

In *Koelner Zeitschrift fuer Soziologie und Sozialpsychologie*, only three articles discussed Eastern European issues, all of them authored by Western sociologists (Mueller 1995; Schienstock and Traxler 1993; Srubar 1991). In *Zeitschrift fuer Soziologie*, there was one article by a Hungarian scholar on a purely theoretical topic (Pokol 1990), three articles on Central and Eastern Europe during the period of transformation, all written by Western scholars (Heidenreich 1994; Kalthoff 2000; Srubar 1994), and one article on the same subject written by a Pole (Sztompka 1993). In *Revue Francaise de Sociologie,* there was one historical article on the region, authored by a Swiss scholar (Coenen-Huther 2000).

The situation is a little different in the international sociological journals. *International Sociology,* the official journal of the ISA, was particularly open to scholars from all regions of the world, including Central and Eastern Europe. There were three articles on the region authored by Western scholars (Brym 1992, 1996; Kupferberg 1996), and twenty-one articles authored by at least one Central and Eastern European scholar (Andorka 1991, 1993; Blom et al. 1991; Buchner-Jeziorska and Evetts 1997; Duka et al. 1995; Filippov 1993; Genov 1997b; Grekova 1996; Kharkhordin 1994; Kloskowska 1992; Lakis 1995; Nickolov et al. 1992; Pommersbach and Wozniak 1991; Racz and Zetenyi 1994; Sawinski and Domanski 1991b; Sztompka 1990, 1996b; Tomka 1998; Yakubovich and Kozina 2000; Yanitsky 1999; Zielinski 1994). Half of them were historical papers, much less than in the national journals. In the *European Sociological Review,* there were ten articles on Central or Eastern Europe written by Western authors (Carroll, Goodstein, and Gyenes 1990; De Graaf 1991; Hernes and Kundsen 1991; Kluegel, Mason, and Wegener 1999; Pickvance 1997; Roller 1994; Szydlik 1994; Trappe and Rosenfeld 1998; Van Eijck and De Graaf 1995; Voelker and Flap 1997), as well as ten papers written by at least one Central or Eastern European author (Flere 1991; Ivancic 2000; Mach, Mayer, and Pohoski 1994; Robert 1991a; Saar 1997; Sawinski and Domanski 1991a; Szakolczai and Fustos 1998; Titma and Saar 1995; Toka and Dronkers 1996; Vecernik 1991). Out of these twenty, fifteen are based on historical material. In *European Societies,* published by the ESA only since 1999, there are five articles on Central and Eastern Europe (Alapuro and Lonkila 2000; Clarke 2000; Gijsbert and Nieuwbeerta 2000; Radaev 2000; Van Duin and Polackova 2000). Two of them were authored by at least one scholar from the region, those by Radaev and Polackova. Interestingly, in an article written by Westerners comparing class cleavages in Western and Eastern Europe, among sixty-nine sources quoted, only six were authored or coauthored by scholars from the Eastern region (Gijsbert and Nieuwbeerta 2000). Unfortunately this has been typical of the approach of Western sociology to Central and Eastern Europe.

The conclusion of this analysis is not that the Western, and international, sociological periodicals publish too few articles on Central and Eastern Europe, or that they are not open to authors from this region. The conclusion is that these journals did not consider the transformations of Central and Eastern Europe as something of particular import. And, when they published analyses of the region, they had more confidence in Western scholars than those indigenous to the region, even if these outsider scholars did not know the languages, or do their research first hand. Ironically, this trend continued the relative lack of interest and regard for sociological scholarship that was common in the West and internationally during the period of Communist domination. When work is done on the region, there is often a striking division of labor when the articles are based on empirical field research. The empirical part of the research is often carried out by local Eastern European scholars, while the Westerners come up with the general idea for the research and the money to finance it.[5]

SOCIOLOGY AT THE DAWN OF A NEW MILLENNIUM

With the collapse of the Soviet Union and the end of Communist rule in 1989, the climate for sociology has changed radically. Neither Central and Eastern European sociology nor its Western counterpart anticipated the precipitous and complete collapse of the Soviet Union. In hindsight, however, Poland was at the forefront as a harbinger of things to come. In the early 1980s, Polish sociology was politicized by the Solidarity movement and many of its members were active participants in helping to bring about Poland's independence. Throughout Central and Eastern Europe, sociologists have found themselves with a new independence, facing a new set of challenges, but also with new opportunities.

An immediately pressing question has been and continues to be that of resources. With the economic crises facing the former Soviet Union and most of the region's nations, universities and research institutes have suffered huge losses in state support and are scrambling to find new sources of revenue. This accounts for the widespread emergence of private and profit-oriented sociological research companies throughout the region. This is a parallel with the situation in the United States, where for several years now, as public funding has become increasingly tight, academic and scientific institutions have also been soliciting support from private foundations and corporations. Many of the major American universities have entered into contractual relations with corporate interests and established auxiliary profit-oriented research and development units. Their European counterparts are beginning to move in the same direction.

Once again, the impact of these great social changes on sociology has been uneven across the region. In some countries, for example, Poland, Russia, Hungary, and Romania, with well-developed academic and scientific institutional structures, firmly rooted sociological traditions, and large resource pools, sociology has been able to reestablish itself among other disciplines and to reinhabit an important role in the academic and scientific establishments. In other nations like those of the Baltic States, this has been more problematic. One common trend has been the establishment of private market-oriented sociological enterprises, selling their services to newly emerging political parties and politicians and collecting information for Western corporations. The result has been a virtual explosion in opinion polling and similar forms of survey research, directed not by state and Party officials, but by market forces.

A continuing problem for the newly independent, and in many cases newly established, smaller countries, has been in what language to work. For sociological communities in countries like Poland, with large populations and a significant critical mass of intellectuals in the academic and scientific establishments, this has never been a problem, even during the period of Soviet domination. However, for countries such as Lithuania, Latvia, and Estonia, with relatively small populations and intellectual establishments, it has been a continuing challenge. For example, in Lithuania most of the sociology was written in Russian and many sociological terms were not even translated into Lithuanian until the mid-1970s. Now the question concerns English, and the challenge is how to maintain an indigenous national tradition of sociology and a Lithuanian heritage in the face of the onslaught of Western culture.

National and regional differences continue to be present in the social sciences. For instance, European sociology continues to differ from American sociology both in theory and in the empirical issues to be studied (Muench 1991). And, Central and Eastern European sociology remains different from Western European sociology, even if nowadays many scholars from the region tend to stress growing similarities more often than remaining differences. The modern but presocialist history, the predominantly agricultural character of societies of Central and Eastern Europe still determines many facets of social life. Common socialist history is a living history. The economic, political, and cultural life of today is still being analyzed in relation and opposition to the past, overcome only a little more than a decade ago. There is also the common experience of the transformation to various forms of democracy and a market economy. Aspirations are also common, for example, access to the European Union and to NATO. The manner in which the sociology of Central and Eastern European countries reflects and responds to these issues remains a question to be resolved by history yet to be made.

Just as Central and Eastern European sociology gained new freedom from the intellectual orthodoxies of old masters, a whole new set of influences has emerged. This is no longer a unique set of influences as was the case during the Cold War, but a set faced by every sociological community around the world, and therefore impacting the development of world sociology itself. During the Cold War it was generally assumed, at least in the West, that there existed two sociologies, each with very distinctive characteristics. However, it is becoming increasingly clear that there has always been only one sociology, albeit with a diversity and multiplicity of national traditions contributing to an increasingly global disciplinary development and discourse. The great restrictions and obstacles imposed by state and Party officials notwithstanding, Central and Eastern European sociology was an embattled but nevertheless continuing and vibrant contributor to this discourse, and now occupies a unique perch from which to offer even greater contributions to its continuing development as we begin the next millennium. Its response to the great transformation since 1989 has been its history in the making.

NOTES

We would like to thank our contributors Mikko Lagerspetz, Franc Mali, Peter Robert, Karel Turza and Ognjen Caldarovic for their helpful comments and suggestions concerning this introduction.

1. For a more detailed account of the history of sociology in Central and Eastern Europe from the end of World War II up until the period of perestroika and glasnost, see Keen and Mucha 1994b.

2. For a selected bibliography of this body of literature, see our previous work, cited above.

3. Despite our many efforts, we were not able to localize the program of the First Conference and therefore we cannot say anything about the presence of scholars from the region at its major events.

4. For our analysis we examined two American, two British, two German, one French, and three international journals. We looked for a) articles on Central and Eastern Europe, particularly on the transition period that began in 1989, and later the period of stabilization of political democracy and market economy; and b) articles by authors who identified themselves as affiliated with research and/or educational institutions of the part of Europe we are interested in. It must also be kept in mind that the Western "national" sociological periodicals publish a relatively large (at least in comparison with Central and Eastern European periodicals) number of articles on foreign countries and papers authored by "foreign" scholars.

5. We want to note that Eastern and Central European sociologists, like their Western colleagues, also published articles on the region in international, interdisciplinary Western periodicals specializing in this area, for instance, *East European and Slavonic Review* (published by the University of London since 1922), *East European Quarterly* (published by the University of Colorado since 1967), *East European Constitutional Review* (published by the University of Chicago Law School since 1992, and *East European Politics and Societies* (published by University of California–Berkeley since 1992).

2

Unhandy Sociology: The Case of Belarus

Wanda Rusetskaya and Olga Tereschenko

Belarusian sociology, which was ruined in the 1930s, was revived in the middle of the 1960s as a result of the processes of democratization inspired by Nikita Khruschev in the Soviet Union. In 1965, the Central Committee of the Communist Party of Belarus (CC CPB) passed a resolution on the development of concrete sociological research in Belarus. That same year, the Central Committee created its own Public Institute for Sociological Research.

In 1967, the Laboratory for Sociological Research was established at Belarusian State University (BSU). In 1968, the Center for Concrete Sociological Research was established by the National Academy of Sciences. Several other research groups developed at other large universities and enterprises. Georgy Davidyuk, Eugeny Babosov, and Konstantin Buslov were among the first organizers of sociological institutions in Belarus. All of these institutions enjoyed financial support from the state and also conducted some commercial research for different governmental bodies and enterprises. The main areas of research were public opinion, effectiveness of propaganda, living standards of different social groups (working class, collective-farm peasantry, intellectuals, women, etc.), sociology of work, and the sociology of youth and education.

Nonetheless, up until 1989, sociology in Belarus, as in all of the Soviet Union, was not regarded as an independent science. Its status was that of a section of Marxist-Leninist philosophy and so-called Scientific Communism. Sociology was denied the right to have its own theory and even history. Any sociological theory was considered to be a bourgeois one and hostile to social-ism. The discipline was officially designated as "Marxist-Leninist Empirical So-ciology." During this period, the training of professional sociologists was not carried out on a regular basis. However, from time to time, philosophy faculties of large universities, Belarusian State University among them, provided some groups of their students with an opportunity to take several courses in empiri-cal sociology.

A special feature of sociological education at BSU was a close cooperation be-tween the professors with teaching appointments and those with research posi-tions in the Laboratory for Sociological Research. Teachers participated in the research of the Laboratory, and researchers taught some courses. As a result, the Belarusian school of sociology has become one of the best in the former So-viet Union, and maintains its strong traditions. During this period, several im-portant books were published, the most famous of them being the textbook *Prikladnaja sociologija* [Applied Sociology] (Davidyuk 1979), and *Slovar' prik-ladnoi sociolgii* [Dictionary of Applied Sociology] (Davidyuk and Shulga 1984), the first book of its kind to be published in the former USSR.

During the last decade of the twentieth century, the process of decommu-nization of the humanities was expanding in Belarus, just as in other countries of the Eastern Block. Sociology was freed of ideological dictates and the neces-sity to submit topics of research for the approval of the various bodies of the Communist Party. All executive positions in research and educational institu-tions became elective offices filled through democratic procedures. Finally, the consideration and creation of new research institutions and centers and chairs of sociology no longer had to be scrutinized by the Party. None of these mani-festations of decommunization were accomplished through the closing of so-ciological institutes, or accompanied by visible resentment or retaliation against sociologists formerly active in the Communist Party. Instead, during the last decade, decommunization led to the creation of new research and edu-cational institutions.

Thus, in 1990, at the very beginning of the transformation process, the Na-tional Academy of Sciences in Minsk created a new Institute of Sociology out of the previously existing Center for Concrete Sociological Research. In the new Institute, headed by Evgeny Babosov, in addition to studies of public opin-ion and living standards that were traditional for Soviet sociology, studies of social stratification, social policy, demography, sociology of work, culture, edu-cation and science, sociology of conflicts, crises, and catastrophes, sociology of deviant behavior, social psychology, and sociology of personality were carried out.

The Laboratory for Sociological Research has proved to be a real hotbed of the Belarusian professional sociological community. At one time or another, all well-known Belarusian sociologists of the elder generation participated in the activity of the Laboratory. In 1996, it was reorganized into the Center for So-ciological and Political Research, headed by David Rotman. The main areas of specialization of the Center are political sociology, sociology of youth and education, sociology of deviant behavior, sociology of religion, and market research.

During the mid-1990s, about two dozen new institutes and centers for sociological research, both state-supported and private, were created in Minsk and other cities of Belarus. The biggest state-supported institutes created were the Minsk Scientific Research Institute of Socioeconomic and Political Problems, and the Minsk Institute for Political Studies. Among private sociological institutions created, the most currently renowned are the Independent Institute for Social, Economic, and Political Studies, in Minsk, a private research agency, Novak, also in Minsk, a center for development of social resources, Orakul, in the city of Gomel, a city association, the Humanitarian Initiative, in the city of Mogilev, and a center for research and education, Logos, in Brest. Some of the heads of these institutes were professional sociologists who came from the main sociological centers, while others came from politics, economics, and commerce.

Private institutes do not have support from the state. They conduct research for Belarusian and foreign customers, including Gallup, the United States Information Agency, European Barometer, and various other commercial interests. Some of the private institutes belong to the Association of Belarusian Think Tanks, and receive grants from Western foundations for the development of sociological research to be made available to the public. They regularly publish the results of their studies in the mass media.

In the second part of the 1990s, there appeared several new specialized sociological journals, such as *Socioligja* in 1997, and *Zerkalo* (Mirror) in 1998. During the decade, a number of books on sociology were also published in Belarus (Babosov 1992, 1993a, 1993b, 1995, 1996; Danilov 1997; Elsukov and Shulga 1991; Shavel 1996; Sokolova 1994, 1998a). Most of these books, written by Belarusian authors, were published in Russian. While the official language of Belarus when it was part of the USSR was Russian, since the disintegration of the Soviet Union, there have been two official languages, Russian and Belarusian. However, Russian has remained the main language of science and education. One important reason for the dominance of Russian in sociology books has been the relatively small market for books in Belarusian, compared to the much larger Russian market, which is reputed to be unlimited.

During the Soviet period, the Belarusian sociological school established a serious tradition of empirical research. However, following the transformation, Belarus sociologists got a chance to significantly expand the range and topics of their research to include fields previously forbidden or ignored. Investigation of socioeconomic change has been of tremendous interest, not only for sociology, but also for adjacent disciplines such as economics, demography, and political science. Problems of social inequality, social stratification and mobility, the formation of new social groups and strata, and those of the labor market, employment and unemployment, have been investigated by the Institute of Sociology of the National Academy of Sciences (Babosov and Buschik 1999; Babosov, Buschik, and Evelkin 2000; Buschik 1999; Tarasov 1999; Shavel 1996; Shavel, Rubanov, and Smirnova 1998; Sokolova 1998b), at Belarusian State University (Danilov 1997), and by the Scientific Research Institute of Socioeconomic and Political Problems, in Minsk.

Nevertheless, development of research of this kind in Belarus cannot be considered successful enough. Socioeconomic studies require substantial financial support. In addition, the national government bodies, institutions of local government, industrial enterprises, and business corporations that contract these studies become owners of the information obtained. Government authorities often consider publication of the data pertaining to the socioeconomic sphere and changes of social structure undesirable, and the results of research commissioned by private organizations are considered classified commercial information. Furthermore, independent sociological centers primarily occupy themselves with political studies and public opinion polls, without paying enough attention to socioeconomic studies.

The most complete information about socioeconomic changes in Belarus is available through the Ministry of Statistic and Analysis, which has significantly increased its workload during the late 1990s. For the first time in Belarus, it has conducted a panel survey of households using the methods of the World Bank. Since 1998, it has published *Economic Tendencies in Belarus*, a quarterly statistical review. However, much of the published data are incomplete, and the results of analyses are not published at all.

A second important area of research has been the impact and consequences of the Chernobyl catastrophe. It includes several significant aspects: living conditions for people who remain in the polluted territories, resettlement and readjustment of migrants from the Chernobyl area and those who participated in the clean-up, and post-Chernobyl demographic, medical, psychological, and ecological problems. The credit for the Chernobyl studies is shared by the Gomel Sociological Center (Zlotnikov, Zlotnikova, and Kasyanenko 1991; Zlotnikov 1994) and the Institute of Sociology of the National Academy of Sciences (Babosov 1993a, 1993b, 1995, 1996; Shavel and Smirnova 1998).

The study of nationalism and ethnic relations is a new field for Belarusian sociologists. It gained ground only after the dissolution of the Soviet Union. Belarus does not suffer from acute interethnic and interreligious conflicts. According to the 1999 Population Census, Slavs constitute 98 percent of the entire population. Among them are Belarusians (78 percent), Russians (13 percent), Poles (4 percent), and Ukrainians (3 percent). In the first half of the 1990s, large-scale studies of the status of the Belarusian language and culture were carried out. The attempt of the first post-1989 government of independent Belarus to pass a law making Belarusian the only official language of the state, and to convert the educational system to it, met with strong resistance on the part of various layers of the society. Sixty-three percent of the population of Belarus, including 59 percent of ethnic Belarusians, consider Russian their mother

language. This was one of the causes of the defeat of the nationalistically oriented democratic forces in the first presidential election in 1994.

The emphasis in ethnic studies shifted to the investigation of the national
mentality and the evaluation of its impact upon the velocity and efficiency of
economic and social reforms, as well as to the exploration of bordering communities, such as Belarusian–Russian, Belarusian–Polish, Belarusian–Ukrainian,
and Belarusian–Lithuanian. Studies of national and cultural development and
interaction have been carried out at the Institute for Sociology (Babosov
1998a), at the Center for Social and Political Studies at Belarusian State University (Novikova 2001), at Grodno State University (Rozenfeld 1999), at the
Gomel Sociological Center (Zlotnikov 1993), and at Gomel State Polytechnical
Institute (Kirienko 1999). In Brest, sociologist Sergei Yaskevich heads the Academy of National Minorities.

After 1989, gender studies became one more new and rather special field for
Belarusian sociologists. From the very beginning it was developed as an interdisciplinary field of study. Sociologists who specialize in very different fields,
such as social stratification, deviant behavior, media, and nationalism, consider
aspects of gender inequality in their fields. Centers for gender studies focus
their attention on women's education, teaching gender relations in various disciplines such as sociology and organizing seminars and conferences. Since 2000,
the Minsk Center for Gender Studies, which is affiliated with a women's non-
state institute, Envila, has published the bulletin *Inoi Vzgljad* (Another View),
and Belarusian gender studies scholars have published some interesting works
(Gapova and Usmanova 2000; Tchikalova 2000).

Practically all sociological centers in Belarus have teams helping to design
programs for political deputies at all levels, developing tactical schemes for election campaigns, and also, upon the request of some of the deputies, working out
recommendations as to how they should best contribute to the development of
regional and national policy. The only trend of research that ceased to exist following the transformation was the study of the leading and guiding role of the
Communist Party. Marxism was forced out of the intellectual center to its pe-
riphery, so to speak, not only in the mass consciousness, but also in the theoretical interests of sociologists and philosophers. While some professors of
philosophy belonging to older generations still stick to Marxism in their academic courses, professors of sociology refer to Marxism only as one of the perspectives of classical and modern critical sociology.

A special feature of the last decade was the development of qualitative and
mixed methodologies of social research. Soviet sociology followed the positivist
paradigm, so it never used qualitative methods that were considered to be un-
scientific. Both an interest in personality studies and the development of market research gave rise to wide use of biographic methods, discourse analysis,
focus groups, and the case study.

During the last decade, radical changes took place in the teaching of sociology
in Belarus. In 1989, the Chair in Sociology and the Department of Sociology

were created at the Faculty of Philosophy and Economics at BSU. Albert El-sukov became the first head of the chair of sociology and the head of the Department of Sociology. From the very beginning, professors of the chair consisted for the most part not of professional teachers of philosophy, but rather experts in practical sociology, with experience in the Laboratory for Sociological Research at BSU or the National Academy of Sciences's Institute of Sociology. This has made the chair not only the leading institution of sociological education in Belarus, but also one of the best chairs of sociology in the former USSR.[1]

Between 1990 and 1993, chairs of sociology appeared at practically all universities in Belarus. In effect, this was a part of the process of the general decommunization of the humanities. However, it is worth mentioning that the majority of these new chairs in sociology were converted from former chairs of Scientific Communism. This accounts for the fact that during the early years, the teaching of sociology in the majority of the universities was on a rather low level. Positive tendencies began to develop after 1994, when the first graduation from the Department of Sociology at BSU took place, and there appeared young teachers with professional training in sociology.

The Department of Sociology at the BSU remains the only institution in Belarus where undergraduate professional training in sociology exists. Every year, it receives between 100 and 120 applicants for admission, but only admits about 30 freshmen. Two to three applicants apply for every position available in postgraduate studies. Seven to ten new postgraduate students are admitted every year. In Belarus, the Soviet system of university education, whereby initial professional training covers five years and the level of education obtained is rather similar to an M.A. degree, remains in place.

Not only do the students of the Faculty of Philosophy and Social Sciences show interest in sociology, but so do those of many other specialties. However, the number of students interested in adjacent specialties, such as social work, communications, social philosophy, and social psychology, is much larger. Training in these specialties is now offered in some universities, including BSU. In 2000, the Center for Gender Studies, at the European Humanities University in Minsk, opened an M.A. program in Gender Studies, the first one of this kind in the former Soviet Union.

Prior to the beginning of the 1990s, Marxist-Leninist sociology was taught only in the humanities faculties. Nowadays, courses of sociology are made available to students of all faculties at all universities. Many faculties teach a number of specialized areas such as economic sociology, sociology of politics, sociology of conflict, sociology of culture, sociology of religion, sociology of management, and sociology of communications.

Universities nowadays enjoy more freedom in the humanities than ten to fifteen years ago. The curriculum for the Department of Sociology at BSU is developed by the Chair of Sociology, and is approved by the Rector of BSU. Syllabi for each of the separate courses are created by the professors and approved by the Chair. There exists a standard syllabus for the introductory course in sociology, approved by the Ministry of Education in 2000. It contains basic requirements pertaining to the contents of the course and allows for the further development of the basic course if desired by a university.

Professors of sociology mostly use textbooks written by Russian authors (Frolov 1999; Kravchenko 1997a, 1997b, 1997c, 1997d; Osipov 1998; Radaev and Shkaratan 1996; Yadov and Semenova 1998) and Belarusian authors (Babosov 1991, 1998b, 2000a, 2000b; Babosov and Tereschenko 2000; Danilov and Rotman 1997; Elsukov 1993, 2000; Sokolova 1998a; Sokolova and Kobyak 2000; Sokolova, Kobyak, and Alexandrova 2000; Titarenko 1998), as well as foreign literature in Russian translation (Bourdieu 1993; Breton and Proulx 1995; Champagne 1997; Coser 2000; Giddens 1999; Noelle 1993; Noelle-Noiman 1996; Smelser 1994; Sztompka 1996b).

The relations between academic sociology, university centers, and private sociological centers have ranged from close and cooperative partnerships and business relationships, to acute rivalries. Competition has encouraged everyone to reach for a high level of quality in their research and for reliability and representation in their data. From the formal and ideological point of view, the state-supported sociological institutions and independent ones are in adversarial positions. However, in practice this has not really interfered with cooperation on an individual level. The roots of this cooperation can be traced back to student days, as the great majority of Belarusian sociologists that are now active are graduates from the Faculty of Philosophy, and in later years the Department of Sociology at BSU. Members of research institutes and centers work as professors at BSU and many other universities. Professors and researchers from universities work part-time and as consultants for private research companies.

Belarusian sociologists have carried out a number of joint projects with sociologists from Central and Eastern Europe, especially from the Newly Independent States, the Baltic States, and Poland. In Russia, the main partners of Belarusian sociologists are the Institute of Sociology and the Institute of Social and Political Studies of the Russian Academy of Sciences in Moscow, the Institute of Sociological Studies at the University of St. Petersburg, and the sociology departments at the universities in Moscow and St. Petersburg. The Russian journal *Sotsiologicheskiye Issledovaniya* (Sociological Studies) dedicated one of its issues to the publication of works by Belarusian authors (Toschenko 1998). The most significant project, carried out in collaboration with sociologists from the former USSR, was the longitudinal study of the lives of differing generations, *Social'noe rassloenie vozrastnoi kogorty* (Titma 1997). The study was begun in 1983. The third wave took place in 1993, the fourth wave in 1998. Sociologists from Estonia, Latvia, Lithuania, Belarus, Ukraine, Tajikistan, and some regions of Russia, including Moscow, participated in the latter two waves.

In Poland, Belarusian sociologists have collaborated with the Institute of Religious Studies at Jagiellonian University, the Institute of Sociology at the

University of Bialystok, the Institute of Philosophy and Sociology and the Institute of Political Studies of the Polish Academy of Sciences. Results of these studies have been published in various journals and proceedings of conferences (Stasiak and Zglinski 1995).

Joint research and cooperation in education are also carried on with some sociological centers of the West. There are two joint projects in the Institute of Sociology at the National Academy of Sciences. One, on problems of the labor market, is with the Group for Transforming European Society Studies at the University of Nanterre (France). The other is with the Academy of Communication in Diemen (Netherlands), studying the consequences of the Chernobyl catastrophe. A similar problem has been the focus of the joint project conducted by the Gomel Center for Development of Social Resources, Orakul, and the Department of Rural Sociology at Cornell University (U.S.A.). The Center for Sociological and Political Research at BSU has been involved in a EU International Association (INTAS) project concerning problems of living standards, nationalism, and religiosity.

Between 1993 and 1997, the Department of Sociology at BSU took a part in the Trans-European Mobility Program for University Students (TEMPUS) with colleagues from the University of Provance (Marsel), the University of Stendal (Grenoble) in France, and the University of Lincolnshire and Humberside in Great Britain. As the result of that project, the Department of Communication was opened at the Faculty of Philosophy and Social Sciences at BSU. In 2001, the Department of Communication was awarded a new TEMPUS grant, along with the University of Provance (Marsel), the University of Stendal (Grenoble), the University of Paris III, and the University of Malaga, for development of postgraduate studies in communication at BSU. The Department of Sociology also has an international program in Jerusalem (Israel). Twice a year, professors from the Department go there for lectures and examinations. A number of sociologists from BSU have also taken part in international exchange programs. Oleg Manaev, a Fulbright Professor, is an associate editor of the *European Journal of Communication*.

The financial support of sociological research and education springs from various sources. Research projects carried out by centers of sociological research operating within the framework of the National Academy of Sciences and in-state educational institutions are, for the most part, financed out of the state budget. The second source of financing is commercial research ordered by enterprises, companies, and local and foreign agencies. A third source is research grants from local and foreign foundations. However, the opportunity for receiving grants from Western foundations is quite restricted because of the sanctions against Belarus. Usually, they are awarded to independent sociological institutions or individual sociologists who are involved in political studies. If it were not for the sanctions of the European Community against Belarus, the participation of Belarusian sociologists in international programs could be more significant. The sanctions hinder international contacts and the dissemination of democratic ideas and values in Belarus.

Sociology is not well recognized by the Belarusian authorities. Involvement of sociologists in the development of fundamental problems of national and local policy is rather rare. The most successful examples have been the participation of researchers from the Institute of Sociology in designing a consistent development strategy for the Republic of Belarus, the preparation of the government's economic and social policy for 2000–2002, and in designing a plan for the socioeconomic and sociopsychological rehabilitation of territories and victims of the catastrophe at Chernobyl. Sociologists have also served as experts in the creation of some sections of the Constitution of the Republic of Belarus.

Sometimes sociologists are also requested as consultants for government institutions, political parties, and commercial enterprises and companies. Among local governing authorities, the Minsk City Council has taken the lead in the use of sociology. The Minsk Scientific Research Institute of Socioeconomic and Political Problems participates in all significant social and economic programs and projects of the Council. Regional sociological centers do some work for regional governments and councils.

In conclusion, Belarusian sociology has at its disposal enough local and metropolitan research centers, as well as qualified researchers, to play a more significant role in the social processes of the state. Professional training in sociology has been strong and flexible. It provides a good basis for the expansion of sociology to new areas of social life. However, it is well known that the prospects of sociology are closely related to the fate of the rest of the society. An authoritarian state needs neither a lot of qualified sociologists, nor a well-developed institutional structure of sociology and set of sociological research centers. For this reason, the growing force for democratic and liberal processes remains the primary condition for the successful development of sociology in Belarus.

NOTE

1. A department of sociology consists of undergraduates studying sociology as a specialization. Unlike the American case, "chair" does not refer to an administrative head but rather to the unit as a whole and consists of professors and postgraduate students. A chair is a research unit, whereas a department is a teaching unit. Chairs of Sociology exist at most of the universities. The only department of sociology in Belarus is at BSU.

3

Bulgarian Sociology: Lights and Shadows at the Dawn of the 21st Century

Vyara Gancheva

Sociology in Bulgaria was not established as a generally recognized "nonphilo-sophical science of society" until the 1960s and 1970s (Genov 1994). Its prede-cessors were the studies of Ivan Hadzhiyski (Hadzhiyski 1974) and the founding of the Bulgarian Scientific-Sociological Association in the 1930s. The reason for this relatively late institutionalization was the initial rejection of so-ciology as a so-called bourgeois science during the 1950s. In 1959, the Bulgar-ian Sociological Association was founded, and, under the leadership of Zhivko Oshavkov, the first large-scale sociological research projects began (Oshavkov 1968, 1976). The theoretical framework for these projects was the understand-ing of society as a sociological structure (Oshavkov 1976). This theoretical par-adigm, which dominated Bulgarian sociology during the socialist period, provided the intellectual foundations for the national school in sociology, as well as the professionalization of several generations of sociologists. After 1968, several chairs of sociology were established, along with the Institute of Sociology at the Bulgarian Academy of Sciences.

The Seventh World Congress of Sociology, which took place in Varna in 1970, is indicative of the prestige of Bulgarian sociology at the time. To date, Bulgaria remains the only Eastern European country that has hosted such a prominent forum. The sessions of the International Varna Sociological School became the center for discussions among scientists from the region (Genov 2001, 36).

The totalitarian state legitimized sociology in exchange for the science's service as a handy instrument that supported the establishment. This "marriage with authority" was in fact a deal that secured a luxurious and elite existence for sociology, including funding, social interest, an inflow of young cadres, and international contacts (Dimitrov 2001; Dragonov 1991). The umbrella of the socialist state over sociology offered a host of other advantages, such as the establishment of a large professional organization and university departments.[1]

Before 1989, as a result of its ability to legitimize the existing order, Bulgarian sociology accumulated a number of advantages. However, after 1989, the moniker "sociological," which had been equated with "socialist," was thereby stigmatized, and the previously dominant structural paradigm fell into disrepute. According to Georgi Dimitrov, "the official Bulgarian sociological school disappeared because it was not really sociological, but was rather constituted of the party line. In its place, formerly marginalized sociological perspectives and areas, i.e., of everyday life, of phenomenology, and of the history of sociology, became institutionally legitimate" (2001).

Following 1989, the entire social order collapsed. This provided Bulgarian sociology with an opportunity for modernization, but it was not taken advantage of immediately or completely. The reasons for the delay, and the resulting marginality of the social sciences, had to do with the difficulty of breaking the grip the previous paradigm held over the discipline and the dominance of obsolete concepts and institutions that divided university teaching from academic sociology.[2] These circumstances contributed to the delay of the rehabilitation of sociology. Petar-Emil Mitev pointed out this paradoxical contradiction between "the higher social needs and the unexpected potential of sociology as compared to the developed countries of the West. At the same time we encounter one-sided understanding and an overall lower realization of sociological information" (1995, 122).

In search of a balance between the negatives and positives of the crisis, Mitev says that after 1989, we can talk about a "sociological expansion" (1995, 122). It was characterized by an abrupt widening of the theoretical basis of sociology, the overcoming of the deficits of rationality and information in the society, and the upgrading and modernizing of the methodological arsenal of empirical sociology. This included the introduction of qualitative methods, focus groups, life histories, and open-ended interviews, in lieu of the anonymous questionnaire.

A thematic broadening was also a part of the sociological expansion, as new, previously risky areas of investigation become legitimate subjects of sociological analysis, for instance, unemployment (Genov 1999a), poverty, homelessness, crime (Mantarova 2000), and marginalization. Progress was also marked by research into the formation of new social and political groups (Dimitrova 1998; Nikolov 1999; Patchkova 1996). Ivan Stefanov defined posttotalitarian sociology as a "science of the new group structures and the differentiated collective subject, which is different from socialism in which the trends toward social homogeneity hindered the formation of a more lasting group identity" (1996, 127).

Some new developments in sociology included the analysis of religious and ethnic identity (Fotev 1994) and of the media. In addition, special attention was paid to language studies. For example, Liliyana Deiyanova (2000) recognized two stages in the post-Communist discourse of Bulgarian sociologists. The first marks the transition to the positions of socially engaged intellectuals, with their typical propaganda speech. The second stage, after 1995, is the transition to the positions of experts who offer varying perspectives and options. According to Deiyanova, these two stages coincide with the periods of the existential and pragmatic politics and are thus the two major periods of sociological discourse after 1989.

In 1997, with the state's financial crisis, the rate of sociological expansion slowed down and some signs of professional regression began to develop. By then, however, the catharsis of sociology, the discovery of new topics, as well as the boom in the publication of translated and national sociological literature had already taken place. The post-1989 transition generally spurred the rehabilitation of sociology, its opening to the international social scientific community and its transition from a monoparadigmatic status to a multiparadigmatic one.

UNIVERSITY SOCIOLOGY

During the last twelve years, university sociology in Bulgaria has developed quickly. There has been an increase in the number of students and teaching professors, and the educational system was decentralized. There are now six university sociology chairs, and many other departments offer sociology courses. This has entailed the development of many new sociology courses, some required, others optional. Bachelor's degrees (eight semesters of study) and master's degrees (two more semesters) were introduced in 1998, along with corresponding state requirements for completion of the degrees.

This rapid development of sociology in the universities was a result of the social and cognitive transformations after 1989. A leading role was played here by the development, beginning as early as 1967, of a series of specializations in sociology at the University for National and Global Economy (UNGE) and by the established traditions of the sociology program at Sofia University. The sociology curriculum was initiated at Sofia, in 1976, by Lyuben Nikolov. The first master's program in sociology was also developed at Sofia, in 2000. After 1989, based on the number of newly accepted students, we can definitely talk about a sharp increase in the sociology major at the university. As a whole, it is reasonable to assume that more than 2000 students have studied sociology during the last twelve years.

An important feature of university education in sociology after 1989 was its decentralization, which was realized on both the institutional and a paradigmatic level (Zakharieva 1996). In spite of uniform state requirements, the chairs of sociology at Sofia University, South-West University, the UNGE, Plovdiv University (established in 1995), the New Bulgarian University, the Slavic University (founded in 1995 and later closed) each established their own sociological perspectives. However, the dilemma of whether to emphasize the narrow specialization of sociologists or to spread sociology among a number of other disciplines is yet to be resolved. There is a lack of standardized university mechanisms requiring periodical changes in the university curricula. And, there has been insufficient attention to the practical application of what students have learned.

After 1989, sociology courses were offered as electives in the secondary schools. In response, university faculty published a sociology textbook for the eleventh grade (Grekova et al. 1992), and an introduction to sociology manual for tenth- through twelfth-grade students (Grekova et al. 1997). The modernization of higher education in sociology was also supported by a number of new textbook publications (Dimitrov 2001; Genova 1996, Genov 1998). In addition, specialized educational literature spurred the formation of a variety of disciplines: social work, social psychology, sociology of the personality, and history of sociology (Fotev 1993; Todorova 1999). Internet technologies also have been a part of university education in sociology. An Internet project sponsored by the Socrates Program, "Transformation in a Comparative European Perspective," involved the participation of the Bulgarian Academy of Sciences, Sofia University, and South-West University in a European master's course in sociology, together with the University of Lund, Goethe University, and Bucharest University.

INSTITUTIONAL HERITAGE: OBSTACLE OR OPPORTUNITY?

The appearance of new sociological institutions and the survival of old ones within the new environment must be discussed in connection with the distribution of resources, relationships with the ruling elite, and the structuring of preference and limitation of choice. The balance of power between the old and the new elites is visible in the competition among the new institutions in a society where the state is the source of political authority. After 1989, hundreds of workplaces for sociologists in enterprises and organizations (in addition to some 400 to 500 in the mid-1980s) were eliminated. A number of sociological institutes were closed or their personnel were significantly cut. This resulted in discontinuity and losses of institutional memory. But, it also spurred a diversification of sociological institutions. A salient example is that of the National Institute for Youth Research, which existed from 1969 until 1992. Following its close, its members became the founders and members of many private and state sociological entities such as the National Center for Public Opinion Research (NCPOR), Gallup, the Institute for Social Critique, the Center for the Study of Authority and Society, the Center for the Study of Ideology at Sofia University, the Center for Market and Social Research, and the Ivan Hadzhiyski Private Sociological Institute. The appearance of numerous nongovernmental organization (NGO) sociological think tanks, for example, the International Center for the Problems of Minorities and Cultural Relationships (IMIR), the Center for the Study of Democracy (CSD), the Center for Liberal Strategies (CLS), the Independent Club Future Alternatives, and the Association for the Development of the Middle Class, also contributed to competition among sociologists.

A sociological institution that did not fare well was the Bulgarian Sociological Association (BSA). In the mid-1980s, the BSA had 1,500 members, as many as the British Sociological Association. In 1990, 760 sociologists participated in the Fifth Congress of the BSA. However, by 2000, the BSA had only 115 members. In 1994, the BSA and the Institute of Sociology at the Bulgarian Academy of Sciences were the co-organizers of the first meeting of sociologists from the Balkan countries. In 2000, the BSA and the Institute initiated a regional network of sociologists from the Balkan countries.

The Institute of Sociology of the Bulgarian Academy of Sciences, founded in 1968, remains the biggest academic research center in sociology in Bulgaria. Its major activities include basic and applied research in the areas of global and regional social trends, national development, and international comparative sociological analysis. Many of the collaborators in the Institute also teach at different universities around the country. Areas of instruction include general sociology, history of sociology, and sociology of knowledge, crime, religion, gender, science and technology, and marginalization.

The emergence of new sociological institutions in the aftermath of 1989 was followed by a large increase in sociological publications. A number of journals and publishing initiatives accompanied the institutionalization of new departments and intellectual circles. New sociological journals included *Izbor* (Choice), a journal for politics, philosophy, and ethnology, *Iztok-Iztok* (East-East), and *Kritika I Humanizam* (Critique and Humanism). Many state and private agencies started publishing annual reports and bulletins. In addition, the outlook and contents of the old periodicals changed. The oldest journal, *Sotsiologicheski Problemi*, established in 1968, used to publish six issues a year. Since 1992, it has been publishing only four thematic issues per year, often with a substantial delay. In 1995, due to financial problems, the journal *Sotsiologicheski Pregled* (Sociological Review), a bulletin since 1977, ceased its activity.

In 1996, the publication of the *Entziclopedichen retchnik po sotsiologiya* (Encyclopedia of Sociology) was one of the foremost events for Bulgarian sociology in that period. The encyclopedia consists of 551 articles in which 186 of the world's most prominent sociologists are featured. It also includes a listing of sociological literature and a list of sociological terms translated into English, German, French, Spanish, and Russian (Mihaylov and Tilkidzhiev 1996).

In post-1989 Bulgaria, there has been neither a state strategy for the development of science, nor an effective mechanism for financing scientific research. The funds that institutions like the Institute for Sociology, Sofia University, and the National Center for Public Opinion Research get from the state budget are extremely meager, only sufficient for salaries. The National Fund for Scientific Research only funds two to five sociological projects a year. This has led to a decrease in the number of scientific studies in the universities and institutes, undermined the prestige of sociology, and reduced the inflow of young people, particularly young males, into sociology.

The financing of sociological studies comes mainly from foreign foundations such as the Open Society Foundation, the Friedrich Naumann Foundation, Friedrich Ebert Foundation, Konrad Adenauer Foundation, and the Macarthur Foundation, as well as from organizations such as the King Boduen Fund, the German Marshall Fund, the Poland and Hungary Assistance for Reconstruction of the Economy (PHARE), the United Nations Development Program, and the United States Agency for International Development. Numerous individual and collective projects were financed by scholarships from Fulbright, NATO, and Central and Eastern European programs. Projects financed from abroad are only evaluated indirectly, on the basis of reports, articles, and business trips. Not surprisingly, the level and type of the foreign research financing available largely determines the areas and topics of the studies conducted.

RELATIONS AMONG ACADEMIC, PUBLIC, AND PRIVATE RESEARCH CENTERS

Economic liberalization and democratization in Bulgaria, after 1989, led to the appearance of numerous state, private, and nongovernmental sociological research centers. They developed in response to the higher demands for market research and public opinion polls (Atanasov, Molhov and Tchengelova 2001). Globalization and the interests of multinational corporations stimulated some of the newly developed centers for public opinion and market research. These included agencies that represent large international research firms like the Bulgarian member of Gallup International Balkan British Social Surveys (BBSS Gallup), Gesellschaft fur Konsumforschung Bulgaria (GfK), and Sova–5, renamed Sova–Harris. Other agencies, such as the Institute for Marketing and Surveys (IMAS), Market Test, Vitosha Research, Alpha Research, the Agency for Socioeconomic Analyses, and the Agency for Social Analyses are sponsored by national private interests or enterprises. They deal with quantitative and qualitative surveys, focus groups and in-depth interviews. Their presidents are members of various global and regional professional organizations. Many of their researchers are members of national organizations such as the Union of

Scientists in Bulgaria, the Bulgarian Sociological Association, the Association of Advertisement Agencies, and the National Association of Marketing Researchers in Bulgaria. There are also state-supported institutions, for example, the National Center for Public Opinion Research (NCPOR), which is under the control of the Parliament and is primarily funded through the state budget.

After 1989, many foundations and associations, founded by academic and university professors, formed their own specific research profiles. For example, the Civil Institute Foundation, which mainly includes scientists from Sofia University, conducted several studies of the civil sector (Dimitrov 1998). The Institute for Social Critique, uniting academic and university researchers, established a strong publishing program for the translation of sociological works. The Association for the Development of the Middle Class (AMCD) was involved in studies of stratification and inequality (Tilkidjiev 1998). The Association for Contacts and Cooperation–East European Self-Support (ACCESS) specialized in ethnic and political studies (Macariev 1999). A number of nongovernmental organizations (NGOs), such as the Center for the Study of Democracy (CSD), the Center for Liberal Strategies (CLS), the Center for Social Practices (CSP), the Foundation for National and Global Development, and Economics 2000 are also prestigious intellectual centers dealing with sociological research.

It often happens that NGOs, private agencies, and state institutions have the same clients. That is why relations among the sociological institutions are ambivalent; they are relations of both cooperation and competition. Experts point out that in 1995 alone, sociological information worth between two and three million dollars was sold on the Bulgarian market. Since 1989, the size of the tested samples of the population has been increasing between 4 to 5 percent annually. Approximately 30,000 to 40,000 people were taking part in sociological field studies at the beginning of the 1990s. In the mid-1990s, 90,000 to 100,000 persons participated in personal interviews, and as many more in telephone interviews (Mitev 1995, 123). By the end of the 1990s, BBSS Gallup alone was conducting 100,000 personal interviews each year.

BBSS Gallup is the biggest company for market and public opinion surveys in Bulgaria. It is associated with Taylor Nelson Sofres (TNS). Since 1992, BBSS Gallup has been conducting 1,000 monthly national surveys consisting of face-to-face interviews, telephone surveys, media surveys, advertisement monitoring and press-clipping, consumer panels for households, and ad hoc quantitative and qualitative research projects for commercial, social, political, and multinational clients.

Since 1999, Vitosha Research, founded in 1991, and owned by the Center for the Study of the Democracy (CSD), has been a partner of Gallup-Hungary in the project Euro Barometer. Vitosha Research carries out the sociological program of CSD, and in the year 2000, it conducted forty-five social, marketing, and media public opinion surveys, as well as 19,000 face-to-face interviews and thirty focus groups. Since 1999, the company has also participated in a number of national and international projects.

To sum up, post-1989 sociology in Bulgaria discovered new methods and new types of research. The competition among state, private, and nongovernmental entities that conduct sociological research has led to the emergence of a pluralistic sociological market and the marginalization of academic and, to a certain extent, university sociology. The sociology that serves the media, advertisement, and political markets has been given a particularly strong stimulus under these circumstances.

ESTABLISHMENT OF A NEW RESEARCH FIELD: GLOBAL-LOCAL INTERACTION

In the late 1980s, the issue of global trends and globalization was on its way to becoming the key issue of modern sociological discourse. This development informed the proposal, in the summer of 1989, to establish a new department, Global and Regional Development, at the Institute of Sociology. Because of the narrow professional horizons of the academic decision makers, the proposal met resistance. However, once institutional approval was given, the department was able to profit from the new social and intellectual developments in the field during the early 1990s. The rising tide of studies on globalization facilitated research on the painful transformation of Bulgarian society in the context of processes in Europe, and on a global scale. Cooperation with the Vienna Centre for Research and Documentation, the International Social Science Council, UNESCO (United Nations Education, Science, and Culture Organization), the United Nations Development Program, and with scientific programs of the European Union provided for a full agenda of research, publication, and other scientific activities in the social sciences. A constructivist approach based on the concept of social interaction fostered theoretical advancements in the study of systemic and actor-related dimensions of social transformation, and of the perception, assessment, and management of risks.

The results of these studies are documented in twenty-nine books, sixteen of them published in English. Their content can be tentatively placed into three groups, all of which related to the interplay between local (subnational), national, regional (subcontinental and continental), and global factors, actors, and trends. The first group covers the studies on the development of Bulgarian society in the context of regional (Eastern European, Southeastern European, European) and global relations and processes. Especially notable in this group were the first three Bulgarian *Human Development Reports* prepared by the department and commissioned by the United Nations Development Program (Genov 1995, 1996a, 1997a). These reports attempted the first holistic assessment of the causes and consequences of the complicated transformation of Bulgarian society.

The second group of studies and publications covered the large technological, economic, political, and cultural variations of the Southeast European region (Genov 1991, 1993, 1996b, 2000a; Genov and Becker 2001; Kertikov 2001). The leading topic in this context was belated modernization and the efforts to cope within the context of continental and global processes. The third group of publications focused on the transformation of Eastern European societies and their adaptation to global trends. Most of these publications were the outcome of the United Nations Educational Scientific and Cultural Organization–Managing of Social Transformation (UNESCO–MOST) international comparative project Personal and Institutional Strategies for Coping with Transformation Risks in Central and Eastern Europe (Genov 1999a, 1999b, 2000b). This cooperation brought to Sofia the first Summer School sponsored by UNESCO and the International Social Science Council, which was held in 2000, on the topic of International Comparative Research Programs in the Social Sciences. Given this background of intensive research, international scientific cooperation, and numerous publications, one can expect further intensification of research on global-local interactions and growing recognition of the achievements in this field of study.

A series of studies on Bulgarian society, conducted after 1993 by the Department of Global and Regional Development, on social risks, tensions and conflicts, addressed the "increasing difficulties of large groups to identify themselves with the ongoing social transformation" (Genov 1994, 11). Research on unemployment, increasing inequality and social stratification, and crime warns about the high cost of the reforms (Mantarova 2000). In a 1996 publication, Duhomir Minev and Ahthoni Vendov pay special attention to the conflict between the "organizational model" and the "normative model" in the process of restructuring economic power, the merging of economic and political power, the processes of "hidden nomenclature privatization," and anomie. According to them, the transformation in Bulgaria turned out to be devolution rather than evolution, and economic reforms resembled a mutation of the system. A particularly worrisome tendency was the lack of socially oriented elites, while selfish oriented elites flourished. Through anomie, they weakened normative changes and contributed to low civility and low effectiveness of the democratic political institutions (Minev 2000, 192–193; Minev, Fotev, and Vendov 1996, 280–281).

The existence of acute and mass anomie in Bulgaria is registered by both national and international comparative studies (Vladimirov et al. 1998). The economic crisis, the dramatic decrease in the GDP, and the period of hyperinflation (1996–97) led to the introduction of a Currency Board in the country. It is a paradox that this time the failure of the state represented a time of success for sociologists, who had noticed the signs of "the erosion of the organizational, economic and social rationality and effectiveness of the changes," or in other words, the "transformation of the transformation" (Minev, Fotev, and Vendov 1996, 289).

SOCIOLOGY AND SOCIAL TRANSFORMATION

It is now obvious that nobody anticipated or was prepared for what Zbigniew Brzezinski has characterized as the big failure of socialism. There was a vacuum of orientation and a lack of a counterelite in Bulgaria. Sociologists failed to predict the revolutions from above. However, at least in Bulgaria, the sociological elite played an active role in the political transformation. The major opposition party, the Union of Democratic Forces, which was founded in 1989, was given office space by the Institute of Sociology.

In other words, sociologists did not predict the social transformation, but rather supported its social processes. But how effective was this support? As Nikolai Genov observed of the Bulgarian model, "the challenge of the necessary, the completed, and the to-be-completed changes in the country turned out to be much more intensive than the informational, organizational, and moral abilities of the social actors to deal with this challenge" (Genov 1994, 15–16). Mitev defines the results of the transformation so far as "proto-democracy." According to him, proto-democracy marks the existence of the basic elements of a democratic political system but at the same time the lack of important conditions for them to fully function (Mitev 1998). The aim of the political transformation is the "consolidation of democracy," a situation in which the new democratic institutions would be irreversible, and internally and externally acknowledged. However, the forging of democratic institutions in the countries of Central and Eastern Europe, especially in Bulgaria, where genuine experience in democratic politics is very limited, has been and still is problematic for democratic consolidation. Yet, as Genov noted, the attempts at a direct transfer of the institutional models of the West does not necessarily offer an easy solution, but rather often contributes to an increase in the complexity and to new difficulties in the practical management of the social processes (Genov 1999b, 103).

The magnitude of the service of sociologists as experts, after 1989, is impressive. Between 1995 and 1999, associates of the Institute of Sociology took part in 127 studies of national importance and provided advice to different state or nongovernmental organizations on 229 occasions. A major proportion of the sociologists working outside of the academic community lead private organizations and NGOs that deal with consultancy and expert activities. Sociological expertise was most visible in the areas of economics and politics, probably because of the growing public interest in these issues.

There were two main tendencies in the role of sociologists as experts after 1989. They both were related to sociology's turn toward the media, political, and advertising markets. The first tendency was the politicization of expert reports. It was especially obvious in preelection surveys and prognoses in the first years after 1989. Several public scandals resulting from preelection prognoses by sociologists took place at that time. The sociologists in question, in line with their political preferences, apparently erred frequently in favor of their parties. This politicization confirmed the validity of Dorothy Nelkin's law of expert studies: the more important the sociopolitical consequences of an expert study are, the more probable it is for the expert study to be polarized along the pre-vailing political line. More recently, a second tendency, towards commercializa-tion, has gradually replaced the political one.

CONCLUSION

To summarize, in the words of a CNN advertisement for Bulgaria, the devel-opment of Bulgarian sociology after 1989 is "a treasure to discover." The hunt for this treasure is a challenge, but allows us to acknowledge the following lights and shadows of Bulgarian sociology after 1989. These include the boom in research, both national and international, but also of theory without empir-ical support and facts without theoretical explanation. The blossoming of intellectual freedom, but also of intellectual corruption. The emergence of com-petition and diversification among and between sociological institutions, but also the commercialization and politicization of sociological expertise. Greater publicity for sociology, but also a regression in professional development. The emergence of a multiplicity of paradigms and the flourishing of private socio-logical institutions, but also an atrophy of state support for sociology.

In Bulgaria, the process of the formation of a new identity for the so-called posttotalitarian sociology took place against the background of sociology's de-velopment during socialism, when it clearly had apologetic functions. The proximity of sociology to the institutions of authority in socialist society was a valuable source of funds and power, but it undermined sociology's neutrality and independence. It remains questionable whether or not sociology can regain the public trust, and whether or not it is too dependent on foreign resources and interests.

After 1989, sociologists in Bulgaria either took part in the ruling regime or engaged in a "lateral attack," cautioning against risks. Yet, neither support of the changes through integration within the official structures, nor "prescrip-tions for social survival" managed to prevent social risks (Nikolov 1999). The ambiguity of the sociologist's position, either included or excluded from the so-cial game, suggests that sociologists often found themselves in a position simi-lar to the Greek prophetess Cassandra. Like her, they could predict the future, but nobody listened to them.

Eadem mutata resurgo (Altered, I ressurect the same), the epitaph on Bernoulli's tombstone, aptly characterizes the case of Bulgarian society and its sociology since 1989. Hungarian sociologist Pal Tamas once characterized the situation as "a science in crisis for a society in crisis" (personal communication) Nonetheless, the identity crisis of Bulgarian sociology holds the potential for a psychotherapeutic, rationalizing development, both in its own right and as a part of the society. The coincidence of the identity crisis with sociology's open-ing to global society and science is a chance to realize this potential. It depends on the sociologists whether any dividends will be extracted from the crisis, because, according to the principle of bimodal symmetry, an organization cannot achieve its external aims if it has not achieved those aims internally. It is high time to realize that our schemes for the rationalization of society are possible only after we first apply them to sociology.

NOTES

Special thanks to Bulgarian sociologists Nikolai Genov, Ivan Evtimov, Georgi Dimitrov, Jelka Genova, Andrei Raichev, Kolio Koev, Ivan Chalakov, Asen Iosifov, and Petar-Emil Mitev for their cooperation and support.

1. In places where no source is mentioned, information came from interviews conducted by the author with several Bulgarian sociologists, including Nikolai Genov, Ivan Evtimov, Georgi Dimitrov, Jelka Genova, Andrei Raichev, Asen Iosifov, and Petar-Emil Mitev.

2. In Bulgaria, as in many Central and Eastern European (CEE) countries, "academic" refers to association with an academy, such as the Bulgarian Academy of Sciences. These academies, which are separate institutions from the university, represent a combination of learned society, made up of the most outstanding scholars and scientists in the country, and research institute. In many CEE countries, the Czech Republic excepted, academies of science have graduate programs within their research institutes, and some have undergraduate programs.

4

Croatian Sociology after 1990: Toward New Institutionalization?

Ognjen Caldarovic

INTRODUCTION

Sociology has existed as a professional field and a university subject in Croatia for many years. As early as 1913, it was taught as a university subject at the Faculty of Law at Zagreb University (the equivalent of a school of law at an American university). During the Communist period, sociology was taught in all of the schools at the university, albeit many times under different names: Basics of Society, Introduction to Marxism, Introduction to the Science of Society, Basics of Social Sciences. This means that sociology as a general subject, and in many cases also as a specialized one, was taught at all schools of Zagreb and at other universities in the Republic of Croatia (then part of the former Yugoslavia). It also should be mentioned that sociology (sometimes under the general rubric of social sciences) was and still is a required subject in all secondary schools.

As a result of the specific social, political, and economic development of the former Yugoslavia, that is, the break with Stalin in 1948, the development of self-management and self-government, and the political nonalignment between the two blocks, there was not the same kind of strong reorientation in sociology as occurred in other Soviet-dominated Central and Eastern European nations. Instead, a slow and steady professionalization of sociology and sociologists took place in the 1960s and 1970s and was strengthened in the 1980s and 1990s. In the 1990s, sociology in Croatia was a competitive social science, and sociologists as professionals were active in many areas of society, including politics.

Today, many Croatian sociologists are active in the International Sociological Association and the European Sociological Association. There is institutional cooperation with other sociological centers in Europe and in the U.S.A. Also, there are several international educational centers in the country, for example the Interuniversity Center for Postgraduate Studies in Dubrovnik, and the Croatian International Center of Universities. At these centers, many courses, conferences, seminars, and symposia take place on a yearly basis. Scholars from all over the world have a real chance to exchange ideas, opinions, and the results of their current research.

In the continuation of this analysis of sociology in Croatia after 1990, we will throw some light on the institutional framework and give basic information concerning the position of sociology in the universities in Croatia. We will also provide information on major journals and publishing houses as well as on the variety of perspectives in Croatian sociology.

THE INSTITUTIONAL FRAMEWORK OF CROATIAN SOCIOLOGY

In Croatia, there are several universities. The major and the oldest one is *Sveuciliste u Zagrebu* (University of Zagreb), which was founded in 1669. There is also the University of Split, the University of Rijeka, and the University of Osijek. The Ministry of Science and Technology of Croatia is the principal financier of the university education system. In the Croatian educational system, there is a *numerus clausus* (quota system) for each university and group of study. Recently, at the Faculty of Philosophy at the University of Zagreb, the number of applicants in sociology has been three to four times more than the quota allows to be enrolled. In the academic year 2000–2001, for example, 450 applicants competed for only 60 places! The Ministry of Science and Technology sets the quotas but only funds a portion of the number of places it allows. For example, in a given year, out of 50 places provided for the study of sociology at Zagreb University, only 35 will be funded by the Ministry of Science and Technology, and the remaining 15 students will have to pay for themselves. The general tendency in financing has been to increase personal financing by students and to decrease state funding.

At the moment, sociology as an independent field of study at the undergraduate level can be found at the Faculty of Philosophy at the University of Zagreb (as an independent major or as one of two equal major concentrations), the Faculty of Philosophy at the University of Split (as one of two compulsory equal subjects), and in the Department of Croatian Studies at the University of Zagreb (as one of two equal compulsory subjects). Postgraduate and doctoral programs are available at the Faculty of Philosophy at the University of Zagreb.

Sociology is also one of the subjects required as a part of the curriculum of other schools at the universities. Courses required usually range from general sociology to applied sociology related to the major field or discipline of a given school. For example, at the Faculty of Engineering and Shipbuilding at Zagreb University, there is General Sociology, but also Sociology of Organizations and Industrial Sociology. At the Faculty of Medicine, there is Sociology of Medicine and Sociology of Mental Health. At the Faculty of Economics, apart from General Sociology, there are courses in Sociology of Tourism, and Economic Sociology. At the Faculty of Architecture, there is Urban Sociology and Social Ecology. There remains some question concerning the credentials of the instructors who teach sociology at these different schools at the university level. In many cases they are not professionally educated sociologists, but rather "retooled" sociologists.

For many years, the major and main institution for teaching sociology has been the Department of Sociology at the Faculty of Philosophy of University of Zagreb. Sociology as an independent field of study was established there in 1963. At the very beginning, the staff came mostly from the philosophy department, and the fruitful exchange of ideas, orientations, people and the like lasted for years. Most came with a social philosophical background. One of the most distinguished social philosophical orientations at the department was known as the Praxis School, a Marxist approach highly influential in the 1960s and 1970s. Today, however, the social philosophical orientation in sociology is increasingly being replaced by the applied, professional, and experimental orientations.

In 2001, there were twenty lecturers at the department, eleven full professors, two associate professors, and three assistant professors. For many years, the system of study has followed the American model. There are core courses in sociology, along with electives that can be chosen from several schools at the University of Zagreb. In this sense, the study system is well adapted to the changes required for articulation with the European Union.

As might be expected, sociology has had a stronger presence at some university schools (faculties) than others, so it is worth mentioning where the stronger subdepartments or concentration of sociologists can be found in Croatia. In Zagreb, at the Faculty of Political Sciences, Faculty of Law, Faculty of Medicine, and Faculty of Economics a higher concentration of sociologists as lecturers and researches can be found. This is also the case, albeit in smaller concentrations, in other university towns like Split and Rijeka.

MAJOR RESEARCH CENTERS AND INSTITUTIONS

There are several university research institutions for sociological research, mostly located in Zagreb. The Institute for Social Research in Zagreb is the oldest institution of this kind. It was established in 1963, and today has many specialized groups for different fields of study, such as sociology of education, rural sociology, urban sociology, transition studies, and social structure. More than thirty researchers are permanently employed in different scientific positions carrying out several research projects. The principal financier of this institute is the Ministry of Science and Technology, but some projects also have been conducted for independent entrepreneurs, firms, and agencies.

The Institute for Applied Social Research, *Ivo Pilar*, in Zagreb, is a newer research institution established in 1992. It is an independent research institution with more than sixty research and administrative staff members. It competes with other research institutions for scientific projects and research tasks at the Ministry of Science and Technology, which is also the principal source of its funding. Other institutions support the work of the institute as well. It covers many subjects and does research on public opinion and also conducts projects for independent entrepreneurs and companies. It has departmental units in several other Croatian cities, including Split, Rijeka, and Pula.

The Institute for Migration and Ethnic Studies in Zagreb is also one of the older research institutions, with approximately forty employees. Because of the rather large number of Croatians living abroad, and the large number of workers who migrated to the countries of Western Europe as so-called guest workers in the 1960s, migration studies is one of the oldest areas in the discipline. The institute is engaged in research on external and internal migration, and the principal financier is the Ministry of Science and Technology, along with some independent agencies and alliances.

The research unit in the Department of Sociology at the Faculty of Philosophy in Zagreb also represents a strong sociological research institution. Each university professor in the Department of Sociology at the Faculty of Philosophy is usually engaged in different research projects that are carried out mostly through this research unit. It also competes for funding from the Ministry of Science and Technology and from time to time accepts research projects financed by other sources.

There are also several independent research offices and centers, privately owned and directed toward the independent sector. They are mostly in the field of marketing research and public polling, but occasionally conduct more elaborate sociological studies as well. At the moment, there are several institutions of this kind. Also, some bigger factories and enterprises have their own smaller research centers, as do major newspaper companies that conduct their own public polling.

THEORY AND RESEARCH

In the 1960s and 1970s, many classical research topics were of typical interest among the former Yugoslavian and Croatian sociologists. These included the study of migration, the study of social structure and stratification, and, most of all, studies of industrial sociology, with an emphasis on self-management, self-government, and participation. Many research projects in these areas were organized in cooperation with scholars from abroad. This included several comparative studies, along with several international meetings at different places in the former Yugoslavia. The strong influence of the Praxis School must be mentioned as well as many seminars and summer philosophy and sociology schools held each year on Korcula Island.

At the ideological level, Marxism was an implicitly adopted ideological orientation that influenced the curriculum at the universities during the 1960–70 period. However, the Praxis School was critical of the theoretically dogmatic "base and superstructure" version of Marxism. Its critical Marxist orientation dominated the education of philosophy and sociology students during the period from 1960 to 1980. After 1990, Marxism remained as one of the theoretical orientations in sociology, and the influence of humanistic Marxism as the legacy of the Praxis School still maintains a presence in the curriculum, especially in philosophy.

After 1990, the focus of research topics changed toward the new problems facing the country. The most difficult problems that were studied, and are still being studied, have been those related to the characteristics and consequences of the war that broke out in the former Yugoslavia in 1991. The great number of refugees, displaced persons, and returnees; the problems of peaceful reintegration, new adaptation, and ethnic relations of the former sides during the war, and now in peace; and housing questions were among the most important topics of sociological interest and research. It should also be stated that because of the turbulent situation in the country and the many political negotiations involving a large number of issues, domestic and international, sociology has yet to play an appropriate role in the investigation of the dynamic social scene. Instead, the state and the Croatian government have made many decisions prematurely, expediently and with little or no knowledge of the potential unintended consequences of the measures to be proclaimed.

Because of the lack of financial resources in general, as well as the much more important problems in the country, the interest for basic, long-term sociological research diminished to a certain extent during the 1990s. Still, many pragmatic and more applied research projects, for example, on the politics of the housing of the war returnees and on some aspects of cultural transition and economic transformation (privatization) of the country, were carried out. Also, many companies carried out market research projects, as well as many opinion polls concerning elections, communal matters, and the popularity of politicians and public figures. Recently, there have been some renewed efforts to restart the investigation of social structure in the countries of the former Yugoslavia, but this has yet to be settled and organized.

The Croatian Sociological Association was established in 1963, and currently has approximately 200 to 300 members, though most of them are not very active. Members of the association form sections around different subjects such as religion, medicine, urban studies, rural sociology, and the association organizes an annual meeting of sociologists at which current research and other topics are presented and discussed.

There are several clearly professional sociological journals, as well as many other journals, not strictly sociological, that publish sociological issues and themes. All of them are published four times a year. The *Revija za Sociologiju* (Sociological Review), founded in 1963, is among the oldest professional journals and publishes articles in Croatian, as well as in English and Slovenian. Editorial control is in the hands of the Croatian Sociological Association and the Department of Sociology of the Faculty of Philosophy in Zagreb. *Sociologija Sela* (Rural Sociology), established in 1958, is another of the older professional sociological journals. It publishes mostly in Croatian, but also in English. The Institute for Social Research at the University of Zagreb is its editorial home. *Migracijske Teme* (Migration Themes), founded in 1970, is a journal published by the Institute for Migration and Ethnic Studies and is also one of the oldest journals of its kind.

Drustvena Istrazivanja (Social Research), founded in 1992, is published by the Institute for Applied Social Research, *Ivo Pilar*. It publishes primarily empirical research, but also some theoretical articles, in Croatian and also in English. *Polemos* (War), a new journal founded in 1998 and devoted to the problems of society and war and to the sociology of armed forces and society, is published by the Croatian Sociological Association and the publishing house Jesenski and Turk, which is located in Zagreb. *Socijalna Ekologija* (Social Ecology), founded in 1992, is a journal published by the Department of Sociology of the Faculty of Philosophy in Zagreb and the Croatian Sociological Association. It publishes works mostly in environmental sociology.

Jesenski and Turk, a newly established publishing house that specializes in sociology and, in a broader sense, the social sciences and humanities, appeared in Zagreb after 1990. It was established by a group of professional sociologists of the younger generation who found their professional and market interests coming together in the establishment of a professional sociological publishing house. Over the past decade they have published approximately 100 titles, ranging from literary criticism to hard sociology. Around 60 percent of the published titles are translations (e.g., Kuhn 1999; Mouzelis 2000; Reich 1999; Rifkin 1999; Ritzer, 1999). Their most recent activity is a series of translations in the form of a scientific pocket book. The series includes translations of titles by Icon Books in Cambridge, England, published mostly in 2000–2001 (i.e., Heaton 2001; Horrocks 2001; Sardar 2001; Sim 2001; Wright 2001). They have also translated one of George Ritzer's textbooks (1997).

THE FUTURE OF SOCIOLOGY IN CROATIA

There are several major problems concerning the future of sociology as a profession in Croatia. The weak and insufficiently visible presence of sociology in the society is probably the most important and general problem. Sociology as a profession is not yet recognized as an autonomous discipline, different from, say, social work. As a result, sociologists have not yet been perceived as professionals who have their own disciplinary identity and distinctive place in the social scientific division of labor, and who can contribute a particular type of expertise to the research and understanding of society. Mostly, they are perceived under the general category of social scientists that can offer passing observations on any given current situation. The mass media, for example, will often turn to sociologists for a short commentary on the sociological aspects of this or that situation of current interest. This lack of recognition of sociology, coupled with widespread unemployment caused by the war, the privatization process, and a destroyed and uncompetitive economy, has resulted in little demand for professional sociologists in any area of society. For example, of late, less sociologist have been able to find jobs in the general economy, its firms, enterprises, and factories, than ever before. However, this situation is likely to change due to the many transformations that are taking place in the economy and everyday life, areas hardest hit by the privatization process.

Young sociologists typically must try to apply for working positions at secondary schools, where they can teach compulsory subjects like sociology, ethics, sometimes philosophy, and other related subjects. However, they have to compete with the graduates from the Faculty of Political Science, and more recently with the graduates from the Department of Croatian Studies as well as some other areas of specialization. The more ambitious and prosperous students can try to find positions at an institute or the university, but, because of the restrictive policy of the state in the field of higher education and the small percentage of the state budget devoted to higher education, generally less than 1 percent, there are few openings. For this reason, a scientific career at the university or research institutions does not look very promising. Nor is it very attractive with small salaries, weak and complicated possibilities for making progress, and relative lack of job security, especially at the scientific institutes. Because of this, there has been a general brain drain of any kind of young professionals during the last ten years. In the future, this fact could have a devastating effect on the country's intellectual potential, and the impact is already being felt. Nonetheless, with the growth of the civil society, as well as the strengthening of democracy, a better position for sociologists, and for sociology as a scientific discipline, can be expected in the future. However, this will most probably only take place after a painful and long process, with no clear end yet in sight.

5

Sociology in the Czech Republic after 1989

Miloslav Petrusek

It is an interesting and historically indisputable fact that events in the academic society of Czechoslovak sociologists were the harbinger of the principal political change of regime that occurred after November 17, 1989, in what was then Czechoslovakia. In December of 1988, a plenary session of the Czechoslovak Sociological Society took place in Prague.[1] In those days, the Society had 639 regular and 280 associate members, of which about 300 participated in the plenary session. After the traditional speeches of the official academic representatives, who did their best to avoid the fact that perestroika was under way in the Soviet Union, a discussion followed. In that discussion several members of the Society mentioned two facts. One, Czechoslovak sociology had parted with its own democratic tradition and had become a manipulated science unworthy of comparison, not only with European science or even Polish sociology, but also with Russian and Bulgarian sociology. And, two, the personalities who had played an important part in the revival of sociology in the second half of the 1960s had been excluded from participation in sociological congresses for the previous twenty years.

Following these provocative speeches, the elections for deputies in the governing bodies of the Czechoslovak Sociological Association were held. The traditional procedure suggested by the secretariat of the Central Committee of the Communist Party, that a vote be taken by raising hands and simply following the instructions from the authorities, was overruled by a proposal to first secretly nominate the members of the board, and then to vote. As a result, the majority of the officially sanctioned representatives failed to be elected, and instead one-third of the new members elected came from the so-called grey zone.[2]

Even though this fact was characterized as a revolt against the regime, no repression followed, as there was neither the strength nor the political will for such action anymore. A paradox is that the Czech Sociological Society played a similar, though not so glorious, role during the division of the common state of Czechs and Slovaks. The Slovak Sociological Society separated from the Czechoslovak Sociological Society and became an independent body as early as 1990. Since that time, both national sociologies have developed separately and relatively independently of one another.[3]

NORMALIZATION AND THE DEVELOPMENT OF CZECH SOCIOLOGY

To be able to understand the development of Czech sociology in the last decade, one must examine its evolution. In the years from 1970 to 1989, Czechoslovak sociology was probably the worst hit by the aftermath of late totalitarianism. This was the logical result of two conditions. First, the very fact of the Prague Spring of 1968, when Czechoslovak society showed an unusual solidarity in its resistance to the occupation by the Warsaw Pact allies. And second, the fact that sociologists such as Pavel Machonin, Jaroslav Klofac, Jirina Siklova, and Miloslav Jodl were among the most engaged in political activities during the Prague Spring and had prepared new action programs for the reorganization of society.

The result of the Prague Spring was the so-called normalization, which meant the regression of society back to the shape of the late 1950s. It can be characterized as a late totalitarian regime, lacking drastic repression in the form of political trials, providing citizens with a relatively high standard of living, cultivating civic apathy, and making contacts with Western democratic societies absolutely impossible.

In sociology, this situation was reflected in several ways. There were dramatic personnel purges, as sociologists were expelled from the Communist Party, dismissed from academic posts, and downgraded to manual jobs such as window cleaners or laborers. Leading representatives of the field in the 1960s, including Jaroslav Klofac, Pavel Machonin, Irena Dubska, Miloslav Jodl, and Jindrich Fibich, were thus forced to part with sociology. Many others, such as Zdenek Strmiska, Jaroslav Krejci, Vaclav Lamser, Bedrich Loewenstein, Karel Macha, and Ivan Svitak, emigrated. Paradoxically, all those who left were replaced not by younger, ambitious graduates in sociology, committed to the regime, but by a group one generation older, which had not won recognition in the 1960s and belonged to the second team: Karel Rychtarik, Marie Hulakova, and others.

Contacts with world sociology were disrupted. Interaction with Western and Polish sociology was completely severed, and contacts with Russian sociology were strictly monitored and required Party approval. In addition, from 1971 to 1989, not a single translation of any sociological book of Western origin was published. Translations of works by Eastern Block authors were carefully censored, for example, *The History of Sociological Thought* by Jerzy Szacki (1981). Books by Jurij Nikolajevitch Davydov and others were not permitted to be published. A further problem was that the technological infrastructure was obsolete. For example, the Faculty of Journalism, which became the Faculty of Social Sciences in 1990, possessed only one personal computer.

However, between 1970 and 1989, the institutional structures of sociology did continue to exist. *Sociologicky Casopis* (Journal of Sociology) was published and the Czech Sociological Society continued its existence. The Sociological Institute of the Academy of Sciences merged with the Institute of Philosophy, and the Institute for Public Opinion Surveys was remodeled into an information service for the Communist Party's Central Committee. The majority of the so-called resort research institutes (i.e., those working for particular ministries) continued to work on elementary investigations of work behavior and industrial relations, but they were decimated personally and professionally. Not only did Czechoslovak sociology cease to be a rival to other national sociologies, its representatives showed no interest whatsoever in such intellectual encounter and confrontation.

Beginning in the late 1980s, a certain loosening could be felt, and attempts to liberate sociology from Party pressure and state supervision occurred. In January 1988, Josef Alan established the Sociological Initiative, the aim of which was an independent and qualified evaluation of the social situation. In 1987, the journal *Sociologicky Obzor* (Sociological Horizon), edited by Josef Alan and Miloslav Petrusek started to be secretly published as a *samizdat*. In it, the first critical analytical studies of the state of society, as well as ideologically unbiased information about current trends in Western sociology, appeared.

In Brno, a group of sociologists and translators worked secretly to publish translations of Western literature from the Dahrendorf list. Ralf Dahrendorf had compiled a list of approximately one hundred titles of basic sociological and also some philosophical literature to serve as a guide for undercover editorial activities. This literature was supposed to represent a basic intellectual foundation for a new open society. Under the Communist regime, forty-six books were translated, the majority of which were published by official publishers after the November 1989 change of regime. Among these were classical texts by Alexis Tocqueville and contemporary texts by Daniel Bell, Raymond Aron, Hannah Arendt, and others.

ATTEMPTS TOWARD A RESURRECTION: THE CLASH
BETWEEN ECONOMISTS AND SOCIOLOGISTS

The fact that sociology as an institution survived the era of normalization was more of a double-edged sword than a foundation stone for future construction. It was not by chance that the change in 1989 was labeled the velvet revolution. There was no will to bring the representatives of the past regime to justice, no decommunization of sociology as such. The most compromised representatives of Marxist-Leninist sociology, which, in fact, not only had nothing to do with Neo-Marxism, but did not even have a clear notion of it, departed to work in the private sector. Many became entrepreneurs, some of them quite significantly in the sphere of the entertainment industry. Others began to work for independent publishers or in the left-wing press. The Communist Party was not abolished, although the Communist regime was declared criminal. Unmerited academic titles were taken away from their holders.

A more important milestone was the introduction of the screening, or lustration, law that stipulated that some top-ranking posts could not be filled by personnel whose collaboration with the secret police was provable. The law itself met with rather sharp resistance, not only among the potentially afflicted, but also among some members of the dissent for whom it represented a violation of human (or even civil) rights. Nonetheless, many exponents of the former regime resigned from their leading posts, or did not attempt to get new ones for fear of being compromised.

It is important to note that while during the Prague Spring the participation of sociologists was significant and the participation of economists relatively small (the group of prominent revisionist economists around Oto Sik was by far not as influential as it had seemed in the late 1960s), the events of November 1989 and afterward were directed by liberal economists (Vaclav Havel being partly in opposition against them). The aim was to create a market economy, following the radical liberal model that was the foundation for the economic policy of Margaret Thatcher. Advocated by Vaclav Klaus, an exceptionally well-educated Czech economist and later prime minister, it was met with sharp disagreement by a number of sociologists who cherished the idea of fostering a moderate form of a welfare state. However, the liberal economic strategy offered many the chance to get rich quick, as it was based on voucher privatization, an undoubtedly Czech invention. In the effort to provide every state enterprise with a private owner, state property was divided up into thousands of vouchers, which were then quickly snapped up by so-called investment funds. As a result, the majority of citizens never became owners, and a considerable proportion of the privatized property was subject to an almost monopoly-like concentration and to corrupt behavior.[4]

It was within the context of these socioeconomic circumstances, when the Czech Republic gradually lost its early leading role as a poster child for privatization and became just another regular applicant for membership in the European Union, that a certain hostility between a large portion of economists and sociologists developed. This attitude found extreme expression in Vaclav Klaus's publications in which he expressed his aversion to sociology by labeling it, following in Friedrich von Hayek's footsteps, "an abortive attempt at social engineering," and later "a strange science that does not understand the meaning of what it doubts" (Klaus 2000). Sociologists did not react openly (except Petrusek 2000), but Klaus's attack, directed against the entire discipline, strengthened the position of those sociologists who had criticized the course of reform, calling it abortive privatization or stolen privatization, that is, those sociologists who had sought alternative solutions and to create new, modernizing transformation strategies capable of finding the way out of a "blind alley leading most likely to a relative backwardness" (Mlcoch, Machonin, and Sojka 2000, 197). However, the most serious political problem from a practical point of view was the discrepancy between the liberal economic rhetoric and the social democratic policy that was pursued by the first post-November governments. Luckily enough, the clash between the economists and sociologists did not find its expression in any administrative steps against sociology, although there was an attempt to abolish the whole Academy of Sciences (including the newly independent Institute of Sociology) as a Soviet-type institution.

INSTITUTIONAL CHANGES FROM 1990 TO 2000

Although the post-1989 transformation left practically all the sociological institutions that had been established in the 1960s in place, without making any significant structural changes, it was necessary to make several changes in their personnel and focus. An independent Institute of Sociology of the Academy of Sciences of the Czech Republic was cut out of the Institute of Philosophy and Sociology. Within the newly established Institute of Sociology, not only was the head changed (the first director was Jiri Musil, followed by Michal Illner), but so too was the range of topics and the structure of research objectives. Initially, the institute concentrated on the analysis of transformation-related processes and social inequalities (especially income), on the changes in political structures and voting behavior, and on the sociological aspects of parliamentary procedures. Later, a Department of Gender Studies was established, winning quick recognition not only in the Czech Republic but abroad as well.

The departments of sociology at three universities, Charles University in Prague, Masaryk University in Brno, and Palacky University in Olomouc, got rid of their odious titles as departments of Marx-Leninist sociology, and were returned to their traditional simple name, sociology. The most compromised ideological representatives of the past regime left the departments more or less voluntarily, and the less compromised sometimes remained in their posts. Many of those who had been previously expelled, particularly between 1970 and 1972, returned. The return was not painless however. Some prominent dissidents had lost touch with their field, through no fault of their own, and were not well accepted, especially by the students. The mentality, psychology, and demands of students had changed, a direct consequence of the fact that the students had discovered the world, acquired new language skills, and gotten into contact with world sociological literature.

In addition to the traditional sociological workplaces, new ones emerged. The former Faculty of Journalism of Charles University was transformed into the Faculty of Social Sciences (the first deans being journalist-dissident Cestmir Suchy, and sociologist Miloslav Petrusek). Apart from sociology, social policy, international relations, and mass communications began to be taught there. At the Faculty of Philosophy, a Department of Social Work was established. In Brno, a new Faculty of Social Studies, with an orientation similar to that of the new Prague faculty, was formed (the dean being Ivo Mozny). Sociology also returned to some regional universities, schools of economics, and other fields.

It can be said that the rate of tuition has gradually stabilized on a level comparable with many European universities. Also, contacts with Western European and American universities have become frequent and matter-of-fact. On the other hand, contacts with Polish sociology, which were once a significant source of inspiration for the development of Czechoslovak sociology (having substituted in a way for the missing contact with Western and non-Marxist literature), as well as contacts with Russian sociology, have all but disappeared. This fact is reflected in a certain one-sidedness of topics. With the intent of publishing in Anglo-American journals, some Czech authors choose topics general and generic enough for a Western reader to understand. From the Czech point of view, the results are frequently absolute banalities or downright mystifications.

Unfortunately, the traditionally good personal and working contacts between Czech and Slovak sociology have also almost completely vanished. The relative advantage of Czech sociology, the fact that it was or could be a bridge between Western and Eastern sociology, has been lost. As evidence of this is the fact that, since 1990, not a single Polish or Russian sociological book has been published, something which cannot be said about the literature in political science or economics.

During the first decade of freedom, *Sociologicky Casopis*, published by the Institute of Sociology of the Academy of Sciences, also focused mainly on transformation-related topics. These included the study of social inequalities and the lingering of egalitarian trends, which apart from being part of the Czech tradition, were strengthened by the egalitarian policy of the era of so-called real socialism. The dispute over social inequality became the key theoretical and research topic of Czech sociology. In this debate, *the fact* of social inequality was not denied. Rather, the issues of the legitimization of inequality and the degree of socially acceptable inequality that would not lead to social upheaval were dealt with. Apart from that, studies dealing with the political structure of society, and its changes with special regard to left-wing and right-wing extremist groups, appeared. Special editions of the journal were published that focused, for example, on the phenomenon of old age in the society under transformation, or on housing and social policy. In cooperation with the reestablished Institute of Tomas G. Masaryk (named for the founder of Czech-oslovak sociology) within the Academy of Sciences, special issues were published on the occasion of the anniversaries of Masaryk's birth and death. The Masaryk Institute also began to publish his collected works (the most important are Masaryk 1995, 1998, 2000, 2001a, 2001b). This was the third attempt at publishing them, as the first one had been interrupted by the Nazi occupation in 1939, and the second one by the Communist coup d'etat in 1948. Masaryk is analyzed not only within the context of world sociology and philosophy, but also within the context of the crisis of modern man.

In the late 1990s, an English version of *Sociologicky Casopis*, the *Czech Sociological Review*, appeared. It is a collection of the most interesting papers from *Sociologicky Casopis*, together with new texts focused on acquainting readers abroad with the specific features of the development of Czech society. A very important fact is that together with the authors of the older and middle-aged generation, new and young authors publish their papers here (e.g., Martin Kreidl, Klara Vlachova, and Dusan Luzny). All of these sociologists studied for some time at universities abroad. The papers in the *Czech Sociological Review* are usually published in thematic editions, dealing, for example, with the issues of youth, Czech-German relations, voting behavior, income inequalities, and gender and the status of women in Czech society.

In 1991, a new and specialized publishing house of sociological literature, *Sociologicke nakladatelstvi* (SLON) came into existence. Much to their credit, they published the first sociological analysis of the causes of the collapse of the Communist system in the Czech Republic (Mozny 1991). The principal question of the analysis was why was it that the political upheaval in Czechoslovakia occurred so late, and at the same time why was it so easy? It argues that the conditions for the change were prepared for by changes in family behavior and in the structure of human and social capital. The first books to be published by *Sociologicke nakladatelstvi* were textbooks aimed at filling the information void of the last two decades as quickly as possible. Two of the most successful were an introduction to sociology, by Jan Keller (1992), and a series of monographic works covering topics including the sociology of the family (Matousek 1993; Mozny 1999), employment as a social problem (Mares 1994), youth considered at high risk for involvement in delinquency and drug abuse (Labath 2001), sociology of medicine and the social status of the patient (Kapr and Koukola 1998), the sociology of bureaucracy and organization (Keller 1996), inequality and poverty (Mares 1999), social policy (Potucek 1995), the study of civic community and therapeutic community (Hartl 1997), and social movements (Znebejanek 1997).

All of these books shared several significant features. Their authors were well acquainted with the foreign literature. But, they also took into account the specific features and problems of Czech society. They aimed at opening topical issues that were felt to remain unsolved. And, they were written by authors both from Prague and elsewhere. This last point is very important since Czech sociology has become polycentric. The once dreaded Prague centrism, which was the result of the Communist state's necessity to have all potentially critical or dangerous sociological activities under control, has disappeared.

The appearance of the above listed books, together with some others published by other publishers, dealing with environmental, social, economic, and political issues, enabled sociology to enter a wider public discourse. Step by step, sociologists have gained respect in Czech society. They are asked to give expert analyses and to contribute to the media. Some sociologists have even taken prominent political positions, representing parties ranging from liberal and conservative to social-democratic. Even the followers of the former regime, the so-called old Communists, have established their own sociological club.

The activity of translators should not be omitted, either. Works by Raymond Aron, Daniel Bell, Anthony Giddens, Zygmunt Bauman, Pierre Bourdieu, and others have been released. For the first time in sixty years, translations of classical sociology are being systematically published, such as works by Emile Durkheim, Marcel Mauss, Georg Simmel, and Thorstein Veblen. Nonetheless, if we compare our situation with the state of affairs in Poland or even Russia, we must admit we still lag behind.

Of course, as in other post-Communist countries, funding, not only of publishing, but also of teaching and research activities, is a grave problem. In the beginning, great assistance came from abroad (e.g., the Open Society Fund). Later on, during the time of the great, but rather overhyped economic boom, the assistance declined. Today, all sociological activities, research, teaching, and publishing, receive funding from state resources, especially in the universities. Such activities also receive funding from both state and private grants, and last but not least, from foreign institutions. For example, the Salda project, the translation of French sociological texts, was supported by French grants, and other similar projects have been supported by the German Goethe Institute. Nevertheless, state universities still lack the funds that would enable them to accept a higher number of the applicants interested in the humanities, including sociology. The ratio of the number of applicants to the number of students that can be accepted still ranges from 4:1 to 10:1.

After November 1989, some private institutions focusing mainly on research appeared on the scene. An example is the Center for Empirical Research, which carries out both basic and applied sociological research, including commissioned surveys based largely on representative samples. Unfortunately, their topics are rather stereotypical: the popularity of politicians, voting preferences, and attitudes of people toward issues related to both internal and international politics. Nevertheless, in most cases these surveys are of high quality and offer sociologists plenty of data to be examined. The Institute for Public Opinion Surveys, which has recently become part of the Academy of Sciences, gradually but radically changed from being a strictly ideological institution in the service of the state and Party to a bonafide research organization bearing comparison with similar institutions abroad.

Public opinion polls, carried out either by private firms or by the state Institute for Public Opinion Surveys, have provoked discussion among leading Czech sociologists Petr Mateju and Pavel Machonin (see Machonin and Tucek 1996; Mateju and Vlachova 1999). The polls have been sharply criticized by some as biased, banal, and trivial, while praised by others as a source of information for longitudinal studies of attitudes. In support of the latter perspective is the fact that the election results corresponded more to preference polls than to the predictions from basic theoretical research, which assumed that the right-wing orientation of Czech politics would be supported by the nascent middle class.

Strangely enough, the newly acquired freedom and democracy had a negative impact on the Masaryk Czech Sociological Society. Under Communism, this voluntary association of sociologists had carried out activities, such as the exchange of opinions and meetings with expelled colleagues, that official institutions could not provide, and which almost disappeared from the professional scene. Following the euphoria of the early 1990s, when the Society took back its traditional name, Masaryk and when contacts among people in general and scholars in particular seemed to flourish, a major setback occurred. The Society, which under the totalitarian regime had roughly 1000 members, dwindled to only about 300 formally registered members, and all the important sociological activities began to take place at the universities and research institutes instead of within the Society. So far, all attempts to revitalize the Society have failed, as it has had little to offer, particularly to the younger generation of sociologists. From an original ten sections, only two are in operation today, one dealing with the sociology of agriculture (led by Vera Majerova), and the other with social deviance (led by Kazimir Vecerka).

PARADIGMATIC DIFFERENTIATION OF CZECH SOCIOLOGY

Immediately after the velvet revolution, Czech sociology was rather limited in terms of areas of focus. The dominant issue was transformation, its theory, analysis, and criticism. Nevertheless, in the late 1990s, due to the emergence of the middle-aged and younger generations, sociology became more broadly differentiated. At first, this differentiation developed as a result of a split between the macro and micro levels of analysis of the transformation. An interest in biographic data emerged, different from the standard empirical analyses based on large surveys. This research dealt with local history, that is, the events between the 1948 coup d'etat and the present as perceived both by participants in these historically important events and by ordinary people. Biographic sociology yielded its first harvest when a large monograph based on the autobiographies by selected sociologists was published (Konopasek 2000).

The biographic perspective also greatly influenced (especially in Prague) the teaching of sociology, and sharpened the conflict between quantitative (e.g., Hynek Jerabek, Jan Rehak, and Blanka Rehakova) and qualitative (Zdenek Konopasek and his school) sociologists. In Western sociology, this conflict withered away long ago. In addition, it was only within the framework of this dispute that the issue of postmodernism entered Czech sociological discourse. Vaclav Belohradsky and Miloslav Petrusek participated as moderate advocates of the legitimacy of the term "postmodern society." Postmodern discourse seems to be quite fruitful in the context of media studies and the nascent analysis of popular culture.

Until recently, Czech sociology had not been clearly differentiated in a way corresponding to Western sociologies. Only with great difficulty could individual sociologists and their works be placed within the paradigmatic axis suggested, for example, by George Ritzer. At the macro level, several essential issues have been articulated and become the subject of serious discussion and dispute. These include the relationship between conditioned historical causality (social causality) and the realization of projects and programs prepared beforehand by social and economic elites. The doyen of Czech sociologists, Pavel Machonin, tried to reconcile both approaches within his concept of "social experience" (Machonin 1997). Another issue has been the relationship between national and international sociology. The gist of this dispute is the relevance of some comparative surveys in which respondents are asked essentially irrelevant questions.

A third issue that has emerged has been the relationship between the nascent middle class and social and political stability. Here the dispute is between the supporters of the overestimated proportion of the middle class among the population and its stabilizing function, and the representatives of the conflict perspective, who warn against the danger of social tension and upheavals. A fourth issue is the relationship between right-wing and left-wing sociology, or to put it more clearly, a variant of the classical dispute over the possibility of a value-free sociology versus the social commitment and engagement of sociologists.

Beginning in the late 1990s, the first large attempts at putting the social and political transformation of Czech society into a broader perspective appeared. Four main streams of thought can be traced. The traditionalist, drawing from classical sociological theory and influenced by contemporary literature, was led by Pavel Machonin and Milan Tucek. These sociologists initiated an updated version of a 1967 study of the stratification of Czech society (Adamski and Machonin 1999; Machonin and Tucek 1996; Mlcoch, Machonin and Sojka 2000), and later developed a schema, based on modernization theory, which identified the objective parameters of social status (Machonin 1997).

The market economy (one feels tempted to say Fukuyamian) stream, stressed the positive aspects of social and economic transformation and the significance of liberal and conservative political orientations for the stability of society (Vecernik 1998). This research team, headed by Petr Mateju, also prepared the *Report on the Development of Czech Society 1989–1998*, which indicated that people's attitudes toward the transformation had changed from enthusiastic to disillusioned (Vecernik and Mateju 1998).

There was also a stream, led by Josef Kabele, inspired by social constructivism and aimed at explaining the basic social processes of transformation as processes of social construction and narration (Kabele 1998). And finally, there was a third stream, led by Martin Potucek and Lubomir Mlcoch, pointing at the problematic aspects of the Czech economy and seeking (in cooperation with sociologists and economists) solutions in policy close to those expressed in the latest works by Anthony Giddens (Potucek 1999). A historical-sociological synthesis of the development of Czech society between 1918 and 1992 was outlined by Pavel Machonin and Jaroslav Krejci in their book (1996). It can only be regretted that, since 1968, no serious theoretical discussion has occurred and the problems of general sociology have been addressed only sporadically (Musil 2001; Nohejl 2001; Petrusek 1991, 1993, 1994; Subrt 2001).

RETURN OF EXILED CZECH SOCIOLOGISTS

It would be highly ungrateful not to mention the role played by the exiled Czech sociologists in the reconstruction of Czech sociology. Emigration from Czechoslovakia to Western democratic countries took place in two waves. The first occurred after the 1948 Communist coup d'etat, and the second after the crushing of the Prague Spring of 1968. From the first wave, it was especially Jiri Nehnevajsa, Zdenek Suda and Jaroslav Krejci (see Machonin and Krejci 1996), all exiled to the United States, who assisted in the development of the teaching of sociology and the supply of sociological literature. From the second generation, Ilja Srubar (Germany) and Vaclav Belohradsky (Italy) should be mentioned. Some of the exiled sociologists have returned to the Czech Republic permanently, but the majority of them commute between their old and new homes. One can but express happiness at the fact that the Czech Republic can once again offer them a home to which they can return to at any time and where they can help Czech sociology make its first absolutely free moves.

NOTES

1. In the Czechoslovak Socialist Republic (the official name of the state between 1960–90, then the Czech and Slovak Federative Republic until 1992), an interesting asymmetry existed. On the one hand, there were "Czechoslovak" institutions, such as the Czechoslovak Academy of Sciences, the Czechoslovak Communist Party, and the Czechoslovak Sociological Society, that had no solely Czech equivalent, i.e., no Czech

Academy of Sciences, no Communist Party of Bohemia and Moravia. On the other hand, independent Slovak organizations did exist. So, there was no separate Czech Sociological Society, only Czechoslovak and Slovak. The same held for the Communist parties. This absurd asymmetry played a very negative role during the struggle to maintain a common state for Czechs and Slovaks.

2. The term "grey zone" was coined by Jirina Siklova, to designate the people who were not exactly dissidents but were in one way or another persecuted by the Communist regime (spies were set on them or they were fired from work, etc.), or who carried out activities considered subversive or illegal beyond the "official" dissent represented by Vaclav Havel and a number of Czech intellectuals, particularly writers. This grey zone was represented by institutions which were tolerated, although sometimes dissolved, by the regime, e.g., the Institute for Future Forecasting, the Future Forecasting Society, and the research institute *Sportproag*. It was in these institutions that sociologists, economists and environmentalists, such as Vaclav Klaus and Milos Zeman (who later became prime ministers), and Josef Vavrousek (who later became the minister of the environment), met to discuss various possible future prospects of Czechoslovak society. The idea of pluralistic democracy and a market economy was generally accepted. The idea of "pure capitalism" of the Western type only received limited support. The most common vision was that of a "third way," which would avoid all the undesirable effects of capitalist development, such as the devastation of the environment.

3. It is regrettable, and this should not be understood as an expression of injured nationalist pride, that contemporary Slovak sociology more or less ignores three circumstances important for its development, namely, 1) that "Slovak sociology" was founded in the 1920s purely and solely by Czech sociologists, and quite distinguished ones (Inocenc A. Blaha, Emanuel Chalupny, and others); 2) that the best Slovak sociologists of the "classical period" were the supporters of the idea of "Czechoslovakism," the idea that there is one Czechoslovak nation differentiated only by language (Anton Stefanek); and 3) that the development of Slovak sociology between the 1960s and the 1990s was characterized by fruitful cooperation between Czech and Slovak sociologists. Since the process of normalization took a milder course in Slovakia, some grey zone sociologists could publish there, i.e., Josef Alan, Miloslav Petrusek, and Josef Vavrousek.

4. In the interest of historical truth, it is necessary to say that restoring capitalism was not discussed in November 1989, nor in the months that followed. The majority of the society was rather allergic to that. What did require special attention was the issue of restitution, that is, the return of property stolen from its rightful owners by the Communist regime. In some cases, these restitutions were rather dramatic since some buildings were functioning as schools or kindergartens, while others had been previously purchased from the state (Holy 1996, 2001).

6

Estonian Sociology of the 1990s: In Search of an Identity

Mikko Lagerspetz and Iris Pettai

INTRODUCTION

Estonian sociologists have produced few retrospective, meta-level analyses of the national development of their discipline. The few analyses are short and leave much unsaid (e.g., Saar, Titma, and Kenkmann 1994) or are very recent and deal only with limited subsectors of sociology (Vihalemm 2001). This situation has been created by the same factors that determined the overall development of Estonian sociology long into the 1990s. First of all, the small community of social researchers lacks a common forum for publication and professional debate.[1] When publishing or making presentations in conferences, Estonian sociologists do not think of each other as addressees, but rather of the wider public of lay academicians or an international audience of social researchers.

Second, and more importantly, the idea itself of comparing and assessing the strengths and weaknesses of different theoretical approaches, typical of contemporary Western sociology, seems new and alien. The Soviet view of knowledge in general, and of social research in particular, was based on the positivist assumption that reality as such does not need to be interpreted, but revealed. The theoretical tool for this was, of course, Marxism-Leninism. Regardless of whether an individual researcher silently disapproved of that official doctrine (as most Estonian sociologists did), he or she shared its quest for objective empirical knowledge and considered theoretical debate as largely irrelevant for his or her everyday work.

A third factor can be found in the educational foundations of the profession. Until 1989, sociology could only be studied on the postgraduate level, by aspirants for the Soviet Candidate of Sciences degree (Ph.D. equivalent). This training took place within research groups and institutions functionally separate from the ordinary university education, and was closely connected with specific research themes. The educational backgrounds of the aspirants varied. Typically, they had completed their university diploma in psychology, history, or the mathematical disciplines. Accordingly, the sociological training received by the elder and middle generation was closely related to practical research methods and to issues central in their specific subdisciplines. When achieving their academic degrees, they possessed, at most, a rather superficial overview of the more distant fields of sociology.

There are, however, some signs of change. They are being brought about by a change in the institutional setting and funding practices, by the emergence of academic study programs in sociology, by international contacts, and by the growth of a new generation of sociologists with new kinds of experiences and concerns. This analysis of Estonian sociology in the 1990s is, among other things, an attempt to document and explain these changes.[2] We have had to rely on our own perceptions and judgments of the work of our colleagues, and also on what could be the essence and rationale of our discipline in the postsocialist world. As any historical treatment with some pioneering ambitions, it certainly can be accused of being subjective.

THE INSTITUTIONAL STRUCTURE OF ESTONIAN SOCIOLOGY DURING THE 1990S

In Estonia, sociology as a profession and an academic discipline became institutionalized much later than in Western or Northern Europe, or in the larger countries of Central and Eastern Europe. Before Estonia's Sovietization, in the 1940s, and the reemergence of sociology under Soviet conditions in the 1960s, sociological treatments of social issues were written by theologians, philosophers, natural scientists, and particularly by geographers. During the late 1930s, the final years of the country's first independence period lasting two decades, sociology courses were taught at the Department of Philosophy of the University of Tartu. The teacher, Ilmar Tonisson (1911–39), had studied at the London School of Economics (Vooglaid 1995). The journalist and politician Eduard Laaman (1888–1941) wrote popular analyses of Estonian contemporary history, applying the theories and methods of Werner Sombart and Max Weber among others (Laaman 1936). Along with many other developments of the young republic, this modest beginning of a sociological tradition was interrupted by Estonia's occupation by Soviet troops in 1940, and by its subsequent incorporation into the Soviet Union as a union republic.

The development of sociology during the Soviet period can be divided into two phases. The first phase lasted from the mid-1960s to the closing down of the Sociological Laboratory of the University of Tartu, in 1975, after a conspicuous dissident trial. The second phase stretched from that event until the creation of the first independent public opinion and market research companies in the late 1980s, just prior to the reestablishment of Estonian independence in 1991. During the first ten years, an emerging community of researchers acquainted itself with the idea and the methods of empirical social research, and also came to test the limits that the regime set on such an endeavour. During the late 1970s and 1980s, sociologists concentrated on refining their methodology and professional practice within the narrow space allowed for them by the rulers. The 1990s included a continuation of the previous phase, the appearance of some new impulses, and, above all, a thorough transformation of the environment in which social researchers were acting.

The restoration of Estonian independence, in August of 1991, was preceded by a long, albeit peaceful political struggle between the Soviet central power and Estonian politicians and social movements. Mass media censorship was gradually abolished during the period of 1988–90 (Lagerspetz 1996, 84). Limited market mechanisms and small-scale private enterprise had already been introduced during the perestroika period beginning in 1987. Immediately before and shortly after the declaration of independence in 1991, several reform initiatives were launched including price liberalization (1990), currency reform (1992), restoration of nationalized property (1991), and decollectivization of agriculture (1991). The rapid restructuring of economic life created a demand for more research in labor force mobility and employment, focusing not only on the level of individual economic organizations or social groups (e.g., youth) as hitherto, but on the macroeconomic level as well. With the emergence of private enterprise, a need for advertising and marketing strategies arose. The establishment of new political parties during the same years created a market for public opinion polls.

Not surprisingly against this background, even before independence, the first organizations for public opinion and market research began their activities. The enterprise now known as EMOR Ltd. was established in the spring of 1988, and went private in October 1990. At present, it is partly owned by the Finnish enterprise Management Development Consulting (MDC) Gallup Finlandia, and is by far the largest enterprise of its kind in the Estonian polling market. Along with its daughter enterprises, EMOR holds a market share of about 75 percent. It competes with two other major enterprises, Saar Poll Ltd. and *ES Turu-uuringute AS* (Estonian Surveys, Ltd.). All three have established a nationwide Estonian network of interviewers. They have also been eagerly introducing new methods of data collection, many of which are applications of computer and Internet technology. The largest polling firms work in accordance with the International Code of Marketing and Social Research Practice, and have all established close relations with foreign partners.[3] In 2001, the estimated value of the opinion and market research market amounted to 70 to 80 million crowns (4 to 5 million USD), and according to experts there is still room for growth. Relying on a growing market of clients and filling a relatively well-defined niche, the commercial survey companies currently form the most successful part of the profession.

After relying on the services of a private firm for some years, the Statistical Office of Estonia has also created a permanent network of interviewers. An independent research institute, the Estonian Institute for Future Studies (est. in 1992), frequently touches sociological issues in its research projects, including socioeconomic development scenarios for the near future in Estonia.

Other major changes in the institutional structure of sociological research have been related to a growing role of universities as centers of research. The overall research policy of the state defined universities as central structures in the organization of research activities, leading to an administrative reorganization of research groups. In 1995, the government decided to reorganize the previous Academy of Sciences as an independent academy, whereas the large majority of its previously existing research institutes had been incorporated within the universities. In 1996, a data archive serving social researchers throughout the country was established at the University of Tartu. In 1998, the Institute of International and Social Studies, including research sections in sociology, political science, and international relations, became a part of the Pedagogical University (previously the Pedagogical Institute) of Tallinn. Funding, which previously was allotted to research institutions directly from the state budget, became based on separate projects. About 85 percent of the Institute's budget for 2000 consisted of financing from state funds for research projects. The remaining amount consisted of funding for research projects commissioned by different branches of government (plus one EU grant).

This shift toward project focused funding has influenced all academic research. Obviously, it seriously reduces the social and economic security of a researcher, if he or she is not a member of a university teaching staff. It also discourages the planning of theoretical, long-term research with no immediate practical application. On the positive side, the resulting dependence on publishing and reporting clearly furthers scientific communication.

Academic education programs on a university diploma level in sociology were introduced for the first time in 1989, when a Department of Sociology was created at the University of Tartu (led by Professors Paul Kenkmann, Liina-Mai Tooding, and Mikk Titma). In 1992, another program was opened at the Estonian Institute of Humanities in Tallinn, an independent university established in 1988 (Professor Mikko Lagerspetz). The Pedagogical University of Tallinn started educating sociologists in 1997 (Professor Juri Kruusvall). The total number of students starting their studies each year for the B.A. degree is about sixty, of which a majority have to pay a fee for their studies, even in the two state-run universities. All the study programs follow the general Estonian educational standard, which until 2000 stipulated a study period of four years for a B.A. degree, and an additional two years for a Master's degree. The actual average time of study is slightly longer. Only a minority of those graduating with a B.A. degree continue in the M.A. study programs. The new educational standard, enacted in 2000, reduces the total period of study by one year, but has yet to be implemented by the individual university faculties.

Most of the senior teaching staff of the universities received their basic education in other disciplines, and became acquainted with sociology through working experience in various research institutes. As of 2001, no dissertation had been presented for a Ph.D. degree in sociology, although in principle programs for doctoral study do exist. However, issues closely related to sociology have been treated by doctoral dissertations in neighboring fields of study, such as psychology and journalism (Kruusvall 1994; Kutsar 1995; Vihalemm 1999). Several social scientists of the younger and middle generation have opted for doctoral and other postgraduate training outside Estonia, often in Finland. In order to strengthen the domestic possibilities for doctoral study, the creation of an interuniversity doctoral school in social sciences was initiated in early 2001. The limited availability of doctoral training is not only characteristic of the social sciences, but is a general feature of the educational system as a whole.

Sociology courses have been introduced as parts of other academic study programs in related disciplines as well. For example, it is taught in connection with studies of political economy and business administration. The Faculty of Economics of the Technical University of Tallinn includes a sociology department (Professor Marje Pavelson), and several independent law and business schools teach organizational studies and introductory courses in sociology. The demand for sociology courses in these institutions has created an important extra working opportunity for some members of the sociological community.

Academic education has mostly relied on Anglo-American textbooks in the original language (i.e., Giddens 1997). To some extent, the accessibility of foreign books and journals has compensated for the absence of original Estonian literature. The proximity of the Estonian and Finnish languages allows many teachers and students to study Finnish sources as well. In 2000, a translation of a U.S. textbook was published, providing universities with the first Estonian-language introduction to sociology in textbook form (Hess, Markson, and Stein 2000). The only attempt made by Estonian authors to write an original introductory textbook can be regarded a failure, as the book incorrectly equates sociology with the very narrow field of organizational studies (Graf and Paul 1997). Due to the absence of general treatises, many central theoretical concepts still lack adequate Estonian translation.

Until 1996, social scientists could publish their findings in Estonian in a series of proceedings, *Humanities and Social Sciences*, published by the Estonian Academy of Sciences. Since then, it has been reorganized as *Trames: A Journal of the Humanities and Social Sciences* (published in English). The cultural journals *Akadeemia* and *Vikerkaar,* both published by the Estonian Writers' Union, continue to serve as vehicles for publication in Estonian. The Statistical Office, the universities, and the research institutes have their own series of publications. In the late 1990s, a rather important role was played by the annual United Nations Human Development National Reports, which have been able to engage many prominent social scientists as authors, and which also attract wide attention by the media and by politicians. Recently, a journal, *Riigikogu Toimetised,* with political, juridical, and sociological content was launched by the chancellery of the Estonian parliament.

In 1990, the Estonian Association of Sociologists was founded. It has consistently had about sixty members, a majority of which are engaged in research, either at academic institutions or at polling firms. The Estonian Association is a member of the International Sociological Association. In November 2000, the first national conference of social sciences was organized by the Institute of International and Social Studies of the Pedagogical University of Tallinn.

RESEARCH THEMES AND METHODS

In the 1990s, much of Estonian sociology continued the research themes initiated during previous decades. Characteristically, many sociologists who started their career in a certain field of research during that time are still the key figures in that area. It almost seems that new fields of research only emerge with the appearance of new researchers.

The postsocialist abandonment of official Marxism, in the 1990s, took place rapidly and without much discussion. Even the concept of class disappeared from sociological discourse for a decade, not to be reintroduced until the year 2000. Obviously, the obligatory use of Marxist terminology and quotations never had much to do with the researchers' real scientific aspirations. As a result, the postsocialist abandonment of official Marxism in the 1990s did not radically change the existing practices of inquiry.

As Estonian sociologists had grown used to working not *on the basis of* a general background theory on society, but *in spite of* it, sociology of the early 1990s rather seemed to avoid explicit theoretical foundations. A 1997 volume of media research in Tartu can be seen as signaling a turning point, as it consciously uses evolutionist and culturalist grand theories as a basis for interpreting Estonian society (Lauristin and Vihalemm 1997). During the second part of the decade, constructionist and interactionist approaches were introduced, mainly as a result of international cooperation (Lagerspetz 1996; Paadam 2000; Ruus 2000; Vetik 1999; Vihalemm 1999). These schools of thought seem to have considerable appeal to the youngest generation of researchers, but to date have remained somewhat marginal.

Initiated in the mid-1960s, mass communications is among the oldest fields of sociological research in Estonia. The media and market research company Baltic Media Facts Gallup Media was established in 1992. Later, it was merged with the polling firm EMOR. It was able to outcompete the research groups of Estonian Television and Estonian Radio, which mainly dealt with the monitoring of media audiences, and have now ceased their activities. The Department of Journalism and Mass Communications at the University of Tartu has remained the center of academic research in this field (Vihalemm 2001). Some of the research has been concerned with the history of mass communications in Estonia. As explanations for historical developments are often sought in modernization processes, even this part of mass media studies has relevance from a sociological point of view. A major result of this research field was the publication, in 1993, of a joint collection of articles by authors from the three Baltic countries and Norway (Hoyer, Lauk, and Vihalemm 1993).

The possibilities of media research in approaching the postsocialist transition have been thoroughly examined by Marju Lauristin and Peeter Vihalemm. In a joint project with Swedish and Finnish researchers, they have published what probably is the most comprehensive presentation that has yet been published in Estonia on the country's society and recent history (Lauristin and Vihalemm 1997). The book is also among the rare attempts by Estonian scholars to interpret their results with reference to a so-called grand theory. The authors rely heavily on Inglehart's (1990) theory of postmaterialist values, as well as on Huntington's (1996) notion of the clash of civilizations.

Media has also formed a part of the research material by sociologists not interested in the media as such, but rather in its contents as indicators of political and cultural change. Studying social problems discourse, Mikko Lagerspetz has used, among other sources, printed and underground media (1996), as well as journalists' own perceptions as presented in group interviews (Lagerspetz, Loogma, and Kaselo 1998). Raivo Vetik (1999) has examined the construction of ethnic identities in Estonia through an analysis of printed media.

Research on youth and education was likewise initiated in the 1960s. An impressively long-lived research tradition is that of longitudinal research on the life careers of high school graduates. Led by Mikk Titma, the first whole cohort of high school graduates was interviewed in 1966, and five follow-ups were performed, the latest in 1991 (Helemae, Saar, and Voormann 2000; Silver and Titma 1996). Preparations for a sixth round of interviews were started in 1999. A similar longitudinal research project with a new cohort was started in 1983, and initially included a comparison between sixteen different regions of the former Soviet Union. In 1997–99, the project still included eight countries, and was financed by U.S. sources and coordinated by American researchers (Titma 1999, 18). These longitudinal projects offer rare possibilities to test hypotheses on the mutual effects of such factors as education, values, life plans, migration, family relations, occupational career, and income, As a result, the rapid social mobility that took place during the first six years of Estonian independence (1991–97) can be analyzed in detail. They have even motivated mass media discussion on the existence of a "winner's generation" in Estonia.

In the sociology of youth, the values of youth and juvenile delinquency have been the traditional areas of research. In the 1990s, the other side of the phenomenon of deviance, the social control system, was studied by Judit Strompl (2000). Both the redefinition of the research object and her "ethnographic" research method are novel in this field of research in Estonia. Youth subcultures, which had received almost no attention by sociologists, are being discovered by the youngest generation of researchers, particularly within the context of drug abuse and risk behavior (Allaste 2001).

From the beginning, research into the population's living conditions was one of the central research areas of empirical sociology in the Soviet Union. In Estonia, a series of representative surveys of the working-age population was initiated in 1966, by the Sector of Sociology of the Estonian Academy of Sciences. With intervals of five years, the research group (now within the Institute of International and Social Studies of the Pedagogical University of Tallinn) has conducted similar surveys. They include a common core set of questions that enable comparison over a period of more than three decades. During the 1990s, the survey was conducted in 1993 and 1998, with samples of 1,867 and 2,317 respondents respectively (Narusk 1995, 1999). The results of these surveys have been used as a basis for analyses of a very wide range of issues.

In part as a result of a close cooperation with Finnish sociologists, in the 1980s this research was incorporated within the lifestyle conceptual framework. In this field, some new important approaches have emerged in the 1990s, often initiated by Anu Narusk of the Institute of International and Social Studies. The original aim of gathering reliable statistics on living conditions has gradually been replaced by a more subject-centered approach to find out about the motives, resources and strategies of people living in the midst of rapid social change. Traditional survey research into living conditions has been supplemented by a series of open-ended interviews, mapping the resources and coping strategies available for families in the conditions of postsocialist economic and social transformation (Assmuth and Kelam 1998; Narusk and Hansson 1999; Paadam 2000).

Dagmar Kutsar, of the Unit of Family Studies at the University of Tartu, has examined how the negative economic and social effects of the postsocialist transformation are reflected on marriage and family (Kutsar 1995, 2000; Kutsar and Trumm 1998). Within the sociology of labor, a yearly labor force survey has been introduced by the Statistical Office of Estonia. On the basis of these data, analyses on the relations between economy, the labor market, and the educational system have been produced (Eamets 1999; Loogma and Terk 1999; Voormann 1995).

As a novel phenomenon in the postsocialist context, the development of civil society and nongovernmental organizations belongs to the newest fields of research. Again, we can see a gradual refocusing of the research efforts, analogous to the change that took place in the sociology of living conditions and lifestyles. In the early 1990s, the aim was a quantitative mapping of the field (Aarelaid-Tart and Tart 1995). Later, attention was directed to the resources, objectives, and functioning environment of civil society and its organizations (*Filantroopia* 1998; Lagerspetz 2001; Lagerspetz, Ruutsoo, and Rikmann 2000).

Last but not least, research on interethnic relations and integration has become an important topic. During Soviet rule, the ethnic composition of the Estonian population, which until 1940 had been relatively homogenous (the proportion of ethnic Estonians was near 90 percent), was transformed due to migration from other Soviet republics. At present, the ethnic Estonians' share of the population is around 65 percent. Among the other ethnic groups, Russians are the most numerous. Until just before independence, the topic of ethnic relations was a taboo theme in public discussion and social research. During the 1990s, the importance of the subject was acknowledged both by politicians and social scientists. Much of the research has been carried out with the financial support of the Soros Foundation and foreign embassies. Since 2000, research also has been commissioned by the government.

The research on ethnic relations has focussed on several issues. The number of people belonging to ethnic minorities, their legal status, and their demographic composition have been subject to thorough discussion (Kirch 1997). There has been discussion of the different ethnic groups' identities, their mutual attitudes toward other groups, and their readiness for integration (Vetik 1999; Vihalemm 1999; Pettai 2000). The population's opinions on government policies and legislation has been investigated (Kruusvall 1998a, 1998b). Finally, research has attempted to assess the possible strategies of influencing public opinion in favor of interethnic integration (Heidmets 1998). As a result, an integration program for the years 2000–2007 has been worked out by social scientists and subsequently adopted by the government.

SOCIOLOGISTS IN SEARCH OF A ROLE IN SOCIETY

In modern societies, social scientists, perhaps like intellectuals in general, have largely adopted one of two major roles available. One is that of the professional offering technical assistance for the decision makers. The other includes criticizing social development from a putatively autonomous position, legitimated by scientific discourse. The developments described in this article show a sociological community oscillating between these two roles. During the revolutionary period of the late 1980s, some sociologists were active in politics. When looking at the developments of the 1990s, it appears, first and foremost, that sociologists rarely applied their research results to public argumentation on policy decisions. And, not surprisingly, decision makers seemed to lack both interest and confidence in research results that contradicted their own political credo. During the 1990s, much government policy has adhered to the Thatcherite sentiment that "such a thing as society does not exist," as quoted by a politician of the government coalition in a leading weekly (Herkel 1999).

In minor issues however, when making decisions or public statements, politicians often lacked any consequent party guidelines to which to turn, but sought guidance in what they regarded as public opinion, their ratings and other findings of the frequently occurring opinion polls. In some sense, one might say that more research on Estonian society is being conducted now than ever before. On the other hand, the knowledge provided by surveys is fragmented, largely concerns topics such as party politics, consumer preferences, and media attendance, and has little relevance for any deeper understanding of society.

However, some very recent changes might be discernible. Growing stratification, deepening poverty, and an alienation of the people from public power have been among the themes publicly discussed by sociologists during the past few years. The growing visibility of sociological perspectives in politics and the media is probably not only due to an enhanced self-reliance of the profession, but is connected to a more widespread dissatisfaction with the neoliberalist reform policies and individualist rhetoric that have dominated Estonian political life during the 1990s.

A division can be made between two distinct types of social science methodology. According to Dag Osterberg (Brante 1989), one type of social research aims at gaining exact results by means of operationalization and quantification, and follows the model of the natural sciences. This approach, which Osterberg calls social statistics, has as its research object an aggregate of individuals rather than society (1989). Sociology, on the contrary, is interested in social phenomena such as societies, communities, and interaction, and thus has an object of knowledge that is not reducible to the individual level. If Estonian social research is examined with the help of this division, we will find that most of it will not qualify as sociology proper in Osterberg's sense. This fact is probably related to the sociologist's role in social engineering.

The rapid transformation of society, for example, the country's membership negotiations with the EU, has enhanced the need for different kinds of statistical information. In designing their reform policies, decision makers often turn to statistical series on economic and social conditions. At the same time, the very transformation process itself creates new difficulties in the production of reliable statistics (Leifman 2000). For instance, the reorganization of the institutions collecting raw data, and a diminished validity of the previously used statistical categories may render it impossible to maintain the old routines of data collection. When the reliability of official statistics is lowered by such circumstances, they can be partially compensated for by professionally conducted survey research.

A major reason for the relative absence of truly sociological research questions has been, however, the lack of opportunity to get acquainted with sociological theory. It was not until the 1990s, that the opening of university programs in sociology created an opportunity for the exposition of different theoretical approaches. The second part of the decade also saw the graduation of the first generation of Estonian sociologists with a thorough basic education in the discipline.

To sum up, the following general trends of development can be discerned in the Estonian sociology of the 1990s. First, opinion and market research companies were established as an important institutional branch of sociology, clearly separate from academic research. Second, a portion of academic inquiry continued the research themes from previous decades, while new issues and approaches were introduced during the second part of the 1990s, mostly due to impulses from outside Estonia. Third, the research community still does not seem ready to create its own research agenda independent of the state and individual clients of research. In our opinion, this is not only due to the scarcity of resources, but also to sociologists' insecurity on the status and identity of their discipline.

Estonian sociology's long-prevailing empiricism has provided it with little discursive means of self-legitimation, and of basing its agenda on other arguments than the immediate needs expressed by state institutions or the market. However, the social developments of the latter part of the 1990s seem to emphasize the need for a more independent formation of research agendas. Estonia's relative macroeconomic success has been accompanied by the marginalization of large groups in society, a development not always acknowledged by government agencies. In the near future, problems related to social capital, marginalization, and alienation from institutional politics will need to be solved by sociologically well-informed development strategies. In short, the need for sociological research is growing, and it is also to a growing degree being acknowledged by the political elite. Along with these considerations, the creation of academic education in sociology and the gradual emergence of a theoretically informed sociology might foreshadow the beginning of a new, more self-conscious phase in the development of sociology in Estonia.

NOTES

1. In 2001, the Estonian Association of Sociologists had about sixty members, while the overall population of Estonia that year was 1.4 million.

2. In addition to the sources referred to in the text, during the winter 2000–2001 we received written and oral information from a number of Estonian social scientists, institutions, and research administrators. We want to thank the following people and

institutions: Marje Joosing, Juhan Kivirahk, Juri Kruusvall, Erkki Rannik, Andrus Saar, Liina-Mai Tooding, Raivo Vetik, Peeter Vihalemm, Rein Voormann, Eesti Konjunktu-uriinstituut, ES Turu-uuringute AS, Saar Poll Ltd., Sociology Departments of the University of Tartu, the Estonian Institute of Humanities, and the Pedagogical Univer-sity of Tallinn, and the Institute of International and Social Studies of the Pedagogical University of Tallinn. It goes without saying that the authors alone are responsible for the claims and interpretations presented in this article.

3. EMOR Ltd. is also represented in Latvia, Lithuania, Ukraine, and Belarus, and is a member of the Gallup International Association. Saar Poll Ltd. has cooperated with sev-eral academic institutions in carrying out research projects. It has also cooperated with Research International, Gesellschaft für Konsumforschung (GfK), Gallup International, and Gallup Worldwide. ES Turu-uuringute AS (Estonian Surveys, Ltd.) is owned by the Finnish Taloustutkimus Ltd., and cooperates with the international enterprise chain GfK. Eesti Konjunktuuriinstituut cooperates with the Institute for Economic Research in Munich, the Swedish National Institute of Economic Research, and with the Finnish Statistical Office. It is a participant in the Centre for International Research and Eco-nomic Tendencies Survey.

7

More Evolution than Revolution: Sociology in Hungary, 1990–2000

Denes Nemedi and Peter Robert

THE INSTITUTIONAL ENVIRONMENT OF HUNGARIAN SOCIOLOGY

When we look back to the last decade of Hungarian sociology in the twentieth century, we must conclude that the collapse of Communism did not provoke a rupture in the development of the discipline. The relative continuity can be explained by characteristics of the transformation in Hungary. In the economic sphere, the planned economy and state ownership of the means of production were replaced by the market and private ownership. In the aftermath, the economic performance of the country went through a serious crisis. There was also rapid political transformation and democratic institutions were created.

However, the Hungarian state socialist system was never as repressive as in other countries. Political freedom and freedom of speech were less restricted than in the German Democratic Republic, in the Soviet Union, or in Czechoslovakia after 1968. This was the case for the freedom of sociological research and thinking as well, even though there were repressive measures. For example, a group of sociologists and philosophers, including Ivan Szelenyi, Istvan Kemeny, Agnes Heller, Ferenc Feher, and Gyorgy Markus, had to leave the country in the mid-1970s. But later, in the 1980s, sociologists could take critical stances, for instance on the Marxist approach to the social structure. As a result, Hungarian sociology, which was in certain respects quite developed and up-to-date in the 1980s, did not need any serious political cleaning up. Nobody was dismissed or suddenly put on pension. Changes were more gradual.

One of the most important continuities that survived the collapse of the former regime was the institutional duality of Hungarian science, the separation of academic research and higher education. On the one hand, the academic research sphere is directed by the Hungarian Academy of Sciences (HAS) that governs a network of research institutions, including one of sociology. On the other hand, departments of sociology exist at many universities and they do the teaching. The largest departments can be found in Budapest. These are the Institute of Sociology of the Eotvos Lorand (ELTE) University, consisting of seven departments or chairs, and the departments of sociology at the University of Economics and at the Technical University. Several departments of sociology can be found in provincial towns at the universities of Debrecen, Szeged, Pecs, Miskolc and Godollo. And, in the mid-1990s, a new Catholic university was established, in a suburb of Budapest, where sociologists are also trained without paying any tuition.

In the field of research, new private research institutes were created in the 1990s, mostly in the field of public opinion research. They focus on marketing research, although some of them, such as *Tarsadalomkutatasi Intezet* (TARKI), *Szonda-Ipsos*, Median, and Gallup, carry out scientific research as well. Its Data Archive represents the academic face of TARKI, and is available for researchers as well as doctorate students. Many of the private institutions do fieldwork for several empirical academic research projects. After completing university, trained sociologists can find employment in the private sphere more easily than in the public one.

After the changes introduced in the 1990s, the system of scientific qualification also took on a dual character. Doctoral programs have been established at the universities. In sociology, two doctoral programs exist in Budapest, at ELTE University, and at the University of Economics. A Ph.D. is the basic requirement for a research position in the Academy of Sciences, or for a lecturer position at a university. Above this level, there are two routes for promotion. Through the Academy, one can get the title of Doctor of Science, which is a precondition to becoming a member of the Hungarian Academy of Sciences. Through the university, one can complete a German-type habilitation, a second published dissertation. This can lead to full professorship at the university. Recently, government institutions have shown a clear preference for candidates advancing though the Academy.

The basic professional body in sociology is the Hungarian Sociological Association. It has approximately seven hundred members, and also has several research committees. Approximately two hundred of its members are doing research in some form. The Sociological Committee of the Hungarian Academy of Sciences plays an important role in promotion and support of sociology in Hungary. A new institution in social sciences, the recently created Rudolf Andorka Social Science Society, also supports sociological and demographic research and provides fellowships to junior and senior scholars.

STUDYING SOCIOLOGY IN HUNGARY

In the 1990s, there was a huge educational expansion at the tertiary level in Hungary, including a disproportionate increase in the number of students studying sociology. In 1990, there were 222 students studying sociology at two institutions (about 0.2 percent of all students). By 2000, the number of sociology students had risen to 1856, studying at seven institutions (about 0.6 percent of all students). While in 1990, sociology was taught only in Budapest, by 2000, 54 percent of sociology students were studying at four provincial universities. Tuition for tertiary education was introduced in the mid-1990s, but has since been abolished. Now, the first diploma is tuition free.

Though there is no singular standard curriculum of sociology at the universities, all students do have to take ten semesters, and they must write a thesis in order to obtain a diploma. This is practically an M.A. program, as no B.A. program in sociology exists in Hungary. Courses in sociology probably have the most comprehensive character at the ELTE University. The largest staff and Faculty of Sociology are in the Institute of Sociology at ELTE. The second biggest sociology department, at the University of Economics, has some focus on the sociology of economics in the curriculum. At the provincial universities, the sociology curricula are less developed.

Since 1992, the postgraduate (Ph.D.) training of sociologists has taken place in the two doctoral programs. The curriculum of the Ph.D. programs consists of a period of course study and a period of writing the thesis. Since the language of the Ph.D. program (and all undergraduate programs as well) is Hungarian, doctoral students are almost exclusively Hungarians, though there are some students from neighboring countries. The number of Ph.D. students rose from 67 in 1995, to 134 in 2000, but only twelve theses had been defended by 2001. The number of grants available for Ph.D. students is limited, and Ph.D. students have to pay a rather high tuition.

FINANCING SOCIOLOGY IN HUNGARY

From the viewpoint of material circumstances, the dual system of academic institutions and universities is rather expensive. Not surprisingly, a major feature of the system is a large deficit in the budget. The financial situation is worse for teaching than research. The latter can apply to different sources and institutions for funding. Similar opportunities hardly exist for the improvement of the material circumstances of lecturing. As a result, the small computer labs, the few computers relative to the large number of students, and the outdated versions of software have led to a decrease in the quality of education at the universities.

The National Foundation for Scientific Research (OTKA) is the main institution that supports research work. Research funds are available for two to four years. Applications are subject to a process of blind review, and a committee makes the final decision. In principle, the system is competitive. However, the small size of the field seriously limits the anonymity and competitiveness of the review process.

In addition to OTKA, research is funded through the Ministry of Education. The amount that is available from this source is limited. Other government agencies and ministries also commission sociological studies and public opinion research on various topics. Since this research is more applied, this form of research funding provides more opportunity for private research institutes than academic institutes. Sociological research is barely supported by the private sphere. As an exception, the Soros Foundation should be mentioned. There are also some intergovernmental and European programs that occasionally support sociological research, such as the French-Hungarian Scientific Exchange Program called "Balaton."

Even though OTKA only provides part of the funding for sociological research, an account of its funding support during the 1990s gives some idea of the trends and magnitude of sociological research funding in Hungary. The social sciences got 20 percent of the OTKA budget, and sociology got roughly 4 to 5 percent. Funding was at a relatively high level in 1992, equaling approximately $393,000 (in 1992 dollars). Following a two-year period of decline, it reached a new peak in 1995, equal to 191 percent of the 1992 amount. It was at its lowest in 1996, with only 36 percent of the amount of 1992 in real value. In 2000, it was 65 percent of the 1992 value.

The distribution of these funds between Budapest and the provinces reflected the general geographical pattern of Hungarian science. Eighty-nine percent of the funds went to Budapest, even though 61 percent of the students and 38 percent of professors in sociology study and teach in the provinces! The funds were rather evenly distributed between the two main types of locations of sociological research. The universities received 45 percent of the funds, and the research institutes 49 percent. Not surprisingly, social structure studies and economical sociology (in a broad sense) received the highest amounts among the main branches of sociological research (15 percent and 19 percent, respectively). None of the other branches received more than 10 percent.

Due to the lack of funds and to the relative smallness of the field, publication possibilities are also limited in Hungarian sociology. The leading journal is *Szociologiai Szemle* (Sociological Review). The Hungarian Sociological Association publishes it, in Hungarian, four times a year. Every year, a selection of the best articles is published, in association with the Rudolf Andorka Social Science Society, in an English language edition, *Szazadveg* (End of Century). Other journals are *Tarsadalomkutatas* (Social Research), which appears less regularly, and *Esely* (Chance), specializing in social policy issues.

Sociological books published in Hungarian are mostly translations, though in recent years original works by Hungarian authors have appeared in greater numbers. The most important publishers are *Osiris, Uj Mandatum* (New Mandate), collaborating with ELTE, *Aula* (which is associated with the University of Economics), and *Szazadveg*, which also publishes books.

FOCAL POINTS IN HUNGARIAN SOCIOLOGICAL RESEARCH

To assess the relative weight and importance of the branches of research in Hungarian sociology, we have analyzed the thematic distribution of articles appearing in *Szociologiai Szemle* from 1991 to 2000. The character of this journal was strictly disciplinary. As a result of its editorial policy, 90 percent of the authors were Hungarian, some living and working abroad. Some foreign coauthors also appeared. These Hungarian authors produced 92 percent of the articles. The only thematic areas producing more then 10 percent of the articles (multiple-coding was permitted) were economic sociology in a broad sense (23 percent), social structure (23 percent), sociological theory (19 percent) and political sociology (10 percent and more important in the first half of the decade, declining to 7 percent in the second, but even so remaining the fourth biggest area). Accordingly, these are the areas we have selected for qualitative analysis.

Before presenting this analysis, we would like to mention some interesting details about the authors. Not surprisingly, about two-thirds of the authors were men, reflecting the male dominance in Hungarian science. Seventy-one percent of the authors lived and worked in Budapest, including 82 percent of the "productive" authors, that is, those who published two or more articles. The concentration of scientific capital in Budapest is remarkable because, as we mentioned, 54 percent of sociology students study at provincial universities. Even though their shares of the OTKA funding are equal, the university researchers produced slightly more articles than those colleagues working in research institutes, that is, 4 percent more articles. The universities, with 33 percent of all authors, produced 55 percent of the "productive" authors, while the research institutes produced 32 percent of the "productive" authors.[1] This disparity reflects the fact that research institutes moved away from academic research toward market demand oriented research.

THEORETICAL APPROACHES IN HUNGARIAN SOCIOLOGY

While the number of articles classified as "theoretical" was rather high in *Szociologiai Szemle*, they constitute a most heterogeneous set. Therefore, in this section we try to give a concise picture of broad theoretical orientations rather than commenting just upon the articles of *Szociologiai Szemle*. The thesis that the transformation opened up specific theoretical possibilities in Hungarian, or for that matter, Eastern European sociology, was proposed by Anna Wessely and Gyorgy Csepeli (Wessely 1996). The possibilities for Eastern European sociologists emerged from the fact that they preserved the sense of sociology's public relevance and a flexible language capable of mediating between conceptual frameworks and lived experience (Wessely 1996, 17). According to Pal Tamas (1994), the project of modernity was disintegrating in the West, while it remained alive in the East. However, the theoretical potential of Eastern European sociology was not realized, as the proponents of the thesis themselves have acknowledged (Wessely 1996, 18–19). Perhaps the failure was due to the so-called colonization of Eastern European sociology by Western colleagues. According to this view, Eastern European social scientists found themselves reduced to the auxiliary role of data suppliers. The most talented (or perhaps the most fortunate?) young scientists were afforded access to a Western-style training, which alienated them from Eastern realities (Csepeli, Orkeny, and Scheppele 1996, 113–116).

The collective theoretical memory of Hungarian sociology was not very different from that of sociology in general. The heroes worshipped in Hungary were more or less the same as in other countries. However, the pattern of fluctuation in attention paid to them was distinctive of the development of sociology in Hungary. In the early years of Hungarian sociology, Max Weber was one of the model sociologists and he was the preferred subject of theoretical publications. Weber was most interesting as a critic of bureaucracy (and consequently of state socialism), and as a source of a non-Marxist theory of capitalism. In recent times, as the first issue lost its significance, and the second one as well, interest in Weber declined.

During the Communist era, Emile Durkheim never served as camouflage for political and social criticism. Rather, he was the ideal hero of serious scientific work. One of the authors of this paper published a historical-epistemological analysis of his sociological theory of knowledge (Nemedi 1996). However, despite the strong presence of Durkheim in the teaching of sociology, nowadays there is nothing especially Durkheimian in Hungarian sociology.

Among modern sociologists, Jurgen Habermas and Pierre Bourdieu are the most present in Hungarian sociological discourse. Habermas's influence in Hungary was due to his analysis of the "public sphere" (his book was translated in 1971), which provided the tools to construct an ideal model of public communication in critical opposition to the then actually existing socialist restricted public sphere. His influence was very much visible in theories of mass communication (Angelusz 1983). The theory of communicative action also received some serious interpretative-theoretical attention (Felkai 1993; Nemedi 2000). Bourdieu's fate was different. He was also an important figure in the 1970s. His approach and theory inspired empirical research on education and stratification. Even now, his theory of capital and capital conversion is utilized rather often, but his theoretical work has never been submitted to serious analysis.

As far as theory is concerned, the success story was that of rational choice theory. Toward the end of the 1970s, it was already being effectively propagated by Laszlo Bertalan and Laszlo Csontos (Csontos 1999). Its impact continued to grow in the 1990s. The relative importance of rational choice theory can be seen from the fact that twenty-three articles from the sixty-six coded as "theory" in *Szociologiai Szemle* dealt with it, mostly from a sympathetic point of view. The earlier interest in the Hungarian tradition of social research (Litvan and Szucs 1973; Huszar 1979; Nemedi 1985) declined in the nineties as a consequence of this opening toward Western research programs.

INVESTIGATING SOCIAL STRUCTURE IN LIGHT OF SYSTEM TRANSFORMATION

In the 1990s, one of the focal points in Hungarian sociology was the empirical investigation of the social structure. Approaches of studies varied as researchers analyzed the increase in social inequalities. This included educational inequalities, the emerging class relations, including a new entrepreneurial class, and the transformation of rural society in the countryside.

The late Rudolf Andorka (1996) provided the first social analysis of the transformation. His article on the increase of social inequalities since the collapse of socialism was based on the Hungarian Household Panel Survey, carried out through the collaboration of the Department of Sociology at the University of Economics and the Social Research Center (TARKI). The main result was not surprising: social inequalities grew in the first half of the 1990s, as differentiation in income increased and more people lived in poverty. A valuable feature of the article was that the analysis of the poor was based on various measures and concepts of the poverty line. Several demographic and other groupings appeared as being in risk of poverty: old people but not all of the pensioners, families with several children, those with a low level of education, those who were unemployed, and those belonging to the Roma Gypsy ethnic group (Andorka and Speder 1996).

Disappointment was a basic phenomenon in Hungary, perhaps more than in other postsocialist societies. Zsuzsa Ferge (1996) offered a plausible explanation for this, based on data from the international Social Costs of Transformation (SOCO) Project. Before 1990, compared to other countries, Hungary was more democratic and less depressed. Consequently, Hungarians have won less freedom while at the same time, like other people in other former socialist countries, they have lost a lot of safety. However, the relative balance was more negative for Hungarians.

Public opinion research data provides evidence that Hungarians expected the government to contribute to solving the social problems in such fields as health, education, unemployment, and the pension system. However, research on the role of government revealed that people did not know much about the use of taxes, and the real choices the government must make when deciding how to use funds. The research tried to explore public attitudes concerning different options by means of which people could take greater care of themselves instead of always waiting for governmental solutions (Csontos, Kornai, and Toth 1996).

When analyzing social structure under socialism, several sociologists have written about "stratification" because the term "class" had a bad connotation in the Hungarian sociological literature (Andorka 1982; Ferge 1996; Kolosi 1987). Approaching the problem from the viewpoint of class identification, Robert Angelusz and Robert Tardos (1995a, 1995b) concluded that the use of the term class makes the empirical results questionable and misleading, even in the post-socialist era. People have negative attitudes toward the term "working class," while the term "middle class" has a new "wishful thinking character." Peter Robert (1997, 1998) suggested the introduction of a neo-Weberian class system developed by John Goldthorpe, widely used for analyzing social structure in industrial societies. Though only occasionally, this class scheme has started to appear in the publications of TARKI, in the publications of the Central Statistical Office, and in a new book by Tamas Kolosi (2000). A further step into a more careful class analysis of Hungarian society required the investigation and comparison of various classifications and an empirical test of their validity (Bukodi 1999; Bukodi and Robert 1999). These studies showed that certain features of the traditional structural cleavages like "blue collar–white collar" distinction were still relevant for Hungary.

Not surprisingly, the entrepreneurial class, as a new class in postsocialist Hungary was an attractive research topic. Kolosi and Akos Rona-Tas (1992) carried out one of the first empirical analyses of this kind. The authors tested several hypotheses in their study, such as "interrupted embourgeoisement" (Szelenyi 1988), the "big coalition" between the new economic elite and the former political elite (Hankiss 1989, 1990), and the very similar concept of "political capitalism" (Staniszkis 1991). Their results did not indicate a large influence of parental inheritance in becoming an entrepreneur, or at least it did not seem true that the former Communist *nomenclatura* could convert its political capital into economic capital. However, cultural capital and human capital investments turned out to be crucial resources for starting private business in postsocialist Hungary. Other research carried out by Kolosi (2000) shows that various types of embeddedness, such as managerial position or participation in the "second economy" before 1990, were also useful for later economic success.

The study of educational inequalities has a strong tradition in Hungary and continued to be an important research topic for the 1990s as well. The analysis by Peter Robert (1991b) demonstrated that the effect of social background hardly declined over time during the decades of socialism. The article by Szelenyi and Aschaffenburg (1993) put larger emphasis on the role of institutions in creating and maintaining inequalities. They interpreted the persistence of educational inequality as evidence for the "new class" theory.

An explanation for the persistence of educational inequalities can be found in the fact that cultural inheritance was more characteristic under socialism, while the possibilities for financial reproduction were more limited. In the 1990s, however, under the conditions of emerging market relations, financial capital tended to play a more important role for educational attainment. Moreover, completion of college or university may not be an appropriate indicator for good prospects in the labor market. It matters more what kind of diploma was completed. Ferenc Gazso (1997) argued that only the offspring of high status families with good material background had the best chance to receive real marketable degrees in the 1990s.

THE TRANSFORMATION OF RURAL SOCIETY

As Hungary is overcentralized both in economic and in political-cultural respects, the transformation of rural society and of agriculture became an important issue for sociological research in Hungary in the 1990s. Istvan Harcsa, Imre Kovach, and Ivan Szelenyi (1994) investigated this problem in historical context. The authors argued that the agricultural crisis in the 1990s was a consequence of the economic recession as well as of the failure to implement reforms earlier in the 1980s. They also criticized the manner of privatization and compensation, as well as the general economic policy in which agriculture was not adequately maintained and supported in Hungary. This led to the emergence of a new agrarian proletariat with highly limited life chances.

Another important study by Andras Csite and Imre Kovach (1995) analyzed the transformation of agriculture and rural society in comparison with other nations. The institutional differences of privatization and the financial inequalities were compared in six former socialist countries: Bulgaria, the Czech Republic, Hungary, Poland, Russia, and Slovakia. In the 1990s, privatization led to significant differences in the distribution of wealth, and rural societies became highly segmented.

RESEARCH IN ECONOMIC ORGANIZATIONAL SOCIOLOGY

Research in the field of economic organizational sociology had a strong focus on the decrease of the population in the labor force, and the consequences of this decline. A special emphasis was put on unemployment. The first overview of the topic was provided by Janos Kollo (1992). In the beginning of the 1990s, unemployment in Hungary was high compared to other nations. On the macro level, risk of becoming unemployed had a strong relationship to privatization. On the micro level, low educational level, older age, and Roma ethnicity increased the risk of unemployment. Regional differences were also substantial. Those who were unemployed had few chances to find new employment.

In the 1990s, unemployment became a way of life for many people in Hungary. Using open-ended interviews, Agnes Simonyi (1995) investigated the life course and adaptation strategies of unemployed people. Some of the respondents had previously had several jobs, others had worked for just one employer for most of their lives. The majority of unemployed persons were skilled and had a middle level of education. Their survival strategies were based either on state redistribution sources or on informal exchange relationships outside of the market.

The informal labor market was analyzed by Endre Sik (1999a, 1999b), who carried out research using participant observation. In this segment of the labor market, occasional workers are hired. Sik directly observed the setting where "buyers," the potential employers (or their representatives), and "sellers," the potential employees, actually meet. The sellers are mostly men, with little education, and frequently homeless. Most of them are Hungarians who came from territories where the Hungarian minority lives in neighboring countries, for example, Slovakia and Romania. The buyers are entrepreneurs in construction who hire these people for hard unskilled manual work. The participant observation was regularly repeated over four seasons. The author describes the main features of the supply and demand sides of this market, including an analysis of the fluctuation of wages and the factors influencing negotiations over wages, such as type of work, season, and ethnicity of the worker.

In the case of the emergence of self-employment in the 1990s, two mechanisms were present at the same time. Employees moved into self-employment as a consequence of "pull factors," like low wages and lesser independence associated with the employee position. The fear of losing a job or the fact that job loss had already occurred acted as "push factors," leading to forced self-employment. Maria Frey (1995) analyzed the institutional background of the process in which the unemployed tried to establish a private business. Although formal labor programs supporting these new enterprises were not well organized, two-thirds of the new enterprises that emerged from unemployment were able to survive.

Privatization became a driving force in the increase in self-employment. Terez Laky (1992) investigated the features of this process in the beginning of the 1990s. The group pushed to self-employment by privatization turned out to be very heterogeneous, but the majority of them had no financial capital for any serious business. Consequently, by definition, these people can hardly be labeled as entrepreneurs. According to Laky, the Hungarian small business is of "too micro a level" in international comparison. In addition to full-time self-employment, part-time self-employment also appeared when participants already had a paid job. In these latter cases, the main capital was even less of a financial character and tended to be some special skill. This type of private business does not help to decrease unemployment since it does not lead to the creation of new jobs. Middle-level or larger business represents a very small fraction of the private sphere in Hungary.

Research on the economic elite included two opposing perspectives. Szelenyi (1995) argued that the economic transformation did not allow the development of a capitalist class of owners in Hungary. Instead, a managerial class took the leading position in the postsocialist period. As a result, the Hungarian system can be labeled as managerial capitalism. On the other hand, research carried out by Kolosi (2000) showed that, by the end of the 1990s, a new capitalist class had indeed emerged in Hungary. Various types of continuities in civic values, accumulated cultural capital, networks of positions, and educational levels played a significant role in the development of an economic elite. Being female was a disadvantage, but previous experience in management, ownership, and wealth increased the probability of entering into an elite position in the managerial era.

The character of the new, postsocialist economic elite was definitely influenced by the professional changes in socialist management during the decades of socialism. Already during the socialist period, managers with a working class origin and political trustworthiness had been replaced by managers with educational and professional competence (Lengyel 1994). Balazs Vedres (1997) also analyzed this process, focusing on managers with either technical or economic backgrounds. He found that an important feature of the emergence of the new managerial class was an upgrade of economic knowledge in contrast to technical skills.

SOCIOLOGICAL REFLECTIONS ON THE POLITICAL TRANSFORMATION

A relatively large number of articles in *Szociologiai Szemle* dealt with political sociology and the sociology of social movements. However, they, too, proved to be an extremely heterogeneous collection of themes and approaches. We believe that this fact reflects the relative weakness of political sociology in Hungary. We have selected three themes in political sociology that were studied in Hungarian sociology.[2]

Gyorgy Konrad and Ivan Szelenyi's *The Road of the Intellectuals to Class Power* (1979b), the best-known Hungarian social science book before 1990, treated the classical question of power and tried to give a sociological answer to it.[3] It identified the intellectuals as the emerging ruling class in state socialism. The book certainly had a lasting impact on the study of the transformation of elites, even if its special predictions were proven false by history. An alternative theory was presented by Elmer Hankiss (1989, 1990) who predicted the emergence of a "great class coalition" consisting of members of the party elite and state bureaucracy, managers of state owned enterprises, and wealthier private entrepreneurs. While Hankiss did not return to his thesis, this model of political capitalism had some influence on later studies.

Szelenyi continued to publish on the "ruling class" problem. He identified three class positions, the intellectual elite, private entrepreneurs, and the working class, along with three political fields that occupied the space between class positions (Kolosi et al. 1991; Szelenyi and Szelenyi 1991). These were the liberal political field existing between the elite and the entrepreneurs, the national-Christian field between the entrepreneurs and the working class, and the social-democratic field between the elite and the working class. Later, based on his idea of managerial capitalism, Szelenyi and Janos Ladanyi proposed as a political antidote a new social democratic policy based on a broad coalition (1995, 1996).

Power and conflicting social groups and strata are at the center of the many publications by Erzsebet Szalai (1994, 1996, 1999), mostly based on qualitative data. Her basic conviction was and is that there was, toward the end of state socialism, a new technocratic elite emerging that was the main protagonist of the transition period.

MASS COMMUNICATION AND POLITICS

Already during the period of state socialism, a rudimentary form of opinion research was developed by the Center of Mass Communication Research, which was attached to the Hungarian Broadcasting Company. After the transition, the majority of people in opinion research moved into new commercial opinion research companies, producing information for the market and for political actors. A minority remained in the social sciences proper. An outstanding example of scientific research in this field is the work of Robert Angelusz (2000). Angelusz is concerned primarily with the visibility of social processes (social optics), and analyzes structures of the public sphere from this point of view. The problem he is starting from is that the correct perception of the social environment is nearly impossible. According to Angelusz, the structure of communication is one of the factors that explain differences in visibility. Visibility depends on the transmissibility of channels connecting the informal and public spheres of communication, with good visibility resulting from a high level of thematic synchronicity. Obviously, there is a good deal of mostly latent normativeness in Angelusz's approach.

ETHNICITY AND NATIONALITY

Two aspects of nationality and ethnicity are highly relevant in the Hungarian context, the problems of the Roma minority, and those of the Hungarian minorities in neighboring countries. The Roma problem was the focus of interest of Istvan Kemeny's research group, which was formed during the state socialist period and was subjected to repressive measures. Kemeny and his collaborators, Gabor Kertesi and Gabor Havas, conducted empirical research in the field (see Kemeny 1999). The problem has many ramifications extending to issues of unemployment, housing, education, and social policy.

The national question and problems of minorities are at the center of the research of the group led by Gyorgy Csepeli and Antal Orkeny. In the early 1990s, Csepeli (1992) developed a theoretical scheme for the analysis of national identity based on the distinction between state nationhood, characteristic of Western Europe, and cultural nationhood, the Eastern European variant, centering on culture, language, and folk (see also Hagendoorn, Csepeli, and Dekker 2000). Csepeli's approach was openly normative, considering the Western type of nationhood as the better one, while arguing that the Eastern variant promotes prejudice and ethnic conflict. The empirical research conducted by Csepeli and his coworkers is social psychological, and is focused on attitudes and discovery of typical configurations of national identities and beliefs, mostly among the Hungarian minorities and the local majorities in the neighboring countries (Csepeli, Orkeny, and Szekelyi 2000).

THE INTERNATIONAL EMBEDDEDNESS OF HUNGARIAN SOCIOLOGY

The Hungarian Sociological Association provides a framework for the participation of Hungarian sociologists in the international scene. The Hungarian Sociological Association is a member of the International Sociological Association (ISA) and of the European Sociological Association (ESA). Several Hungarian sociologists are individual members in these institutions. One of our colleagues, Gyorgy Lengyel, is a member of the board of the ESA. Several Hungarian colleagues participate in the activity of the research committees of the ISA, or in the activity of the research networks of the ESA. Three Hungarian institutions, the Department of Sociology of the University of Economics, the Institute of Political Sciences of the Hungarian Academy of Sciences, and TARKI, are members of the European Consortium of Sociological Research (ECSR).

International conferences provide good opportunities for Hungarian sociologist to meet with the international scientific community. In 1995, the second ESA conference was held in Budapest. The Hungarian Sociological Association organizes conferences every year. During the last ten years, these conferences were mainly national ones. However, the 1992, 1994, and 1999 conferences had an international character. The 1999 conference aimed to provide an overview of the ten-year period of transformation of the system. Unfortunately, the proceedings are not available.

Since any concluding remarks would be rather superfluous at the end of this rather compressed overview of certain developments in Hungarian sociology, we would like to call attention to the ambiguous existence of the national sociological entities in the relatively small countries like Hungary. Sociology, which was once conceived as the critical consciousness and conscience of "its" society, is becoming an international research machine. While the role sociology (and other social sciences) has in national education systems gives credence to the existence of separate national scientific communities, the realities of international research make these national boundaries irrelevant. Of course, for reasons of convenience, sociologists deal mostly with "their own" societies. But the real networks of science cannot be grasped in national terms. The integration of the sociologies of former socialist countries into Western science networks is proceeding fast, and will change the shape of science in that part of the world as well. The contours of the new scientific arrangement cannot be clearly drawn yet, but we feel that new realities are emerging. Perhaps the authors of a subsequent review in ten or twenty years will be able to analyze those developments.

NOTES

1. The rest is constituted by students and unknowns.

2. For lack of space, we have not covered other areas where some work was done, that is, the sociology of social movements (Szabo 1998), and political socialization (Csepeli et al. 1993).

3. It was published by a Western Hungarian publisher in 1978, in English and French (Konrad and Szelenyi 1979b, 1979c). Translations appeared in 1979, and the first edition in Hungarian in Hungary came out in 1989 (Konrad and Szelenyi 1989).

8

Sociology in Latvia after 1990

Aivars Tabuns

DECOMMUNIZATION OF SOCIOLOGY

The decommunization of sociology in Latvia was fostered by the replacement of the scientific elite in the beginning of the 1990s. This was facilitated by a nostrification (recertification) of academic degrees that had been conferred both before and after the restoration of statehood took place. Some scientists did not submit their work for nostrification, and some of those who did were not nostrified. Most scientists who were not nostrified nevertheless continued to pursue their academic activities as lecturers at universities or as researchers.

It is useful to point out that the nostrification procedure had more of a symbolic meaning than a practical one. Marxism for most Latvian sociologists was nothing more than bijouterie. Pro forma references to the most recent congress of the Communist Party always had to be made, and some quotation from Marx had to be inserted in the introduction of a paper. In the introductions of papers in the 1990s, more references to other authors began to appear, although often those quotations had rather weak relationship to the content of the papers.

To a large extent, the decommunization of the academic elite was also influenced by a reorganization of funding and research priorities. Under the old system, scientific institutions received their financing directly. Now, the norm is to give grants for specific projects. The principal investigator of a proposed project submits a request to the Latvian Council of Sciences (LCS), and those projects that are given high ratings in an independent peer review process receive grants from the Council.

Because its resources are not sufficient to cover all of the expenses for a research project, the grants financed by the LCS for the most part only cover salaries of researchers and the rent. This means the researchers themselves must find the necessary additional funding. In most instances, researchers get these resources from the funds and scientific programs of other countries (e.g., Soros Foundation and the Fifth Framework Program of the European Union), or by taking part in applied research projects that are financed by state government or institutions affiliated to it. At the moment, Latvian sociologists do not receive funds for social analyses from private sources.

A high scientific standard, competitiveness at the international level, and the quality of international contacts serve as the main criteria for defining research priorities. A special financing agreement was introduced to facilitate the participation of Latvian scientists in international activities, as well as to give additional support for the best doctoral students in both the universities and the research institutions. Those scholars who were not nostrified are not eligible to be elected to grant review committees or to serve as principle investigators of funded projects.

In the mid-1990s, some scholars who had received their Ph.D.s in Western Europe joined the academic elite. In the late 1990s, in order to facilitate a more rapid replacement of the academic elite, the existing system of two levels of doctoral degrees (Dr. and Dr. with habilitation degree) was replaced with that of a single doctoral degree that enables young scientists to obtain administrative and academic positions at universities and institutes more quickly. Currently, there is a great emphasis placed on the preparation of Ph.D. students.

CHANGES IN TEACHING SOCIOLOGY

In September of 1990, a new class of sociology students was accepted at the University of Latvia. Unlike during the previous era, when sociology students majored in philosophy and specialized in their field only during the last two years of study, current training programs correspond to the curricular structures which are characteristic of Western European universities. Two other public institutions, the Academy of Culture, and the University of Agriculture, also have undergraduate sociology students. All sociology programs must be accredited by a commission of experts that consists of two representatives from universities in Western Europe and one representative of a university from the Baltic States. Successful accreditation allows universities to issue diplomas that are recognized abroad.

The competition for the state-financed scholarships in sociology programs at the universities is rather fierce. There are about seven to twelve candidates for every scholarship available. At the moment, approximately one-half of all sociology students must pay tuition fees or rely on student loans. Students (undergraduate, graduate, and postgraduate) in sociology programs at the University of Latvia have an opportunity to acquire more knowledge and experience in Western universities, though mainly in the Scandinavian countries. Students from other study programs at the University of Latvia, and in other universities as well, may take sociology courses, though they are more likely to be the elective ones. In turn, sociology students often take courses in study programs such as political and communication sciences.

Demand for sociologists in Latvia is not that high, and therefore, after graduation, most sociology students find jobs in state administration or other organizations. Typically, however, it is the ability to use sociological research methods that is more in demand than theoretical knowledge. Most graduate students work during their study years.

A number of full text databases, as well as sociological journals and monographs, are available to students, though limited due to financial constraints. In their studies, students mostly use works published in English, not in Latvian. Until very recently, none of the Western sociology textbooks were translated into the Latvian language. Some local textbooks are available to students, but they serve only as a mere introduction to basic concepts and terms in sociology. The translation of some works into Latvian is proceeding with the financial support of the Soros Foundation, including works by authors Jean Baudrillard, Michel Foucault, Anthony Giddens, Erving Goffman, and Anthony D. Smith. Apart from this initiative, the Latvian Council of Sciences is also providing support for the publishing of scientific books, as well as the development of sociology courses that will be available for students on-line.

At the present moment, undergraduate students have rather limited opportunities to acquire practical skills in the field of sociology, that is, they are not sufficiently involved in research projects. Most universities do not possess sufficient financial resources that would allow students to prepare high quality bachelor's and master's theses. The situation is somewhat better regarding the preparation of postgraduate students. Most postgraduate students have an opportunity to study at Western universities, and to take part in research projects led by professors at these universities.

RELATIONSHIPS BETWEEN ACADEMIC SOCIOLOGISTS AND PRIVATE RESEARCH CENTERS

The main feature of the transformation of the institutional environment of Latvian science was the liquidation of the system of control that the Latvian Academy of Sciences (LAS) used to exert control over the scientific institutes. The institutes are now independent from the Latvian Academy of Sciences. Since February 14, 1992, the Latvian Academy of Sciences has been functioning as an association of scientists and acts as a nongovernmental organization. The main aims and tasks of the LAS include active participation and consultation with the government in establishing Latvian science policy; publishing of scientific literature, development of scientific terminology, and maintenance of scientific standards; organization of congresses, conferences, discussions, and competitions; popularization of scientific achievements; maintenance of international contacts of Latvian scientists; and protection, maintenance, and perfection of research ethics, principles, and traditions. However, the LAS is not authorized to distribute state science budget funds.

The structure of research centers also has been changed fundamentally. In large part this was due to a lack of resources that led to the liquidation of many facilities at universities, companies, and government agencies. In addition, privately run research centers began to emerge, many of which conduct marketing research in addition to sociological work. Academic research centers, institutes run by universities, and private research centers owned by Western companies all regularly take part in competitions to carry out research projects for state and international organizations. Academic sociologists are typically more oriented toward analytical research, while private companies tend to do public opinion surveys.

Most of the leading sociologists at Latvian universities have created their own private centers or collaborate with such research centers. Thus, possible conflicts between centers run by universities and private companies have been avoided. Both kinds of centers also have an opportunity to receive research grants from the Latvian Council of Sciences.

The largest private company in Latvia is Baltic Data House (BDH), the largest center for market and social research in the Baltic States, and an affiliate organization of one of the leading research companies in Europe, Taylor Nelson Sofres. BDH serves more than two hundred clients and provides information necessary for marketing and management decisions, as well as public administration. Currently, there are thirty-one full-time employees working at BDH. In 2001, BDH carried out more than 120 research projects. In 1993, in collaboration with Finnish Gallup Media, BDH founded a company named Baltic Media Facts. In 2000, building on one of BDH's academic and social research departments, the Institute of Social Sciences was established. Its major research areas are public policy analysis, analysis and evaluation of public information campaigns, and comparative sociological studies. By and large, these centers have valuable collections of data and good international contacts as well. The quality of the research done by both universities and private companies is pretty much the same.

SOCIOECONOMIC TRANSFORMATION AS A RESEARCH TOPIC

Research projects of a socioeconomic character in Latvia are funded by a number of international organizations (e.g., the United Nations Development Program and the World Bank), various ministries or their affiliated organizations, and the Latvian Council of Sciences. Sociological research projects financed by the LCS tend to focus on issues related to the transformation of Latvian society in the post-Communist era. This includes research on social structure and the dynamics of social change (Tabuns 1998c), the background of new economic, social, and political relations, and social stratification (Dobelniece 1997; Rungule, Pranka, and Trapenciere 1998; Trapenciere et al. 2000), the emergence of new social groups, ethnic processes, and national relationships (Dribins 1994; Ezera 1999; Karklins and Zepa 1996; Tabuna 1997; Tabuns 2001; Vebers 1996, 2000), attitudes toward national, regional, and European integration (Broks, Tabuns, and Tabuna 2001b; Tabuns and Tisenkopfs 2001), the mobility of young people and their integration with social structures (Koroleva 2001; Koroleva and Rungule 1997; Koroleva et al. 1999; Tisenkopfs 1995a, 1995b), and the employment and quality of life of women (Broks 1999; Koroleva 1997; Tabuns and Sanita 1999; Zarina 1995).

Research into the society's institutional reforms is being done in connection with the establishment of a democratic system of politics (Broks et. al. 1997; Lakis 1997; Tabuns 1998a) and the involvement of residents in the political process (Karklins and Zepa 2002; Tabuns and Tabuna 1999, 2000; Vebers 1998; Zepa 1997, 1999a, 1999b). Research is also being done on the international integration of Latvian science, as well as qualitative and quantitative changes that have been occurring in science as a social institution (Tabuns 1997, 1998b; Trapenciere, Ashmane, and Krutskih 1994). Research in the area of social policy is aimed at the analysis of balanced agricultural policies (Tisenkopfs 1998b, 1999a, 1999b) and public policy (Eglite 1995; Menshikov 2001; Tisenkopfs 2001b).

Several grants also have been given for research into the agents of social change. Research is being done on the establishment of new social identities (Tabuns 2001; Tisenkopfs 1995a, 2001a; Zepa 1997, 1998), the hereditary nature of traditions (Broks, Tabuns, and Tabuna 2001a), the role of historical memory (Broks, Tabuns, and Tabuna 2001a; Skultans 1997; Tisenkopfs 1993; Zirnite 2001), and strategies of action in the present day (Tisenkopfs 1995a, 1997).

If the development of various subsectors of sociology is analyzed, one can see that limited amounts of research are being done in the following areas: ethnosociology, the sociology of youth and education, social structure and social change, the sociology of rural and regional development, the sociology of politics, the sociology of deviant behavior and criminology, gender and family sociology, the sociology of science, social anthropology, the sociology of mass communications, social policy and social work, urban sociology, and the sociology of the environment. Because of a lack of money, no work is being done in sociological theory and history, the methodology of sociological research, work, industrial, and economic sociology, the sociology of lifestyles and culture, the sociology of organizations and social administration, and the sociology of religion.

From 1998 until 2001, one of Latvia's leading sociologists, Talis Tisenkopfs, was the chief editor for the *Latvia Human Development Report* (Tisenkopfs 1998a, 1999c, 2001b). Many Latvian sociologists were involved in this project. Thanks to this collaboration, it was possible to include a rather wide spectrum of themes in the series of reports, that is, public policy processes, globalization, and the role of the individual, the state, and the private sector in human development.

On a regular basis since the beginning of 1991, private research centers have carried out public opinion surveys in which respondents are asked to evaluate social and economic aspects of the development of the Latvian state, privatization, and macroeconomic policies (see Baltic Data House, www.bdh.lv). Through collaboration with the International Social Survey Program, and funded by the Latvian Council of Sciences, eight research projects have been carried out in Latvia on topics including national identity, the role of government, family and changing gender roles, religion, inequality, environment, and social relations and support. These studies have allowed researchers to do comparative analyses of these processes in Latvia (Zepa 1999a, 1999b; Tabuns 2001).

NATIONALISM AND ETHNICITY AS A RESEARCH PROBLEM

Analyses of identity formation among the Latvian population have been of great interest among scholars for one important reason: Latvia is the most ethnically divided country of Eastern Europe. Different surveys demonstrate that there are marked differences in the ways in which various sectors within the Latvian population develop identification with an ethnic group, the state, and the political regime. Work on these issues has been based on data from several different studies carried out between 1991 and 2001. Some of the studies overlapped with those of political science, and others with the sociology of culture.

These studies have focused on several different facets of the problem. Some have focused on the formation of new national, state, and regime identities in Latvia, and the links between political and ethnic pluralism. This has included analysis of the role of ethnicity in political mobilization during the transition to democracy, and the various manifestations of ethnicity in self-consciousness, attitudes, behavior, ideology, and politics (Tabuns 2001; Vebers 1996; Zepa 1997).

There also has been comparative research on national identity characteristics in Latvia and other European countries. This research has attempted to assess the most important similarities and differences in identities on the social and demographic group and national levels (Tabuns 2001; Zepa 1998). Related to identity formation, research has been done that intended to investigate the Latvian population's attitudes toward regional and European integration, and to analyze the factors that influence links between Latvia and other European countries (Tabuns 2001; Tisenkopfs 2001a). Most researchers argue that identities are constantly challenged, negotiated, reconstructed, and maintained. They think that identities are not just a relatively fixed set of traits of an individual, and that there is not merely one and only real national identity of the Latvian people.

THE DEVELOPMENT OF THE PROFESSION OF SOCIOLOGY

For the most part, Latvian sociologists are involved in carrying out short-term projects, and therefore they are frequently compelled to shift their research themes and expertise. This intermittent "retooling" of sociologists is further fueled by the fact that the state and its affiliated institutions may occasionally order research projects in fields in which Latvian sociologists have no prior experience. Sociologists affiliated with various institutions and universities frequently join projects with ever-changing research tasks. And, many sociologists may occasionally and simultaneously take part in several projects whose research objectives may be unrelated to one another. As a result, the institutional structure of Latvian sociology has developed a somewhat amorphous shape. On the one hand, the low level of specialization may occasionally have a negative impact on the quality of research. On the other hand, in many instances the breadth of sociologists trained in such a manner offers a wider and deeper perspective on social reality than the perspective of their colleagues who are more narrowly specialized.

Academic debates between Latvian sociologists take place very rarely, primarily because most of them are overloaded with their own projects. The largest public debate was devoted to the identity problem, but only a few sociologists participated in it. Public attention has also been achieved by regular conferences, organized by the Institute of Philosophy and Sociology, on democracy and ethnopolitics. Latvian sociologists have also organized a series of theoretical seminars.

Approximately thirty scientific articles are printed each year in Latvian publications. Articles by Latvian sociologists also have received regular exposure in Latvian social and humanities journals. Publications such as *Latvijas ZA Vestis* (Proceedings of the Latvian Academy of Sciences) and *Humanities and Social Sciences: Latvia* can be mentioned in this respect. The interest of the scientific public has also been aroused by research reports from the Institute of Philosophy and Sociology, and from the Baltic Data House. The limited number of potential authors and readers discourages the publication of an academic sociological journal.

During the 1990s, Latvian sociologists published several articles in international journals, while countless articles were printed in social science books that were published in other countries in the English, Russian, Polish, Finnish, German, and Swedish languages. English was the predominant language of international publication.

Data standardization and harmonization is a very crucial issue in Europe right now, and Latvia must deal with this issue as well. Otherwise, opportunities for data comparison will disappear very quickly. The development of the social sciences at this point is being hampered to a great extent by problems with terminology. To resolve this problem, work has begun on preparing a dictionary of sociology. A smaller explanatory dictionary, meant for schoolchildren, has already been prepared (Zepa and Zobena 1996).

Proposals have been developed for a code of ethics for Latvian sociologists. Efforts must be undertaken to ascertain that all organizations that are doing sociological or market research in Latvia give official recognition to this code. This would not only improve relations between data users and providers, but it would also help to achieve better links among the organizations that engage in this kind of research. A generally recognized code of ethics also would serve as a control for those persons whose research quality is not up to snuff. Then, the inclusion of data in the social sciences archive would become an important indicator of the quality of an organization's data, and of the willingness of the respective organizations to subject themselves to external control. There is an urgent need to establish a neutral institution of expertise and review, which would provide expert analysis of data quality for any and all data users.

INTERNATIONAL RESEARCH COOPERATION

Before the 1990s, there was good cooperation with Baltic and Russian social scientists. Since then, these contacts have narrowed and become irregular. Nonetheless, with the more frequent involvement in various research projects and conferences abroad, and thanks to the new opportunities to obtain the results of studies done in other countries, Latvian sociologists have more chances to obtain necessary information and to get insights about the social processes in other Central and Eastern European countries than they did under Soviet rule. Except for some isolated cases, however, most joint research projects carried out by sociologists from these countries do not receive Western financial support. Only some joint projects between Latvian and Polish sociologists can be mentioned here as exceptions.

During the 1990s, as cooperation with the North and West widened, the research partners of Latvian social scientists also changed. Latvian sociologists were able to study Western sociological theories, and the diversity of theoretical approaches used by them grew. But, at the same time, many sociologists did not notice that they sometimes accepted theories that contradicted one another. While this situation "let a thousand flowers boom," many of these flowers were poorly rooted. Sometimes it appeared that authors did not make any efforts to critically evaluate the theories they used in their work. That is, they seldom tried to verify these theories with empirical data. Furthermore, researchers rarely used methodological strategies that could confront the theories and challenge their assumptions or conclusions.

In the area of quantitative research, Latvian sociologists typically use questionnaires that have been developed and already validated in other countries. Thus, the data obtained in Latvia is comparable with the data obtained by social scientists in other countries. This also considerably facilitates the interpretation of the data and the evaluation of results.

In October 1996, the Latvian Social Science Data Archive (LSZDA, www.lszda.lv) was funded. The archive has a range of cultural, historical, social, scientific, educational, and financial objectives. It is intended to provide Latvia's scientists and other interested persons access to data archives of foreign countries, as well as to help foreign archives and social scientific investigators to obtain information about Latvia. The current task of LSZDA is to improve its services by offering users new types of data sets (gathered from Latvia and other regions), as well as to improve the information on the existing data sets.

Latvian sociologists regularly participate in significant international projects, and most have spent time at Western research centers, working with foreign colleagues on the preparation of collective monographs. The following projects must be mentioned specifically: the International Social Survey Program (ISSP), Paths of a Generation (a longitudinal project involving people who graduated from high school in 1983), the World Values Survey and European Values Survey, and the UNESCO project, Management of Social Transformation (MOST). Latvian researchers have also participated in the Central and Eastern European Barometer (CEEB) program, as well as other major research projects.

International research contacts have been established largely on the basis of participation by Latvian sociologists at international conferences and seminars. Each year, Latvian sociologists present papers at between twenty and thirty such events. Several Latvian sociologists have lectured at foreign universities. At the same time, many Western sociologists take part in projects directed by Latvian sociologists.

CONCLUSION

In my opinion, the development of the discipline of sociology in Latvia during the 1990s was influenced more by exogenous factors than endogenous factors. As a consequence of the funding policy of the Latvian government, scholars had rather limited opportunities to carry out their own research projects. In addition, due to inadequately low stipends for postgraduate students and wages for lecturers, graduates from universities were not interested in pursuing postgraduate studies.

The development of sociology was also considerably influenced by the greater involvement of Latvian sociologists in various international projects. Social demand for empirical studies and the subject matter of these studies was largely determined not by national institutions but rather by international organizations. Those scholars who were unable to get involved in international projects had rather limited opportunities to find funding to pursue their own research. Unfortunately, the cooperation between sociologists and national government agencies and organizations in Latvia is far from ideal. Nor have sociologists managed to develop good relationships with local government.

Nonetheless, sociologists were involved in the preparation of several important documents, including the National Development Plan, the state program Social Integration in Latvia, and the Latvian Poverty Reduction Strategy. And, the mass media has had a very friendly attitude toward sociologists, who have been afforded great opportunity to comment on the social and political situation. Sociologists frequently publish their articles in the leading newspapers and journals. For these reasons, not only their own colleagues, but also the mass media and scholars from different countries have been involved in the evaluation of the qualifications of Latvian sociologists. Only by winning recognition and trust have Latvian sociologists been able to claim their place among the academic elite. As a result of this increased exposure and scrutiny, public trust of sociology has increased during the last several years.

9

Lithuanian Sociology, 1990–2000

Anele Vosyliute

LITHUANIAN SOCIOLOGY BEFORE 1989

In Lithuania, sociology first appeared in its prescientific stage after World War I, at Kaunas University and the Kaunas Theological Seminary. A department of sociology was opened at Kaunas in 1922. The focus of sociological reflection was on the problems of the economic, social, and political situation and on reforms of the new state. In their writings, sociologists were using the concepts of Auguste Comte, Karl Marx, Herbert Spencer, Charles Darwin, Pitirim Sorokin, Maxim Kovalevskij and others (Saulys 1920; Leonas 1939). The problems of integrating the people into the active social life of an independent Lithuanian Republic (1918–40), the formation of a civilized man, and the development of a national consciousness appeared to be key concerns.

After World War II, Soviet Communist doctrine rejected the scientific heritage and traditions of the social sciences. It was assumed that the problems of society could be understood only from a "historical materialist" perspective. As Vaclovas Bagdonavicius and Palmyra Katinaite have noted:

Soviet Lithuania had to be protected not only from the overall effects of capitalism, dangerous to the whole Soviet empire, but also from some specific attributes due to her own spiritual heritage and historical path. The Catholic faith, which the occupational structures failed to subdue, and a strong immigrant community, whose relations with the oppressed homeland were never completely severed even though there were harsh restrictions, constituted two major "domestic" issues of concern for the Soviets (1997, 7).

Therefore, philosophy and the social sciences had the goal of criticizing "harmful bourgeois ideology" and the religious worldview, as well as the "reactionary nature of nationalism."

During the Soviet period, sociological studies were carried out at the Sociological Research Laboratory (established in 1965) at Vilnius University, at the Sociological Research Laboratory at Kaunas Politechnical Institute (beginning in 1966), and from 1969, at the Department (changed to Institute in 1977) of Philosophy, Sociology, and Law of the Lithuanian Academy of Sciences. These investigations were directed toward the social problems of socialist production, mostly in industrial enterprises, and the socialist way of life (*Darbininkas* 1972; *Darbininkas iriiimone* 1974). Studies also examined the creation of social development plans for the collectives and towns (*Siauliu* 1980; *Druskininkai* 1985; Jonaitis 1987), as well as national comparative longitudinal research on the attitudes of youth and other investigations of areas such as family and recreation.

REDEFINITION OF THE DISCIPLINE AFTER 1990

Postsocialist Lithuania found itself engaged in the process of democratization, with national freedom, economic, social, and cultural reforms, and the emergence of a new reality. This included the development of a pluralistic system of public opinion and political perspectives, changes in attitudes toward state and private property, resulting from the emergence of new institutions of the market economy, and new concepts of everyday lifestyles. New social movements, for instance, those of landowners, women, businessmen, and peasants, provided a vehicle for the expression of new needs and interests.

The broadening of social horizons and the diversification of patterns of economic, political, and cultural life in the country contributed to a concomitant transformation in the dynamics of sociology. Its relationship with and ideological influences from the Soviet Union declined as the necessity to become autonomous, in order to measure up to the standards of Western science, increased. However, because of the small number of scholars in the country having sociological credentials, there was no general removal or replacement of personnel or leadership within the discipline. Only a few sociologists in leadership positions had been active as members of the Communist Party in the pre-1989 period. With the transformation, only the perspectives and the problems to be investigated were changed. For example, during the process of nostrification (the recertification of Soviet-time diplomas and degrees within the context of the newly emerging post-Soviet Lithuanian institutional structures), practically all dissertations were accepted as meeting the qualifications for academic title.

The new independence in Lithuania brought radical changes to the environment of social scientific thought and its paradigms. The new structures and features of society necessitated changes in sociological research methodology and the rethinking of the subject matter of sociological investigations. In response, the epistemological foundations of science, and the theoretical and methodological problems of sociology, have been an important topic of analysis (Valantiejus 1999; Grigas 2001).

In the beginning of the period of social transition, sociologists were a dominant force. Sociologists, together with politicians, were active participants in creating new social development projects intended to help the nation to become a respected member of the international community. Sociologists were involved in new administrative, communications, and educational institutions and structures. Through the mass media, they were active in the public discourse in which new meanings of social change and cultural life were discussed. Along with journalists and the leaders of social movements, associations, and political parties, sociologists participated in the creation of an open public sphere. Through it, their writings and data were able to influence public opinion and the formation of civil society.

The Institute of Philosophy, Sociology, and Law (in 1995, its name was changed to the Lithuanian Institute of Philosophy and Sociology) became not only a popular center of intellectual activity, but also a place for theoretical and political discussions directed to the analysis of the foundations for a new civil society. Some of its members were active participants in the main social and political movement, *Sajudis*, and three were signatories of the Independence Act. Sociologists were also active as researchers. They analyzed the participation of the leaders and the people in the political events, and the changes in their attitudes toward the new reality (*Lietuva* 1990).

Social scientists became, in a way, stewards for those concepts and terms that could articulate and reflect the new activities and practices of the people. As a result, theoretical discussions on citizenship and democracy and the new social mobilization in the country took on a special importance. Concepts such as "modernization," "pluralism," "democracy," "nation state," "civil society," "new identity," and "social change" were used not only in the analyses of sociologists, but frequently in common usage as well.

Not surprisingly, the new social historical context created a flux in the national, cultural, religious, and political identities of the people. New meanings and narratives of identity, which had been hidden as dangerous during the Soviet time, such as those of expatriate, believer, and dissident, accompanied and accentuated the emergence of new issues in public discourse, and enriched social investigations. During the transformation, sociologists, whose research tasks during the Soviet period had been largely commissioned by the largest manufacturing enterprises, began to engage in dialogue and communication with a multiplicity of different institutional and social actors. The reformation of scientific institutions and the creation of a new identity for sociologists was supported and influenced by market relations and interests. A greater range of choice of possible fields of research opened up, but at the same time there was an internal "brain drain," as academics were able to use their expertise to shift into careers in politics or business. However, with the opening of sociology departments at the universities, new opportunities emerged within the academic world, especially for senior sociologists with academic degrees. Many of them became professors or lecturers.

The formation of a new identity for sociology has occurred against the background of a newly established intellectual freedom, but one might also argue, anarchy. This intellectual freedom has been particularly characteristic of the younger generation of sociologists, who are more open to foreign influences. Their intellectual goals and orientations tend to be more individualistic, and primarily focused on the contemporary social context, distant from former national achievements, problems, and contradictions.

Scientific and cultural exchange is very important for the development of the social and cultural capital of small countries. But, the indigenous authors have reasons to be worried by foreign competition because they can be forced out of the social scientific and culture fields through the importation of materials and texts from abroad. In the long run, this can lead to an erosion of the mother tongue and of domestic culture.

The central structures in the organization of sociological research activity in Lithuania are the Institute of Philosophy and Sociology, and the departments of sociology at Vilnius University, Vilnius Pedagogical University, Vytautas Magnus University, Kaunas Technological University, and Klaipeda University. Since 1990, there has been a process of decentralization going on. The Lithuanian Sociological Society, of which the Kaunas branch is very active, organizes conferences and publishes sociological materials. There are two journals for the publication of sociological papers, *Filosofija: Sociologija,* published, since 1990, by the Lithuanian Academy of Sciences, and *Sociologija* published by Klaipeda University and Vytautas Magnus University, since 1997.

In 1990, several public opinion centers, such as *Vilmorus* (www.vilmorus.lt), *Baltijos tyrimai* (Baltic Research www.Balttyr.lt), and later *Socialines informacijos centras* (SIC www.sic.lt), were established. These private agencies for public opinion and market analyses have attracted the public's attention, and their data have been useful in public discussions and in decision making. Changes in public opinion were analyzed by Vladas Gaidys and Danute Tureikyte (1994).

THE TEACHING OF SOCIOLOGY

The teaching of sociology is a new phenomenon in Lithuania. The first postwar sociologists of the country had no higher education in sociology. But, they were enthusiastic, and through individual work and postgraduate studies they acquired their scientific qualifications. Following independence from the Soviet Union, the universities in Lithuania abolished the teaching of scientific Communism and dialectic and historical materialism. New departments of sociology, and curricula, were established. In the beginning, this was difficult due to the lack of lecturers, textbooks, programs, and literature. The core curriculum of sociology at the universities followed the model of Western countries. With the help and influence of Western educational institutions, the training of sociologists has been successfully established at the universities, and the quality of education has improved. There are still some problems, such as a lack of Lithuanian textbooks in general sociology. In their absence, several textbooks have been translated from English into Lithuanian. Among the most used is the text by Leonard Broom, Charles M. Bonjean, and Dorothy H. Broom (1992). Texts by Peter Berger and Neil Smelser, the latter translated into Russian, are also used.

B.A. studies exist at Vilnius University, Vytautas Magnus University, and the Vilnius Pedagogical University. M.A. and Ph.D. studies exist at Vilnius University, Vytautas Magnus University, and Kaunas Technological University. Doctoral studies also exist at the Lithuanian Institute of Philosophy and Sociology. In Lithuania, there are about three hundred students studying sociology, of which about half are fee paying. Fewer than 10 percent are doctoral students. Between 1990 and 2001, approximately ten doctoral dissertations were presented for a Ph.D. degree in sociology. Also, some Lithuanian students are studying at foreign universities. Currently, given the state's limited support for research, teaching positions in sociology are more stable and offer a greater guarantee for the future than do research positions. Scientific researchers are paid poorly and state support for research is comparatively very limited.

DEVELOPMENT OF THE SOCIOLOGICAL COMMUNITY

At the beginning of the transformation, the theoretical and methodological perspectives of sociologists were first influenced by the opportunities to participate in international scientific conferences and world congresses of sociology, and then later by access to the international literature. At the beginning of the decade, the writings of sociologists were largely descriptive. Now, because of their better qualification, Lithuanian sociologists are increasingly using more conceptual analysis in their work, analyzing social change (Taljunaite 1995), post-Communist revolution (Saulauskas 1998), gender (Juozeliuniene and Kanopiene 1995, 1996), social mobility, the welfare state, Pierre Bourdieu's field of power, Anthony Giddens's theory of structuration, and the postmodern theory of Zygmunt Bauman and others (Grigas 2001).

The Baltic Branch of the Soviet Sociological Association was originally found in 1975. The independent Lithuanian Sociological Society (LSS) was established in 1990, and there are now approximately 120 members. A majority of the members are working as researchers or as lecturers. During the decade of the 1990s, the LSS organized four conferences that were each attended by between 100 and 120 members of the Society. In their papers, the participants analyzed the most important problems of Lithuanian society (Grigas 1996b; Vosyliute 1998, 2001b). In 1991, the LSS became a member of the International Sociological Association. It is also a member of the European Sociological Association. During the decade, a few Lithuanian sociologists were able to participate in sociological congresses and conferences abroad. Some published articles abroad (Juozeliuniene 1993, 1997, 1999; Juozeliuniene and Kanopiene 1995).

The academic and educational institutions maintain close relations with research and study institutions and governmental and nongovernmental organizations of other countries, and they participate in international projects. The Lithuanian Scientific Fund, the Soros Foundation, and various Western assistance programs have been the main supporters of these academic exchanges. Academic contacts and cooperation with the international research communities enabled Lithuanian sociologists to become conversant with the research projects and pedagogical ideas of Western countries. These programs were first taken advantage of by younger scholars who spoke English, German, or French.

During the last decade, the State Science and Studies Fund of Lithuania has supported several sociological projects, including research on the social, cultural, and educational needs of Lithuanians living in neighboring countries, the social memory of women, and the problems of national minorities in Lithuania. It has also supported the publication of collections of articles presented at the conferences of the LSS between 1990 and 2001.

MAJOR RESEARCH AREAS

The new research interests and orientations of Lithuanian sociologists have been related to the challenges facing the nation and the state during the transition. For example, the development of a national consciousness as a precondition for sovereignty was important. The situation and the role of the nation and nationhood at the level of the state, as well as globally, was analyzed by Romualdas Grigas (1995). With reference to theories of modernity, Grigas explicated the concepts of nation and nationhood. He examined their sources and discussed their relation to the structures of the contemporary state, and an open and civil society. He also provided a theoretical analysis of the sociodynamics of the nation, its social heritage, and the environment that influences it (Grigas 1993).

The conceptualization of an open society, including the problems of democracy and social identity, was investigated by Irena Juozeliuniene (1993). The attitudes of Lithuanian society toward minorities, their representatives in the political parties, their image in mass media, and new social and ethnic identities were also of great interest (Grigas 1996a; Kasatkina and Leoncikas 2000; Motuzas 2000).

Juozas Algimantas Krikstopaitis (1997) analyzed the causes of the decay of trust in the posttotalitarian condition, as the painful process of change in values takes place. Lina Astra and Bronislovas Kuzmickas (1996) compared national value types and their features. Their study, conducted in 1993–94, provided an opportunity to outline the worldviews of different generations. Such sociological attention to the question of values, that is, changes, values conflicts, and the manifestation of political, material, and ethnic values, is characteristic of the transition period (Mitrikas 1999).

The history of sociology has been another important area of research (Vosyliute 1996–2000). In this work, the sociological ideas, theoretical views, and research orientations of many Lithuanian sociologists were evaluated and analyzed. It is only the decline of the hegemony of the socialist paradigm that has made the resumption and restoration of a national sociology with its own roots possible.

Since 1990, the role of the Catholic Church has become more important. The religious life of the people is open and free, and many books and periodicals on religious philosophy, social issues, history, and education have appeared. In response, sociologists have analyzed levels of religiosity, religious minorities, and the changing strength of the role of religion (Juknevicius 2000; Ziliukaite 2000).

Discussions of national identity, citizenship, political culture, civil society, globalization, and the nation-state were very popular in both the mass media as well as in sociological analyses. Particular interest was directed to the evaluation of the country's development and readiness for the possibility of integration into the European Union. The attitudes of Lithuanian youth toward European integration are among the most positive in East and East-Central Europe (Krukauskiene 2000).

The sociology of culture was also an important research topic, though it was analyzed mostly at the Institute of Culture and Arts. Vytautas Kavolis (1992, 1994), a sociologist and cultural scholar, exerted significant methodological influence on issues such as civilization, the sociology of art, nationalism, cultural meaning, and modernization (see also Valantiejus 2000). Algirdas Gaizutis (1998) examined the theoretical foundations of the sociology of art, the development of the aesthetic attitudes of the people, and the importance of cultural factors in society. Cultural identity, evaluation of culture and its values, cultural needs of the population, and the social position of artists were studied by Arvydas Matulionis (2000).

Market reforms, the problems of entrepreneurs, and changes in society's structure were also very important issues of sociological research. The features of the situation of business and the difficulties, problems, and obstacles to its development in Lithuania have been investigated by Antanas Klicius (2001). Meilute Taljunaite (1995) investigated the creation of an effective private sector with liberal values, and the attitudes of people toward private ownership. Taljunaite (1999) also examined the new social structure, that is, the formation of a middle class and the emergence of different social groups, social mobility, and occupational change. The significance of the role of different elite groups, that is, political, economic, bureaucratic, public, and private enterprise, and banking, and their problems and worldviews were analyzed by Kestutis Masiulis (1997) and Irmina Matonyte (2001). Sociologists, mostly from the Institute of Labor and Social Research, also gave attention to the rapidly growing unemployment (*Aktualus* 1999; Gruzevskis 2000).

During the decade, the orientation of family research also changed. The main methodological and theoretical trends of social and sociological investigations were analyzed by Juozas V. Uzdila (2001). Family research revealed changes in the family's formation processes, the role of women, and the status of the children. Recently, Vlada Stankuniene (1997) investigated new features of the demographics of the Lithuanian family and its households, the ethnic composition of families, children as a value, changes in fertility and its regulation, support for families, work and family, and the dilemma of the status of the housewife. This research was done between 1989 and 1995, as part of an international project of the United Nations Economic Commission for Europe, which involved twenty countries.

In Lithuanian society, we can also see the formation of new roles for women (Juozeliuniene 1999; Juozeliuniene and Kanopiene 1996; Purvaneckas and Purvaneckiene 2001), and changes in styles of life and consumer needs and interests (Vosyliute 2001a). Some research has investigated gender segregation in the labor market, violence against women, and the existential problems of women (Kanopiene 2000; Seduikiene 1999; Vosyliute 1999).

CONCLUSION

During this decade, significant changes have occurred in sociological institutions, research methodology, and areas of interest. As the result of decentralization, several departments of sociology at universities and several public opinion centers were founded. New thematic orientations and a new elite within the sociological field emerged. The tradition of positivistic, empirical sociological research continues to exist. However, this strategy is too expensive for the state institutions to maintain, and trust in the qualitative approach is increasing. The integration of Lithuania into the EU will support the improvement of scientific standards, as well as increased participation in international projects.

During the 1990s, Lithuanian sociologists were exposed to the broad experience of world sociology. They were able to identify themselves with the entire world of the sociological community and the sociological heritages of its many different branches. Scientific help and financial support from the West provided the Lithuanian scientific community opportunities to participate in a wide range of studies, grant and scholarship programs, and conferences. However, native sociologists remain worried because of the domination of the English language in these scientific exchanges, threatening the survival and maintenance of mother tongues and of domestic culture. They are also concerned about increasing stereotyping of indigenous investigators.

The writings and the data of sociologists have a chance to influence public opinion. Their voice is an active agent in the struggle against social incivility and cultural stagnation. Their discussions and works on the processes of personal and collective identity formation are very important. In the future, the creation of an information society and the development of intellectual culture will involve more reflection about society. In these endeavors, sociologists will serve as useful experts, as social authorities and critics, and as an important form of symbolic analytic capital for the country.

10

Macedonian Sociology in the 1990s: Between the Old Conceptions and New Challenges

Petre Georgievski and Mileva Gurovska

INTRODUCTION

Macedonia, as a geographical and ethnic unit, was under Ottoman occupation until the outbreak of the Balkan Wars in 1913. With the signing of the Versailles Treaty after World War I, Macedonia was divided among Bulgaria, Serbia, and Greece. During World War II, in the part that was annexed by Serbia, called Vardar Macedonia, through their own struggle, and allied with the other Yugoslav peoples, the Macedonian people created their own legitimate nation-state. This newly created state was formally inaugurated on August 2, 1944, at the First Session of the Antifascist Council for National Liberation. The Macedonian state voluntarily became part of a federation with the other five Yugoslav states. In the early 1990s, the Socialist Federative Republic of Yugoslavia (SFRY) was dissolved. The Macedonian people, through a referendum organized on September 8, 1991, clearly expressed themselves in favor of an independent state. Today, the Republic of Macedonia is a parliamentary democracy.

The beginnings of sociology in Macedonia can be traced back to December 16, 1920, when the Faculty of Philosophy was founded in Skopje, as an affiliation of Belgrade University. Articles on sociology and social research were regularly published in the 1930s. Among the first sociological research studies was that carried out by the Polish ethnosociologist Jozef Obrebski, who stayed in the Porece region in Macedonia in 1932–33. He studied the local folk culture and traditions.

One of the first Macedonian sociologists to write on the contemporary sociology of that time was Boris Arsov. In 1936, Arsov defended his Ph.D. thesis at the Sorbonne in Paris, entitled *Economic Life in Macedonia in the 19th Century*. Arsov was the founder and editor-in-chief of the journal *Luc,* a monthly magazine about cultural, economic, and social issues, started in Skopje, in 1937. In it, he published analytical texts on certain aspects of the life of particular social groups, the customs and culture of Macedonia, as well as reviews and outlines of works by well-known sociologists from Francophone sociology. Arsov was involved in such activity until the outbreak of World War II. From the end of the war until his death in 1954, he could not work in the field of sociology because it then was considered a bourgeois science, and as such, illegitimate. At that time, sociology was replaced by historical materialism, which was studied as a separate subject at the social science faculties of the University of Skopje, which were established in 1949.

Sociology was only introduced at the faculties of the University of Skopje in 1960, as a subject taught only as a part of the general education requirements. The profession of being a sociologist was not yet institutionalized. Its institutional establishment in Macedonia occurred in 1966, with the founding of the Institute for Sociological and Political-Juridical Research at the University of Skopje. The Institute's staff consisted mainly of lawyers and philosophers interested in empirical research. The Institute offered postgraduate studies in sociology, as well as political science. The Institute's research was focused on the transformation of villages, a comparative analysis of social stratification and mobility in Macedonia and Slovenia, conflicts in the work process, the social origins of the pupils in secondary schools, religion and religious sentiments of the rural population, a comparative analysis of electoral systems in Macedonia and England, and public opinion. This research, although theoretically based, had a quantitative orientation.

From the mid-1960s until the mid-1970s, sociology in Macedonia developed with an accelerated intensity. In 1975, a Department of Sociology was established within the Faculty of Philosophy at the University of Skopje. The primary activities of this department were to educate students in the field of sociology. This department was later renamed as the present-day Institute of Sociology. The aim of this transformation was to broaden its activity and to link education with research activity. During this early period, sociologists were primarily employed as sociology teachers in secondary schools. At the time, the possibility for employment of sociologists in other jobs related to sociology was still small, in part due to the generally high unemployment (36 percent) that for many years has been a structural characteristic of the society.

The tendencies in the development of sociology up until the period of the 1990s are characterized by a significant delay in achieving a professional and academic status, compared to the status it had in other republics of the SFRY, and a strong influence of the Belgrade and Zagreb schools of sociology. As a result, Macedonian sociology was, to a significant extent, a passive segment of

Yugoslav sociology. And, in Macedonia, the textbooks and other sociological literature that were predominant came from the developed sociological centers in the SFRY, resulting in a low level of contact with sociologists in other countries.

The only active sociological communication maintained outside the SFRY was cooperation with the Institute of Sociology at Jagiellonian University, begun as early as 1978, through the initiative of professors Wladyslaw Kwasniewicz and Petre Georgievski (Nezgoda 1979). After 1990, formal cooperation with the Institute of Sociology at Jagiellonian University did not continue in the same manner as before. However, permanent connections have continued on a more individual level, and some attempts are being made to renew the Krakow-Skopje Seminar, beginning in 2002.

Macedonian sociology, shaped in the mold of the Yugoslavian sociology of the time, shared the latter's characteristics. Thus, the dilemma expressed in the commonly used phrases "between Marxism and sociology" or "somewhere between East and West" was also a feature of Macedonian sociology. This feature of sociology, which was rooted neither in the East, with its dogmatic courses of revised Marxism, nor in the West, which was always ready to criticize, emerged from the sensibility of the society itself, which did not want to be either the former or the latter.

SOCIOLOGICAL RESEARCH DURING THE TRANSITION

The radical and swift social transformation and the independence of the Republic of Macedonia from the SFRY, in 1991, quickly brought changes to sociology, first in the sociology curriculum, and afterward in the shift toward contemporary theoretical and methodological paradigms. During this period, most Macedonian sociologists made efforts to undertake study visits to developed sociology centers around the world, and to participate in international conferences.

The changes in social conditions and the adaptation of contemporary theoretical and methodological approaches could be the topic of a separate meta-sociological study. In practice, the change of the dominant paradigm under which sociologists had previously worked, and the change from the model of the so-called actually existing or real socialism toward a democratic model of society, produced an authoritarian and ethnocentric tendency, which was not adequately studied by sociologists. Although there have been some studies of Macedonian society in the transition period (Aceski 1995, 1997; Georgievski and Skarik 2000; Trajkovski 2000), there still has been no systematic study of the evident autocracy and ethnocentrism in political practice. More attention has been paid to certain issues in political sociology, such as the institutions of electoral democracy and democratic structures in Macedonia (Mircev 1991; Mircev and Mihajlovski 1995).

A complex and long-term project was carried out on the *Changes in the Social Structure in Macedonia*, with a particular focus on university education (Georgievski 2002). This research was a continuation of studies carried out before the 1990s, though broadening the topic to include issues such as poverty and values. In fact, the topic of poverty, which had not been explored at all in the period before the 1990s, became one of the more frequent themes in sociological research (Jakimovski, Tacheva, and Dimitrievska 1999). These studies are distinctive because, in addition to the use of a quantitative approach, which had previously been dominant, they also integrated a qualitative approach.

Taking into consideration the overall Balkan context during the transition period, the ethnic conflicts in Bosnia, Croatia, Serbia, and Kosovo, one need not provide any special explanation for the appearance of ethnic relations as one of the main themes in Macedonian sociology, as well as in other sciences dealing with society (psychology, law, social policy, etc.). Many of these studies were financed by foreign nongovernmental organizations (NGOs) from the United States, the Netherlands, and Germany. One of the better theoretically grounded research studies on ethnic groups was carried out by Marija Taseva (1997, 1998).

One of the topics that was intensively investigated at the very beginning of the transition was the study of the family life of Macedonian immigrants to Canada. The aim of this study was to establish their identity as well as the level of their integration into the new social environment (Petroska 1996). Topics relating to emigration have their due place in Macedonian sociology because presently there are more Macedonians living abroad than in their own native country.

Differentiation according to gender, that is, a study of change in the social status of women, became a particularly interesting issue in the transition period. The so-called feminine issue was studied during the period of socialism; however, it was seldom separated from the ideological proclamation of the formal equality between men and women. From the more recent studies that treat this issue, we would particularly like to point out studies on marital mobility that used statistical methods (Jovanovik 1997), and studies on the vertical occupational mobility of women, which used qualitative methods (Gurovska 2001).

The intelligentsia, their social existence, and their role, was another topic that came to the fore as a result of the transition. After the 1987 Krakow Seminar on the intelligentsia and their role in contemporary conditions, this topic was further elaborated (Korubin 1994, 1999). In addition, in a very short time span following the beginning of the 1990s, deep changes took place in the social structure. Even in the first years of the transition period, there was already a new stratum of rich people ("nouveaux riches") and a new elite who were at the vanguard in the creation of new values. Coupled with the widespread disintegration of families and a generally endangered existence throughout the society, this has led to an enormous rise in deviant activity, that is to say, the use of drugs and alcohol, the establishment of the drug market, prostitution, corruption, and the so-called gray economy. These manifestations are increasingly present in sociological analyses (Georgievski and Stojanovski 2000; Stojanovski 1998).

With regard to topics from economic sociology, there have been no systematic sociological studies so far. Studies made by economists are still dominant. The rise in entrepreneurship and the structural transformations in economy and in the market are topics treated in a descriptive and programmatic manner. In this context, we would like to single out studies of the diffusion of new technologies and the penetration of the multinational companies into this sector of the Macedonian sociocultural environment (Chalakov, Gurovska, and Glodeneau 2001; Gurovska 2001).

Finally, during the transition period, research on themes present in the previous period has also continued. This includes the analysis of development in urban centers in the Republic of Macedonia and topics connected to the transformation of the village (Jakimovski, Bubevski, and Matilov 1995). Topics that had often been treated in the previous period and remain the case are the family and changes it has undergone in transitional conditions (Petroska 1994), and topics connected to demographic tendencies, family planning, and ethnically mixed marriages (Jovanovik 1997).

THEORETICAL AND METHODOLOGICAL ORIENTATIONS

The widespread thematic innovation and broadening of sociological research was followed by the abandonment of the previously dominant Marxist sociological paradigm, and by a switch toward other theoretical and methodological paradigms. However, the process of transformation still continues. A bibliographical analysis shows that Marxist references are being abandoned, and references from works by well-known Western European and American authors are more frequent. Here, we would like to state one paradox. Even though the well-known sociology textbooks in Western countries accord significance to the study of Karl Marx (Smelser 1988; Haralambos and Holborne 1995), former orthodox Marxists who are now sociologists and analysts have fully rejected Marx. They do not even want to mention his name.

With regard to research, it can be concluded that the macro-level of analysis is still dominant, while the meso- and micro-levels are neglected. This orientation has resulted in the use of deductive theory, which prefers a quantitative, that is, positivist approach. Inductive theory, such as grounded theory, has received little attention. As a result, qualitative research approaches (or even a combination of quantitative and qualitative), such as the case study, the biographical method, and action research, have not been sufficiently developed in Macedonian sociology.

The switch from the Marxist theoretical paradigm toward other theoretical paradigms, such as structural functionalism, symbolic interactionism, and interpretative sociology, as well as the real need for the application of qualitative and combined methodological approaches and procedures, is called for in the textbook *Sociologija* (Petroska 1998). For the first time, in this textbook, a collective work, the teaching of the concepts of social base and social superstructure, as a theoretical foundation for understanding social structure, is not mentioned. This textbook was written following the example of well-known Western sociological textbooks (e.g., Conklin 1987; Haralambos 1989; Light and Keller 1975). Taking into consideration the topics selected, apart from the basic concepts and theories employed, the Macedonian social context and data from empirical research in Macedonia are used. In addition to this textbook, other sociology textbooks were published (Aceski 2000; Cokrevski 2000; Tonovski 2000; Trajkovski 2000). The textbook *Socioloski teorii* (Taseva 1999) addresses the development of the theoretical aspect of sociology in Macedonia.

A paradox can be observed when talking about abandoning the Marxist framework and the wider affirmation of contemporary theoretical paradigms. Namely, in the period when the Marxist paradigm was predominant, almost all classic works of Marxist scholarship were translated into Macedonian. This was not the case with other sociology classics. Even today, there is a significant lack of translated foreign literature (classical and contemporary). This has had notable impact on the development of sociology in Macedonia, which, in this respect, is behind the other sociological communities in the neighborhood, in Serbia, Croatia, and Bulgaria. In order to overcome the lack of literature, but also to contribute to a theoretical and epistemological improvement in sociology, the Institute of Sociology at the Faculty of Philosophy organized several international symposia. Particularly significant were the symposium devoted to Emile Durkheim, entitled *Durkheim and Contemporary Sociology* (in 1998), and to Max Weber, *Max Weber and the Understanding of the Contemporary World* (in 2000). However, a return to the classics of sociology did not mean a pure reproduction of their perceptions, but rather a synthesis with current tendencies in contemporary sociological theory and methodology, and an attempt to give a diagnosis of certain current social issues.

The social reality that a society in transition was facing, presented a great challenge to sociologists. In response, two international sociological symposia were held. The first was *Cultural Pluralism and Social Organization* (in 1994), where it was pointed out that although the phenomenon of culture had become topical in modern sociology, because of integrative and global processes, an ethnic particularism, which results in fragmentation and separation, lies behind this phenomenon in the societies of the Balkans (Mladenovski 1995). The second symposium, entitled *Transition and Reconstruction of Societies*, was held immediately after the NATO military intervention in the region (1999) and was organized in cooperation with the International Association of Francophone Sociologists. Among other contributions, this symposium emphasized the ever-present tendency in sociology toward an active role for sociologists in the construction of societies (Bardech 2001).

ACADEMIC AND PROFESSIONAL STATUS IN SOCIOLOGY

In the initial period of social transition, in order to adhere more closely to the standards of the European countries, the need to change the sociology curriculum at the levels of graduate and postgraduate studies was recognized. In fact, the sociology textbooks mentioned above were a result of the already modified curriculum, which has been amended twice, first in 1992, and again in 1996. These changes were made based on a comparative analysis of curricula in several countries, as well as on the Macedonian experience and the existing human resources. Comparisons were made with the curricula from the Institute of Sociology of Zagreb University, Jagiellonian University, Belgrade University, the University of Arizona, and Evry University (France).

Changes of curricula mainly related to an increase in methodology courses, and their separation into two parts, Sociological Methodology I, oriented toward a quantitative approach, and Sociological Methodology II, oriented toward the qualitative approach. Furthermore, the curriculum was broadened with new sociological subdisciplines in addition to those that had already existed in the previous period, that is, rural sociology, urban sociology, social anthropology, sociology of religion, sociology of education, political sociology, sociology of family, and sociology of labor. Several new areas were introduced, including sociology of culture, sociology of business, social ecology, and sociology of communications. Hence, the result was a more comprehensive knowledge in particular areas of sociology, allowing for a broader range of themes to be elaborated. In the context of the development of subdisciplines, several textbooks were published, for example, on sociology of law (Cokrevski 1994), on rural sociology (Kartalov 1996), on the sociology of education (Georgievski 1996), and a collection of translated texts in the form of anthologies on the sociology of the city (Aceski 1995) and anthropology (Mladenovski 2000).

Despite the modifications carried out, the postgraduate sociology curriculum still has not been standardized. The current project, under the umbrella of the European Union's Trans-European Mobility Scheme for University Students (TEMPUS) Program, is aimed at the development of these curricular standards. It includes the departments of sociology in Belgrade, Novi Sad, Nis, and in other universities from European countries. Also underway is a research project in cooperation with the Institute of Sociology at the Sofia Faculty of Philosophy (Bulgaria) under the umbrella of the Soros Foundation. This project, with a broad range of activities, is aimed at an evaluation and standardization of the graduate sociology curriculum.

Redefining the secondary-school curriculum also has resulted in certain changes in the teaching of sociology at this level. A team of sociologists was formed to create basic materials that would facilitate the socialization of the youth population for coexistence in a civil society. In vocational secondary schools, excluding high schools and economic secondary schools, sociology, which had been taught for more than thirty years, was replaced by Education on Civil Society. In 1998, a textbook on civil education, edited by Dimitar Mircev, was published.

Although ten years have passed since the beginning of the transition period in Macedonia, there are still no private educational and research institutions in the country. This is mainly a result of the delayed passing of the Law on Higher Education, which was only passed in 2000. The first private university in Macedonia will be the Southeastern European University, also to be know as van der Stoel University, located in Tetovo. This university involves four types of study, Law, Public and Business Administration, Communications, and Education. There is no information on what place the teaching of sociology will have there.

With regard to providing services in the field of sociology, the Institute for Sociological and Political-Juridical Research and the Institute of Sociology at the Faculty of Philosophy are still active. Both institutions act within the framework of Cyril and Methodius University. Their relation in the market is one of two rival institutions, primarily in the area of research. However, one should note the difference between the Institute for Sociological and Political-Juridical Research, which is primarily a research institute with only postgraduate studies as education-related activity, and the Institute of Sociology at the Faculty of Philosophy, which is primarily an educational institution that provides education on all levels and already has been active in the market for sociological research.

The market for activities in the field of sociology still does not determine the quality of services offered or provided. Most of this research is quick, instant survey research, lacking consistent theoretical and methodological foundations. The primary problem here is the fact that state bodies are the main clients ordering such survey research. And, typically, research contracts are awarded more on the basis of membership or affiliation with the ruling political party or other personal connections, rather than on the merits of the projects themselves or their research designs.

The successful completion of the transformation of Macedonian sociology, as a science, a profession, and a teaching activity, will depend on the level of reforms in the economic and political system, that is, to what extent they provide a realistic material and democratic framework for its faster development. Some flaws in the development of Macedonian sociology could be repaired by more thorough and systematic attention to the theoretical and methodological foundations of sociological research. This could be done, for example, by the use of complementary methodological approaches and a strategy of triangulation encompassing all three levels of sociological theory, micro-level theory, meso-level theory and macro-level theory. In addition, an ongoing assessment (internal and external) and standardization of all levels of study are necessary. This would enable further realization of the standards of the developed sociology centers throughout the world, and greater communication with them.

11

Polish Sociology, 1990–2000: Society after a Breakthrough, Sociology in Evolution

Janusz L. Mucha

By the end of the 1920s, Polish sociology was already a well-organized academic discipline. Since then, it has continued to function and develop as a fully institutionalized discipline, albeit with one break during World War II, and another during the Stalinist period of 1948–56. During the socialist period, everything, including sociology, was subordinated to the political authorities. Many sociologists (though the proportion was smaller than in other social sciences) belonged to the Communist Party.[1] After 1980, effective Party control over sociology decreased.

During the socialist period, overrepresentation of Marxism was institutionally enforced. Political and ideological control over sociology was particularly severe outside the main academic centers. Widespread censorship was very harmful for sociological research and publications. One of its most significant important consequences was the removal of some topics from sociological discourse, for example, the political organization of society. Piotr Lukasiewicz coined this phenomenon "limited sociology" (1991, 48–49). However, beginning in 1976, in order to get around the censorship, there emerged a "second circulation" of underground publications in Poland.

The political control over sociology began to disappear as a part of the great transformation of Polish society that began in 1989. The rudiments of a market economy emerged. The country opened both economically and politically to foreign goods, services, and investments, as well as to foreign ideas and institutions.

Small private enterprises mushroomed and commerce bloomed. While many sectors of the socialist economy collapsed and unemployment grew very fast, many new occupations also emerged. Political parties were legalized, procedural democracy was introduced, and free national and local elections were organized. Gradually, Poles were able to travel without visas to all European countries. Many Western magazines began to print Polish-language editions, more and more Western books were translated, and Western TV channels became easily available. Ethnic and sexual minorities became active. In other words, with the transformation, a new and free civil society emerged as both the precondition of a free sociology, and the subject matter of its research.

THE DECOMMUNIZATION OF POLISH SOCIOLOGY

In the new social and political situation, those who had earlier represented and supported the ancient regime (including Marxist social scientists) were labeled as post-Communists. Their right to participation in the public life of the so-called new Poland came under question. However, the historical and political criteria that were used by the newly liberated sociological community in accepting or not accepting sociologists who were active participants of the Polish public life of the pre-1989 period are not very clear. Many sociologists who were active in the Communist Party until its dissolution in 1990, and who were teachers of a more or less apologetic Marxism, continue to be very active in the discipline's public life. There has been no strong resistance to this development among scholars who were connected with the pre-1989 democratic opposition.

However, this lack of a deep decommunization of sociology has caused some concern among scholars who consider it to be an indication of a more general lack of coming to terms with the socialist past. A discussion of this problem was published in the influential right-wing daily Zycie. Zdzislaw Krasnodebski, a Polish sociology professor in Germany, observed that there was no debate on the relationship that had existed between the social sciences and Communism in Poland, "Its lack resulted in the fact that the academic community has not taken any steps—intellectual or institutional—against even the most corrupted persons. Nobody was fired, nobody was criticized in public" (1998: 11). In several of the following issues of Zycie, the views of a small number of scholars of various pre-1989 biographies (Ireneusz Krzeminski, Leszek Nowak, Jerzy Szacki, Antoni Dudek) were published. They stressed that, in 1998, it was too late to start any decommunization of sociology, that Polish scholarly mediocrities had not been of only a Marxist character, and that many current sociological mediocrities also represented a clearly anti-Marxist outlook and could be found in the right-wing and pro-Church intellectual circles. In addition, they underlined the fact that ideological "conversions" were a natural consequence of deep social transformations and were not necessarily only the result of opportunism. Discussion has not continued. Most likely, a full decommunization will come only with the generational transition that is inevitable due to the simple fact of human mortality.

TRANSFORMATION OF SOCIETY AND THE EVOLUTION OF SOCIOLOGY

Perhaps most importantly, systemic transformation has meant, among other things, the end of censorship of sociological research projects and publications. Other changes, of a much less political character, followed. A new structure of research financing was introduced. As a result, the main source of funds is the State Committee on Scientific Research (KBN). Unfortunately, state funds are extremely limited and, as of yet, no indigenous private funding for research has emerged to supplement that of the state. The KBN distributes its funding through blind reviewed competitions for research, publications, and conference grants. Foreign foundations, like the Research Support Scheme of the Central European University (funded by the Soros Foundation) and the Friedrich Ebert Foundation, provide research and publication grants in the field of sociology as well.

Along with the broader society, academic life has also been democratized. Now, officers of the universities, as well as of the research institutes of the Polish Academy of Sciences (PAN), are democratically elected. Since the mid-1990s, competitive searches have been organized for the position of editor-in-chief of *Studia Socjologiczne* and of *The Polish Sociological Review*. However, to date no Polish journal has succeeded in entering the "Philadelphia list" of the most respected journals, nor in being listed in *Current Contents*, the weekly bulletin of the Philadelphia Institute for Scientific Information.

After 1989, rapid growth occurred in the number of sociological books on the market. Many new publishing houses specializing in the social sciences emerged, for instance Nomos in Kraków, ZYSK in Poznan, and Oficyna Naukowa and Scholar in Warsaw. The dominant position on the market is held by IFiS PAN (Instytut Filozofii i Socjologii Polskiej Akademii Nauk) Publishers, which belongs to the largest sociological institution in Poland, the Institute of Philosophy and Sociology of the Polish Academy of Sciences.

Several other new and important publishing initiatives also appeared after 1989. The most significant was the *Encyklopedia Socjologii* (Encyclopedia of Sociology). Initial work was begun in 1991, by a team led by Wladyslaw Kwasniewicz. The first of four volumes came out in 1998, the most recent, and third, in 2000. The Committee on Sociology initiated other research and publishing enterprises as well, addressing issues such as European integration (Mucha 1999b) and the morality of Polish society (still in progress).

In an unanticipated development, a new sociological authority has become widely visible and popular in the media. With the new openness, and resulting interest in social life, in local and national elections and politics, and in the economic market, the media has turned to sociology for expertise. In the Warsaw media, sociologists comment on nearly all events. One might even speak of the pathology of this sociological authority as respected professors appear in five-second spots to quickly present a table, a figure, or their opinions on the most current events, all too often without any basis in actual research findings. The very term "sociology" has become well known to the general public, and is generally identified with survey and market research. Sociologists have also become recognized as experts in the field of social problems such as unemployment, poverty, and crime. As a result, demand for their services is quite strong, leading to an explosion of university programs in the sociology of social problems.

After the breakdown of socialism in Poland, the number of university students increased rapidly. Sociology has emerged as one of the most popular disciplines. There are a large number of candidates in the M.A. programs in sociology at the established public universities, where studying is free of charge. Master's programs in sociology have also been developed at the newer academic centers created since the transformation. Thirteen public institutions of higher education (including all the universities but the two youngest) have these programs. A master's degree in sociology is also offered at the nonpublic (tuition must be paid) Collegium Civitas in Warsaw. A bachelor's degree in sociology is also available in many nonpublic schools, including the College of Social Sciences and Economy in Tyczyn, the College of Business and Entrepreneurship in Ostrow Swietokrzyski, the College of Management and Social Sciences in Tychy, and the Warsaw School for Social Psychology.

Altogether, at the B.A. and M.A. levels, there are approximately eleven thousand students majoring in sociology. However, as is the case with other attractive university disciplines, there are not enough senior professors in Poland to educate all of these students in accordance with the state's quality of education requirements. Many faculty members have several academic jobs. Young scholars' promotions are often delayed because they do not have the time to do the research that would allow them to obtain their habilitation degree. Furthermore, with the growing unemployment of people with higher education, it is not clear where the graduates of sociology will work in the future (Kwasniewicz 1998).

In addition, there are problems with Polish textbooks. Private schools publish their own texts, but they are of a relatively low quality and the circulation is small. There are no good, widely accepted Polish textbooks in general sociology. To date, the most important texts have been translations of undergraduate texts published in America, Britain, and France (Bauman 1996b; Giddens 1998; Goodman 1997; Mendras 1997; Turner 1998). In addition, a translation of Jonathan H. Turner's *The Structure of Sociological Theory* was made available in 1985, Peter Berger's *Invitation to Sociology* in 1988.

Several new areas of specialization have emerged within the general major in sociology. The most important are social policy and social work. B.A. and M.A.

degree programs in these areas are offered by public and private schools. However, these programs must be paid for by students, and they are usually extramural, that is, the students come to the university only twice a month for a weekend and they are expected to study at home. A unique, but important development, has been the establishment of a two-year postgraduate interdisciplinary program in Gender Studies, offered by the Institute of Applied Social Sciences of Warsaw University.

Doctoral studies in sociology are a relatively new phenomenon. They existed in some Polish universities before 1989, but have grown only recently. In addition to the major universities, they have emerged in two private schools. Doctoral studies in sociology at the Central European University (Warsaw Branch) started in 1997. In the academic year 2000–2001, there were 26 postgraduate students coming from eleven countries, mostly from Central and Eastern Europe, but also from Mongolia and Kirgistan in post-Communist Asia. The Graduate School for Social Research at the Institute of Philosophy and Sociology of the PAN was founded in 1992. In the academic year 2000–2001, 162 persons from seventeen countries studied philosophy and sociology at the doctoral level.

Even without the requisite infrastructure, new teachers, adequate textbooks, new lecture halls, Polish scholars have tried very hard to maintain or even increase the quality of education in this new situation of dynamic development in higher education. A semiformal process of accreditation of individual academic disciplines was started in 1998, and was carried out by the University Accreditation Commission, which is independent of the Ministry of Education. Sociology programs at Adam Mickiewicz University in Poznan, the University of Lodz, Warsaw University (its Institute of Sociology), Jagiellonian University in Kraków, Nicholas Copernicus University in Torun, Silesian University in Katowice, the Catholic University of Lublin, and the University of Wroclaw were all granted accreditation in 2000. The process of accreditation was preceded and prepared for through the work of the Conference of the Institutes of Sociology (KIS), an informal body that has been analyzing and coordinating syllabi and teaching standards since the mid-1990s.

SOCIOLOGICAL RESEARCH AFTER THE REVOLUTION

Until 1989, there were three survey centers in Poland, all controlled by the state's Communist authorities, the Social Opinion Research Center (CBOS), the Public Opinion Research Center (OBOP), and the Media Research Center (OBP). None is a state agency any longer. CBOS became a foundation. Forty percent of OBOP belongs to public television, while the rest is in foreign hands. And, OBP has become a research department of Jagiellonian University. These centers regularly publish bulletins that are available in major research libraries. In addition, since 1989, several new private public opinion and market research centers have also emerged. They were founded by academic sociologists and by sociologists who used to work for the state-owned centers.

Today, the most important public opinion research centers (in order of market share) are OBOP, the Sopot Social Research Center (PBS), which was founded in 1990 and is fully in Polish hands, and CBOS. The latter is the largest research center and many of its surveys are directly financed by the government. The most important market research centers (again in order of market share) are SMG-KRC Poland Media S.A. (founded in 1990, 52 percent of the capital in Polish hands), Pentor (founded in 1991, 40 percent in Polish hands), OBOP, and CASE (founded in 1993, fully in Polish hands) (Warsaw Business Journal 2000). The findings of these commercial firms are often used by academic sociologists, particularly by specialists in the fields of economics and advertising.

Because some professors of sociology are members of supervisory boards and some are part-time employees, research methods new to Poland, such as the focus group, sometimes enter the academic education process via these commercial research centers. In the early 1990s, survey specialists founded a Research Committee on Public Opinion at the Polish Sociological Association, but it soon disappeared and two separate bodies were organized in it place, the Polish Association of Public Opinion and Market Research (PTBRO), in 1994, and the Organization of Public Opinion and Market Research Companies (OFBOR), in 1997.

An analysis of Polish sociological research production during the last decade, particularly in comparison with former decades, gives the impression of a retreat from theory as such, as well as an interest in the general methodology of the social sciences. Before 1989, there were many books on theory. Since then, only a comparatively few theory books have been published. These include books on the sociology of Pierre Bourdieu (Jacyno 1997), on interpretative sociology (Piotrowski 1998), on the concept of the definition of the situation (Manterys 2000), on new trends in exchange theory (Sozanski, Szmatka, and Kempny 1993), on new trends in the sociology of knowledge (Zybertowicz 1995), and on the role of theorizing in sociology (Misztal 2000). Moreover, many empirical studies were inspired by theory. Here, I am particularly referring to "grounded theory," and, more generally, interpretative sociology in its applications as a background for qualitative social research (Konecki 2000; Wyka 1993). Several studies have been based on the biographical method (Czyzewski, Piotrowski, and Rokuszewska-Pawelek 1996; *Kultura i Spoleczenstwo* 1995), rational choice theory (*Studia Socjologiczne* 1998, 2000), theories of social change as a background for the analysis of systemic transformation (Rychard 1993; Wnuk-Lipinski 1996), and postmodernism in the analysis of cultural change (Kempny, Kapciak, and Lodzinski 1997). Zygmunt Bauman, very influential in Poland as elsewhere, has also had several of his books translated into Polish (1991, 1995, 1996a, 1996b). As is evident from the listing above, since the early 1980s, Marxism has ceased to be an important theoretical issue for sociologists educated in the major academic centers. No single ideological framework for sociological analysis has replaced it.

The methodological interests of many Polish sociologists has turned from a more general and philosophical interest in the methodology of the social sciences to a much more specific focus on the development and application of specific research techniques, both qualitative and quantitative, but especially survey research. This has been accompanied by an increasing interest in the ethical aspects of research methods (Konecki 2000; Wyka 1993). Several books on various methods were published and widely discussed within the sociological community (Domanski, Lutynska, and Rostocki 1999; Konecki 2000; Lutynska 1993; Sulek 1990). Special issues of *Kultura i Spoleczenstwo* were also published (1993, 1999). In 2000, a textbook for the Statistical Package for the Social Sciences was published (Gorniak and Wachnicki 2000). And, *Ask*, a periodical devoted purely to methodology of social sciences, has been in publication since 1995.

The most detailed "raw" sociological information on Polish society is available through the Polish General Social Survey (the PGSS), which is modeled on the American General Social Survey (GSS). Since 1992, this project has been a permanent research program of the Institute of Social Studies of Warsaw University, and is funded by the KBN. The PGSS covers individual attitudes and value systems, and social orientations and behavior, as well as the demographic, economic, occupational, and educational differentiations within Polish society. The survey used to be conducted on a yearly basis, but since 1997, it has been done every other year. It maintains the same methodological standards and identical coefficients from year to year, making systematic analysis of social trends possible.

An important aim of the PGSS has been the noncommercial dissemination of data and methodological documentation to the entire community of social scientists throughout Poland, as well as to other interested persons and institutions. Data from 1992 to 1997 are also available on the Internet (www.iss.uw.edu.pl). Another aim of the program has been to provide social scientists in Poland with data and coefficients directly comparable with findings from other countries. Since 1992, the PGSS has included sets of questions from the International Social Survey Program (ISSP), which is conducted in twenty-nine countries.

Since 1989, sociologists have studied the socioeconomic transformation of Poland. Several components of this broad research area are important. The first important research area has been the analysis of changes in the economy in the domestic and international realms, using an application of neo-institutionalist theory (Jakobik 1997; Morawski 1998; Rychard 1993). A second important research area has been the analysis of the privatization of state-owned enterprises (Jarosz 1993), and later the analysis of relations between new foreign owners and Polish workers (Jarosz 1997). The attitudes and new social roles of individual workers, of trade union members, and of employee self-governance activists were also studied during this period (Gaciarz and Pankow 1997).

Privatization of the Polish economy has meant not only the selling of already existing state-owned companies to private investors (both Polish and foreign), but also the emergence of new, mostly small, private firms (Reszke 1998). A third important sociological issue connected to the economy is industrial relations in the new context of a free market and democracy, in still existing state-owned enterprises, in companies sold to foreign investors, and in small private firms. The new role of trade unions in all types of enterprises has also been studied (Gieorgica 1998; Kozek and Kulpinska 1998). A fourth important research problem in the socioeconomic area has been the emergence of new styles of consumption (Sikorska 1998).

The systemic transformation of Polish society has brought not only generally positive but also obviously negative social consequences, such as poverty, joblessness, organized crime, and corruption. Scholars from Silesian University in Katowice have studied the psychological aspects of poverty as well as the poverty in the "old industrial areas" (Wodz 1993). Scholars from the University of Lodz have concentrated on poverty in the larger cities. A new type of poverty has been distinguished from previously existing forms, and the poverty of Poland's larger cities has been examined within the context of a comparative analysis of poverty in larger Western European cities. Relations between poverty and gender, and between poverty and unemployment have also been studied (Warzywoda-Kruszynska and Grotowska-Leder 1998). The Institute of Philosophy and Sociology of the PAN focused on the historical and cultural aspects of poverty (the so-called culture of poverty), particularly in the rural settlements of the former state-owned farms that were liquidated in the early 1990s. This research was conducted on the basis of biographical interviews and oral histories of families (*Kultura i Spoleczenstwo* 1998; Tarkowska 2000).

Joblessness came to Poland in the early 1990s. By the end of the decade unemployment had risen to 16 percent of the labor force. In 1993, a tentative summary of first findings on unemployment research was published (Borowicz and Lapinska-Tyszka 1993). In another study in the early 1990s, joblessness was examined as not only an economic and structural issue, but also as a moral phenomenon (Marianski 1994).

There have also been several interesting sociological works on new, post-1989 forms of criminal activity, including organized crime, drug crime, and Internet crime. The problem of corruption has also been studied, since according to international agencies such as Transparency International, corruption is very widespread in Poland (Siemaszko 2000).

Sociologists were particularly interested in the dynamics of class structure in the 1990s. The relative social position of the working class deteriorated, and a new class of the unemployed, and a new business class emerged. Since the beginning of the transformation, many scholars and politicians have agreed that a democratic market society requires a large and strong middle class. The question arose as to whether this functional requirement had already been met by

Polish society, and of what the character of this middle class is or should be. Henryk Domanski (1994) put Poland in an international context and analyzed the role of the "old" and "new" middle class as compared to stable Western democratic market societies. He also discussed the question of which groups could be called middle class in the Poland of the 1990s, and to what extent these groups were crystallized. An edited collection by Jacek Kurczewski and Iwona Jakubowska-Branicka (1994) was devoted to the old (coming from the socialist times) and new (post-1989) private entrepreneurs. The central issue of this book was whether a new ethos of this business class has emerged, and what their everyday life patterns, career ideals, and attitudes might be. *Kultura i Spoleczenstwo* (1994) published a special issue devoted to the same problems. (see also Bryant and Mokrzycki 1995).

At the end of the decade, a special issue of *The Polish Sociological Review* (2000) on the death of classes in Poland came out. It contained an international discussion of Domanski's article on the existence of classes in Poland. In the context of class analysis, a research project on social structure and personality under conditions of systemic change should also be mentioned (Slomczynski et al. 1996, 1999).

Since 1989, intensive studies have been conducted on the world of Polish politics and its various aspects. These projects were carried out during the last decade by teams of scholars of various political backgrounds and allegiances, and belonging to different generations. In the early 1990s, a study linking the legitimization problems of the previous and the new political leadership was carried out (Ziolkowski, Pawlowska, and Drozdowski 1994).

Political parties have been an important subject matter for sociologists. Parties in the Western democratic sense are a completely new phenomenon in Poland (Grabowska and Szawiel 1998; Kubiak 1997; Kubiak and Wiatr 2000). The first systematic sociological studies of economic and political elites were conducted in Poland at the end of the previous decade, and, during the 1990s, they became very popular. Some research projects were of an international character (Szelenyi, Treiman, and Wnuk-Lipinski 1995). Most of the Polish studies on political elites concentrated on members of parliament (Frentzel-Zagorska and Wasilewski 2000; Wasilewski and Wesolowski 1992). Election research has been another area of political sociology in which Polish scholars were very active from the first days of the transformation (Grabowska and Krzeminski 1991; Kolarska-Bobinska, Lukasiewicz, and Rykowski 1990; Markowski 1999; Raciborski 1991, 1997).

A related area of study has been research on the public sphere outside of the purely political. A large project was devoted to the functioning of the legal system in Poland during the whole decade of the decomposition of the socialist system and the building of civil society (Kojder et al. 1989–93; Turska et al. 1999). Since the spring of 1989, a civil society has been developing in Poland. At that time, the main actors in the public arena were the regional Citizens' Committees, a wide anti-Communist social grassroots movement (Borkowski and

Bukowski 1993). Local participation in public life, in the form of rural and urban councils, was studied by Barbara Lewenstein (1999). The ecological movements were also a subject matter of sociological investigations (Glinski 1996).

Gender research has emerged as a new phenomenon in Poland. There are two empirical research centers in Warsaw dealing with gender. The first has studied social inequalities between men and women within the socioeconomic realm, particularly in the job market (Domanski 1992; Titkow and Domanski 1995). In the second center, Renata Siemienska has been interested in the political aspects of gender relations (1997, 2000).

From the very beginning of the great transformation, Polish sociologists have studied the role of culture in postsocialist economies and societal change (Jawlowska, Kempny, and Tarkowska 1993; Sztompka 1999). Public discourse issues such as new ideological debates, new kinds of mental and political correctness, and new types of cultural exclusions were particularly important targets of analysis (Czyzewski, Dunin, and Piotrowski 1991; Czyzewski, Kowalski, and Piotrowski 1997; Lewenstein and Pawlik 1994).

Religiosity is another important subject of investigation in Poland. Since 1989, the institutional role of the Roman Catholic Church has strengthened, but at the same time many completely new religious phenomena have emerged. These have been connected with the new openness toward the West and the Far East, as well as with an increasing sense of insecurity and fear. Many articles on these topics have been published in periodicals like *Nomos*, *Przeglad Religioznawczy*, and *Wiez*, but only a small number of books have appeared so far (Borowik 1997; Borowik and Zdaniewicz 1996). Sociologists have also studied the New Age movement and its sects. Important summaries of their findings are presented in a dictionary of new religious and para-religious movements prepared by Tadeusz Doktor (1999), and in a collection edited by Marian Kempny and Grazyna Woroniecka (1999).

Since the end of the 1980s, Polish scholars have systematically analyzed the country's ethnic composition. The democratization of the 1990s meant a great revival of the already stable and institutionalized ethnic minorities that altogether constitute about 5 percent of the total population of Poland (Babinski 1997; Sadowski 1995). There is also a large, but new ethnic minority in Poland, the Germans. It is new in the sense that until 1989, the Communist authorities had denied the very fact of its existence, so it was impossible to do any research on it. Under the new political conditions, several academic centers have studied this group (Kurcz 1995). Polish border areas were also investigated (Goldyka 1999).

The Jewish minority, which constituted about 9 percent of the population of prewar Poland, has also been studied. Due to the Holocaust, and subsequent waves of emigration after the war, partly voluntary and partly forced, only a few thousand Jews still live in Poland. The attitude of other Poles toward this group is also a new research topic (Krzeminski 1996). At the end of the 1990s, a number of books discussing all the ethnic minorities that live in Poland became available (Chalupczak and Browarek 1998; Szczepanski 1997). Also, several special issues of *Kultura i Spoleczenstwo* were devoted to this subject.

Research projects in the field of ethnicity have been theoretically conceptualized in various ways. In the 1990s, most of them were conceptualized in terms of the strengthening of ethnic identity under new social and political conditions. These projects were a continuation of the programs initiated at the end of the previous decade by Malgorzata Melchior (1990) and by Ewa Nowicka (1990). During the 1990s, another approach emerged, a research program on cultural relations as seen from the vantage point of the minority groups themselves (Mucha 1999a). After 1989, Poland became a country of destination for many immigrants, and this new process also became a topic of social analysis (Grzymala-Moszczynska and Nowicka 1998).

As an early culmination of the transformation of Polish society, it is likely that by the year 2005, Poland will join the European Union. This will constitute a serious economic, political, structural, and cultural challenge. In anticipation of this development, one of the most researched topics has been the attitude of Poles toward entry into the European Union (Skotnicka-Illasiewicz 1997). The problem, however, is not only what the Poles think about Europe, but also whether or not Polish society is "objectively" prepared for access to the Union (Hausner et al. 1998; Mucha 1999b; see also Domanski and Rychard 1997; Domanski, Ostrowska, and Rychard 2000).

Still another important body of research deserves separate remarks. It is a part of a research project that has continued for about twenty years under the title "The Poles." Various teams led by Wladyslaw Adamski studied living conditions and activities in Polish society during that period of time (Adamski 1998; Adamski et al. 1999).

The history of sociology also has been an important research topic during the last decade. In 1995, a large team of scholars led by Jerzy Szacki published an anthology of the works of fifty-seven Polish sociologists who had been active during the previous one hundred years (1995). The following year, Nina Krasko (1996) published a book on the institutionalization of sociology in Poland between the 1920s and the 1970s. During the whole decade, Wlodzimierz Winclawski worked on the biobibliographic dictionary of Polish sociology and presented his findings at various conferences. Winclawski built the Archive of Polish Sociology in Torun, which is a joint venture of the Polish Sociological Association and Nicholas Copernicus University.

Between 1990 and 2000, four congresses of Polish sociology were held. The first of them, the Eighth Congress, was organized in September 1990, one year after the beginnings of the thorough and radical economic reforms that brought significant structural transformations to Polish society. The theme of the Congress was "Breakthrough and Challenge: Theories of Social Change and the Experience of Contemporary Times." The Ninth Congress, on "People and Institutions: Emergence of Social Order," was held in 1994. In 1997, the Tenth

Congress, on "Silesia-Poland-Europe: Changing Society in the Local and Global Perspective" was organized. The Eleventh Congress was held in 2000, and its topic was "Fate and Choice: Legacy and Perspectives of Polish Society."

THE PRESENCE OF POLISH SOCIOLOGY IN THE INTERNATIONAL ARENA

The international presence of Polish sociology has been far below its potential and merits. This observation can be supported by an analysis of several major Western (international and national) sociological periodicals during the 1990s.[2] In the *British Journal of Sociology,* only one article by a Polish sociologist was published (Kolarska-Bobinska 1994).[3] In the *American Sociological Review,* one article with four Polish coauthors was published (Kohn et al. 1997). In the *American Journal of Sociology,* one article with one Polish coauthor was published (Kohn et al. 1990). And, in *Zeitschrift fuer Soziologie,* one article by a Polish author was published (Sztompka 1993).

The situation was somewhat different with international periodicals. *European Sociological Review* published two articles by Polish authors (Mach, Mayer, and Pohoski 1994; Sawinski and Domanski 1991a). *International Sociology* published seven (Buchner-Jeziorska and Evetts 1997; Kloskowska 1992; Pommersbach and Wozniak 1991; Sawinski and Domanski 1991b; Sztompka 1990, 1996b; Zielinski 1994). And, while there were no articles published by Polish sociologists in *European Societies,* the journal emerged only in 1999.

In addition, few Poles served as members of the ruling bodies of the International Sociological Association (ISA) and of the European Sociological Association (ESA). During the World Congress of Sociology in 1994, Piotr Sztompka became the first Polish member of the ISA's Executive Committee in many years. Since the Congress in 1998, he has served as the ISA's vice president.

The ESA began to take shape at the beginning of the 1990s. During the First European Conference of Sociology held in Vienna, Austria, in 1993, a Steering Committee of the ESA was organized by a group of volunteers, which included Wladyslaw Kwasniewicz from Poland. The first formal elections were held at the Second Conference in Budapest, Hungary, in 1995. Janusz L. Mucha was elected to the Executive Committee. At the Fourth Conference in Amsterdam, the Netherlands, in 1999, Elzbieta Halas became an Executive Committee member. At the Vienna conference, Wlodzimierz Wesolowski gave a plenary lecture, and at the Budapest conference Piotr Sztompka delivered a plenary lecture and Jolanta Kulpinska gave a semiplenary lecture.

The education of foreigners in the field of sociology can be also considered as evidence of an international presence. The Graduate School for Social Research at the Polish Academy of Sciences and the Central European University (CEU) are the major actors on the international education scene in Poland. Since the academic year 1993–94, the CEU's Department of Sociology (located in Warsaw) has granted M.A. degrees in cooperation with the University of Lancaster, England. In 2000–2001, there were forty-five students in the M.A. program, among them seventeen from Poland, six from Russia, six from Romania, five from Bulgaria, and five from Lithuania. In addition, there were students from Canada, the United States, and post-Soviet Uzbekistan, Kazakhstan, Armenia, and Albania. The Graduate School for Social Research has only a Ph.D. program. Both schools use English as the language of instruction, and both intend to continue the old tradition of attracting young people from Central and Eastern European countries to study sociology in Poland.

There is no centralized official cooperation between sociologists from Central and Eastern Europe. However, the Polish Sociological Association invites colleagues from other countries of the region to its congresses, and sociologists from the region participate in joint research projects and in joint publications.

CONCLUSIONS

The liberal, democratic political system of the 1990s allowed Polish sociology to study everything and anything that was important in transforming Poland. Sociology has provided Poles with significant information and interpretation of a society in the process of radical change. And, while the discipline has continued to operate largely within the old institutional frameworks, these frameworks have evolved systematically. Only those research centers that were extremely closely connected with the former political system were dissolved. Nonetheless, within this institutional continuity, many important changes, resulting from the transformations in society, have occurred in Polish sociology.

Since society changed quite dramatically, sociology had to keep up. The implementation of democratic and liberal political rules provided a crucial foundation for a newly established freedom of research in the social sciences. During the 1990s, there were no political limitations on the intellectual activities of Polish sociologists. There was no visible attempt, or even real possibility, to impose a single research paradigm on sociologists, as had been the case earlier with Marxism.

Significant economic limitations on sociological research, which also existed prior to the transformation, continued. And, they can become more pressing when foreign foundations reduce or withdraw support for research and publications. Foreign financing can also cause problems, particularly if the intellectual interests of non-Polish sponsors deviate from those of the Polish scholars whom they fund. Finally, due to the political and economic transformations, a nonacademic professionalization of sociology took place. New sociological occupations emerged.

In comparison with the last two decades of the socialist system in Poland, not only have some new research areas of sociological research emerged, but also some previously important areas have ceased to be of interest to sociologists.

There used to be much more research on youth and on the rural population. Both of these collectivities are very important for the future of Polish society, and for its chances to successfully participate in a unified Europe. More studies would seem to be necessary. In the late 1980s, the sociology of social movements was very active in Poland. Initially, this was largely the sociology of anti-Communist opposition. In the 1990s, once the anti-Communist movements completed their tasks, sociologists ceased to be interested in this field, even though the number of social movements has been growing. Some problems, crucial in the last decades of the twentieth century and the beginning of the twenty-first century, and hotly debated by Western sociology, such as globalization, are relatively rarely discussed by Polish scholars.

At the end of 2001, one can be quite optimistic about the future of Polish sociology. This is a restrained optimism however. The advantages of the openness of liberal society are counterbalanced with the disadvantages of its economic problems. If the salaries of university-based scholars continue to be very low, they will have to continue to work more than one job and have less and less time for reading, thinking, and doing original research, the lifeblood of the academy. As a result, their teaching will be of a lower quality. If the fraction of the state budget devoted to scholarly activities remains as small as it is now, there will be no research funds, no money for books and periodicals, or for participation in international conferences.

These problems are not specific to sociology, but apply to all academic disciplines in Poland, and no doubt throughout Central and Eastern Europe. After more than ten years of the new, democratic political system, it seems that the solution to this problem does not depend on the particular political orientation of the series of governments that have been in power. It seems that, currently, Polish society in general does not see any reason to invest more in research and teaching at the university level. Given the increasing importance of knowledge and information in the global economy, this is a potentially self-defeating strategy. The future of Polish society, and its sociology, will depend in large part on whether or not this sensibility changes and greater resources are provided for research and education.

NOTES

Many Polish scholars read this text in various stages. I am very grateful particularly to Anoni Sulek, Andrzej Kojder, Wladyslaw Kwasniewicz, and Henryk Domanski.

1. Until the mid-1980s, I considered myself to be a Marxist. Until the declaration of martial law in Poland on December 13, 1981, I was a member of the Polish United Workers' Party.

2. Books have not been taken into account in this analysis due to the difficulty of collecting systematic information about them. It should be borne in mind, though, that

scholars such as Piotr Sztompka and Jadwiga Staniszkis have published influential books in respected Western presses that refer to Polish society.

3. In this text, the term "Polish sociologist" means a scholar who worked at least half-time in Poland during the last decade and who in his or her publications presented himself or herself as a person institutionally connected with Poland.

12

Sociology in Romania since 1989

Ilie Badescu and Radu Baltasiu

The decommunization of sociology in Romania began as early as 1966, at the same time as its rebirth in the sphere of higher education. Lectures based on Western bibliographies were introduced into the curricula. Marxist theory was implicitly amended through the inclusion of Weberian theory of organization and authority. Similarly, Emile Durkheim's theories of social control were widely presented. Furthermore, in the field of sociology of education, the ideas of Pierre Bourdieu and Jean Claude Passeron and their disciples in France were extensively taken into account, theories on reproduction and symbolic violence. In the sociology of work, the same was happening with the theories of Georges Friedman and with those pertaining to the Chicago school of sociology. In the field of methodology, there was a strong interest in empirical research methods, such as the work of Paul Lazarsfeld. In social problems, Robert Merton's work received a lot of attention. The sociology of culture, of arts, and of literature were influenced by Western cultural anthropology, for example Claude Levi Strauss's structural anthropology, as well as the work of Bronislaw Mali-nowski, Alfred Reginald Radcliffe-Brown, and Alfred Kroeber. In this manner, Western schools of thought and theories always accompanied the Marxist perspective.

Only Miron Constantinescu continued his Marxist perspective during the period 1966–72. Constantinescu was the high-ranking official and intellectual responsible for the return of sociology to higher education in 1966. He had been a Communist since the interwar years, despite his membership in Dimitrie Gusti's royally sponsored sociological field research teams. Given his high position in the Communist Party, and the relatively more liberal political environment that followed in the aftermath of the withdrawal of the Russian troops from Romania in 1958, Constantinescu was able to support the continuing development of sociological research and education in Romania, until 1978, when it was once again virtually outlawed. And even though the higher education institutions of sociology were once again disbanded, lectures in the sociology of art and literature, and rural and industrial sociology managed to survive at the Faculty of Philosophy, the Faculty of Literature, and the Polytechnic University, as well as at small centers of research affiliated with the Academy of Social and Political Sciences.

In 1990, sociological education was reinstitutionalized yet again, with the establishment of the Faculty of Sociology, Psychology, and Pedagogy at the University of Bucharest, and in other main public higher education centers in Cluj and Iasi. In the years that followed, new departments of sociology were established at universities in Timisoara, Oradea, Brasov, Sibiu, and Craiova. The major public universities, that is, the University of Bucharest, Alexandru Ioan Cuza University in Iasi, and Babes Bolyai University in Cluj, now offer a fully developed curriculum in sociology, including master's degrees and Ph.D. programs.

Also in 1990, publication of *Sociologie Romaneasca* (Romanian Sociology) was resumed. The journal, founded by Dimitrie Gusti during the interwar period, was a continuation of the *Arhiva pentru Stiinta si Reforma Sociala* (Archive for Science and Social Reform), originally founded in Iasi, in 1918, by Gusti and economist Virgil Madgearu. Madgearu eventually went on to become one of the highest-ranking politicians of the National Peasant Party (PNT).

The Quality of Life Institute, the only institution in Romania to deal with the problem of poverty in a systematic way, was also founded in 1990. The Institute, affiliated with the Romanian Academy of Sciences, was the result of the efforts of Catalin Zamfir. She was a minister of labor and work in 1990, and after 1989, the initiator of social policy studies in Romania. Currently among the most important research institutions are also the Institute for Social and Geopolitical Studies, founded by Ilie Badescu, the Center for Urban and Regional Sociology, one of the most powerful private institutes for public and marketing surveys, lead by Dorel Abraham, and the Institute for Marketing and Surveys (IMAS), another well-established private research institute. Several new journals also appeared, including the *Revista de cercetari sociale* (Journal of Social Research), *Revista Romana de Sociologie* (Romanian Journal of Sociology), and *Calitatea vietii* (Quality of Life), as well as others published by private or academic research institutions.

After 1990, the teaching of sociology was oriented toward a reconstruction of Dimitrie Gusti's Bucharest School of Sociology, as well as some other schools of thought that developed in Cluj and Iasi in the interwar period. A new development in the teaching of sociology has been the broadening of the new curriculum to include anthropology, social policy, marketing, public relations, advertising techniques, and human resources. Since 1989, several new areas of sociology also have been initiated. These include Christian sociology, also known as "sociology through the eyes of faith" (with similarities to the work of Tony Campolo and David A. Fraser), structural analysis, conflict resolution, international relations and geopolitics, community justice administration, and economic sociology.

Sociology has become a very attractive discipline for students. Starting with only a few dozen students in 1990, more than 1500 now enter the major universities to study sociology each year. The main state faculties are the University of Bucharest, Babes Bolyai University in Cluj, and Alexandru Ioan Cuza University in Iasi. Two major private universities with sociological faculties have also joined the picture, Spiru Haret University and Hyperion University, both in Bucharest. The public universities are considered to be of a higher quality than the private ones. They are very competitive and only accept the best candidates. The remaining candidates go to the private schools. All students must pay tuition, which is higher at private than at public schools. That said, in general tuition is not very high and university education is accessible.

At the beginning of the 1990s, sociology as a discipline was institutionally linked with psychology and pedagogy. In the following years it became more closely connected to social work. Nowadays, at the main university, the University of Bucharest, sociology is taught at the Faculty of Sociology and Social Work. Students can enroll in a three-year program and earn a graduation diploma from the College of Social Work, with specializations in community social work, probation, or social pedagogy. There is also a four-year program culminating in a university degree in sociology or in social work. Finally, there are five master's programs, in European Social Policy, Social Policy Development, Community and Regional Development, Social and Health Services Management, and Community Justice Administration.

Following 1989, a new integration between research institutes and academic sociology began to develop. As a result, many prestigious researchers are also professors at the university, and an increasingly significant number of student teams are included in research projects being conducted at the research centers and institutions.

Professors at the university have founded most of the private research institutes, such as the Center for Urban and Regional Sociology (CURS), the Institute for Marketing and Surveys (IMAS), and the National Institute for Opinion and Marketing Studies (INSOMAR). These institutes are focused primarily on opinion polls and market research surveys. Many academicians also are involved in private research projects related to marketing, consulting and political analysis, and surveys. As a result, a significant portion of important sociological research receives its support through private funding. Since 2001, the government has been increasingly interested in sociological research being carried out at the universities, mainly on topics regarding poverty and European integration.

Poverty and the sudden deindustrialization resulting from the transformation was a major core focus of sociological research during the 1990s (Sandu 1996a, 1996b; Zamfir and Preda 2000). There was also interest in family (Mihailescu 1999), in social policies and the process of European integration (Zamfir and Zamfir 1995), and in ethnicity and interethnic relations (Badescu et al. 1995; Wats 1993; Zamfir and Zamfir 1993), as well as sociological analyses of the political philosophy of the Reform (Zamfir 1999). Some significant research and doctoral theses also focused on the transition and underdevelopment (Badescu et al. 1995).

However, taken as a whole, relatively few of the daring objectives identified by preeminent representatives of Romanian sociology in the early days of transition were addressed. For example, in 1992, the Rector of the University of Bucharest wrote:

Given the number and complexity of social problems in Romania, the list of social science priorities is a very long one. The new social and political situation calls for urgent action in the following areas: In the economic field, the transition from a centralized state economy to a market economy, a new system of balances between sectors, a new price system, consideration of the future of major industrial firms which make little or no profit, a new system of ownership, industrial reorganization, the training of key personnel and specialists who will be able to master the mechanisms of a market economy, a new system of motivations for the workers ... , and the development of domestic and international marketing. (Quoted by Mihailescu 1992: 153)

With few exceptions, we have not yet developed a significant theory on transition, and almost no sociological understanding of the almost mystic phenomena of the economy. At the same time, with few exceptions, there was and continues to be virtually no direct involvement or consultation of sociologists in decision making and the formation of economic policies in Romania. The social logic revealed by sociology has not yet been able to accommodate the logic of politics.

Since 1993, the problem of nationalism and ethnicity has been the subject of scientific scrutiny in Romania. This began with a joint effort, supported by the United States Project on Ethnic Relations, of the University of Bucharest, University of Timisoara, CURS, the Ministry of Labor and Social Protection, the Institutes of Sociology and of Psychology of the Academy of Sciences, and the Sociology Institute of the Academy (Abraham, Badescu, and Chelcea 1995).

The study was intended to determine and to measure the feelings of the population toward several ethnic groups, including Hungarians, Roma, and Jews. The main conclusion of the project was that the causes of the conflicts were social and not ethnic. At the time of the analysis, only 7 percent of the population had the perception that ethnic conflicts had occurred in the previous twelve months. Fifty-one percent of those that considered there to have been ethnic conflicts believed that the source of these tensions was interpersonal relations. The next most important causes of conflict were felt to be property affairs and politics. This was the case irrespective of the ethnic composition of the region (Abraham, Badescu, and Chelcea 1995, 22–24). Since then, other studies have been carried out on this matter but were far less complete and did not result in any significantly different findings.

Another important conclusion of the study was that the rise of ethnic minorities and the development of ethnic confrontation as a pattern of interethnic relations, whenever it takes place, is not a purely local phenomenon. Rather, it is an expression and consequence of the dynamics associated with the metropolitan frontier, that is of the process of the resettlement of the geopolitical frontiers. For example, the breakdown of the former USSR once again raised the question of geopolitical frontiers. Under these circumstances, the war in Yugoslavia broke out, the political map of Czechoslovakia changed, and the nostalgic zone of the former Austro-Hungarian Empire was revived (Abraham, Badescu, and Chelcea 1995, 24). The level of anxiety in the face of a changing frontier and the threat of war was relatively high at the time of investigation. Regardless of ethnic membership or region, about one-third of the population was concerned about the problem.

After 1990, the international outreach and collaborative efforts of Romanian sociology were directed exclusively toward Western countries, mainly the United States, Canada, France, Germany, The Netherlands, the United Kingdom, and Sweden. This cooperation was motivated, at first, by the eager intellectual need to close the gap or "the missing link" caused by the forced communization after World War II. Another important motivation for this cooperation was financial. For example, each year from 1991 to 1999, four to sixteen Romanian students and professors took advantage of the Trans-European Mobility Scheme for University Students (TEMPUS) project to study for six to twelve months in Western Europe.[1] Each year since 1998, between eleven and eighteen students have participated in exchanges with Western universities through the Socrates Program.[2]

TEMPUS and Socrates also brought important logistical resources to Romanian universities. The Faculty of Sociology and Social Work in Bucharest has carried out most of these projects. Currently, the Faculty has research, doctoral, and teaching partnership agreements with the following universities: Patras University and Thessaloniki University (Greece), Anglia Polytechnic University (United Kingdom), Hogheschool Sittard (The Netherlands), Chisinau State University (Republic of Moldavia), the University of Barcelona (Spain), Lund University and Umea University (Sweden), and Tiffin University and Case Western Reserve University (United States).

Between 1999 and 2000, an international distance-learning project was established with the assistance of Anglia Polytechnic University, Umea University, and Tiffin University. TEMPUS provided support for the European portion of the project, while the United States Agency for International Development and the Council of International Programs supported the American one.

During the last decade, an increasing number of sociologists were involved in local and national agencies of development, in international projects in Romania with the International Monetary Fund (IMF) and the World Bank, and with nongovernmental organizations (NGOs) and other foundations, such as the Dimitrie Gusti Foundation for Science and Social Reform. In general, sociologists were involved in political and social life in two ways. Some were directly involved, as politicians acting in parliament or in the government, for example in the reform of education beginning in 1995 and in the Agriculture Sector Adjustment Loan (ASAL) program with the World Bank. Others were, and some still are, presidential or prime minister's advisers. Some were more indirectly involved, collaborating with different governmental or international agencies in developing and implementing new laws and social projects such are those regarding child protection, probation, unemployment, minorities, and handicapped people.

The financing of sociology is still a relatively difficult problem in Romania. The government has supported very few serious research projects, and the Academy of Sciences is continually challenged by chronic funding shortages. Several of the major research projects carried out since the transformation were begun only after 1998, when the World Bank initiated a three-year funding program for academic research. Between 1999 and 2000, the project had a budget of 1.7 million dollars, of which the Romanian government covered 30 percent. However, most of the sociological research carried out in the 1990s was done using public funding from the former Ministry of Research and Technology and the Romanian Academy of Sciences, despite their chronic under funding.

Since 1997, a relatively new and flexible source of research funding has been from the National Council for Higher Education Research, which supports young researchers and professors. The Council is funded from the national budget. Major sources of educational funding have been the TEMPUS project, the Socrates Program and LEONARDO (a European vocational training program begun in 1995). The United Nations Children's Fund, the United Nations Development Program, and the PHARE program (a pre-accession program financed by the European Union) have also been involved in financing research and education in Romania, including sociology.

Romanian sociology has made a new start since 1990. The field of this science is very provocative as Romanian society is trying to rediscover itself again, after fifty years of Communism. However, since sociology did not have a good reputation in the public sphere, part of its legitimate field of discourse has been encroached upon by so-called political analysts. They have no specific qualifications, and are loud and hasty in their analyses. The good news is that Romanian sociology is surely developing at a satisfactory pace and gaining recognition and legitimacy in the society at large. Private companies, and more importantly, the government have begun at least to ask for, if not always to carefully listen to, the results of professional sociological studies. There is no doubt that Romanian sociology has already had some success in fulfilling its huge responsibility as the mirror of the society.

NOTES

1. TEMPUS is a higher education cooperation scheme between the European Union and CEE Partner Countries launched in 1990. It was intended to respond to the needs for reform in higher education in Central and Eastern European countries as well as to facilitate the transfer of credit and students between countries.

2. Socrates is a European Community Action Program in the field of education that is intended to strengthen the European dimension of education, to improve knowledge of European languages, and to promote cooperation and mobility in higher education throughout all of Europe.

13

The Return of Russian Sociology

Valery Mansurov and Mikhail Chernysh

Prior to 1991, there was no such thing as an autonomous and independent Russian sociology. There were quite a number of sociologists that were based in the Russian Federation, but they all belonged to one big pool of social scientists that worked under the aegis of Soviet sociology. They were supposed to toe the line of scientific Marxism, a peculiar strain of theory that emerged in the totalitarian society and was used to justify the increasingly nonsocialist reality of the late Soviet Union. Mikhail Gorbachev's perestroika made a big dent in the armor of Soviet-style Marxism, but could not do away with it altogether. The inertia of Marxism weighed heavily on the minds of Russian social scientists, who were both puzzled and inspired by the advent of Gorbachev's new thinking.

In 1988, there was a big institutional breakthrough in the life of Russian sociology. For the first time in its history, Russian sociology was accepted as a full-blooded science without any qualms or reservations. Tatyana Zaslavskaya took the leadership of the Russian Sociological Association on behalf of the reformers, and did her best to promote a new approach toward the ongoing social change. This act of acceptance, which came in the form of a special edict by the Central Committee of the Communist Party, proved to be a boost and an inspiration for a number of social scientists that had hitherto stayed on the sidelines of Soviet sociology despite their high informal status within the profession. Boris Grushin, Vladimir Yadov, Andrej Zdravomyslov, and Leonid Gordon started asserting their own, largely critical views of Soviet society, views that drew inspiration from empirical research and data as well as historical analysis. Owing to their critical approach, a number of new concepts made their way into the parlance of Russian social science. For the first time in their lives, Soviet sociologists could freely use theoretical perspectives, which had been developed by social scientists in the West, for the analysis of their own society.

While the Politburo of the Communist Party was torn between the reformers and the hardliners, the social scientists were engaged in the lively discussion of Soviet totalitarianism and its short-term and long-term impact on society. This discussion came to be reflected in a series of high-profile books that made Soviet totalitarian society the object of criticism. The first of these books was entitled *A Stray Path Not Accepted* (Afanasyev 1988). From the rather multifarious contents of the book, it was hard to conclude what was meant by "stray path." However, the spirit of the publication unmistakably pointed toward the Soviet totalitarian practices that had warped the natural course of societal development and had been the cause of its many ills.

The general approach of the book's contributors boiled down to a fairly simple string of arguments. In the wake of the revolution, Russian society was subjugated by a small clique of marginal revolutionaries, the Bolsheviks, bent on the establishment in Russia of a socialist society. The Bolshevik mind was permeated by a concoction of radical ideas, among which the Marxist approach was dominant. The revolutionaries imposed their violent dictatorship upon Russia, bringing the country to an almost total collapse. The dictatorship led to the demise of all alternative thinking in society and laid the basis for the Stalinist regime and the purges. While critical of Stalin and his "deformations" of socialism, the book's contributors insisted that there existed the possibility of a different socialism, one that would have a "human face." This would be the only right path for Soviet society to tread.

The book made a noticeable impact on Soviet intellectuals and proved to be the initial volume of a whole series that set out to cleanse Soviet social science of the vestiges of falsified Marxism and to reestablish a positive, fact-oriented research as the mainstream of Soviet social science. The discussion of socialism with a human face and its chances in Soviet society continued until August 1991, when a right-wing putsch occurred and in its wake the Soviet Union ceased to exist. In place of the old empire, a cluster of newly independent states emerged, each with its own policy in the field of social science.

INSTITUTIONAL CHANGE

During the years 1990–99, there were three major institutional changes in sociology. The first one consisted of the rapid spread of sociology into the realm of higher education. In 1991, a Department of Sociology was opened at Moscow State University. Later, similar departments were set up at the prestigious

Academy of Management and the Higher School of Economics, the University of St. Petersburg, Altai State University, and in some others. Today, every university in Russia has either a department or a chair of sociology. Approximately 200,000 students are currently taking sociology courses in the Russian Federation, and about 11,000 of them major in sociology at the B.A. and M.A. levels.

Such quick growth of sociological education demanded trained qualified personnel to fill the teaching positions. The staff for the departments was often recruited from the pool of instructors who had previously taught Marxism-Leninism or Scientific Communism. These teachers often encountered many problems trying to adjust to the new way of teaching and the new theoretical approaches. With the collaboration of the Ford Foundation and other basic sociological institutions, retraining courses were set up at the Institute of Sociology of the Russian Academy of Sciences to help them overcome these problems. The growth and spread of sociology also included the establishment of new degree programs in graduate education. From 1994 onward, the contingent of Candidates (Ph.D.'s) and Doctors (Ph.D.'s with the habilitation degree), as well as professors of sociology started to grow.

The fast growth of the departments and faculties (schools) of sociology, along with the discipline's inclusion among the list of obligatory subjects at most higher education institutions, created a demand for more teaching materials. Initially many institutions chose a strategy of using manuals and textbooks written by Western colleagues. Then, Russian authors started to publish their works with the valuable assistance of the Soros Foundation. Nowadays, many universities issue their own manuals. During this period, the first full-scale sociological dictionary was published, as were a number of other sociological reference books.

The second direction of institutional change affected the institutes of the Academy of Sciences. In 1991, the Institute of Sociology of the Russian Academy of Sciences, until recently the only formally recognized sociological institution in the Russian Federation, was split into two institutes, the Institute of Sociology, headed by professor Vladimir Yadov, and the Institute of Social and Political Studies, headed by professor Gennadij Osipov. The two institutes came to have different approaches toward society and sociology.

This division was inevitable because in the early part of perestroika, the original Institute of Sociology gave birth to two conceptions of social change in the Soviet Union. Both conceptions regarded change as inevitable, but were poles apart as far as the means of carrying out reforms were concerned. The first conception, supported by Professor Yadov, argued for the necessity to dismantle most of the institutions of power that had been created in the Soviet period and to change the foundations of the existing order. It had a sound logic behind it since the retardation of the process of change could result in a backlash from Party bureaucrats. The second conception, by Osipov, stressed the importance of seeing the reforms through the prism of lost and acquired opportunities as far as the population was concerned. It called for the preservation of stability and order, given that the continued progress of reforms could jeopardize the living standards and survival opportunities of the majority of the population. In the conditions of those days, the adoption of this conception could have allowed for the massive comeback of the trenchant Party apparatus.

It is notable that, for the first time, the conflict between the two schools was resolved in a democratic way. On March 26, 1991, the Presidium of the Russian Academy of Sciences created the Institute of Social and Political Studies, with Osipov as its director. As a result, both conceptions of change were formally recognized and legitimated. At the end of the decade of the 1990s, the Institute of Sociology was split once again, this time on a geographic basis. The St. Petersburg affiliate became an independent Sociological Institute of the Russian Academy of Sciences, headed by Sergej Golod. The Institute of Sociology also became the basis for a new teaching institution, the State University of Humanities. Hence, an integration of research and teaching occurred when the professors and associates of the research institute received a chance to test their ideas against the judgment of students and graduates.

In analyzing the institutional change of sociology in Russia, it is difficult to bypass the role of private research and marketing organizations, the third major area of change in sociology. Most of them came into being in the early stages of the reform process, as a result of cooperation between relevant Western networks and Russian researchers. A large part of the latter came from the Academy of Sciences and other scientific institutions seeking a means of survival in the new era. The close cooperation and financial obligations that these new institutions had to maintain with Western partners and clients demanded a closer look at the methodology of the social sciences than had been conducted up to this point in time. Commercial marketing research enterprises wanted better samples both of Russia as a whole and its individual regions. This demand was expressed and addressed in a number of seminars, held between 1993 and 1995, with participation by experts from Western institutions such as the University of Michigan. A number of students also went to Michigan to study the art of sampling. For the first time, the complexity of making a sample in a country so variegated as Russia became obvious to many Russian sociologists and their Western partners. Nowadays, Russian sociology and marketing research are much more qualified in the field of sampling, a crucial prerequisite for any valid and reliable social research.

Another contribution by commercial research to sociology came in the form of a renewed interest in qualitative studies. In the Soviet Union, qualitative methods were only used on rare occasions, and when employed they were subject to castigation by the authorities. The reason for this was that qualitative studies, being explorative in nature, often brought results that could not be properly interpreted within the framework of socialist doctrine, and could not be placed within the old-style Marxist theory. The other reason was that qualitative studies were regarded by many Soviet sociologists as having little support from basic science such as mathematics. The commercial researchers proved through their practice that qualitative methods could be treated on a par with quantitative ones, and that they could provide explanations of different phenomena that could be as enlightening and often more manageable than proven quantitative methods.

THEORETICAL EVOLUTION: FROM CRITIQUE TO ANALYSIS

The previous analysis provides a partial explanation for the changes that occurred in the role of theory in Russian social science. In the socialist society, any discussion of theory other than orthodox Marxism was not allowed and could bring about harsh reprimand or even administrative punishment from the authorities. Multiple perspectives existed only in the forms taken by the critique of bourgeois science. Very few translations of classic or modern works by sociologists were published. Even Max Weber's works were confined to the so-called *spezkhran*, special library halls accessible only to Doctors of Science or to researchers with special permissions. These conditions cannot be regarded as a proper environment for a lively academic discussion of sociological issues.

With the birth of the contemporary Russian state, there was an abolition of all bans on social theory, and the community of social scientists was given free access to contemporary sociological theory. This access occurred through two major channels. First, colleagues from Western countries flocked to Moscow and exposed Russian social scientists to their theoretical perspectives. In the span of the ten years that separated the acme of perestroika and the postcrisis year of 1999, Anthony Giddens, Jurgen Habermas, Pierre Bourdieu, Immanuel Wallerstein, Samuel Eisenstadt, and many other eminent modern scientists visited Moscow and used the opportunity to lecture to Russian scientists at various institutions. Further exposure to theory was made possible by the active participation of Russian scientists in various international events. For instance, the size of the Russian delegations at the congresses of the International Sociological Association in Bielefeld (1994) and Montreal (1998) were second only to those of the hosts. In addition, new laws of publication and the growing demand from teachers and students led to the release of a flow of translations of sociological classics into the Russian book market. To date, most of the classic works of sociology have been translated into Russian, and more modern works are being constantly introduced to Russian readers.

The critique of bourgeois sociological theory fell into oblivion, and a smoldering discussion turned into a fire with the release of a five volume *History of Theoretical Sociology*, written by a group of social theorists, with Yurij Davidov as editor (1997–2000). The discussion was a marked departure from the type of critique characteristic of the old Soviet system, and centered on the relevance of sociological theory in the context of Russian social change. It was obvious that the Russian Federation was implementing reforms that intended to lead it to capitalism. It was also obvious to many observers that the newly emergent Russian capitalism was not what many supporters of the change had expected. The difference between the hope and the reality made for a gap that sociological theory was called upon to fill.

The authors of *History* made a thorough examination of classical sociological theory of capitalism, particularly of the works of Max Weber and Werner Sombart. Previously, the role of Weber had been trivialized and reduced to the core of his theory of the Protestant ethic. In line with the theory, some Russian (but not only Russian) sociologists had started looking for Protestant values in Russian society, ignoring the basic assumption of Weberian theory that tied together existing values and basic religious archetypes. Obviously these attempts discovered few Protestant values in the changing Russian society. Ironically, the Communist system with its emphasis on self-restraint and the ideal looming ahead had more in common with the Weberian type of attitudes toward labor and wealth than the new Russian so-called crony capitalism that stressed pleasure and the enjoyment of wealth rather than hard work and desire for salvation.

In other words, in order to generate a viable explanation of early Russian capitalism, the works of Max Weber had to be reexamined beyond the trivial level. Yurij Davidov, who authored the articles on Max Weber in *History*, presented Weber's theory on two types of capitalism. The first type relied on an archaic value structure and stressed the importance of financial speculation as a source of wealth. This kind of capitalism was an omnipresent phenomenon that went hand in hand with any social order and any structure of production. The second argued that it was the accumulation of wealth that led to capitalism and industrial production, not the industriousness of peasants. To make capitalism possible, a new system of values was required that might emerge as the result of a unique cluster of circumstances, which would not reappear in a contemporary society. It would be close to impossible to reproduce this cluster and such an experiment would not make any sense in the conditions of modern Russia.

Thus, Weber, as treated by Yurij Davidov, came out as a critical invective aimed at both the "new Russian rich" that had squandered the country's wealth, and at the Russian bureaucrats who expected the general misspending of resources to turn at some point into economic growth. It was also an argument against the tide of Marxist reasoning that kept appearing in contemporary Russian literature. While not openly invoking Marx, some authors, particularly belonging to economics, claimed that the period that Russia had been going through could qualify as a phase of the primary accumulation of wealth. One needed only to wait and eventually the accumulated wealth would flow freely into economy in the form of private investment and thereby create economic growth. The facts of life dealt a heavy blow to these arguments. Instead of freely flowing into the Russian economy, the accumulated wealth flowed out of Russia and into the more prosperous and less hazardous economic environments that most Western economies provided. The outflow of capital became a known fact and a big problem for Russian leaders, a problem for which no adequate solution has so far been found.

Davidov (1997–2000) countered this use of the Marxist theory of primary accumulation, arguing that it originally had been a moral argument that was supposed to justify a takeover of capitalist property by the working class. The theory of primary accumulation, claimed Davidov, was not embedded in the logic of Marxist economic analysis and could not be inferred from any of its arguments. This train of thought is an illustration of the new critical current in Russian sociology that made its appearance in the wake of the reforms and their unexpected consequences.

It would be wrong to claim that Marx and Marxist arguments were completely ousted from the theoretical baggage of Russian sociology. After a few years of reforms, Marxist theory returned, not as an ideology that imposed its matrix upon society, but rather in a more traditional manner as a pattern of critical argumentation leveled against rampant social injustice and inequality. The new Marxist argument is based on the concept of alienation, which was interpreted as Marx's basic teleological argument. Marx was no longer regarded only as a proponent of an anticapitalist revolution, but also as a philosopher who sought a solution to the eternal problems of humankind, consisting in an inability to achieve a "natural community." The latter was regarded by him as a harmonious type of human existence that was utopian if viewed within the context of capitalist society (Marx 2000). An anticapitalist revolution was only one way of solving the problem, economic development and gradual increase in the usage of machinery could be another one.

The elements of this theoretical debate are just one illustration of the changing pattern of perception of Marxist theory in the Russian sociological community. In the debate, Marx appears as a sociologist whose theories were being modified and transformed by scholars who wanted their own ideas, whatever they were, to be supported by his work. He was no longer the ultimate icon of the previous Soviet period, but a tormented thinker on an equal footing with other thinkers who had often had better answers to many contemporary problems.

Another case that illustrates the evolution of Russian sociology in the post-Soviet period is research in the field of social structure and social stratification. In fact, prior to perestroika, the concept of social stratification could not be used in any of the studies conducted by Soviet sociologists. Every society was to be regarded as class based, including Soviet society and the societies in Eastern Europe. However, unlike classes in the capitalist countries where there was supposed to be a division into the exploited and the exploiters, the classes that were supposed to be present in those socialist societies were qualified as friendly ones. The official class-based analysis assumed that a socialist society had two big classes, and one "layer," that were set in a hierarchy of proximity to the society's fundamental values, that is, the working class, the collective farmers, and the so-called socialist intelligentsia (Rutkevitch 1982). The difference between these groups was supposed to diminish as society progressed toward its stated goal of advanced socialism and Communism. This concept bore the name of social homogeneity.

Even in the 1970s, it was obvious that this concept could not provide an adequate explanation of the many problems that plagued socialist society. It could not explain why there were so many workers who engaged in manual, routine, and dirty work. Nor could it explain the existence of the nomenclature, and the gap in the living standards between the elite and the rest of the population. Any discussion of the matter was strictly forbidden. Even in the all-Union census, Party functionaries were defined as workers rather than bureaucrats.

Obviously these problems did not go away because of the ban. They were raised beyond the Soviet Union and became the subject of many sociological debates, which only some Soviet sociologists had word of. There were many sociologists that tried to breach the social homogeneity theory by proposing ideas that did not openly contradict the official dogma, but bit off some of its most preposterous corners. At one point, Ovsej Shkaratan argued that in a society of developed socialism, the socialist intelligentsia could be regarded not as a separate layer but as a progressive part of the working class (Blyachman and Shkaratan 1973). Vladimir Yadov outlined new possible dimensions of social differentiation in a famous monograph *Man and His Work* (Chelovek i ego rabota 1967). Professor Leonid Gordon concentrated on the cultural aspect of social differentiation (Gordon and Nazimova 1985).

The real demise of the social homogeneity theory happened when glasnost became a possibility. Journalists rather than social scientists made a dent in it by exposing many of society's existing injustices and many of the hidden and muted principles of social differentiation. In the post-Soviet period, studies of social structure once again became the main object of study, but in a totally different way. Attempts were made to abandon the Marxist approach and to shape social structure studies in the form of social stratification research. The logic behind the tendency was purely epistemological, because in reality a formerly egalitarian society was gradually moving toward one of more pronounced social differences for which only social stratification theory could account, but which it could not adequately explain.

Attempts to provide a meaningful explanation came from a number of authors. Tatyana Zaslavskaya came up with a theory that amalgamated social positions and the inclination to support the ongoing reforms (Zaslavskaya and Ryvkina 1991). Her analysis presented conflicting data that pointed to sizable groups that were prepared to support the reforms and a large part of the population that regarded the reforms in a passive, but hostile way. Natalya Tikhonova viewed social differentiation in the tradition of Pitirim Sorokin, as part of various social cycles that generated different shapes of social differences (Tikhonova 1999). Mikhail Chernysh (1994) made an attempt to study lifestyles, particularly in respect to the richer part of the population.

However, more elaborate research with better explanatory outcomes came from the study of specific problems. As was indicated previously, within the framework of the official Soviet doctrine, the intelligentsia was regarded as a separate layer that was different from the classes by virtue of the fact that it had no propriety over the means of production (the working class and the collective farmers were supposed to have it). In the context of Russian sociology, the problem of the intelligentsia's role in society grew into a general problem of professions and professionalization. It was clear that like the society as a whole, the stratum of the intelligentsia was fragmenting into higher and lower strata, successful and unsuccessful professionals. A closer look at the process demanded a change in theoretical approach. A more Weberian stance was assumed so that the conversion of resources into status and well-being could be examined. One approach singled out the state and the private sector as big players in the field providing legitimation for the professions and determining the conditions of their work. This approach toward the study of professions was employed in a research project, "Russian Doctors: Social Attitudes and Strategies for Adaptation to Changes," headed by Valery Mansurov. It was partially due to the fact that much of the sphere of reproduction and culture, medicine, and institutions of higher learning, was in the past and still remains under state control.

The study of elites became another popular area of study. Olga Kryshtanovskaya made an extensive study of the emergence of the contemporary Russian elite, stressing the inequality of access to various resources needed to move up the social ladder. In the study, it appeared that most of the top Russian corporations were founded and run by the members of the old Party nomenclature (Kryshtanovskaya 1998). In other words, the possession of networking resources and state support became a crucial factor in the formation and configuration of the Russian elite. The study also revealed a growing tension between the Moscow elite that harnessed most of the financial resources of the country, and the local and regional elites that became increasingly restless as vital local resources kept falling under the control of Moscow-based companies. The study pointed to an alarming rate at which local elites were building their strength, ousting intruders, and suppressing all possible criticism on a local level. In some areas, local chiefs created authoritarian states of their own, complete with constitutions that stipulated all possible conditions of independence, including a clause calling for a local armed forces. A team from the St. Petersburg Sociological Institute launched another project centering specifically on local elites (Duka 2001).

A totally new aspect of structure studies came in the form of research related to gender. In the Soviet Union, the gender issue was regarded as nonexistent because the socialist state was assumed to have been the ultimate guarantor of the equal rights of the sexes. In the new Russia, a new discourse on the problem was started by a number of researchers. Marina Malysheva (1999) came up with results that pointed to deep built-in gender inequalities in Russian society, including inequality in the level of salary, inequality in levels of professionalization, and other forms of inequality. This research attracted public attention, although it did not receive as much public response as the research on the problem of the elites.

Poverty emerged as another prominent field of research. Leonid Gordon found that poverty was a complex phenomenon that designated a human condition of various origins and characteristics. In the case of younger professionals, poverty could mean a turning point toward the adaptation to the labor market. In the case of the older part of the population, it could signify a permanent state of discomfort and scarce resources. A new phenomenon of relative poverty was discovered that brought into light the conditions of a segment of the population that aspired to maximize the benefits received from various quarters. Svetlana Stevenson made a particularly thorough study of the Russian homeless, a new phenomenon that had either been hidden or nonexistent during Soviet times (Sidorenko-Stevenson 1996). The study provided for the typology of conditions described by the concept. The group of homeless appeared to be divided into segments that were gradually evolving a culture of poverty and the homelessness characteristic of the underclass.

The unfolding of qualitative analysis has been mentioned before, but in the context of theoretical evolution it has a special meaning. Almost nonexistent in Soviet times, of late, qualitative analysis has become one of the most popular methods of exploring various issues of Russia's past and present. Olga Maslova, an expert on methodology, investigated the particular conditions influencing qualitative interviewing within the Russian context (1995). Alongside colleagues from St. Petersburg, Victoria Semenova (1996) undertook a significant biography project focusing on the Soviet past. The advantage of the project consisted in its ability to amalgamate several important social realms, political, economic, and cultural, which all appeared to be closely interrelated. The political realm created the preconditions for the mobility of the large masses of the Russian population into big cities. The influx of former peasants into the urban environment transformed the nature of that environment and dramatically changed the lives of former peasants. The inflated population had to be crammed into communal apartments that constituted a very peculiar world. This world magnified the intensity of human interaction and exacerbated its problems against the backdrop of political control, war, and postwar reconstruction. The decision to move a large part of the population out of communal apartments came not only as a political and economic decision, but also as a cultural turning point signifying the strengthening of the individual and a gradual process of embourgeoisement in the wake of the post-Stalinist thaw. The qualitative study focused on the internal logic and interaction of events that at a later stage led to the demise of the Soviet Union and the emergence of a new Russian state.

Under Communist rule, Soviet sociology, whatever its merits and flaws, had to bypass important issues that the Party found ideologically unacceptable. The study of conflict and particular situations of conflict was one of these issues. Contemporary Russian sociology can no longer ignore the issue given the scale and bitterness of political conflicts unfolding in the post-Soviet space. Evgenij Stepanov (1996) concentrated on the methodology of conflict studies and applied conflict analysis to various conflict situations. The contribution of sociologists toward the solution of conflicts may not yet be evident, but it is bound to become tangible in the years to come when the analysis of the roots and causes of contemporary conflicts becomes the subject of public discussion. Even now, the sociological community contributes their bit to the comprehension of the Chechen problem, drawing attention to its underlying causes and possible solutions (Drobizheva 2000).

The institutionalization of sociology and the upgrading of its status gave a boost to the emergence of new theoretical approaches. A multiparadigmatic approach to the study of social processes is gradually gaining ground, providing for a broad definition of moving forces, dominant factors, and prospects. Society is treated as an objective-subjective reality and the individual is regarded as a product of the system, resulting from a complex interaction of various factors, economic to psychological. At the same time, society is defined as an entity resulting from individual actions integrated into the social process in various ways. It is in the process of social action by individuals that society evolves, not as a result of some unknown mystical or fatalistic forces.

Though the structural paradigm is enjoying widespread popularity in the community of Russian sociologists, it is not the only framework of social investigation. Alongside various linear concepts of development (formational, industrial, postindustrial), there are polycentric and multilinear concepts based on the civilization approach that sees the world as a cluster of poles representing various civilizations. This approach is exemplified by works of Alexander Akhiezer (1997), Svetlana Kirdina (2000), Nikolai Lapin (2000), Vyacheslav Stepin (2000), and Gennadij Osipov (2000a, 2000b). Another trend in Russian sociology is further research into nonclassic sociology (Grigoriev 2001), individual concepts of development, and societal functioning beyond the paradigms offered by Western sociology (Nemirovsky and Nevirko 1998).

We have mentioned only a few directions of theoretical research that constitute the profile of contemporary Russian sociology. The obvious tendency that these cases point to is the move from a monotheoretical research field with a curtailed range of discourse toward a science that employs a broad variety of methods and theoretical approaches, and that spreads beyond specialized institutions into the limelight of public debate. Russian sociology is gradually reducing the distance that has for many years separated it from Western sociology, and its sociologists are finding common footing with colleagues from many countries. After the first enthusiasm caused by the collapse of the Soviet Union dwindled, a new situation has emerged with incentives for the exploration of new issues and methods.

14

In Search of Its Own Identity: A Decade of Slovak Sociology

Bohumil Buzik and Eva Laiferova

SLOVAK SOCIOLOGY BEFORE 1989

The institutionalization of sociology in the Czech lands occurred as a part of the development of science in Slovakia. Along with their political careers, sociologists Milan Hodza and Anton Stefanek were simultaneously engaged in academic activity and were major contributors to the institutionalization of sociology at Comenius University in Bratislava (Laiferova 1995). In 1946, the Sociological Section of the Slovak Cultural Society was founded and began publishing the first Slovak journal of sociology, *Sociologicky sbornik.* During this period, Alexander Hirner, particularly noted for his empirical research, was one of the most productive authors in Slovak sociology (Turcan 2000).

Following the Communist takeover in 1948, there was a serious break in the development of Slovak sociology. Only in the mid-1960s, with considerable support from the Polish sociological community, did Slovak sociology continue its development. Beginning in the mid-1960s, until the so-called normalization in 1970, M.A. programs in sociology at Polish universities were open to Slovak scholars. Polish sociologists also provided translations of literature and collaboration on collective research projects (Pasiak 1997).

A short period of political thaw, at the end of the 1960s, made possible the publication of translations of the work of Western authors. Mostly Czech translations of classical and contemporary authors, these translations served Slovak students as the major sources of knowledge of and contact with the world of Western sociology until the transformation of 1989. It was during these few years that international cooperation and contact reached its height during the Communist period.

In 1964, the Slovak Sociological Association was founded, under the umbrella of the Slovak Academy of Sciences. However, during the Communist period, it was controlled by the Communist Party. Sociologists who were persecuted by the state or excluded from the Communist Party were not allowed to be elected to any of its leadership positions. This restriction remained in place until the historic Second Congress of Slovak Sociologists held in Martin, in 1989. An important contribution to these changes, and of an uncommon critical spirit, was a report by Sona Szomolanyi (1990) on the history of the birth and development of sociology within the Slovak Academy of Sciences. Written in 1988, the report could only be published in 1990.

THE TRANSFORMATION OF SLOVAKIA AFTER 1989

In comparative studies of the countries in transition, Slovakia has been labeled as "a boundary case," located between a group of successfully transforming Central European countries and the countries of South-Eastern Europe (Szomolanyi 1999). With the division of the Czechoslovak Federation, in 1993, a separate, independent and sovereign Slovak state was established. This was accompanied by the transformation of the economy, a process of national integration, and the formation of new political institutions. However, a deep economic decline, high unemployment (more than 10 percent), and low inflows of foreign capital led to the abandonment of the Western model of economic transformation being followed by her newly independent sister state, the Czech Republic, and other countries in the region.

Between 1994 and 1998, there was a search for a so-called Slovak model for the transformation of the economy. It was led by an attempt to identify the national characteristics of the new state, and to transpose them to all spheres of the society in order to unite economic and governmental interests in the creation of a new strata of Slovak capitalists. The period was characterized by attempts to achieve a more active role for the state in the regulation of economic transformation and development, and a higher measure of economic growth to offset an expansion and increase of the expenses of the public sector. However, these efforts continued to be thwarted by low inflows of direct foreign investment.

In 1998, a new government declared a willingness to revise economic policy in accordance with the spirit of classic liberalism and neo-institutionalism (Kollar and Meseznikov 2000). However, due to the fragmentation of political power, the changes actually implemented did not fully live up to these declarations, and the economic policy that was put into place had a constrictive impact. Following a small decrease between 1994 and 1997, unemployment began to grow, exceeding 20 percent in the year 2000. The legal and health systems came to the verge of collapse, and, in a comparative analysis of ninety countries, based on the Consumer Price Index in 2000, Slovakia slipped from fifty-second to fifty-sixth place (Kollar and Meseznikov 2000).

THE PROBLEM OF THE DECOMMUNIZATION OF SOCIOLOGY

In the former Czechoslovakia, the majority of sociologists active at universities and in the academic milieu after 1971 belonged to the Communist Party. This was a result of the massive pressure of strongly ideological sectors of the Communist Party, of Party organization of social scientists and university pedagogues, and of the "normalization" period. In the period following the end of Communist rule (and while still under the aegis of the Czechoslovak Federation), a major change in the institutional structure and personnel of the scientific communities was begun. The mechanisms of appointment to key positions in scientific institutions and the state and public administrations were transformed. Previously politically nominated representatives of institutions were replaced by highly respected scholars whose professional careers had been politically blocked. Sociologists, like a lot of professionals, started to function in spheres that had had no legitimate structures or existence under the Communist system, for example, business enterprises, public opinion research centers, and advertising agencies. Because of cuts in jobs resulting from the transformation in the structure of the economy, mainly in the sphere of previously state-controlled enterprises, some sociologists were forced to leave existing positions and to search for work in other spheres, often outside of sociology.

There was no general decommunization of Slovak sociology during the last decade. Because of the relatively small size of its sociological community, there did not exist any alternative pool of sociologists, that is, sociologists clearly not involved in the Communist system and who could have filled the positions purged of Party members. At the beginning of 1990, in an act of solidarity, those members of the sociological community who had been clearly affiliated with the Party and had lost their jobs after the abolition of its various institutions, were given a chance to begin anew. As a result, decommunization, understood as a conscious effort to eliminate former members of the Communist Party from the discipline or to exclude them from professional positions, never came to pass in Slovakia. A clear boundary line demarcating Party sociologists and non-Party sociologists did not exist prior to the transformation, and does not exist in its aftermath. The differences that do polarize and separate the sociological community today tend to reflect the general polarization of Slovak society in its transformational or countertransformational tendencies.

Because only a Marxist paradigm was accepted in sociology in the former Czechoslovakia up until 1989, an alternative sociology did not officially exist, and access to different perspectives on the social world was unavailable for the majority of Slovak sociologists. This lack of theoretical pluralization, along with a lack of preparedness to accept new conditions, resulted in a theoretical vacuum in sociology and the social sciences. The result has been the lack of a conscious and critical reflection on the social world, typical of extremely empirically oriented sociologists. During the 1990s, a natural political divergence among sociologists began to appear, an understandable phenomenon given the context of general pluralization of the broader society. However, this internal diversification of the sociological community did not lead to communication and discussion, but rather to mutual alienation.

THE IMPACT OF SOCIAL TRANSFORMATION ON SLOVAK SOCIOLOGY

Throughout the 1990s, many changes occurred in the science as a result of social transformation (Kollar and Meseznikov 2000). This was especially the case since the social transformation was accompanied by a noticeable decrease in expenditures on science and research from the state budget, from 0.48 percent in 1993 to 0.38 percent in 1998. There was also a reduction in expenditure from other public sources, as well as from the business sector. The total expenditure on the sciences and research fell from 1.53 percent of GDP in 1993, to 0.86% in 1998. These cuts in funding resulted in a large reduction in the number of positions in institutions and enterprises dedicated to science and research.

The general framework of austerity imposed on the scientific community resulted in a noticeable decline in the number of sociologists, along with a reduction in the number of sociological positions at most state research institutes. The most important nongovernmental organizations for sociological research are the *Institut pre Verejne Otazky* (Institute for Public Issues), and the Social Policy Analyses Center (SPACE). The only new state research agency established was the *Centrum pre Vyskum Rodiny* (International Center of Family Studies), which came into existence in 1992, and attracted some researchers from the academic sphere.

Unlike the case of its neighbors the Czech Republic, Poland, and Hungary, Slovak sociology was not influenced by the return or collaboration of native sociologists who had left the country and become eminent scholars during their exile. A lack of funding to obtain foreign publications and journals has also limited the accessibility and influence of international sociology for Slovakian sociologists. From the institutional point of view, the most important new development has been the establishment of a competitive grants system for distributing funding resources. However, perhaps the most direct impact of the transformation on Slovak sociology came from the partition of the Czechoslovak Federation.

It is possible to characterize the mid-1990s in Slovak sociology as the period of empiricism (Buzik 1997). Between 1992 and 1994, the quarterly journal of Slovak sociology, *Sociologia* (and its English language yearly edition *The Slovak Sociological Review*), was dominated by articles focusing only on the gathering and description of empirical facts, and either absent of any theoretical component or containing only minimum tracks of theory, interpretative schema, or typologies (Buzik 1997). However, Slovak sociology is a rather young science with a traditionally strong tendency to identify sociology with data collection applicable for the organization of the public life (Kusa 1997). At its best, it has attempted to verify scientific hypotheses with empirical research, in order to realize the full potential of sociology as a theoretical-empirical science.

Since 1989, this empiricism has contributed to the establishment of international cooperation with Western sociology. For Slovakian sociology, this cooperation mostly has been limited to the translation of already existing questionnaires, organization of the collection of empirical data, and the publication of their description without their deeper theoretical interpretation. Until the latter half of the 1990s, foreign offers to join international research projects were usually based on financial support from abroad.

Of course, a situation in which only two to four researchers are responsible for an entire research area has a negative effect on scientific discussion within Slovak sociology. In such a small sociological community, strong informal networks develop in which the imperative of solidarity rules, undermining the ability for the critical review of sociological production. This has been another barrier for the development of sociological theory (Kusa 1997).

CHANGES IN UNIVERSITY EDUCATION AFTER 1989

Revolutionary changes at the beginning of the 1990s substantially changed the situation in the sphere of university education. Democratization occurred very rapidly in this sphere. It occurred above all in the liberalization of curricula, the strengthening of the control of pedagogues over the quality and requirements of the educational process, the removal of ideological subjects from teaching plans, an increase in the autonomy of faculties in decision-making processes, and the creation of academic senates as the autonomous and controlling organs of faculties.

During the 1990s, there was a significant increase in the presence of sociology at the university. In part this occurred in response to requests for courses in sociology by several new departments at Comenius University in Bratislava, as well as at other regional universities, such as Trnava University, the University of Pavol Jozef Safarik in Presov and Kosice, and the University of Matej Bel in Banska Bystrica. In the Faculty of Pedagogy of Comenius University, the Department of Sociology of Education and Sociology of Youth was founded by the

Faculty of Public Administration. Some special areas in sociology, such as urban sociology and the sociology of residential zones, are taught at many natural science and technical departments of other faculties and universities. One could say that since 1989, a systematic reconstruction of sociology occurred within the university, permeating all aspects of the pedagogical process, including a reorganization of personnel.

All regular programs of study are tuition free as guaranteed by the Constitution of the Slovak Republic. However, because of limited capacity and financial restraints, candidates must pass a competitive entrance examination in order to be admitted. For foreign students, there is a tuition charge, but it is affordable. Recently, the programs at the Department of Sociology of the Faculty of Arts at Comenius University, and the Department of Sociology of the Faculty of Humanities at Trnava University have been accredited. The programs in both of these departments are master's degree programs that focus on a single area of specialization, but also offer students the possibility to develop their own professional identities on an individual basis. Study lasts five years. Besides core subjects such as theory, history, and methodology of sociology, a selection of topics from a variety of subareas are offered, depending on the interests of particular faculties as well as the needs of the labor market.

The curriculum also includes supplementary disciplines related to the social sciences, such as philosophy, psychology, ethnology, ethics, history. A strong emphasis is placed on the practice of research and the independent development of sociological projects. Graduates of sociology find employment mainly in the spheres of applied research, public opinion research, marketing, counseling, mass media, and to a somewhat lesser extent, in the nongovernmental organization (NGO) sphere. Academic jobs in institutions of a pedagogical or purely research nature are less appealing because of their relatively low pay.

Private universities do not exist in Slovakia yet, because they are not allowed by current legislation. However, the Department of Sociology of the Faculty of the Arts of Comenius University does offer a special, for paid tuition, three-year-long independent study B.A. program in Human Resource Development. In the country as a whole, approximately 250 students are enrolled in the regular programs of sociology. About 80 students are enrolled in the paid bachelor's program offered by Comenius. Given the needs of Slovakia, this is a sufficient number.

The curriculum of particular faculties and departments is not set in stone. The variety of subjects offered has been increasing. This particularly has been the case at the advanced levels of study, as individuals begin to develop their own areas of interest and professional identities. During the academic year 2000–2001, a crucial change occurred in the educational environment at Comenius University with the transition to the European Credit Transfer System (ECTS). The main aim was to open the studies within the Faculty and the whole University to foreign universities (Laiferova 1999).

At the moment, only the Bratislava Department of Sociology of the Faculty of Arts of Comenius University has been accredited for doctoral studies. Programs of doctoral study are offered both on a full-time (three-year-long) basis, and on a part-time (five-year-long) basis for those students who are not able to live in Bratislava and attend full time. These programs are also open to foreign students, as long as they pay tuition.

In 1990, the Committee for Accreditation at the Ministry of Education and Science began evaluating specific fields of sociological study at the universities. However, the most difficult test of the program of the Department of Sociology of the Faculty of Arts of Comenius University was an international evaluation, supported through the Poland and Hungary Assistance for Reconstruction of the Economy Program (PHARE), which it had to pass in 1998.

The quality of sociological study in all of its forms fundamentally depends upon the accessibility of a wide variety of literature, and the availability of technology such as computers and access to the Internet. Slovakian sociology is lacking in these areas. Most of the available literature consists of Czech translations of the works of classic authors and the latest sociological contributions. Slovak sociological literature only partially covers existing requirements. The capacity of libraries is also insufficient, as is access to the Internet. As we enter the twenty-first century, Slovak universities still do not have adequate technological resources and are not able to offer their students academic conditions and opportunities comparable to those of the economically advanced countries.

NEW CENTERS FOR PUBLIC OPINION

Since the beginning of the 1990s, there has been a robust development in the sphere of public opinion research. In addition to the already existing state Institute for Public Opinion Research at the Statistical Office of the Slovak Republic, the Department of Public Opinion Research was founded at the National Enlightenment Center, under the umbrella of the Ministry of Culture. Several nongovernmental commercial agencies also began to work in the areas of market research, public opinion, and electoral polling. These agencies are affiliated under the Research Agencies Association. An important challenge in this area has been competence and professionalism of the staff. In addition to the foreign agencies, Gesellschaft fur Konsumgutterforschuung (GfK) and the Association for Independent Analysis (AISA), which regularly focus on public attitudes concerning contemporary social problems, the best-known Slovakian agencies are the *Metodicky vyskumny kabinet* (MVK), Focus, and Markant.

SOCIOLOGICAL RESEARCH IN THE 1990S

During the 1990s, Slovak academic sociology systematically investigated citizenship and civic society, modernization and the transformation of the society

(Buncak and Harmadyova 1993), urban communities and local democracy (Faltan, Gajdos, and Pasiak 1995), family (Guran and Filadelfiova 1995), youth (Machacek 1996), minorities (Dzambazovic and Vasecka 2000), social ecology, the history of Slovak sociology (Turcan and Laiferova 1997), education (Ondrejkovic 1997), social theory (Schenk 1993), and qualitative methodology (Kusa 1996).

Several other topics and problems were handled on a more occasional basis. These included social stratification (Buncak and Harmadyova 1993), social institutional change, multicultural education, poverty (Bednarik 1995), gender studies and violence against women (Butorova 1996), human resources management, criminality (Ondrejkovic 1999), media influence, religion, social values, labor and working life, population behavior, the brain drain, health and medicine, social identity (Alijevova 2000), and analysis of social networks.

For research on family, the International Center of Family Studies was created as an independent research agency in 1992. Among nongovernmental organizations, the independent Institute for Public Issues carried out longitudinal research on social and ethnic minorities. The Social Policy Analyses Center conducted social policy research.

In terms of international collaboration in sociological research, in addition to the Czech Republic, Poland, Austria, France and the United States, Japan has been a major partner. In the areas of local community studies and industrial relations, cooperation between the Institute of Social Sciences of Chuo University, Tokyo, and the Institute for Sociology of the Slovak Academy of Sciences has been particularly strong. A special form of international cooperation was established between the Department of Sociology of the Faculty of Arts at Comenius University, and Rene Descartes University in Paris, Nicholas Copernicus University in Torun, Poland, and several Austrian universities. Similar cooperation and exchange was established between the Department of Sociology of the Faculty of Humanities at Trnava, with Cardinal Stefan Wyszynski University in Warsaw, Poland. In addition to these bilateral arrangements, Slovak sociology also participates in multilateral cooperation, in projects of UNESCO, the European Union, Trans-European Mobility Scheme for University Students (TEMPUS), and PHARE. From time to time there has been cooperation with German sociologists.

One obstacle to the participation of the Slovak sociological community in foreign projects has been the insufficient amount of publication based on the results of its research. Consequently, the results of Slovak sociological research have not been included in broader scientific discussions, even in cases that deal with special Slovak problems. Such has been the case, for example, with research on the Roma ethnic minority.

Thematically, one can talk about continuity from the socialist area only in research in the areas of family, youth, and urban communities. After 1989, some new themes were developed in Slovak sociology, such as research on political behavior, elective preferences, and the political system (Krivy 1999;

Szomolanyi 1999). Some areas of research initially disappeared after 1989, only to reappear once again in the wake of offers for collaboration from abroad. Among such topics were religion, work and industrial relations, social stratification, and nations and nationality. In every case, Slovak sociologists who joined in these collaborations had not handled these questions before.

One example is the area of religion. Until 1990, it was monopolized by the Institute for Atheism of the Slovak Academy of Sciences. Its results were not generally made public, and for the most part served Party and governmental organizations in the fight against religion. Following the abolition of the Institute, in 1990, religion was not a topic of sociological analysis until 1998, when an opportunity was extended to participate in an international research project with the International Social Survey Program (ISSP).

New topics that emerged in Slovak sociology include modernization, civil society and citizenship, social transformation and transition, and policy. Topics such as modernization and civil society actually emerged just prior to the end of totalitarian governance, and their initial focus was on the reformation of socialism.

THE PROFESSIONAL ORGANIZATION OF SLOVAK SOCIOLOGISTS

The only professional association of Slovak sociologists is the Slovak Sociological Association (SSA), which is also a member of International Sociological Association (ISA). It has served as the organizational foundation for sociological life in Slovakia for more than thirty-seven years since its founding during the socialist era. Its survival under the transformation may largely have been due to economic considerations. In addition, by the end of the 1980s, notwithstanding Party control, it became an organizational base for critical scientific activities against "official" sociology and sociologists representing the official line. In 1989, this scientific activity developed into political activity on the part of many of its members, and it thereby played a part in the social transformation of 1989.

In 1991, after many of the SSA active members had left to national politics or the commercial sphere, an argument among its remaining members, over the function, purpose, and stance of the organization, shattered the Association. As a result, some members resigned their positions in the Executive Committee. During the 1990s, the ongoing process of politicization and commercialization of the discipline led to such a growing fragmentation that the grounds for common communication, necessary to the functioning of the Slovak sociological community, were endangered. Consequently, the interest of the members in the Association's scientific activities and creative dialogue weakened. Theoretical colloquia organized by the SSA started to suffer from a lack of general attention, and were reduced to meetings of a narrow and specialized circle of participants

(Machacek 2000). This breakdown of communication between Slovak sociologists continues to threaten the organization of scientific life and still endangers the unity of Slovak sociology as a national sociology. Recently, since 1998, there appears to have been a more promising reactivation of SSA activity, though mainly limited to the organization of professional conferences, colloquia, and workshops.

As of 2001, the SSA had approximately 150 members. It gives out an award, the Anton Stefanek Award, for the best graduate work in sociology. Since 1991, the SSA has issued a quarterly newsletter, *Sociologicky zapisnik* (Sociological Notebook), with a supplement *Sociologicky spravodaj* (Sociological Reporter). Within the SSA, there is the Club of Young Sociologists, as well as eight research committees, on sociological theory, methodology, sociology of health care, sociology of the army, sociology of youth, urban sociology, sociology of culture, and social pathology. Its head office is in Bratislava, and there is one branch in Kosice.

Every two years, the SSA organizes a conference. During the conference, the Executive Committee is elected. Because of the processes of political differentiation and commercialization following the transformation, the first professional conference in the 1990s did not take place until 1994. Its theme was "Slovakia in the 1990s: Trends and Problems." Themes of following conferences were "Problem Areas of Slovak Sociology" (1996), "Sociology and the Challenges of Modern Society" (1998), and "Lasting Questions: Slovak Social Science between the Twentieth and Twenty-First Centuries" (2000).

INTERNATIONAL PRESENCE OF SLOVAK SOCIOLOGY

Slovak sociologists are members of many international scientific societies. During 1993–94, Professor Juraj Schenk was a member of the ISA's Executive Committee. Ladislav Machacek is a member of the ISA's Research Committee on the Sociology of Youth (RC 34). Aua Kusa is a member of the European Sociological Association's Research Network on Biographical Perspectives on European Societies (RN 1). Peter Gajdos is a member of the York Academy of Sciences, and Lubomir Faltan is a member of a Programming Board of UNESCO and collaborates with Warsaw University. Slovak sociologists are also present on the boards of editors of foreign journals, such as Zuzana Kusa with *BIOGRAF* in the Czech Republic, Vladimir Krivy with the *Czech Sociological Review,* and Ladislav Machacek with *IDENTITY,* in the United States. Since 1995, Slovak sociologists have used the *Slovak Sociological Review,* published twice a year in English by the Institute for Sociology of the Slovak Academy of Sciences, as a vehicle to present their scientific work to the international community.

CONCLUSION

In the aftermath of the transformation, and formal severance from its Czech counterpart, Slovak sociology finds itself facing a challenging future and in search of its own identity. Important developments during the last decade have provided the foundations for this search. Sociology has been accredited as a specialization at two departments of two universities, and it is taught as an autonomous subject at many academic institutions. Since the latter half of the mid-1990s, sociology has been taught in the high schools. Possibilities for applied sociology have increased considerably within the commercial sphere, nongovernmental sector, and to a certain extent also in the state sector. Perhaps most important, following the fall of totalitarian governance, has been its new multiparadigmatic openness, theoretical pluralization, and wider range of international cooperation, mainly with EU countries and the United States. The picture that is emerging is that of a Slovak sociology conditioned by an overlapping of ideal, confessional, political, and cultural concepts, visions, and influences.

15

Sociology in Slovenia: The Challenge of Transition

Franc Mali

Sociology as an academic discipline first appeared in Slovenia at the beginning of the twentieth century. In the aftermath of World War II, with the constitution of a new social and political order in Slovenia, sociology as an academic discipline disappeared from all university curricula. Sociology, as an autonomous program of study, reappeared in the university curricula in 1960–61 (Jogan 1994, 126). The 1960s and the first half of the 1970s are years during which sociology increasingly cultivated its professional profile. In the middle of the 1970s, political pressures from outside of the discipline caused stagnation in its cognitive development, but did not stop its continued institutional proliferation. This was even more the case during the 1980s, when the ideological pressures on sociologists started to diminish. As a result, even before the sociopolitical changes of the 1990s, there had been an increased professionalization and autonomy of sociology as an academic discipline.

The changes, at the beginning of the 1990s, did not lead to a radical increase in the scientific infrastructure, that is in personnel, institutions, and research funding, but the new social circumstances did bring sociologists new social challenges. And, they have been coping with them quite successfully. As we shall note in further discussion, many, though by no means all, of the social and political aspects of the transitional period have been examined in the research investigations of sociologists. During the 1990s, Slovenian sociologists also increased the level of their cooperation with the international research community. Given the relatively small size of the Slovene sociological community, even greater openness to the international arena will be required in the future. In spite of the numerous problems sociology has encountered in the last ten years, such as the lack of financial support for new research projects and a lack of institutional and teaching flexibility, it has made important social and intellectual progress. It could be said that the progress in sociology during this period was not only one of quantitative growth, but of qualitative improvement as well.

SOCIOLOGY IN THE UNIVERSITY CURRICULA

In 1991, at the University of Ljubljana, the Institute for Sociology was affiliated with the Faculty of Sociology, Political Science, and Journalism. At that time, the Faculty of Sociology, Political Science, and Journalism was renamed as the Faculty of the Social Sciences. As a result of this affiliation, some excellent scientists, who had not participated in the education process before this institutional change, were given the opportunity of participating in pedagogical work. Recently, more than ten years after the relocation of sociologists from a governmental institute to integration within an academic unit, there have arisen some critical voices against such an institutional concentration of sociologists. According to these views, such a concentration reduces the competitiveness of the sociologists in big scientific projects, especially under the conditions of the reorganization of the research funding system in Slovenia (Boh 1999, 13).

Institutional unification, at the beginning of the 1990s, did not retard the processes of diversification in sociological topics. It is not possible on this occasion to list every single subject that emerged in the different sociology programs after 1990. However, both higher education institutions of the University of Ljubljana, where sociology has its domicile at the Faculty of Social Sciences and the Faculty of Arts and Humanities, offer a number of undergraduate and postgraduate programs and areas of study in the field of sociology.

At the Faculty of Social Sciences, the university-level study program leading to a bachelor's degree in the field of sociology is divided into three areas: theoretical analysis, human resources management, and social informatics. Cultural studies could be counted as a fourth sociological subprogram at the Faculty of Social Sciences, although the Department of Cultural Studies is formally separated from the Department of Sociology. Cultural studies were introduced at the beginning of the 1990s, mostly with a focus on sociological topics.

At the Faculty of Arts and Humanities, the undergraduate sociological programs are general sociology and sociology of culture. The sociology of culture program prepares students for general social scientific research of culture. In either case, students must combine these two programs with another major (or minor depending on their selection from the sociology programs) from other programs at the Faculty of Arts and Humanities. The number of students enrolling in undergraduate sociological programs of higher education institutions increased moderately during the 1990s, but it has never caught up with the extreme jump in enrollments that occurred in some other fields of the social sciences, for example, economics and management.

In the 1990s, the postgraduate sociological programs at both faculties where sociological study is offered in Slovenia became even more diversified. During the entire period, the Faculty of Social Sciences offered a wide selection of postgraduate sociological studies, with M.S. and Ph.D. degrees in social ecology, sociology of everyday life, gender studies, analysis of European social policies, social work, management of not-for-profit organizations, and social studies of science and technology. The Department of Sociology at the Faculty of Arts and Humanities offers two M.A. graduate programs, sociology of culture and social anthropology.

LACK OF INSTITUTIONAL AND TEACHING FLEXIBILITY

Given the increased variety of postgraduate programs in sociology in the 1990s, and the small numbers of students enrolled in these programs, it would seem necessary to create new forms of cooperation among them in drawing up joint interdisciplinary teaching projects. Unfortunately, there has been too little cooperation between the faculty members and their own departments, let alone among the different higher education institutions.

In the post-Communist countries undergoing transition, the number of specializations at the university is not always in accordance with real demands. It would be difficult to say that sociology in Slovenia has already reached the phase of overspecialization. Nonetheless, the main issues facing sociology today are not how to further increase the number of study programs, but how to achieve their integration and how to adjust their organizational structures. In addition, there is too much of a concentration of academic staff in sociology at the University of Ljubljana. At the second Slovenian university, founded in Maribor in the 1960s, sociology has practically not been developed at all. At Maribor, there are only a few individual sociologists, and they do not have their own independent organizational unit, that is, a department or institute.

Generally speaking, the teaching structure of the university system in Slovenia is still too rigid. The reform of undergraduate study programs in the direction of a credit unit system is still at its beginnings, although such a necessity is being put into place through the European Credit Transfer System, in cooperation with several countries of the European Union. Although some initiatives for change have already been started by individual institutions of higher education, they have not as yet been fully implemented. The inflexibility of teaching efforts is not only the result of internal blockages, but of external bureaucratic pressures as well. The government has the final say on the formal execution of programs and study courses, on staffing plans, and, as a major determinant of research and university policy, on budget allocations to scientific institutions.

Since the beginning of the 1990s, hardly any private institutions of higher learning have been founded. This is the opposite of the situation in some other Central and East European countries, where the number of nonpublic institutions of higher education has increased tremendously in recent times. In Slovenia, the Institutum Studiorum Humanitatis is the first and only nonpublic higher education institution that is authorized to confer M.A. and Ph.D. degrees for accredited study programs in the fields of sociology, anthropology, and other disciplines of the humanities.

SOCIOLOGICAL LITERATURE AND PUBLICATION

In the 1990s, small private and specialized university publishers took the place of former big state publishers in the production and distribution of books in the social sciences. As a result of this proliferation in the number of publishers, there was a significant increase in the publication of scientific books. As early as the late 1980s, the main academic institutions, where social science research and teaching were situated, had already begun their own specialized publishing activities. However, these newer, small and specialized publishers set more professional standards in the production and distribution of social science scholarship.

Although the quantity of literature, both written by domestic authors and translated from abroad, has increased in the last few years, the growing demand from students and professionals has yet to be adequately satisfied. The most important publishers of scientific literature in the field of sociology in the 1990s were the publishing house of the Faculty of Social Sciences, *Znanstveno in Publicisticno Sredisce*, and *Studia Humanitatis*, an independent publishing house. The Faculty of Social Sciences, which has had its own publishing house since 1991, has taken great care in publishing original sociological texts and sociological textbooks from Slovenian authors. In the first half of 2000, the 100th book of this publishing house was released. Of the100 books, about half were written by authors working in the field of sociology. The publishing house also works closely with young Slovenian authors to give them a chance to publish their doctoral dissertations. Though dedicated primarily to the production of the original monographs of Slovene authors, a significant part of its book production (about 30 percent) has also consisted of translations of foreign works.

Since the 1990s, *Studia Humanitatis* has been publishing a series of books featuring Slovene translations of international literature in the humanities and social sciences. The translations appearing in the series have included a variety of world-famous sociological names. Other small publishers, such as *Studentska Zalozba Cf, Analecta, Annales,* and *Aristej* also originated in the 1990s and have focused mainly on edited monographs within the social sciences. They publish from a variety of social scientific disciplines and professions, keeping the emphasis on small and very specialized series, and within their publishing programs sociological literature has an important place.

Slovene sociologists continue to publish their articles primarily in domestic scholarly and nonscholarly journals, and book proceedings. The main sociological journal is *Druzboslovne razprave*, published by the Slovenian Sociological Association. Other social science journals include *Teorija in Praksa, Nova revija, Anthropos,* and *Casopis za Kritiko Znanosti.* Although their was an increasing interest throughout the 1990s to publish abroad, few articles were published in the major international sociological journals, and journal articles from Slovenian sociologists which are indexed by the Institute for Science Information in Philadelphia were, in the 1990s, very rare.

SOCIOLOGY AND THE SOCIOECONOMIC TRANSITION OF SLOVENIA

The 1990s was a period of extremely important socioeconomic and political change in Slovenian society. Slovenia moved toward the establishment of an independent state, democratic politics, and a market economy. The establishment of an independent state is largely a rather straightforward matter of the establishment of the formal constitutional framework for statehood. The latter changes are much more profound, since they include not only significant social transformations, such as the establishment of democratic institutions, and the privatization and liberalization of the market, but also changes in actual ways of thinking and acting. As a result, a wide variety of important social topics emerged during the transformations of the 1990s.

Generally speaking, during the whole period, sociologists exhibited a high awareness of the urgent social issues of transition. Both the theoretically and the methodologically oriented sociologists had become conversant with the international sociological mainstream prior to the changes of the 1990s. As a result, concepts of contemporary sociological theory, such as social functional differentiation and modernization, provided a strong theoretical basis for critique not only of the deformations within the post-Communist system, but also of the Communist system as such during its final years (Adam and Tomc 1994; Bernik 1992; Novak, Tomc, and Adam 1993).

Slovene sociologists thoroughly investigated many of the most important transitional issues. However, many of these issues, such as the reproduction and circulation of elites, the level of democratic development of Slovene society, and the public role of the Roman Catholic Church, were often interpreted in very different and even contradictory ways. To some extent, these differences may have reflected the differing ideological orientations and worldviews of various researchers (Adam and Makarovic 2001, 194). Although some findings of sociologists did attract attention in the public sphere, they rarely became the basis for any major institutional changes. There were also blind spots in sociological investigations, especially concerning some of the more complex and multifaceted issues.

Slovenia was able to avoid the ethnic tensions that characterized the rest of the ex-Yugoslav region. Nonetheless, various dimensions of ethnic conflict and ethnonationalism drew the attention of Slovenian sociologists, especially during the first half of the 1990s (Klinar 1993; Rizman 1993). There were also some sociological studies of nationalism and the emergence of the new nation-state in the era of globalization (Mlinar 1995). Currently, there is an increased interest in issues concerning the integration of Slovenia into the European Union. Slovenian integration into the EU is a complex process that requires a whole range of reforms and transformations. Sociological studies have examined the specifics of the Slovenian case, including its status as a small state and public attitudes regarding European integration. Recently, emphasis has also been put on the relationship between integration and cultural diversity within Europe (Svetlik and Isac 2000), and on formulating a theoretical framework for a system of social indicators of development with which to compare Slovenia with EU countries (Adam et al. 2001).

The issue of social cohesion demands the attention of sociologists in all transitional countries. Unfortunately, this theme has not been investigated in depth by Slovenian sociologists. Slovene sociologists directed more interest to the issues of neocorporatist arrangements (Rus and Zalar 1996; Stanojevic 1996). The neocorporatist model of decision-making processes and institutional negotiations was accepted as a model by which small countries could maintain a dynamic equilibrium between different parts of society, and between global and local tendencies as well. Of course, sociologists continually have stressed that the new forms of neocorporatism cannot be understood only within the framework of the domination of the political subsystem over other parts of society, as was the case in the former Communist countries, but rather as a modern form of social partnership.

The results of the general sociological analysis regarding concepts such as modernization in post-Communist societies served as a starting point for the empirical analysis of elites in postsocialist countries. The characteristics and performance of elites inspired several directions of sociological study in the 1990s. An empirical study of how the new political elite in Slovenia understood democracy, which was carried out at the beginning of the 1990s, introduced a new course of research (Makarovic 1994). In the second half of the 1990s, studies of the characteristics, attitudes, origins, and interdependencies of new elites appeared. This research provoked extensive discussion among sociologists in Slovenia. Evidence of a relatively high level of elite reproduction in Slovenia was interpreted either as a sign of social stability and the proper adaptation of the "old" elites, or to the contrary as a deficiency in the democratic processes of elite circulation (Adam and Tomsic 2000; Iglic and Rus 1996; Kramberger and Vehovar 2000).

The 1990s brought a lot of new social issues that were previously unknown in Slovenia. Many social groups found themselves particularly vulnerable to the social changes resulting from the move toward what can be sociologically termed a "risk society." Among these marginal groups were the unemployed, the poorly qualified or less educated, and families with many children. Slovenian sociologists had some success in the investigation of the issues impacting these groups (Hojnik-Zupanc 1999; Kolaric 1994; Mandic 1996).

It is clear that isolated actions in the context of the "welfare civil society" are not enough to protect the groups at the social margins. There is a necessity to build a whole system of intermediary structures, especially in those sectors of the society where the increasing social inequalities have especially damaging consequences, such as the health and education systems. Issues of the quality of social services have particularly attracted the interest of sociologists. The impact of privatization on the quality of social services was examined. These studies included analysis of the conflict and cooperation between the public and private sectors, and the regulatory role of so-called quasi-markets in the privatization processes. Special attention was given to human rights, theory and research of social capital, elite integration, new public management, and problems of corruption (Rus and Zalar 1999). Other longitudinal research projects in the field of sociology focused on quality of life (Sadar-Cernigoj, Majda, and Trbanc 1994; Svetlik 1996), and on the changes in value orientations and lifestyles of young people and families (Jogan 1995; Rener and Ule 1998; Ule and Miheljak 1995).

Many of the research projects in the field of sociology were based on Slovene public opinion surveys. Sociologists have carried out public opinion surveys in Slovenia on a continuous basis since 1968, when the Center for Public Opinion and Mass Communication Research was founded at the Faculty of Social Sciences. In the 1990s, there was an expansion of longitudinal public opinion surveys, which have been used to investigate an intensive transformation of values in all basic areas of social life (Malnar and Tos 1995; Tos 1999). The role of public opinion surveys, as a basic source of empirical data for social scientists, was strengthened with the establishment, in 1997, of the Social Science Data Archives (Stebe 1997). It acts as a national resource center for empirical data from academic research as well as from government and commercial surveys.

During the 1990s, there was an important shift in the sociology of religion, sociology of art, and sociology of science toward more empirically based investigations of the social dimensions of religion, the arts, and science in Slovenia. These three fields represent a strong theoretical basis for studying culture in its contemporary, that is, postmodern incarnations. The sociologists of religion tried to use empirical data from public opinion surveys to explain the religious situation in Slovenia, taking into account its social context as a small post-Communist country in transition (Flere 1999; Kersevan 1996; Roter 1992; Smrke 1996). The study of the relationships between religious communities and the state have been broadened to include other religious practices and communities in addition to those of Catholicism (Debeljak 1995).

The sociology of science focused its research on the different social dimensions of science and technology, such as scientometric analyses and surveys of scientists' opinions about research and development policy (Kirn 1994; Mali 2000). Recently, in connection with the social studies of science and technology, there have been some studies of the social changes initiated by the expansion of the Internet and of the related information and communications technologies.

INTERNATIONAL COLLABORATION AND ECONOMIC CONDITIONS

In accordance with the increasing processes of scientific internationalization during the last decade of the twentieth century, there was a rapid attempt by sociologists in Slovenia to reinforce the official and unofficial mechanisms of cooperation with scientists from abroad. It has been estimated that each year during the period from 1996 to 1998, research groups in the field of sociology established an average of more than six formal or informal contacts with partners abroad (Splichal and Mali 1999). This number is higher than in many of the other scientific disciplines in Slovenia. Cooperation with numerous eminent sociological centers in Europe was already established before the 1990s, and continued throughout the decade.

Sociologists from Slovenia have been continuously active in the work of the International Sociological Association (ISA) and the European Sociological Association (ESA). However, while they often have served in the role of conveners of working groups, they have rarely appeared as keynote speakers at plenary and subplenary sessions. Only on occasion have they served as members of executive committees of either association. During the 1990s, Mojca Novak, Maca Jogan, Zdravko Mlinar, and Perter Jambrek were the Slovenian sociologists most prominent in the ISA and ESA.

Participation of sociological research groups from Slovenia in some major multilateral research programs funded by the EU and other supranational institutions was quite insignificant. In order for this to change, sociologists, like their other social scientific counterparts, will need greater support from the government. Although sociological research groups have faced many problems in the organization and management of international cooperation (in some research areas they didn't attain even the so-called critical mass required for a relatively balanced international cooperation), they have succeeded in achieving some good results. However, professional contacts with the sociologists of other East and Central European countries, especially within the context of long-range research projects, have been practically nonexistent. And, during the 1990s, professional contacts with the sociologists of other parts of former Yugoslavia were largely discontinued.

In Slovenia, research and pedagogical work in the field of social sciences (including sociology), is mainly dependent on public funding. At the moment, there exist no private foundations of Slovenian origins, which support the funding of the social sciences. In early 1990, two different governmental sources of funding for university staff were established. The staff of the academies received funding for their pedagogical work from the Ministry of Education. Until 1994, the Ministry of Education did not support research activity, which was considered the responsibility of the Ministry of Science. However, since then all teachers at faculties have been entitled to an annual lump sum from the Ministry of Science for their research activities. These funds can be spent for the purchase of literature, attending scientific conferences, visits to other universities or colleagues, and for exchanges and collaboration.

During the 1990s, the academic staff at universities received support for research projects and programs from the Ministry of Science. Funding was distributed largely through a competitive grants system. It did not increase the cooperation between different research teams or contribute to the building of an interdisciplinary approach. The academy's esprit de corps was undermined as a consequence of increased scientific fragmentation. More recently, the introduction of intermediate and long-range funding of programs has attempted to avoid this fragmentation. For example, in the last two years, instead of 1200 separate research projects, 300 research programs were supported. This represented 80 percent of all public scientific funding. Six of these research programs were in sociology.

In 1999, the ministries of education and science were merged. This institutional unification did not result in any change in the relatively complicated scheme of public financing for academic staff. And, public financing of the social sciences has decreased in the last few years, even though, according to the assessment of foreign experts, the share of social sciences in the overall public funding system should be at least twice its current levels (see PHARE 1994, 110).

THE ROLE OF SOCIOLOGY AND SOCIOLOGISTS

In Slovenia, in the 1990s, several factors speak against simplified views on the role of sociologists as experts. Even though many sociologists were involved in applied research projects sponsored by governmental bodies and local communities, it would be difficult to conclude that adequate use of sociological knowledge in policy-making processes has been achieved. The main conclusion of Slovene sociologist during their annual meetings in Nova Gorica, in 2000, was that they, as experts as well as an independent professional group, did not have enough influence on decision-making processes in politics.

Ideally, sociological research should not contribute only to academic debate, but also to rational policy decision making. It might be expected that in

Slovenia, as a post-Communist society in transition, there would be a high demand for the expert knowledge of social scientists to help in the social and political decision-making processes, especially since the vulnerability of politicians and parties in modern times increases with the lack of scientific knowledge. It is for this reason that in developed political democracies scientific expertise is in constant and increasing demand for policy making. However, the reality in Slovenia is often just the opposite, discussions between scientists and politicians appear to be what one could call, metaphorically, a dialogue of the deaf. This metaphor refers to a conversation between people who talk to each other but do not listen to each other.

The responsibility for the lack of interest in the results of sociological research among political decision makers resides in part with sociologists themselves. Opportunity for the transfer of social scientific knowledge to potential users depends on the ability of scientific disciplines to develop the policy implications of their findings. While academic research in the social sciences in Slovenia is divided, both cognitively and institutionally, into disciplines, the problems that confront public policy makers do not always fall under such conventional headings. And, sociological research is often too descriptive and analytical, lacking any problem-solving orientation. In addition, some sociological expertise could be defined as "partisan expertise," when the production and use of scientific knowledge becomes all too quickly a matter of political opportunism. To conclude, in order for Slovenian sociology to continue to develop, it must not only retain its high level of professional identity and development, but it must at the same time improve its cooperation and collaboration with the broader society.

16

Sociology in Ukraine, 1990–2000: A Decade of Firsts

Nataliya Pohorila

INSTITUTIONALIZATION OF UKRAINIAN SOCIOLOGY

It is widely accepted that the 1990s brought an immense change in the development of sociology in the formerly Communist part of Europe. Although sociology, hidden under the guise of philosophy and economics, existed in a semilegal manner in the Soviet Union, it is not until the 1990s that one can speak of sociology as an independent university discipline and briskly developing empirical science.

Sociology was prohibited as a science in the Soviet Union in 1923. In the Ukraine, the first department of sociology, the sociology of labor, was not established until 1967, in Kiev, at the Institute of Philosophy of the Academy of Sciences of the Ukrainian Socialist Republic. Later, four more departments, social psychology, public opinion, methodology, and economic sociology, were opened in the same institute. Until 1991, no sociological activity in the Soviet Ukraine was conducted outside the work of these departments. Each of the five departments listed above only issued one paper every three years, devoted to the one of its institutional topics.

Publications were extremely rare and subject to severe censorship. Each monograph had to include a substantial preface honoring the Communist Party's deeds. No study could be conducted without the permission of a special body within the Central Committee of the Communist Party. Individual monographs appeared after the defense of candidate or doctoral theses. Some of these publications were based on good empirical and methodological foundations. Among the first was a study of occupational prestige among the graduates of secondary schools (Chernovolenko, Osovskyi, and Paniotto 1979). A study of social mobility in Kiev was presented in a monograph by Serhii Makeev (1989). An original approach to the study of value orientations was suggested and implemented in a series of studies by Lidia Sokhan (Sokhan and Tykhonovych 1980).

In 1990, the Ukrainian Sociological Association was reorganized out of the Ukrainian branch of the Soviet Sociological Association, and Vilen Chernovolenko became the first president. In 1991, building on the already existing five departments of sociology, an Institute of Sociology was established within the National Academy of Sciences (NAS) of Ukraine. In 1991, the first national representative survey, focusing on political culture, was carried out under the umbrella of the Institute of Sociology. Later, the Institute of the Problems of Youth, formerly affiliated with the Ministry of Education, was reorganized into the Ukrainian Institute of Social Research, headed by Olha Balakirieva.

It was approximately during the same period, beginning in 1988, that the first public opinion center, a branch of the All-Union Public Opinion Center (VCIOM) was founded in Ukraine. Later, under the directorship of Mykola Churilov, the Ukrainian branch of VCIOM was reorganized into the research institute Sotsiologicheskoe issledovanie (SOCIS) Gallup, the biggest public opinion center currently in existence in the Ukraine. In 1991, another private research institute, the Kiev International Institute of Sociology (KIIS), was founded by Valeriy Khmelko and Volodymyr Paniotto. Plenty of smaller institutes and marketing firms also began to work. The largest public opinion centers, Ukrainian Survey and Marketing Research (USM), SOCIS Gallup, and Amer Nielsen Research (ANR) conduct more than 100 surveys per year. The public opinion center Sotsialnyi Monitoryng, and the Kiev International Institute of Sociology do between 50 and 60 surveys each year.

The first sociological periodical, *Filosofska i sotsiologichna dumka* (Philosophical and Sociological Thought), was begun in 1989, by sociologists working within the Institute of Philosophy. Nine years later, in 1998, a journal devoted only to sociology, *Sotsiologia: teoria, metody, marketing* (Sociology: Theory, Methods, Marketing) was initiated by the Institute of Sociology of the National Academy of Sciences. The turn around time for publication was reduced substantially in comparison with that during Soviet times. In addition, many sociological works began to be published as monographs or articles in political periodicals such as *Politologichni chytannia* (Politological Readings), *Political Thought* (published in Ukrainian and English versions), and *Politychny portret Ukrainy* (Political Portrait of the Ukraine); in economically oriented journals such as *Ukraina: aspekty pratsi* (Ukraine: Aspects of Labor) and *Sotsialna polityka i sotsialna robota* (Social Policy and Social Work); and in scientific bulletins issued by the largest universities. A collection of the best articles by Ukrainian sociologists, published in English, can be found in the digest *Ukrainian Sociological Review 1998–1999* (Ivaschenko 2000).

Several conferences were held during the 1990s. The most important were a conference on youth held in Zhitomir in 1993, four annual conferences on "Dialogue of Ukrainian and Russian Culture" held in Kiev between1996 and 1999, a conference on social work held in Uzhgorod in 1999, an interdisciplinary conference on Ukrainian elites held in Kiev in 2000, a roundtable, "Restructuring of Personality in Unstable Society," held in Kiev in 2000, and the first all-Ukrainian conference "The Problems of Sociological Theory" also held in Kiev in 2000.

The loosening of authoritarian rule in the Soviet Union, in 1985, led to the beginning of the institutionalization of sociological education. Sociological faculties were opened first in the largest universities of Ukraine, for example, Kharkov in 1985, Kiev in 1986, and afterward Dnipropetrovsk, Lviv, Odessa, and Lutsk. Most of these faculties offered five-year programs of study for between twenty and twenty-five candidates. Gradually, the Soviet model of education was transformed into a Western-style system. Most of the universities offer four-year bachelor's degree programs, and either a degree of Specialist with one more year of study, or of Magister (M.A.) after two more years of study. Two universities, Kiev and Kharkov, and the Institute of Sociology of the National Academy of Sciences prepare graduate students for the Candidate of Science (an equivalent of the Ph.D.) and Doctor of Science degrees (equivalent of the German-style habilitation). Following in the footsteps of the universities, many other institutions throughout the country, mostly teacher's colleges, established sociology departments to offer sociology courses to students in other fields.

During the 1990s, more than sixty textbooks on sociology and its separate branches were prepared for the institutions of higher education. The best textbooks were prepared by Nataliia Chernysh (1996), Olena Yakuba (1996), Nataliia Panina (1998) and Iryna Popova (1998). An encyclopedia of sociology was prepared by Volodymyr Volovych and Valentyn Tarasenko (2000). In addition, the computerization of sociology began in the early1990s, and in the second half of the decade, Ukrainian sociologists received access to the Internet.

During the decade, the first Ukrainian students graduated from international programs on "Society and Politics" in Central European University, first, in Prague, and later in Warsaw, and from the College of Europe in Warsaw. Ukrainian scholars and students were well informed and engaged with the most important sociological problems of world sociology, those of globalization, gender study, poverty, and youth, as well as with problems important for its own national sociology, such as entrepreneurship and ethnic identity.

It can be concluded that the past decade was a time of institutionalization of sociological education and of the growth and development of sociology as a theoretical and empirical science. However, despite impressive achievements, the present situation of Ukrainian sociology is far from satisfactory, even in comparison with other Eastern European countries and Russia. Ukrainian universities prepare fewer than 100 sociologists per year at the specialist level.

Altogether, there are only 30 doctors of sociology (Volovych 1998). Except for those at the colleges in Kiev, all students have problems with access to computers and the Internet, and, without exception, all students lack an opportunity to participate in empirical research and analysis of data in actual ongoing sociological studies.

Even though most of the faculties were opened in the mid- to late 1980s, the first sociological graduates at the level of Specialist did not appear in the Ukraine until the early 1990s. As a result, there is still a shortage of lecturers with sociological credentials. Most of the textbooks, except a few of the best ones, are based on the old Soviet courses of sociology. For this reason, students of the leading national universities are taught using translated versions of sociology textbooks by Neil Smelser, James W. Vander Zanden, and Anthony Giddens.

Financial difficulties also handicap the work of the Ukrainian Sociological Association. For this very reason several periodicals were discontinued, including *Ukrainsky ogliadach* (Ukrainian Reviewer) in 1994, and *Filosofska i sotsiolohichna dumka* in 1997. As a result, the quarterly *Sotsiolohia: teoria, metody, marketyng* remains the only academic sociology periodical in the Ukraine, whereas in neighboring Russia there are four periodicals in sociology.

Prior to the transformation, only the most basic works of classic Western sociology, mostly from the pre–World War II period, were translated into Ukrainian. Some additional works, which were translated in Russia, were available in Ukrainian libraries, those of Talcott Parsons, Georg Simmel, Lewis Coser, Gabriel Tarde, Karl Mannheim, Daniel Bell, Hannah Arendt, Jonathan Turner, and Pierre Bourdieu. However, the prominent works of the postwar period, including those of Jurgen Habermas, Niklas Luhmann, Theodor Adorno, Norbert Elias, John Goldthorpe, Anthony Giddens, and many others, were absent both in translation as well as in original editions. Due to Western-based grants, some key works on global change and social transformation in Eastern Europe appeared in either translation or original language versions. However, most of the empirically based analyses and discussions are absent from the Ukrainian academic scene.

Access to the prominent Western periodicals was no better, and things have not improved much during the last decade. Renowned Western journals such as the *American Sociological Review, American Journal of Sociology,* and the *British Journal of Sociology,* are completely absent from university libraries. They can be found only in the Central Scientific Library in Kiev, and even there only those issues published before the 1980s. Even journals of our Western neighbors, such as the Polish *Studia Sociologiczne,* are available only in this library, and only those issues dated before the 1990s.

To a large extent, economic constraints also explain the situation of Ukrainian research institutes. To begin with, it should be pointed out that the traditional distinctions and boundaries between research institute, public opinion center, and marketing company are not applicable in the Ukrainian situation. Most of the currently existing private research companies began in the 1990s, as state-supported research centers. Because of economic difficulties, their development has taken one of two paths. Either these institutions refocused their academic research and public opinion polls, and became purely marketing firms, such as Ukrainian Surveys and Market Research (USM), or they expanded their research portfolios to include any type of study that could attract support, public or private, such as SOCIS Gallup, KIIS, Ukrainian Sociological Institute, and Social Monitoring. As a result, Ukraine lists ten institutes as members of the European Sociological Association of Marketing and Research (ESOMAR). However, none of them conduct surveys unless financing is available from other entities. For example, because of the lack of its own interviewing network, when it has funding available for a study, the Institute of Sociology of the NAS, which was also formally a member of ESOMAR, contracts its surveys from some of the other institutes.

All of these institutes, except the Institute of Sociology and Social Monitoring, which are partially sponsored by the Ministry of Education, are now in private hands. Since the state-owned Foundation for Fundamental Studies finances an abysmally low number of sociological projects, most of nonmarketing studies have been financed by the United Nations, United States Agency for International Development (USAID), the World Bank, and the like.

One of the most acute problems of Ukrainian sociology is the heavy concentration of academic, educational, and empirical life in Kiev. In contrast to neighboring Poland, where established schools of sociology in Lodz, Krakow, Torun, and Poznan offer a reasonable alternative to the Warsaw institutes, in Ukraine there are few influential centers of sociological thought outside of Kiev. The small number of networks of well-trained interviewers that exist in the country are based in and controlled from Kiev. This means that only Kievan institutes have reliable national representative data. The center of publishing life and the best libraries are also concentrated in Kiev.

Fortunately, there is no conflict between the different generations in Ukrainian sociology, no sense of confrontation between the old Marxist sociologists and the new, progressive ones. The reason is that sociology did not appear in Ukraine until the late 1960s, after Khrushchev's "thaw." The oldest professors are still under seventy, and they work in sociology departments. They do not suppress younger sociologists, because they themselves suffered from Communist censorship. And, even in those days, they perceived Communist ideology only as an unavoidable facade to which their work must pay formal homage. There is, however, an observable gap between the generations, since younger sociologist are often well trained in research methods and computing, are typically fluent in English, and are therefore arguably in some sense better prepared than their professors.

DEVELOPMENT OF THEORY AND METHODS

Ukrainian sociological theory has had to take on two tremendously important tasks. First, to comprehend and explain the reality of the social transformation, and, second, to integrate this highly specific and local knowledge with international sociology. The first theoretical monographs and publications made by Ukrainian sociologists, in *Filosofska i sotsiologichna dumka* (beginning in 1989), were concentrated mainly around the theoretical legacy of Western sociology. In the context of an almost complete absence of Western classical sociological literature in Ukraine, the importance of the work of popularizing Western sociology at that time is difficult to overestimate (see Kutsenko 2000; Kutuiev 1999a; Ruchka and Tancher 1992; and Zakharchenko and Pohorilyi 1993). Due to the endeavors of these authors, the Ukrainian reader could learn for the first time about theories of such sociologists as Jurgen Habermas, Jeffrey Alexander, Richard Munch, Randall Collins, Jonathan Turner, Thomas Kuhn, Florian Znaniecki, and Ken Jowitt, as well as about the elitist school, the sociology of culture, and various approaches to social stratification.

The second half of the 1990s was the time when the first attempts at theoretical generalizations of Ukrainian reality were undertaken. Understandably, these were concentrated on the experience of the systemic transition from Communist to democratic rule. These attempts were summarized at the first all-Ukrainian conference "The Problems of Development of Sociological Theory," held in Kiev in December of 2000 (see Shulha 2001), and in the volume of collected works *Ukraine on the Threshold of the Third Millenium* (Shulha 1999). It should be pointed out that Ukrainian theorizing has been focused on the problem of consciousness in crisis, that is, changes in ideology, psychological adaptation, and appearance of various fears and myths amid the wider public. The work of Iryna Popova offers theoretical analysis of crisis consciousness in its temporal dimension (2000). Pavlo Kutuiev (1999b) has conducted research on the dynamics of the post-Leninist state and its influence on the ability of Ukrainian society to become modern and to implement developmental projects.

A different approach to crisis consciousness was suggested by sociologists who shared a psychological background, and who analyzed this problem in the light of the psychological theory of adaptation to changing conditions (Golovakha and Panina 1994; Zlobina and Tychonovych 2001). The approach of the problem from the standpoint of social psychology has engaged sociology in a wider discourse and new associations, providing opportunities for the classification of adaptation mechanisms and life strategy plans on the one hand, and continuing the Durkheimian tradition and Robert Merton's study of anomie on the other.

As is well known, in the Soviet Union, sociological theory was displaced by historical materialism, and theoretical studies were allowed only as critical reviews of so-called bourgeois science. However, access to scientific literature on empirical methods was more open because of its less ideologically threatening character and potential. As a result, several textbooks that were published in Moscow, with the participation of Ukrainian authors, introduced and explained Western methodology quite sufficiently (Andreenkov and Maslova 1990; Yadov 1987). This relatively favorable atmosphere allowed Ukrainian sociologists to make several independent contributions to the development of sociological research tools. Thus, a method of measuring value orientation, encompassing the cognitive and emotional aspect of values, was developed by Valeriy Khmelko (1984). In the same area of the sociology of personality, Yevhenii Golovakha and Nataliia Panina (1997) worked out an integrated index of social well-being, which is a compressed scale composed of several questions on the perceived deficit of various social resources.

When analyzing the restructuring of the Donetsk coal mining industry, Ukrainian sociologists applied a new approach, based on the reports of local experts, to the social assessment of social projects (Patrakova 1999). In the area of data processing, a simple and convenient package of statistical data processing, *Obrabotka Sotsiologicheskikh Anket* (Sociological Questionnaires Processing or OCA), was prepared by Andrii Gorbachyk.

TOPICS OF SOCIOLOGICAL RESEARCH IN UKRAINE

Although national representative surveys have been conducted regularly since 1991, Ukrainian research activity really picked up only in the second half of the 1990s. Ongoing social analysis of the most topical social issues has been conducted since 1994, and is summarized in both Ukrainian and English in the annual review, *Tendencies in the Development of Ukrainian Society 1994–1998* (Panina and Golovakha 1999).

The main difference that characterizes the organization of research in Ukraine is not its division into research institutes and public opinion centers, but instead, a division into basic and applied science. Under this rubric, public opinion polls, marketing, and social work belong to applied science, and are not considered as academic science. In what follows, I will focus on basic science, or academic research, conducted by the leading research institutes for obtaining knowledge that has no pure or immediate market utility.

In economic realm of social life, Ukrainian sociology has focused first and foremost on economic attitudes, that is, opinions of the mass public on privatization and on private business, and estimation of personal economic well-being, expectations for the future, and so on. Many sociological reports on economic attitudes can be found in two major collections, *Ukrainske suspilstvo na porozi tretjogo tysiacholittia* (Shulha 1999), and *Sociology in Ukraine: Selected Works Published during the 1990s* (Golovakha, Panina, and Vorona

2000). Trend data can be observed in the annual report *Ukrainske suspilstvo: monitiryng 1994–1998* (Vorona and Ruchka 1999).

Work on trends among economic indicators is rather rare, since Ukraine lacks reliable data on material well-being for the Soviet period and the first years of perestroika. Even in the *World Development Report* (see World Bank 1997), the Ukrainian cells for the tables of the main economic and social indicators remained blank until 1994. This is why the big question of the sociology of transformation, namely, whether people actually became poorer following the breakdown of socialism, or whether this was just a matter of deterioration in economic attitudes, remained unanswered. An attempt to estimate household property dynamics from 1982 to 1996 was made by Yevhenii Golovakha (1997). The most detailed and reliable data on the structure of incomes, expenditures, and consumption are available only for 1995 and 1996 (*Incomes and Expenditures of Ukrainian Households* 1996). On the basis of these data, collected by the Kiev International Institute of Sociology, for the first time ever the poverty level was assessed in Ukraine using internationally standardized criteria (Makeev and Kharchenko 1999). The relationship between individual income, and education and occupational skills, for the years 1993–96, was examined by Nataliya Pohorila and Kazimierz M. Slomczynski (2000).

A study of the social structure of the Ukrainian population was undertaken in Kharkov by Olena Yakuba (Yakuba et al. 1997). Theoretical conceptualization and empirical studies on social mobility are presented in the edited collection *Podviznost struktury* (Makieiev 1999). This book contains sections on intergenerational mobility, occupational and educational mobility, and changes in the prestige of occupations.

Another topic, new for all post-Communist societies, is private business, or entrepreneurship. The topic of the private entrepreneur, his or her social situation, professional ethos, and lifestyle became one of the most popular in both Ukrainian and Russian sociology. The impressive number of media discussions, monographs, articles, candidate dissertations, and diploma work on this topic is in stark contrast with the relatively small number of registered private entrepreneurs in Ukraine. The works of Olena Donchenko (Donchenko, Zlobina, and Tychonovych 1995) and Gennadiy Korzhov (1999) consider not only the social and psychological portrait of the Ukrainian entrepreneur, but also examine the wider cultural context of entrepreneurship in a society that has no memory of private initiative and is deeply egalitarian in its orientations.

Interesting empirical work in the area of political sociology has been done on political culture (Golovakha et al. 1993), political discontent (Gorbachyk and Lyzohub 2000), and political regionalism (Khmelko and Wilson 1998). However, the core challenge for Ukrainian political sociology is to close the gap between sociopolitical theory and empirical research on political questions. The first steps in this direction were made by sociologists in studies of the Ukrainian elite (Shulha et al. 1998), the role of mass media in election campaigns (Kostenko 1999), the West-East regional split in Ukraine (Stegnii and Churilov 1998), and the status of public opinion in Ukraine (Osovskyi 1999).

The problem of ethnic relations and migration in Ukraine, newly independent, but with a substantial minority population of Russians (22 percent of the population according to the 1989 census), two-dozen other minorities, and a strong West-East ethnolinguistic split, is one of the highest importance. An impressive flow of publications written by philosophers, politicians, linguists, sociologists, pedagogues, and journalists covers a wide range of ethnic questions. Because the nature of the ethnic question requires an interdisciplinary approach, this wide-ranging interest has not been a disadvantage. The work of sociologist Volodymyr Yevtukh (1997) was used as a foundation for Ukrainian policy toward ethnicity. However, as is the case with political sociology, the challenge for the sociological analysis of ethnicity has been the lack of empirically based research on ethnic tolerance and national stereotypes. A study of ethnic tolerance, conducted by the Institute of Sociology of the National Academy of Sciences, and using a Bogardus scale, is the only example of such a study to date (Paniotto 1999).

A solid empirical basis for migration studies was provided by demographer Iryna Pribytkova, who headed the Center for Study of Population in the National University *Kyiv-Mohyla* Academy (Pribytkova and Zholdasev 2000). She studied migration to large cities, labor migration, and the return of Tatars to Crimea, from which they had been repatriated after World War II. Other topics of migration studies are local aspects of labor migration (Rohatiuk 1999) and transitory migration through Ukraine (Volovych et al. 2000).

Among other topics widely discussed by Ukrainian sociologists was the consequences of the Chernobyl catastrophe. A longitudinal study of post-Chernobyl traumatic consciousness was carried out between 1992 and 2000, by the research group headed by Jurii Saienko. The collected findings from studies of material and psychological damage, social policy toward the victims of the catastrophe, media effects on public opinion, and the first epidemiological study on children of the victims are presented in the volume *Post-Chornobylskyj Sotcium: 15 rokiv pisla avarii* (Vorona, Durdynets, and Saienko 2000).

There are many other topics that so far have been only marginally touched by sociologists of Ukraine, such as gender studies, sociology of organization, urban sociology, the nongovernmental sector, immigrants, and sexual minorities. The weak development in these areas is only partially explained by the relatively low relevance of these questions to the current situation in Ukraine. The Ukrainian scientific community and public opinion simply are unprepared to deal with some of these topics. One such subject is gender studies, which has just recently begun to receive some largely theoretical attention (Melnyk 1999; Zherebkina 1999).

INTERNATIONAL COLLABORATION

An acute problem of Ukrainian sociology has been its insufficient integration into the international comparative context. Despite its unquestionable achievements, Ukrainian sociology has remained outside of the international mainstream, largely because of its weak theoretical base, lack of the internationally accepted terminology, deficit of high standards of statistical analysis, and insufficient publishing culture. Sometimes, Ukrainian authors overstate the uniqueness of the Ukrainian case, even though many comparative West-East studies have demonstrated that there are at least as many similarities as differences.

Ukraine does not have the sufficient finances to join the General Social Survey, nor has it participated in any important international comparative survey. In contrast, Russia regularly participates in such studies, and the Baltic countries occasionally take part in them. Given this relatively low level of international participation, the few international projects that have taken place are of great importance for Ukrainian sociology. The most important has been Melvin Kohn's study of "Social Structure and Personality Under the Condition of Radical Social Change," which was a replication of the study on social structure and personality conducted in the 1960s and 1970s in the U.S.A., Japan, and Poland (Kohn et al. 1997, 2000). The Ukrainian data, obtained through a national representative sample of the urban population in 1993, by KIIS, are comparable to an analogous survey done in Poland in 1992. This work represented the first publications in highly acclaimed Western periodicals, in which Ukrainian sociologists had not previously published. The Ukrainian part of the study was repeated in 1996.

Vladimir Shlapentokh, of Michigan State University, guided another big project. His study "Catastrophic Thinking in the Modern World," was conducted in 1998, in Ukraine, Bulgaria, Russia, and Lithuania (see Gaidys 1997; Mitev, Ivanova, and Shubkin 1998; Shlapentokh, Shubkin, and Yadov 1999). Data from international comparisons with the other countries of transition in Eastern Europe can be found in the New Democracies Barometer Projects, collected from surveys conducted since 1991 by the Paul Lazarsfeld Society of Vienna (Gorbachyk and Lyzohub 2000). Of all the former Soviet Union countries, comparative studies with Russia are the most popular, for example, one that illustrates change in public mood before and after the August financial crisis of 1998 (Vorona, Holovakha, and Panina 1999).

Many studies, although not being comparable, are sponsored by U.S.-based institutions. This was the case with the first epidemiological study conducted with the children of victims of the Chernobyl catastrophe, and on the reproductive health of women, sponsored and supervised by the American National Institutes of Health (Bromet et al. 1998). The contributions of prominent Ukrainian scientists now working in the United States, along with those of their colleagues living in the Ukraine, are presented in the book *Contemporary Ukraine: Dynamics of Post-Soviet Transition* (Kuzio 1998). The same publishing house that issued this book, M.E. Sharpe Inc., and its Editor-in-Chief Tadeusz Krauze, also made possible the preparation of two special Ukrainian issues of the *International Journal of Sociology* (Pohorila 1999–2000).

CONCLUSIONS

Since 1990, Ukrainian sociology developed significantly, starting from the very imperfect publications in *Filosofska i sotsiologichna dumka*, and ending with voluminous collected works that summarized the decade. One could say that this was a "decade of firsts" for Ukrainian sociology. For the first time, professional sociologists were graduated from sociology departments in the Ukraine. The Institute of Sociology of the National Academy of Sciences and the Ukrainian Sociological Association came into being. The first translations of sociological classics from the West saw the light. For the first time, a national representative survey was conducted and the tendencies of development were assessed based on national data. The first professional publications, in which many political and ideological problems were discussed openly and thoroughly, appeared. The first participants in international conferences and educational programs brought their experiences back to Ukraine.

There are many "firsts" yet to come. For example, the first entry into a large international project, the first national journal in the English language, the first internationally acclaimed monograph, and the first international conference to be held in Kiev. Many limitations and drawbacks still face Ukrainian sociology. However, one should keep in mind that Western sociology has been developing for well over a century. In Ukraine, just ten to fifteen years ago, one could not even have imagined or begun to anticipate the immense progress and emancipation that has been the legacy of the last decade.

NOTE

The author expresses deep gratitude to Olexii Bielienok of the Institute of Sociology of the National Academy of Sciences of the Ukraine for valuable help in the preparation of this text.

17

Sociology without Society?: Yugoslav Sociology after 1990

Karel Turza

INTRODUCTION

Dealing with Yugoslav sociology after 1990 is complicated not only because it implies an inquiry into a relatively wide and diverse sociological production, but also due to the fact that both the adjective in the title, "Yugoslav," and its relevant noun, "Yugoslavia," refer to an indefinable entity.[1] In 1989–90, the former Socialist Federal Republic of Yugoslavia was far beyond the pale of where most of the Communist countries found themselves after the Berlin wall had fallen. Owing to its position within the so-called socialist community, but also to a modernizing economic project of the then Prime Minister Ante Markovic, SFR Yugoslavia had at the time a real chance to become the avant-garde of transition and an active participant in European integration, achieving thus the status of a respectable and stabilizing political and economic influence in the Balkan region.

This did not happen. On the contrary, ever since 1991, Yugoslavia has been an epicenter of instability in Europe, in fact, a region where the most evil deeds have become part of everyday life. The wars in Slovenia and, especially, in Croatia and Bosnia and Herzegovina, waged between 1991 and 1995, probably were the cruelest conflicts in Europe during the last fifteen centuries. The geopolitical result was the collapse of SFR Yugoslavia. Regarding the *Lebenswelt* (life-world), more than half a million people have been murdered or wounded, about 2 million people have lost their homes, hundreds of thousands of young people have fled abroad, millions have been pauperized, and the economy, culture, science, education, and health care have all been destroyed.

The Third Yugoslavia (the Federal Republic of Yugoslavia that was formed in April 1992),[2] a sad reminiscence (in fact, only by the name) of a country that was probably doomed to disappear, undoubtedly had various positive qualities. However, due to an aggressive "ethnonationalsocialistic" project and its producer, Slobodan Milosevic and his entourage, it has remained nothing but a mere ruin, a simulacrum of a nation-state, a country without society. The latter means that over the past ten years its hallmark has been "sociocide."[3] This furthermore means that the social structure has been reduced to a rudimentary division between the elite and the masses. The very concrete everyday life of the majority of the population has been reduced to mere survival, accompanied by spiritual, cultural, and political impoverishment.[4]

Sociocide in the Third Yugoslavia came as a result of a decisive neglect, rejection, and suppression of the processes of formation and distribution of the main attributes and conditions of modernity. In other former Communist systems, after 1989, these processes have been identified, first, as the transition and then as the transformation by the then power elite (Lazic 2000; Sztompka 1994). Though abstract, the quite practical effects have been a lack of the affirmation and development of a market economy and private property, the objective conditions of modernity. Instead, a type (certainly the worst one) of centralized economy and state property has existed. In fact, a conglomeration of state and so-called social ownership was maintained during the reign of Milosevic, with the addition of a new, "kleptocratic" private property. Instead of another pair of the subjective conditions of modernity, that is, individualism and rationality, their opposites, namely, collectivism (as ethnic nationalism) and irrational (nationalistic) ideology have remained predominant. All these antimodern instances, mutatis mutandis, had been structural premises of the former Yugoslav system as well, but they had been, so to say, restrained and moderated by the openness of the country and its self-government.

This is just a brief account of the nature of high (or late) antimodernity in Yugoslavia, and of its sociocidal consequences. However, it should be emphasized that the concept of sociocide, which is obviously connected with and definitely developed from a theory of modernity and antimodernity, should not be taken for granted (Turza 1966c, 1998). To boast that this is the key that provides answers to all Yugoslav mysteries, certainly would be inappropriate. For, in this intrinsically irrational milieu, every approach based on a rational logic (and on a logic of rationality) sooner or later exposes its insufficiency. And, the concept of sociocide is a rational construction. This does not mean that those conceptions that are underlain by irrational premises (theory of conspiracy, or of an international plot for pounding the Serbs to pieces, for instance) have offered more valuable insights. Sociology alone, with its rational theoretical and methodological structures, has not been able to capture the full complexity of the Yugoslav case.

DECOMMUNIZATION, DE-MARXIZATION, AND THE *MARXISMUSSTREIT*

It is well known that values have an unavoidable influence upon people, upon their beliefs and the ways in which they think and act. Values have the power not only to affect the common people, but also to influence the topics, issues, or themes that are examined by philosophers and social scientists, as well as the way they are treated by these experts. Our interests, as well as our powers of comprehension, have always been more or less determined by the socio-cultural surroundings and value-world to which we belong.

In the former Communist milieus, philosophers and social scientists were not immune to such influences. On the contrary, the "Communist order of life" was very coercive, much more so than the value-worlds of Western countries. The Communist order of life, combined with or undergirded by a variety of Marxism, constituted its inevitable ideal and practical horizon.

In the so-called Second Yugoslavia, there was undoubtedly more room for various theoretical options than in any of the other Communist countries. Nevertheless, Marxism was the general framework of social thought. Since all other options were more or less ignored, the most important theoretical debates existed within Marxism itself. After the fall of Communism in 1989, Yugoslavia, although it was on the margin of the "big bang," as it obstinately remained the Socialist Federal Republic of Yugoslavia, faced the changes that, in relatively quick order, brought about the destabilization and dismemberment of the country. In Serbia and Montenegro, though their power elites pretended, and perhaps even believed, that socialist Yugoslavia would last forever, all spheres of society, including the spheres of ideology and social and political thought, were severely shaken up. In spite of the fact that Milosevic and his comrades did not get rid of their variety of the Communist order of life, and in spite of the fact that they were very powerful people, the fall of Communism (and Marxism) in Serbia and Montenegro commenced.

On many levels, changes in the political map of Serbia and Montenegro (since 1992, the Federal Republic of Yugoslavia), that is to say, political pluralization and parliamentarianization, brought about the institutional fall of the Communist order of life and of the Marxist paradigm. For instance, the Marxist Centers, institutions that had ambitions to work as institutes of social sciences and which existed within the organization of the League of Communists at all levels, including the universities, were quickly closed. Journals, such as *Marksisticka misao* and *Marksizam u svetu*, which were supported by the then League of Communists, and in which sociologists, among others, used to publish their works and were even engaged as editors, also ceased to exist. In 1990, the Institute for the International Labor Movement in Belgrade changed its name to the Institute for European Studies. Departments of Marxism that existed at some universities in Serbia were transformed into departments of philosophy and sociology. Marxism as a subject was driven out of both the universities and the secondary schools. Most of the publishing houses owned by the state excluded classical Marxist works and many of the more recent books based on Marxism from their publishing programs. New, private publishers, many of them established in 1990 and 1991, were from the very beginning oriented toward non-Marxist or anti-Marxist authors in philosophy and the social and historical sciences, including sociology.

Tendencies toward the decommunization and "de-Marxization" of Yugoslav sociology have been investigated by some authors. Aljosa Mimica and Vladimir Vuletic (1998, 71–94) made a bibliographic investigation of articles that had been published in the journal *Sociologija*, a publication of the Yugoslav Sociological Association, between 1959 and 1996. The study consisted of a citation analysis of the works of Marx, Weber, and Durkheim during that period, in order to reveal changes of theoretical orientation and theoretical "tastes" within the Yugoslav (both former and contemporary) sociological community. Their hypothesis, that in the late 1980s and in the first half of the 1990s there had been a drastic decrease of interest in Karl Marx as a referential author, was absolutely confirmed.

Vladimir Ilic (1999) recapitulated a wide discussion that had been carried out among sociologists in the Federal Republic of Yugoslavia over the past several years.[5] He showed that though the critiques of Marxism within Yugoslav sociology had been heterogeneous, two main streams could be clearly identified, nationalistic and nonnationalistic. The discussion was actually initiated by an article by Mladen Lazic (1996), on the action potential of social groups. In the same issue of *Sociologija*, Aleksandar Molnar (1996) published a critical review of Lazic's theoretical position of Marxist structuralism and sociological realism, from a nominalist point of view. Lazic did not react to the Molnar's comments, but some other authors did.

At the same time this discussion was going on, there were disputes on some other problems among sociologists on the left and the right, such as nationalism. Ilic (1999) concluded that the discussion was primarily about Marxism, and that there were some similarities between it and some foreign disputes on history, social theory, left and right, Marxism, and other topics. In his opinion, the Yugoslav discussion had some elements of the so-called *Historikerstreit*, a debate among German historians and social theorists over the historical reinterpretation of Germany in the twentieth century, which had started in 1986, and lasted a decade or so. That is why, I suppose, the title of Ilic's work was "The *Marxismusstreit*: A Recapitulation." One of the main points of his article was that the debate did clarify two different positions from which Marxism was criticized in Yugoslav sociology, a nationalistic one, and a nonnationalistic or liberal one. And, finally, in Ilic's words, "ethnic nationalism in Yugoslav sociological theory was compromised in the debate, and that was its basic achievement " (1999, 523).

In the next issue of *Sociologija*, Molnar denied that the discussion was all about Marxism. According to him, the main problem was "the relation between democratic and authoritarian [totalitarian] power" (Molnar 2000, 107). He believed that the Marxists, that is Vladimir Ilic and Todor Kuljic (Molnar called them "the neoBolshevist school"), remained on a totalitarian theoretical, and by that fact alone, practical position.

The question that remains open is was this discussion really about Marxism or about totalitarianism? In my opinion, it was about both. And, did it contribute in any way to the "decommunization," which neologism I regard as a synonym for another one, the "detotalitarianization" of Yugoslav sociology? And, what about "de-Marxization"? Is it the essential condition of decommunization, or vice versa? These are two different matters, and they are not necessarily the same. For, Marxism as such cannot be generally treated as a totalitarian social theory, nor can it simply be identified with Communism, except from an extreme position of "liberal fundamentalism."

The discussion among Yugoslav sociologists was very interesting, though perhaps occasionally too passionate and exclusive. It seems to me that there was a certain dose of "liberal fundamentalism" in Molnar's theoretical exclusiveness. In his critique, he did not say a word to condemn the ethnonationalistic stream in Yugoslav sociology, a malign, undoubtedly much more totalitarian and authoritarian option than were the theoretical views of his "neoBolshevist" colleagues, Ilic and Kuljic.

ON ACADEMIC SOCIOLOGY

The Federal Republic of Yugoslavia has always been overcrowded with academic sociology. There are four university centers where departments of sociology exist, five, if the Faculty of Philosophy at the University in Pristina, Kosovo is counted. However, since 1998–99, all connections with the Faculty there have been severed. The Serbs, as well as the other non-Albanians, neither teach nor study there any more, and information about what has been going on there is unavailable. The largest and most developed department of sociology is at the Faculty of Philosophy in Belgrade. The others are at the faculties of philosophy in Nis, Novi Sad, and Niksic (Montenegro). These sociological oases undoubtedly are a form of "capital" that might be used for gaining significant scientific and cultural "profit" in different circumstances.

In an impoverished country such as the Federal Republic of Yugoslavia, universities simply share the destiny of the society as a whole. According to some recent investigations, most of the universities have run into debts that significantly exceed the sum that the Ministry of Education has in the budget, and, thus, the faculties where there are departments of sociology share the penury. The problem is both actual and prospective. Interest in sociology among young people in Yugoslavia has seriously decreased over the past ten years, since the probability that one can get a job as a sociologist has fallen to almost zero. In addition, some of the newly predominant cultural values direct young people very much toward material goods and acquisitiveness. Nonetheless, there have always been more than enough candidates who have applied to study sociology. However, while some ten or fifteen years ago mostly excellent and very good high school graduates were interested in the discipline, during the past several years candidates usually have been young men and women whose performance in secondary school has been below average. Many of them are not interested in sociology at all, they just apply to delay facing a bitter truth that in a society that does not exist any more, they are superfluous in almost every sense.

Prediction is a very dubious sociological endeavor. Yet, I will not be in error, I am afraid, if I say that the situation of sociology departments at Yugoslav universities is hardly likely to get better in the near future. Cold comfort is the fact that sociologists in some other parts of Europe, in rich countries with very rich sociological tradition, share similarly pessimistic thoughts.[6]

In spite of all this, some of our professors have not given up. They have refreshed and innovated the curricula, and a few new textbooks enriched with new theoretical insights have appeared (Djordjevic 1996; Mimica 1999; Pecujlic and Milic 1995; Pusic 1997; Zivkovic and Jovanovic 1997; Zunic 1995). Some new areas of study also have been established, for example, gender and society, and sociology of interethnic relations. Regarding translations of Western textbooks, nothing could have been done until recently due to the international sanctions. In 1998, the translation of an extraordinary textbook, *Sociology*, by Anthony Giddens (1998) did manage to appear.

The international sanctions brought about a lack not only of research cooperation with Western sociology and sociologists, but also of any scientific communication.[7] The same might be said for the relations with Central and Eastern European sociology and sociologists. There have been some individual contacts and cooperation, but they have been sporadic and based on private acquaintances or friendships. Owing to this, however, some Yugoslav sociologists have managed to maintain their presence in the international sociological community (see Antonic 1996; Milic 1996; Vejvoda and Kaldor 1999). In addition, in 1995, in a short "intermezzo" between two periods of sanctions, we had the opportunity to listen to Anthony Giddens and Alain Touraine when they visited Belgrade.

NEW CHALLENGES AND TEMPTATIONS

Though my radical thesis is that Yugoslav sociology has lost its subject (society), I must admit that over the past ten years we (sociologists) have had a unique opportunity to witness and examine many events, processes, and phenomena which our colleagues, particularly those from Western countries, will probably never face. Some six years ago, I met an English sociologist who was very interested in the Yugoslav state of affairs. He asked me, "What does living with a hyperinflation of 10,000,000 percent really mean? What does it actually look like?"

I tried very hard to offer a proper answer, but, in vain. I answered the question, but I had the strong impression that the colleague understood very little of what I was talking about. The same thing happened on three or four occasions two years later. Was it due to a lack of words, terms, or categories? Yes, to a certain extent. In fact, the main reason why I was not completely understood was that some terms, phrases, and categories, from very abstract to quite concrete, no longer carried appropriate or applicable common meaning. The word "inflation" for instance, had an almost entirely different meaning to me as compared to an Englishman, or German, or Italian. Theoretically, inflation is what it is. But, until 1993, there wasn't even any theory that might have explained (or described) an inflation of ten million percent or even more, a practical reality that almost ten million people in Yugoslavia actually and concretely experienced in 1993–94.

Let us be less abstract. "Milk," "bread," "meat," "gas," common words for common (banal) things for an English, or German, or Italian sociologist, and, to me? In a later conversation, I asked my foreign colleague, "What would be your reaction if you found out one morning that there was no milk in shops? In the whole city? In the whole country?"

"I would be astonished," he answered.

"And, if there were no bread, meat, salt, sugar, gas, or medicine in the whole country?" I asked.

"That would be incredible, surrealistic," he said.

Thus, to him my questions referred to something that was, actually, unreal. But, since I had lived in such an "unreal" world for many months and years, his and my conceptual systems simply were no longer congruent. Such is the case with many other words, sociological terms, and phrases.

I consider these exchanges with foreign colleagues very important. Several sociologists have faced the same kind of misunderstanding and blocked communication in their endeavor to adequately present, describe, and explain the Yugoslav situation to foreigners. Therefore, I think it should be one of the main priorities of Yugoslav sociology to build up a corpus of precise, rational, and comprehensible articulations of all the unique phenomena which have been our specialty, but might (not that I would wish it on anyone!) become important to some other sociological communities and societies. This should be done for the sake of better mutual understanding as well as for the sake of enriching general sociological knowledge.

Actually, the first step has already been taken. In 1998, a decision was made by the Institute for Sociological Research of the Faculty of Philosophy at the University of Belgrade to produce an encyclopedia of sociology. It will present, in a communicable way, most of our specific, genuinely Yugoslav problems. In the meantime, our sociologists have had to and still must respond to the challenges that the Yugoslav system of human interdependence has imposed and continues to impose upon them.[8] Thus, let us see, in brief, what they have been dealing with.

In order get an overview of Yugoslav sociological production, I have collected the bibliographies and the most important works of some sixteen sociologists who were among the most representative authors in Serbia and Montenegro during the period 1989–2000. These materials reveal the fact that they all, no matter what their major scholarly interests were, spent a lot of time and energy engaged with various ongoing and often strictly political problems. This is not strange at all, given that since 1989, and, especially after 1991, politics in Serbia and Montenegro has become fate. Political questions, problems, and praxis have occupied every segment, even the most intimate, of people's lives. And, all too often, these have been nothing less than matters of life and death. Naturally, sociologists could not avoid this any more than anyone else within the society.

Fortunately, their more often than not only occasional "visits" to the world of the Realpolitik have not suppressed their sociological *Eros*. Their excursions into the political and public realms during the reign of Slobodan Milosevic were initiated primarily by their need to react as true, active intellectuals, rather than by any desire for power, to the stupidities that Milosevic and his political partners were producing in enormous quantities.[9] However, to a certain number of Yugoslav sociologists, the sweet call of power has been irresistible, and they have entered the labyrinth of professional politics. They, regrettably, might be regarded as a confirmation of the Weberian thesis that the political and sociological professions are generally totally incompatible. A similar problem is shared by those sociologists who were unable to resist the call of ethnonationalism. Though they have not ceased to be sociologists, as have many of the former, they have become, or perhaps have just remained, lousy sociologists.

Generally, sociologists have managed to preserve elements of the scientific infrastructure of the discipline by remaining attached to its fundamental theoretical topics, and by continuing to carry out empirical research, at least to the extent that the circumstances have permitted. That is to say, turbulent social, economic, and political waters, and a living which has too often been reduced to desultory and desperate surviving, have not discouraged and led them away from dealing with significant sociological problems. There is no room in this article for mentioning all the authors, not to mention their articles and books, which have contributed to keeping sociology in Serbia and Montenegro alive. However, a list of the topics and challenges which have most frequently occupied the attention of Yugoslav sociologists over the past ten years includes the following: social structure, social crisis, social conflicts, interethnic relations and conflicts, changes in social structure, state and society, elites and social change, civil society, destruction of society, war and society, media and war, cities and war, post-Communist transition/transformation, political pluralism, democracy, urban life and transition, ideological and value orientations, political parties and public opinion, legitimacy, social movements, political protests, culture in general, culture in transition, family and politics, youth, gender studies, globalization, modernity, postmodernity, historical sociology, the history of sociology, methodology, and multiculturalism.

CONCLUSIONS

Considering the very difficult conditions to which the Yugoslav sociology has been doomed, the sole fact that it still exists could be proclaimed as a success. Yugoslav sociologists, who have had to fight with all sorts of things, even with the vanishing of the subject of their own discipline, and who have steadily "worked" for a whole decade against unimaginable challenges deserve every commendation. Even if we agree with Mladen Lazic's radical thesis, that in the Federal Republic of Yugoslavia there are sociologists, but there is no more sociology, we should not forget that the opposite, if it were at all possible, would be much worse. For, sociologists can breath new life into sociology, as well as to contribute to the renewal of society. But sociology alone, whatever it means, cannot reanimate them.

Anyway, all that remains is hope, and not much of that. And even that little bit of hope vanishes when one recalls that Montenegro may, sooner or later, reach its absolute autonomy as a state. In that case, Yugoslavia will not exist any more and, logically, there will be no Yugoslav sociology either. Regarding this, a very significant indication is that over the past few years sociologists in Serbia have used the phrase "Serbian society" more often than the phrase "Yugoslav society." Do these sociologists have a presentiment of something? Do they know something before a political decision is made? Well, it might be. Maybe, due to that, this article should close with an epilogue, such as an epitaph? Alas, I am not at all good in that genre.

NOTES

1. As I am finishing this article (fall 2001), after almost a decade of its existence, no one in the Federal Republic of Yugoslavia can be sure what this entity actually implies. De jure, it still embraces the two federal units: Serbia and Montenegro; de facto, on the one hand, Montenegro has already gained some important attributes of a sovereign state and, on the other hand, the Serbian authorities have no influence at all, particularly after the NATO military action in 1999, over a part of the Serbian territory, Kosovo (or Kosmet). During the past decade, sociologists have made many attempts to analyze the Yugoslav "state of affairs." The concept that I have been using, since 1992, is sociocide (Turza 1992, 1996a, 1996b). Ultimately, it implies that in Yugoslavia, society sensu stricto no longer exists.

2. Yugoslavia was first formed in 1918, and lasted until 1941. The so-called Second (Communist) Yugoslavia was constituted in 1945 and actually existed until mid-1992.

3. There are certain similarities between results of this analysis and of some others in which the focus has been the destruction of society or its parts (see Bolcic 1994; Lazic 1994; Vujovic 1997). The similarity is perhaps most transparent in Vujovic's (1997) notion of urbicide.

4. The fact has been noticed by many social analysts (Golubovic, Kuzmanovic, and Vasovic 1995; Gredelj 2000; Mrksic 2000). According to Mrksic (2000), in contemporary

Yugoslavia some 40 percent of the population is absolutely poor, another 40 percent lives on the edge of survival, about 15 percent could be regarded as a middle stratum, and finally, some five percent are rich.

5. The majority of participants in the discussion published their works in the journal *Sociologija*. They referred to books that appeared in the Federal Republic of Yugoslavia and to some articles published in *Socioloski pregled* and *Nova srpska politicka misao*.

6. For more information, see some articles by leading, mostly German, sociologists (Ralf Dahrendorf, Wanfried Dettling, Dirk Kaesler, Hans-Peter Mueller, Richard Sennett, Gerhard Schulze) that were published in *Die Zeit*, in 1996. Their translations appeared in the journal *Treci program Radio Beograda* (Darendorf 1996; Detling 1996; Kezler 1996; Miler, 1996; Senet 1996; Sulce 1996). It is curious indeed that we, in Yugoslavia, had posed the question "Who needs sociology?" before our colleagues from the West did; or perhaps it is not, since our reason was unique: our sociology had lost its subject, namely, society.

7. In the Federal Republic of Yugoslavia, three sociological associations now exist: the Sociological Society of Serbia, the Sociological Society of Montenegro, and the Yugoslav Sociological Association (the successor to the former Yugoslav Sociological Association of the period 1954–91). Due to the international sanctions of 1992, the (new) Yugoslav Sociological Association (YSA) was excluded from membership in the International Sociological Association (ISA). A few years later, in 1995, the YSA managed to renew its membership in the ISA, though in principle only. Actually, the membership was renewed in 1998. The title role in the YSA readmittance to the ISA was played by Jennifer Platt, a member of the Executive Committee. The relations between the YSA and the ISA still cannot be regarded as satisfactory.

8. Mike Keen wrote, "just as Central and Eastern European sociology has gained freedom from the intellectual orthodoxies of old masters, a whole new set of influences has emerged in the form of the 'invisible hand' of the market" (Kin 2001, 141). In my view this is correct in principle only. In principle, because in this regard also, the Federal Republic of Yugoslavia is the unique case. "Old masters" have remained strong long after the Berlin wall fell, and the "invisible hand of the market" has been too weak, if it has existed at all. However, since the state has not been providing money, and the regime has not allowed privatization of the six Yugoslav sociological research institutes, they exist nowadays as mere wrecks. Those who work in them, if they have no other job, live very poorly. Fortunately, there are international foundations, such as the Fund for an Open Society and Friedrich Ebert Stiftung, which finance certain research projects on which some sociologists work. In addition, political parties and private newspapers and magazines periodically engage some sociologists in public opinion research. There are six or seven private agencies in the Federal Republic of Yugoslavia that use the skills of some sociologists off and on. Finally, some of our colleagues work in nongovernmental organizations (NGOs). All in all, the situation is bad.

9. In my estimation, the majority of Yugoslav sociologists nowadays share the ethos of responsibility that general social problems, or public issues as C. Wright Mills (1959) put it, should never leave them indifferent. Since 1991, many Yugoslav sociologists were

active participants in the public manifestations and protests against the Milosevic regime. Some of them were even beaten and arrested. Their reactions to how the regime was acting also were manifested in many other, more subtle ways, i.e., through petitions, written protests, open letters, articles, pamphlets, and analyses published in independent newspapers and magazines. In addition, some books appeared in which the results of some very critical research appeared (Kuzmanovic 1993; Mihailovic 1999; Milic and Cikaric 1998; Skopljanac-Brunner et al. 2000; Valic-Nedeljkovic 1997). Collectively, protests were articulated within the Yugoslav Sociological Association and its publication *Sociologija*. For instance, special issues of the journal were dedicated to the destruction of cities in Yugoslavia, then, to the great civil protest in 1996–97, to the consequences of juridical destruction of the Serbian universities, and to NATO military action in Yugoslavia (during which Yugoslav sociologists established correspondence with about 800 sociologists around the world in order to inform the international sociological community of the real effects of bombing). *Socioloski pregled* published a similar issue. Yugoslav sociologists also have learned very much about the ethos of responsibility from numerous brave intellectuals who raised their voices against totalitarianism and authoritarian regimes in former Communist countries.

References

Aarelaid-Tart, Aili, and Indrek Tart. 1995. "Culture and the Development of Civil Society." *Nationalities Papers* 23 (1): 153–165.

Abraham, Dorel, Ilie Badescu, and Septimiu Chelcea. 1995. *Interethnic Relations in Romania: Sociological Diagnosis and Evaluation of Tendencies.* Cluj Napoca: Carpatica.

Aceski, Ilija. 1995. *Sociologija na gradot (hrestomatija).* Skopje: Filozofski Fakultet.

———. 1997. *Opstestvoto i covekot vo tranzicija.* Skopje: Ekspres.

———. 2000. *Sociologija.* Skopje: Filozofski Fakultet.

Adam, Frane, and Matej Makarovic. 2001. "Society in Transition as Reflected by Social Sciences: The Case of Slovenia." In *Social Sciences in Southeastern Europe,* ed. Nikolai Genov and Ulrike Becker, 192–222. Berlin: Social Science Information Center.

Adam, Frane, Matej Makarovic, Borut Roncevic, and Matevz Tomsic. 2001. *Socio-kulturni dejavniki razvojne uspesnosti: Slovenija v evropski perspektivi.* Ljubljana: Znanstveno in publicisticno sredisce.

Adam, Frane, and Grega Tomc, eds. 1994. *Small Societies in Transition: The Case of Slovenia.* Ljubljana: Institute for Social Sciences.

Adam, Frane, and Matevz Tomsic. 2000. "Transitional Elites: Catalyst of Social Innovation or Rent-Seekers." *Druzboslovne razprave* 16 (Special Issue): 223–249.

Adamski, Wladyslaw, ed. 1998. *Polacy '95: Aktorzy i klienci transformacji.* Warsaw: IFiS PAN.

Adamski, Wladyslaw, Jan Buncak, Pavel Machonin, and Dominique Martin, eds. 1999. *System Change and Modernization: East-West in Comparative Perspective.* Warsaw: IFiS PAN.

Adamski, Wladyslaw, and Pavel Machonin. 1999. *System Change and Modernization: East-West in Comparative Perspective.* Warsaw: IFiS PAN.

Afanasyev, Yuriy N., ed. 1988. *Inogo Ne Dano: Sudby Perestroyki, Vglyadyvanya v Proshloye, Vozvrashcheniye k Budushchemu.* Moscow: Progress.

Akhieser, Alexander. 1997. *Rossia: kritika istoricheskogo opita: Sotsio-kulturalnaya dinamika Rossii.* Novosibirsk: Sibirsky khronograph.

Aktualus socialines politikos klausimai. 1999. Vilnius: Agora.

Alapuro, Risto, and Markku Lonkila. 2000. "Networks, Identity, and (In)Action: A Comparison between Russian and Finnish Teachers." *European Sociologist* 2 (1): 65–90.

Alijevova, Dilbar. 2000. "Osobnostna identita: kontinuita verzus diskontinuita." *Sociologia* 32 (4): 319–342.

Allaste, Airi-Alina. 2001. "Alternatiivne noorsookultuur-voitjate voi kaotajate kultuur" (with a summary in English). In *Mitte ainult voitjatest,* ed. Leeni Hansson, 142–154. Tallinn: Eesti Teaduste Akadeemia kirjastus.

Andorka, Rudolf. 1982. *A tarsadalmi mobilitas valtozasai Magyarorszagon.* Budapest: Gondolat.

———. 1991. "Hungarian Sociology in the Face of the Political, Economic and Social Transition." *International Sociology* 6 (4): 465–470.

———. 1993. "The Socialist System and Its Collapse in Hungary: An Interpretation in Terms of Modernisation Theory." *International Sociology* 8 (3): 317–338.

———. 1996. "A tarsadalmi egyenlotlensegek novekedese a rendszervaltas ota." *Szociologiai Szemle* 6 (1): 3–26.

Andorka, Rudolf, and Zsolt Speder. 1996. "Poverty in Hungary in 1992–1995." *Review of Sociology* 6 (Special Issue): 3–28.

Andreenkov, Vladimir, and Olga Maslova. 1990. *Metody sbora informatsii v sotsiologicheskom issledovanii.* Moscow: Nauka.

Angelusz, Robert. 1983. *Kommunikaoo tarsadalom.* Budapest: Gondolat.

———. 2000. *A lathatosag gorbe tukrei: Tarsadalomoptikai tanulmanyok.* Budapest: Uj Mandatum.

Angelusz, Robert, and Robert Tardos. 1995a. "Tarsadalmi atretegzodes es szocialispolitikai identifikacio." *Szociologiai Szemle* 5 (2): 85–97.

———. 1995b. "Social Restratification and Socio-Political Identification." *Review of Sociology* 5 (Special Issue): 65–80.

Antonic, Slobodan. 1996. "Democracy and Political Elites in Serbia." *Dialogue: Journal international des arts et des sciences* 5 (18): 49–54.

Assmuth, Laura, and Aili Kelam, eds. 1998. *Saarte elu murdlainetes: Saaremaa ja väikesaared uleminekuuhiskonnas.* Tallinn: Eesti Teaduste Akadeemia kirjastus.

Astra, Lina, and Bronislovas Kuzmickas. 1996. *Lietuviu tautine savimone.* Vilnius: Rosma.

Atanasov, Atanas, Maksim Molhov, and Emiliya Tchengelova. 2001. *Izsledvaniya na obshtestvenoto mnenie v Balgariya.* Sofia: Nazionalen Zentar za izsledvance na obshtestvenoto mnenie.

Babinski, Grzegorz. 1997. *Pogranicze polsko-ukrainskie: Etnicznosc, zroznicowanie religijne, tozsamosc.* Krakow: Nomos.

Babosov, Eugeny M.1991. *Sociologija confliktov.* Minsk: Belarusian State University.

———. 1992. *Chelovek na poroge rynka: Socialnye ozhidanija naselenija.* Minsk: Navuka i Technica.

———. 1993a. *Sociologicheski analiz posledstvij Chernobylskoi katastrofy.* Minsk: National Academy of Sciences (NAS) Institute of Sociology.

———. 1993b. *Socialnaja ekologija I ekstremal'nye situacii.* Minsk: International High College of Radiology.

———. 1995. *Katastrofy: Sociologicheski analiz.* Minsk: Navuka i Technica.

———. 1996. *Chernobyl'skaja tragedija v ee social'nyh izmerenijah*. Minsk: Pravo and Economica.

———. 1998a. *Etno-nacional'nye konflikty: Puti ih predotvraschenija i razreshenija*. Minsk: Institute of National Security.

———. 1998b. *Socilologija: Obschaja sociologicheskaja teorija*. Minsk: Design-PRO.

———. 2000a. *Sociologija upravlenija*. Minsk: Tetra-Systems.

———. 2000b. *Konfliktologija*. Minsk: Tetra-Systems.

Babosov, Eugeny M., and Vasily V. Buschik, eds. 1999. *Dinamika social'nyh processov v uslovijah gosudarstvennoi nezavisimosti Belarusi*, Vol. 1. Minsk: Pravo and Economica.

Babosov, Eugeny M., Vasily V. Buschik, and Georgy M. Evelkin, eds. 2000. *Dinamika social'nyh processov v uslovijah gosudarstvennoi nezavisimosti Belarusi*, Vol. 2. Minsk: Pravo and Economica.

Babosov, Eugeny M., and Olga V. Tereschenko. 2000. *Prikladnaja sociologija*. Minsk: Tetra-Systems.

Badescu, Illie, Dan Dungaciu, Sandra Cristea, Claudiu Degeratu, and Radu Baltasiu. 1995. *Sociologia si geopolitica frontierei*, Vols. 1 & 2. Bucuresti: Floare albastra.

Bagdonavicius, Vaclovas, and Palmyra Katinaite. 1997. "History of Development." In *Science and Art of Lithuania*, Vol. 5, 3–27. Vilnius: Lietuvos mokslas.

Bardech, Sylvie. 2001. *La transition et reconstruction des societes: Actes du colloque d Ohrid*. Paris: Centtre Nationale dela recherche Scientifique.

Bauman, Zygmunt. 1991. *Nowoczesnosc i zaglada*. Trans. Franciszek Jaszunski. Warsaw: Masada.

———. 1995. *Wieloznacznosc nowoczesna, nowoczesnosc wieloznaczna*. Trans. Janina Bauman. Warsaw: PWN.

———. 1996a. *Etyka ponowoczesna*. Trans. Janina Bauman. Warsaw: PWN.

———. 1996b. *Socjologia*. Trans. Jerzy Lozinski. Poznan: Zysk i Ska.

Bednarik, Rastislav, ed. 1995. *Chudoba ako socialny problem*. Bratislava: Medzinarodne stredisko pre studium rodiny.

Berger, Peter L. 1988. *Zaproszenie do socjologii*. Trans. Janusz Stawinski. Warsaw: PWN.

Bernik, Ivan. 1992. *Dominacija in konsenz v socialisticni druzbi*. Ljubljana: Institut za druzbene vede.

Blom, Raimo, Markku Kivinen, Harri Melin, and Erkki Rannik. 1991. "The Economic System and the Work Situation: A Comparison of Finland and Estonia." *International Sociology* 6 (3): 343–360.

Blyachman, Leonid, and Ovsej Shraratan. 1973. *NTR, rabochyi klass, intelligentsia*. Moscow: Nauka.

Boh, Katja. 1999. "Uvod." *Druzboslovne razprave* 15 (Special Issue): 13–16.

Bolcic, Silvano. 1994. *Tegobe prelaza u preduzetnicko drustvo—Sociologija "tranzicije" u Srbiji pocetkom devedesetih*. Beograd: Univerziteta u Beogradu.

Borkowski, Tadeusz, and Andrzej Bukowski, eds. 1993. *Komitety obywatelskie: Powstanie, rozwoj, upadek?* Krakow: Universitas.

Borowicz, Ryszard, and Krystyna Lapinska-Tyszka, eds. 1993. *Syndrom bezrobocia*. Warsaw: IRWiR PAN.

Borowik, Irena. 1997. *Procesy instytucjonalizacji i prywatyzacji religii w powojennej Polsce*. Krakow: Uniwersytet Jagiellonski.

Borowik, Irena, and Witold Zdaniewicz, eds. 1996. *Od Kosciola ludu do Kosciola wyboru: Religia a przemiany spoleczne w Polsce*. Krakow: Nomos.

Botev, Nikolai. 1994. "Where East Meets West: Ethnic Intermarriages in the Former Yu-
    goslavia." *American Sociological Review* 59 (3): 461–480.
Bourdieu, Pierre. 1993. *Sociologija politiki.* Trans. N. Shmatko. Moscow: Socio-Logos.
Brante, Thomas. 1989. "Samhallsteoretiska traditioner." In *Moderna samhallsteorier:
    Traditioner, riktningar, teoretiker,* ed. Per Manson, 381–405. Stockholm: Prisma.
Breton, Philippe, and Serge Proulx. 1995. *Vybuh kamunikacyi.* Trans. A. Maroz. Minsk:
    Belarus Soros Foundation.
Broks, Janis. 1999. "Labour as a Value in a Transitional Society." *Humanities and Social
    Sciences: Latvia* 1 (22): 49–71.
Broks, Janis, Uldia Ozolins, Gunars Ozolzile, Aivars Tabuns, and Talis Tisenkopfs. 1996.
    "The Stability of Democracy in Latvia: Pre-Requisites and Prospects." *Humani-
    ties and Social Sciences: Latvia* 4 (13)/1 (14): 103–134.
Broks, Janis, Aivars Tabuns, and Ausma Tabuna. 2001a. "History and Images of the
    Past." In *National, State and Regime Identity in Latvia,* ed. Aivars Tabuns,
    42–91. Riga: Baltic Studies Centre.
———. 2001b. "National and Regional Integration." In *National, State and Regime
    Identity in Latvia,* ed. Aivars Tabuns, 173–200. Riga: Baltic Studies Centre.
Bromet, Evelyn, Natalia Panina, Gabriela Carlson, Yevhenii Golovakha, Dmytro
    Goldgaber, Semen Gluzman, and Andrii Gorbachyk. 1998. "Psykhichne
    zdorov'ia ditei poterpilych vid Chernobyl'skoii avarii: dosvid epidemiolohich-
    noho doslidzhennia." *Sotsiologia: teoria, metody, marketyng* 6: 25–52.
Broom, Leonard, Charles M. Bonjean, and Dorothy H. Broom. 1992. *Sociologija.* Kau-
    nas: Littera univresitatis Vytaunti Magni.
Bryant, Christopher G., and Edmund Mokrzycki, eds. 1995. *Democracy, Civil Society
    and Pluralism in Comparative Perspective: Poland, Great Britain and the
    Netherlands.* Warsaw: IFiS PAN.
Brym, Robert J. 1992. "The Emigration Potential of Czechoslovakia, Hungary, Lithua-
    nia, Poland and Russia: Recent Survey Results." *International Sociology* 7 (4):
    387–396.
———. 1996. "The Ethnic of Self-Reliance and the Spirit of Capitalism in Russia." *In-
    ternational Sociology* 11 (4): 409–426.
Buchner-Jeziorska, Anna, and Julia Evetts. 1997. "Regulating Professionals: The Polish
    Example." *International Sociology* 12 (1): 61–72.
Bukodi, Erzsebet. 1999. "Osztaly vagy reteg? Torteneti valtozasok, emberi toke, karrier-
    mintak a foglalkozasi osztaly-es reteghelyzet vizsgalataban." *Szociologiai
    Szemle* 9 (2): 28–57.
Bukodi, Erzsebet, and Peter Robert. 1999. "Historical Changes, Human Capital, and Ca-
    reer Patterns as Class Determinants in Hungary." *Review of Sociology* 9 (Special
    Issue): 42–65.
Buncak, Jan, and Valentina Harmadyova. 1993. "Transformacia socialnej sttruktury."
    Sociologia 25 (4/5): 389–403.
Buncak, Jan, and Milan Tucek. 1999. "Life-goals and Strategies of Individuals in the
    Modernization Process." In *System Change and Modernization: East-West in
    Comparative Perspective,* ed. Wladyslaw Adamski, Jan Buncak, Pavel Machonin,
    and Dominique Martin, 239–252. Warsaw: IFiS PAN.
Burawoy, Michael, and Pavel Krotov. 1992. "The Soviet Transition from Socialism to
    Capitalism: Worker Control and Economic Bargaining in the Wood Industry."
    American Sociological Review 57 (1): 16–38.

Buschik, Vasily V. 1999. *Chelovek i obschestvo v uslovijah social'no-ekonomicheskih preobrazovanij*. Minsk: Pravo and Economica.

Butorova, Zora. 1996. *She and He in Slovakia: Gender Issues in Public Perception*. Bratislava: FOCUS.

Buzik, Bohumil.1997. "Od kritiky teorie k empirizmu." In *O kontinuitu a modernu,* ed. Ludovit Turcan and Eva Laiferova, 19–31. Bratislava: Sociologicky ustav SAV.

Carroll, Glenn R., Jerry Goodstein, and Antal Gyenes. 1990. "Managing the Institutional Environment: Evidence from Hungarian Agricultural Cooperatives." *European Sociological Review* 6 (1): 73–86.

Chalakov, Ivan, Mileva Gurovska, and Yon Glodeanu. 2001. *Telematic Communication Technologies Industrial Comparative Study*. Sofija: Bugarska Adademija na Naukite.

Chalupczak, Henryk, and Tomasz Browarek. 1998. *Mniejszosci narodowe w Polsce 1918–1995*. Lublin: Wydawnictwo UMCS.

Champagne, Patrick. 1997. *Delat' Mnenie*. Trans. N. Osipova. Moscow: Socio-Logos.

Chernovolenko, Vilen, Volodymyr Osovs'ky, and Volodymyr Paniotto. 1979. *Prestyzh profesii i problemy sotsial'no-profesiinoii orientatsii molodi*. Kiev: Naukova dumka.

Chernysh, Mikhail. 1994. "Sotsialnaya mobilnost v 1986–1993." *Sotsiologicheski zhournal* 2: 130–134.

Chernysh, Nataliia. 1996. *Sotsiolohiia: kurs lektsii*. Lviv: Kalvaria.

Clarke, Simon. 2000. "The Closure of the Russian Labour Market." *European Societies* 2 (4): 487–504.

Coenen-Huther, Jacques. 2000. "Production informelle de normes: les files d'attente en Russie sovietique." *Revue francaise de sociologie* 33 (2): 213–232.

Cokrevski, Tomislav. 1994. *Sociologija na pravoto*. Skopje: Praven Fakultet.

———. 2000. *Sociologija*. Skopje: Ljuboten.

Cole, Maria. 1998. "Gender and Power: A Comparative Analysis of Sex Segregation in Polish and American Higher Education 1965–1985." *Sociology* 32 (2): 277–298.

Collins, Randall. 1995. "Prediction in Macrosociology: The Case of the Soviet Collapse." *American Journal of Sociology* 100 (6): 1552–1594.

Conklin, John E. 1987. *Sociology: An Introduction*. New York: MacMillan.

Coser, Lewis Alfred. 2000. *Funktsyi sicial'nogo conflicta*. Trans. O. Nazarova. Moscow: Ideja-Press.

Csepeli, Gyorgy. 1992. *Nemzet altal homalyosan*. Budapest: Szazadveg.

Csepeli, Gyorgy, Laszlo Keri, and Istvan Stumpf, eds. 1993. *State and Citizen: Studies on Political Socialization in Post-Communist Eastern Europe*. Budapest: Magyar Tudomanyos Akademia Politikai Tudomanyok Intezete.

Csepeli, Gyorgy, Antal Orkeny, and Kim Lane Scheppele. 1996. "Acquired Immune Deficiency Syndrome in Social Science in Eastern Europe." *Replika* (Special Issue):111–123.

Csepeli, Gyorgy, Antal Orkeny, and Maria Szekelyi. 2000. *Grappling with National Identity*. Budapest: Akademiai.

Csite, Andras, and Imre Kovach. 1995. "Posztszocialista atalakulas Kozep-es Kelet-Europa ruralis tarsadalmaiban." *Szociologiai Szemle* 5 (2): 49–72.

Csontos, Laszlo. 1999. *Ismeretelmelet, tarsadalomelmelet, tarsadalomkutatas*. Budapest: Osiris.

Csontos, Laszlo, Janos Kornai, and Istvan Gyorgy Toth. 1996. "Az allampolgar, az adok es a joleti rendszer fogalma." *Szazadveg* 2 (fall): 3–28.

Czyzewski, Marek, Kinga Dunin, and Andrzej Piotrowski, eds. 1991. *Cudze problemy. O waznosci tego, co niewazne: Analiza dyskursu publicznego w Polsce.* Warsaw: Osrodek Badan Spolecznych.

Czyzewski, Marek, Sergiusz Kowalski, and Andrzej Piotrowski, eds. 1997. *Rytualny chaos: Studium dyskursu publicznego.* Krakow: Aureus.

Czyzewski, Marek, Andrzej Piotrowski, and Alicja Rokuszewska-Pawelek, eds. 1996. *Biografia a tozsamosc narodowa.* Lodz: Katedra Socjologii Kultury Uniwersytetu Lodzkiego.

Danilov, Alexander N. 1997. *Perehodnoe obschestvo: Problemy sistemnyh preobrazovanij.* Minsk: Universitetskoe.

Danilov, Alexander N., and David G. Rotman, eds. 1997. *Operativnoe sociologicheskoe issledovanie.* Minsk: Vedy.

Darbininkas iriimone. 1974. Vilnius: Filosofijos, sociologijos ir teises institutas.

Darbininkas: Gamyba ir laisvalaikis. 1972. Vilnius: Filosofijos, sociologijos ir teises institutas.

Darendorf, Ralf. 1996. "Zasto danas vise nije uzbudljivo biti sociolog: neke druge discipline daju ton." *Treci program Radio Beograda* 107–108, 116–118.

Davidov, Yuriy, ed. 1997–2000. *Istoria teoreticheskoy sotsiologii,* Vols. 1–6. Moscow: Kanon Press.

Davidyuk, Georgy P. 1979. *Prikladnaja sociologija.* Minsk: Vysheishaya Shkola.

Davidyuk, Georgy P., and Karina V. Shulga, eds. 1984. *Slovar' prikladnoi sociologii.* Minsk: Universitetskoe.

Davies, Norman. 1996. *Europe: A History.* Oxford: Oxford University Press.

Davydov, Yury A., ed. 1997–1998. *Istorija teoreticheskoi sociologii,* Vols. 1–3. Moscow: Canon.

De Graaf, Nan Dirk. 1991. "Distinction by Consumption in Czechoslovakia, Hungary and the Netherlands." *European Sociological Review* 7 (3): 267–290.

Debeljak, Ales. 1995. *Oblike religiozne imaginacije.* Ljubljana: Znanstveno in publicisticno sredisce.

Deiyanova, Liliyana. 2000. "Nevazmoznata kriticheska publichnost." In *Medii i prehod,* ed. Georgi Lozanov, Liliyana Deiyanova, and Orlin Spasov, 240–256. Sofia: Zentar za razvitie na mediite.

Detling, Vanfrid. 1996. "O pitanjima (naseg) vremena sve vise sociologa ima sve manje da kaze." *Treci program Radio Beograda* 107–108, 106–110.

Dimitrov, Georgi. 2001. *Universitetski kurs po sotsiologiya: Kraiyat na XX vek.* Sofia: Universitetsko izdatelstvo.

Dimitrov, Rumen. 1998. *Grajdanskiyat sector: Definizii i klasifikaziii.* Sofia: Fondazia za razvitie na grazdanskoto obshtestvo.

Dimitrova, Dimitrina. 1998. *Trudat na jenite.* Sofia: LIK.

Dinkic, Mlakjan. 2000. *Bela knjiga Miloseviceve vladavine.* Beograd: G 17 PLUS.

Djordjevic, Dragoljub B., ed. 1996. *Sociologija—forever.* Nis: Ucenicka zadruga gimnazije Svetozar Markovic.

Dobelniece, Signe. 1997. "Poverty in Latvia during the Period of Transformation." *Humanities and Social Sciences: Latvia* 4 (13)/1 (14): 199–212.

Doktor, Tadeusz. 1999. *Nowe ruchy religijne i parareligijne w Polsce.* Warsaw: Verbinum.

Domanski, Henryk. 1992. *Zadowolony niewolnik? Studium o nierownosciach miedzy mezczyznami a kobietami w Polsce.* Warsaw: IFiS PAN.

———. 1994. *Spoleczenstwa klasy sredniej.* Warsaw: IFiS PAN.

Domanski, Henryk, Krystyna Lutynska, and Andrzej W. Rostocki, eds. 1999. *Spojrzenie na metode: Studia z metodologii badan socjologicznych.* Warsaw: IFiS PAN.

Domanki, Henryk, Antonina Ostrowska, and Andrzej Rychard, eds. 2000. *Jak zyja Polacy.* Warsaw: IFiS PAN.

Domanski, Henryk, and Andrzej Rychard, eds. 1997. *Elementy nowego ladu.* Warsaw: IFiS PAN.

Donchenko, Olena, Olena Zlobina, and Vsevolod Tychonovych. 1995. *Nash delovoi chieloviek.* Kiev: National Academy of Science (NAS) Institute of Sociology.

Draganov, Mincho. 1991. "Balgarskata sotsiologia pri novite istoricheski usloviya: Diskusiya okolo kraglata masa." *Sotsioligicheski Problemi* 3: 3–24.

Dribins, Leo A. 1994. "Nation State and Its Ethnic Policies." *Humanities and Social Sciences: Latvia* 2 (3): 70–93.

Drobizheva, Leokadia, ed. 2000. *Sotsialnaya i kulturalnaya distantsia.* Moscow: Institute of Sociology.

Druskininkai: socialine ir ekologine raida. 1985. Vilnius: Filosofijos, sociologijos ir teises institutes.

Duka, Alexander, ed. 2001. *Regionalne elity severo-zapada Rossii.* St. Petersburg: Aleteya.

Duka, A., N. Kornev, V. Voronkov, and E. Zdravomyslova. 1995. "The Protest Cycle of Perestroika: The Case of Leningrad." *International Sociology* 10 (1): 83–100.

Duke, Vic. 1990. "Perestroika in Progress? The Case of Spectator Sports in Czechoslovakia." *British Journal of Sociology* 41 (2): 145–156.

Durkheim, Emile. 1968. *Suicide: A Study in Sociology.* London: Routledge & Kegan Paul.

Dzambazovic, Roman, and Michal Vasecka. 2000. "Socialno-ekonomicka situacia Romov na Slovensku ako potenciálnych migrantov a ziadatel'ov o azyl v krajinach EU." In *Socialna a ekonomicka situacia potencialnych ziadatel' ov o azyl zo Slovenskej republiky,* 17–62. Bratislava: International Organization for Migration Slovensko.

Eamets, Raul. 1999. "The Labour Market and Employment." In *Estonian Human Development Report 1999,* ed. Raivo Vetik, 66–71. Tallinn: United Nations Development Programme.

Eglite, Parsla. 1995. "Family Policy during Transition Period." *Humanities and Social Sciences: Latvia* 2 (7): 28–47.

Elsukov, Albert N., ed. 1993. *Istorija sociologii.* Minsk: Vysheishaya Shkola.

———. 2000. *Sociologija.* Minsk: TetraSystems.

Elsukov, Albert N., and Karina V. Shulga, eds. 1991. *Sociologicheskij slovar'.* Minsk: Universitetskoe.

Evans, Geoffrey, and Colin Mills. 1999. "Are There Classes in Post-Communist Societies: A New Approach to Identifying Class Structure." *Sociology* 33 (1): 23–46.

Evans, H.D., Jonathan Kelley, and Tamas Kolosi. 1992. "Images of Class: Public Perceptions in Hungary and Australia." *American Sociological Review* 57 (4): 461–482.

Ezera, Ligita. 1999. "The Development of Ethnic Assimilation in Latvia in the 1990s." *Humanities and Social Sciences: Latvia* 3 (24): 83–96.

Faltan, Lubomir, Peter Gajdos, and Jan Pasiak. 1995. *Socialna marginalizacia uzemi Slovenska*. Bratislava: Social Policy Analyses Centerm.

Felkai, Gabor. 1993. *Jurgen Habermas*. Budapest: Aron Kiado.

Ferge, Zsuzsa. 1996. "A rendszervaltas megitelese." *Szociologiai Szemle* 6 (1): 57–74.

Filantroopia ja kolmas sektor Eestis. 1998. Tallinn: Eesti Avatud uhiskonna instituut.

Filippov, Alexander. 1993. "A Final Look Back at Soviet Sociology." *International Sociology* 8 (3): 355–374.

Flere, Sergej. 1991. "Explaining Ethnic Antagonism in Yugoslavia." *European Sociological Review* 7 (3): 183–194.

———. 1999. "Church-State Relations in Slovenia in the Nineties." *Facta Universitatis* 2:23–26.

Fotev, Georgi. 1993. *Istoriya na sotsiologiyata*, Vols. 1 & 2. Sofiya: Universitetsko izdatelstvo.

———. 1994. *Drugiyat etnos*. Sofia: AI Marin Drinov.

Frentzel-Zagoska, Janina and Jacek Wasilewski, eds. 2000. *The Second Generation of Democratic Elites in Central and Eastern Europe*. Warsaw: ISP PAN.

Frey, Maria. 1995. "Munkanelkulibol lett vallalkozok." *Szociologiai Szemle* 5 (1): 87–100.

Frolov, Sergei I. 1999. *Sociologija*. Moscow: Nauka.

Gaciarz, Barbara, and Wlodzimierz Pankow. 1997. *Przeksztalcenia przedsiebeorstw przemyslowych*. Warsaw: Wyzsza Szkola Przedsiebiorczosci i Zarzadzania.

Gaidys, Vladas. 1997. "The Economic Attitudes That Make a Difference." *The Baltic Review* 13: 45–46.

Gaidys, Vladas, and Danute Tureikyte. 1994. *Nuomones 1989–1994*. Vilnius: Filosofijos, sociologijos ir teises institutas.

Gaizutis, Algirdas. 1998. *Meno sociologija*. Vilnius: Enciklopedija.

Gapova, Elena, and Almira Usmanova, eds. 2000. *Antologija gendernoi teorii*. Minsk: Propilei.

Gazso, Ferenc. 1997. "A tarsadalmi folyamatok es az oktatasi rendszer." *Szazadveg* 7 (winter): 73–107.

Genov, Nikolai, ed. 1991. *Society and Technology in the Balkan Countries*. Sofia: Institute of Sociology Department of Regional and Global Development.

———, ed. 1993. *Society and Environment in the Balkan Countries*. Sofia: Institute of Sociology Regional and Global Development.

———, ed. 1994. *Riskove na prehoda*. Sofia: Natsionalno i globalno razvitie.

———, ed. 1995. *Bulgaria 1995: Human Development Report*. Sofia: Institute of Sociology National and Global Development.

———, ed. 1996a. *Bulgaria 1996: Human Development Report*. Sofia: United Nations Development Program.

———, ed. 1996b. *Society and Politics in South-East Europe*. Sofia: Institute of Sociology National and Global Development.

———, ed. 1997a. *Bulgaria 1997: Human Development Report*. Sofia: United Nations Development Program.

———. 1997b. "Four Global Trends: Rise and Limitations." *International Sociology* 12 (4): 409–428.

———. 1998. *Sotsiologiya*. Sofia: Natsionalno i globalno razvitie.

———, ed. 1999a. *Unemployment: Risks and Reactions*. Paris: UNESCO.

———. 1999b. *Managing Transformations in Eastern Europe*. Paris: UNESCO.

————, ed. 2000a. *Labour Markets and Unemployment in South-Eastern Europe*. Berlin: Wissenchaftzentrum Berlin fur Sozialforschung.

————, ed. 2000b. *Continuing Transformation in Eastern Europe*. Berlin: Trafo.

————, ed. 2001. *Perspektivi pred sociologiyata v Balgaria*. Sofia: Universitetsko izdatelstvo.

Genov, Nikolai, and Ulrike Becker, eds. 2001. *Social Sciences in Southeastern Europe*. Paris: International Social Science Committee (UNESCO).

Genova, Jelka. 1996. *Sotsiologiya*. Plovdiv: Plovdivski universitet.

Georgievski, Petre. 1996. *Sociologija na obrazovanieto*. Skopje: Veda Makedonija.

————, ed. 2002. *Promenite vo socijalnata struktura vo Republika Makedonija*. Skopje: Filozofski Fakultet.

Georgievski, Petre, and Svetomir Skaric. 2000. *Transformation between Marginalization and European Integration: Potential and Shortcomings in the Yugoslave States*. Luxemburg: Austrian Institute of International Affaires.

Georgievski, Petre, and Nelko Stojanoski. 2000. *Le status socioeconomique des etudiantes utilisants de la drogue*. Paris: La Sorbonne.

Gerber, Theodore P., and Michael Hout. 1995. "Educational Stratification in Russia during the Soviet Period." *American Journal of Sociology* 101 (3): 611–660.

————. 1998. "More Shock Than Therapy: Market Transition, Employment, and Income in Russia." *American Journal of Sociology* 104 (1): 1–50.

Giddens, Anthony. 1997. *Sociology*. Cambridge: Polity.

————. 1998. *Socjologia: Zwiezle lecz krytyczne wprowadzenie*. Trans. Joanna Gilewicz. Poznan: Zysk i Ska.

————. 1999. *Sociologija*. Trans. O. Shkaratan. Moscow: Editorial.

Gidens, Entoni. 1998. *Sociologija*. Podgorica: CID.

Gieorgica, J. Pawel, ed. 1998. *Zwiazki zawodowe w okresie przeobrazen politycznych i gospodarczych*. Warsaw: Centrum Partnerstwa Spolecznego DIALOG.

Gijsberts, Merove, and Paul Nieuwbeerta. 2000. "Class Cleavages in Party Preferences in the New Democracies in Eastern Europe." *European Societies* 2 (4): 397–430.

Glinski, Piotr. 1996. *Polscy Zieloni: Ruch spoleczny w okresie przemian*. Warsaw: IFiS PAN.

Goldyka, Leszek, ed. 1999. *Transgranicznosc w perspektywie socjologicznej: Kontynuacje*. Zielona Gora: Lubuskie Towarzystwo Naukowe.

Golovakha, Evgeniy, Natalia Panina, and Valeriy Vorona, eds. 2000. *Sociology in Ukraine: Selected Works Published during the 1990s*. Kiev: NAS Institute of Sociology.

Golovakha, Yevhenii. 1997. *Transformiruiushcheesia obshchestvo: opyt sotsiologicheskogo monitorynha na Ukraine*. Kiev: NAS Institute of Sociology.

Golovakha, Yevhenii, and Nataliia Panina. 1994. *Sotsial'noe bezumiie: instoria, teoria I sovriemiennaiia praktika*. Kiev: Abris.

————. 1997. *Integral'ny index sotsialnogo samochuvstviia: konstruirovanie i primenenie v massovych oprosach*. Kiev: Stylos.

Golovakha, Yevhenii, Nataliia Panina, Yurii Pakhomov, Mykola Churilov, and Ihor Burov, eds. 1993. *Politicheskaia kul'tura nasielienia Ukrainy: rezultaty sotsiologicheskikh issliedovanii*. Kiev: NAS Institute of Sociology.

Golubovic, Zagorka, Bora Kuzmanovic, and Mirjana Vasovic. 1995. *Drustveni karakter i drustvene promene u svetlu nacionalnih sukoba*. Beograd: Filip Visnjic.

Goodman, Norman. 1997. *Wstep do socjologii.* Trans. Jedrzej Polak, Janusz Ruszkowski, and Urszula Zielinska. Poznan: Zysk i Ska.

Gorbachyk, Andriy, and Iryna Lyzohub. 2000. *Political Culture of Society under the Conditions of Radical Social Change: A Comparative Analysis of Poland and Ukraine.* Sociological Series, no. 39. Vienna: Institute of Advanced Studies.

Gordon, Leonid, and Alla Nazimova. 1985. *Rabochyi klass SSSR: tendentsii i perspektivi sotsialno-ekonomicheskogo razvitia.* Moscow: Nauka.

Gorniak, Jaroslaw, and Janusz Wachnicki. 2000. *SPSS for Windows: Pierwsze kroki w analizie danych.* Krakow: SPSS Polska.

Grabowska, Miroslawa, and Ireneusz Krzeminski, eds. 1991. *Bitwa o Belweder.* Kraków: Wydawnictwo Mysl i Wydawnictwo Literackie.

Grabowska, Miroslawa, and Tadeusz Szawiel. 1998. *Anatomia elit politycznych: Partie polityczne w postkomunistycznej Polsce 1991–93.* Warsaw: Instytut Socjologii Uniwersytetu Warszawskiego.

Graf, Eha-Mai, and Maarja Paul. 1997. *Uldsotsioloogia.* Tallinn: Pirgu Arenduskeskus.

Gredelj, Stjepan. 2000. "Vrednosno utemeljenje blokirane transformacije srpskog drustva." In *Racji hod,* ed. Mladen Lazic, 171–236. Beograd: Filip Visnjic.

Grekova Maya. 1996. "Restructuring of the Life-world of Socialism." *International Sociology* 11 (1): 63–78.

Grekova, Maiya, Petiya Kabaktchieva, Liliyana Deiyanova, and Georgi Dimitrov. 1992. *Sotsiologiya za XII klas.* Sofia: Prosveta.

———. 1997. *Nezavarchvachta sotsiologiya: Uchebno pomagalo za X–XII klass na SOU.* Sofia: Filosofska fondazia Minerva.

Grigas, Romualdas.1993. *Tautos savigyna.* Vilnius: Academia.

———. 1995. *Tautos likimas.* Vilnius: Rosma.

———, ed. 1996a. *Paribio Lietuva: Sociologine Paribio gyventoju integravimosi i Lietuvos valstybe apybraiza.* Vilnius: Lietuvos filosofijos ir sociologijos institutas.

———, ed. 1996b. *Lietuva socialiniu pokyciu erdveje.* Vilnius: Lietuvos filosofijos ir sociologijos institutas.

———. 2001. *Sociologine savivoka: Specifika, metodai, lituanizacija.* Vilnius:Vilniaus Pedagoginis universitetas.

Grigoriev, Svyatoslav. 2001. *Vitalistskaya sotsiologia: paradigma nastoyashchego i budushchego.* Barnaul: Altaiskiy Gos. Un.

Gruzevskis, Boleslovas. 2000. "Darbas-uzimtumo strukturos kaita." In *Socialiniai pokyciai: Lietuva, 1990–1998,* ed. Aleksandras Dobryninas, 52–73. Vilnius: Garnelis.

Grzymala-Moszczynska, Halina, and Ewa Nowicka. 1998. *Goscie i gospodarze: Problem adaptacji kulturowej w obozach dla uchodzcow oraz otaczajacych je spolecznosciach lokalnych.* Krakow: Nomos.

Guran, Peter, and Jarmila Filadelfiova. 1995. *Hlavne demograficke trendy a rodina.* Bratislava: Medzinarodne stredisko pre studium rediny.

Gurovska, Mileva. 2001. *Sociologija na zenskiot trud.* Skopje: Filozofski Fakultet.

Habermas, Jurgen. 1971. *A tarsadalmi nyilvanossag szerkezetvaltozasa: Vizsgaladasok a polgari tarsadalom egy kategoriajaval kapcsolatban.* Budapest: Gondolat

Hadzhiyski, Ivan.1974. *Izbrani proizvedeniya.* Vols. 1 & 2. Sofia: Nauka i izkustvo.

Hagendoorn, Louk, Gyorgy Csepeli, and Henk Dekker, eds. 2000. *European Nations and Nationalism.* Aldershot: Ashgate.

Hall, John A. 1994. "After the Fall: An Analysis of Post-Communism." *British Journal of Sociology* 45 (4): 525–542.

Hankiss, Elemer. 1989. *Kelet-europai alternativak.* Budapest: Kozgazdasagi es Jogi Konyvkiado.

————. 1990. *East European Alternatives.* Oxford: Clarendon Press.

Haralambos, Michael. 1989. *Uvod u sociologiju.* Zagreb: Globus.

Haralambos, Michael, and Martin Holborn. 1995. *Sociology: Themes and Perspectives.* London: Collins.

Harcsa, Istvan, Imre Kovach, and Ivan Szelenyi. 1994. "A posztszocialista atalakulasi valsag a mezogazdasagban es a falusi tarsadalomban." *Szociologiai Szemle* 4 (3): 15–43.

Hartl, Pavel. 1997. *Komunita obcanska a komunita terapeuticka.* Praha: Sociologicke nakladatelstvi.

Hausner, Jerzy, Miroslawa Marody, Jerzy Wilkin, Andrzej Wojtyna, and Marek Zirk-Sadowski. 1998. *Przystapienie czy integracja: Polska droga do Unii Europejskiej.* Warsaw: Fundacja im. Friedricha Eberta.

Headey, Bruce, Peter Krause, and Roland Habich. 1995. "East Germany: Rising Incomes, Unchanged Inequality and the Impact of Redistributive Government 1990–1992." *British Journal of Sociology* 46 (2): 225–243.

Heaton, John M. 2001. *Witgeinstein i Psihoanaliza.* Trans. Dinko Telecan. Zagreb: Jesenski Turk.

Heidenreich, Martin. 1994. "Die mitteleuropaeische Grossindustrie im Transformations process." *Zeitschrift fuer Soziologie* 23 (1): 3–21.

Heidmets, Mati, ed. 1998. *Vene kusimus ja Eesti valikud.* Tallinn: Tallinn Pedagogical University.

Helemae, Jelena, Ellu Saar, and Rein Voormann. 2000. *Kas haridusse tasus investeerida?* Tallinn: Tallinna Pedagoogikaulikooli Rahvusvaheliste ja Sotsiaaluuringute Instituut.

Herkel, Andres. 1999. Kas uhiskond on olemas? *Eesti Ekspress-Areen* (Tallinn) 29 July: B5.

Hernes, Gudmund, and Knud Knudsen. 1991. "The Iron Law of Inequality: Different Paths, but Same Results? Some Comparisons between Lithuania and Norway." *European Sociological Review* 7 (3): 195–212.

Hess, Beth B., Elizabeth W. Markson, and Peter J. Stein. 2000. *Sotsioloogia.* Trans. Jaan Soontak and Mait Muursepp. Tallinn: Külim.

Hodson, Randy, Dusko Sekulic, and Garth Massey. 1994. "National Tolerance in the Former Yugoslavia." *American Journal of Sociology* 99 (6): 1534–1558.

Hojnik-Zupanc, Ida. 1999. *Samostojnost starega cloveka v druzbenoprostorskem kontekstu.* Ljubljana: Znanstvena knjiznica Fakultete za druzbene vede.

Holy, Ladislav. 1996. *The Little Czech and the Great Czech Nation: National Identity and Post-Communist Social Transformation.* Cambridge: Press Syndicate of the University of Cambridge.

————. 2001. *Maly cesky clovek a skvely cesky narod.* Praha: Sociologicke nakladatelstvi.

Horrocks, Christopher. 2001. *Marshal McLuhan I Virtualnost.* Zagreb: Jesenski i Turk.

Hoyer, Svennik, Epp Lauk, and Peeter Vihalemm, eds. 1993. *Towards a Civic Society: The Baltic Media's Long Way to Freedom.* Tartu: Nota Baltica.

Huntington, Samuel P. 1996. *The Clash of Civilizations and the Remaking of the World Order.* New York: Simon & Schuster.

Huszar, Tibor. 1979. *Tortenelem es szociologia: A cselekvo ember nyomaban.* Budapest: Magveto.

Iglic, Hajdeja, and Andrej Rus. 1996. "Dinamika sprememb v egocentricnih omrezjih slovenskih elit v obdobju 1988–1995." In *Slovenska drzava, druzba in javnost,* ed. Anton Kramberger, 215–227. Ljubljana: Fakulteta za druzbene vede.

Ilic, Vladimir. 1999. "Marxismusstreit: Rekapitulacija." *Sociologija* 61 (4): 499–530.

Incomes and Expenditures of Ukrainian Households in 1995. 1996. Kiev: Kiev International Institute of Sociology.

Inglehart, Ronald. 1990. *Culture Shift in Advanced Industrial Society.* Princeton: Princeton University.

Ivancic, Angela. 2000. "Education and Shifts between Labour Market States in the Transition from the Socialist to the Market Economy: The Slovenian Case." *European Sociological Review* 16 (4): 403–425.

Ivashchenko, Olha. 2000. *Ukrainian Sociological Review (1998–1999).* Kiev: NAS Institute of Sociology.

Jacyno, Malgorzata. 1997. *Iluzje codziennosci: O teorii socjologicznej Pierre'a Bourdieu.* Warsaw: IFiS PAN.

Jakimovski, Jorde, Dusan Bubevski, and Naum Matilov. 1995. *Vlijanieto na industrijalizacijata vrz socijalnite procesi i promeni na selo vo Republika Makedonija.* Skopje: Institut za socioloski I politickopravni istrazuvanja.

Jakimovski, Jorde, Maria Tacheva, and Vesna Dimitrievska. 1999. *Fokusiranje na siromastijata.* Vols. 1 & 2. Skopje: Edinica za razvojot na coveckite resursi pri Svetskata Banka.

Jakobik, Witold. 1997. *Transformacja gospodarki: Spojrzenie retrospektywne.* Warsaw: ISP PAN.

Jarosz, Maria, ed. 1993. *Prywatyzacja: Szanse i zagrozenia.* Warsaw: ISP PAN.

———, ed. 1997. *Foreign Owners and Polish Employees of Privatized Enterprises.* Warsaw: ISP PAN.

Jawlowska, Aldona, Marian Kempny, and Elzbieta Tarkowska, eds. 1993. *Kulturowy wymiar przemian spolecznych.* Warsaw: IFiS PAN.

Jogan, Maca. 1994. "Modern Slovenian Sociology." In *Eastern Europe in Transformation: The Impact on Sociology,* ed. Mike F. Keen and Janusz L. Mucha, 125–130. Westport, Conn.: Greenwood Press.

———. 1995. "Androcentricna ali androgina kultura in (simetricna) druzina." In *Druzine- razlicne-enakopravne,* ed. Tanja Rener, 49–63. Ljubljana: Vitrum.

Johnson, Lonnie R. 2000. *Central Europe: Enemies, Neighbors, Friends,* 2nd ed. New York: Oxford University Press.

Jonaitis, Vytautas. ed. 1987. *Palanga: kurorto vystymo socialines ir ekologines problemos.* Vilnius: Filosofijos, sociologijos ir teises institutas.

Joppke, Christian. 1994. "Revisionism, Dissidence, Nationalism: Opposition in Leninist Regimes." *British Journal of Sociology* 45 (4): 543–562.

Jovanovik, Amalija. 1997. *Opstestvenata polozba i opstestvenata mobilnost na zenite vo Makedonija.* Skopje: Godisen Zbornik na Filozofskiot Fakultet.

Juknevicius, Stanislovas. 2000. "Lietuviu moralines vertybes: tarp Dievo ir Mamonos." In *Kulturologija,* Vol. 6, ed. Arvydas Matulionis, 192–212. Vilnius: Gervele.

Juozeliuniene, Irena 1993. "The Lithuania National Report." In *Democracy and Local Governance,* ed. Betty M. Jacob, 105–123. Hawaii: Matsunaga Institute for Peace.

————. 1997. "Ethnic Identities and Interethnic Relations in Lithuania." *Regional Contact* 2: 194–206.

————. 1999. "Political Systems and Responsibility for Family Issues: The Case of Change in Lithuania." *Marriage and Family Review* 28 (3/4): 67–77.

Juozeliuniene, Irena, and Vida Kanopiene. 1995. "Women and Family in Lithuania." In *Family, Women and Employment in Central-Eastern Europe*, ed. Barbara Lobodzinska, 155–165. Westport, Conn.: Greenwood.

————. 1996. "Gender Roles and Identity." In *Changes of Identity in Modern Lithuania*, ed. Meilute Taljunaite, 223–240. Vilnius: Lietuvos filosofijos ir sociologijos institutas.

Kabele, Jiri. 1998. *Prerody: Principy socialniho konstruovani*. Praha: Karolinum.

Kalthoff, Herbert. 2000. "Entscheiden unter Ungewissheit: Bankwirtschaftliche Standortsuche in Mittel- und Osteuropa." *Zeitschrift fuer Soziologie* 29 (2): 103–120.

Kanopiene, Vida. 2000. "Uzsiemimu segregacija Lietuvos darbo rinkoje." *Filosofija: Sociologija* 4: 57–65.

Kapr, Jaroslav, and Bohumil Koukola. 1998. *Pacient*. Praha: Sociologicke nakladatelstvi.

Karalius, Alvydas. ed. 2000. *Bendruomeniskumas ir savivalda*. Kaunas: Kauno technologijos universitetas.

Karklins, Rasma, and Bigita Zepa. 1996. "Multiple Identities and Ethnopolitics in Latvia." *American Behavioral Scientist* 39 (8): 33–45.

————. 2002. "Political Participation in Latvia, 1987–2001." *Journal of Baltic Studies* 32 (4): 334–347.

Kartalov, Hristo. 1996. *Sociologija na seloto*. Skopje: Filozofski Fakultet.

Kasatkina, Natalija, and Tadas Leoncikas. 2000. *Lietuvos etniniu grupiu adaptacijos konturai ir eiga*. Vilnius: Lietuvos filosofijos ir sociologijos institutas.

Kavolis, Vytautas. 1992. *Moterys ir vyrai lietuviu kulturoje*. Vilnius: Lietuviu kulturos institutas.

————. 1994. *Zmogus istorijoje*. Vilnius: Vaga.

Keen, Mike Forrest, and Janusz L. Mucha. 1994a. "Eastern Europe and Its Sociology." In *Eastern Europe in Transformation: The Impact on Sociology*, ed. Mike F. Keen and Janusz L. Mucha, 1–10. Westport, Conn.: Greenwood.

————. eds. 1994b. *Eastern Europe in Transformation: The Impact on Sociology*. Westport, Conn.: Greenwood.

Keller, Jan. 1992. *Uvod do sociologie*. Praha: Sociologicke nakladatelstvi.

————. 1995. *Dvanact omylu sociologie*. Praha: Sociologicke nakladatelstvi.

————. 1996. *Sociologie byrokracie a organizace*. Praha: Sociologicke nakladatelstvi.

Kemeny, Istvan, ed. 1999. *A ciganyok Magyarorszagon*. Budapest: Magyar Tudomanyos Aakademia.

Kempny, Marian, and Grazyna Woroniecka, eds. 1999. *Religia i kultura w globalizujacym sie swiecie*. Warsaw: Oficyna Naukowa.

Kempny, Marian, Alina Kapciak, and Slawomir Lodzinski, eds. 1997. *U progu wielokulturowosci: Nowe oblicza spoleczenstwa polskiego*. Warsaw: Oficyna Naukowa.

Kersevan, Marko. 1996. *Cerkev, politika, Slovenci po letu 1990*. Ljubljana: Enotnost.

Kertikov, Kiril, ed. 2001. *Balgariya-Makedoniya: Predizvikatelstva na promenite*. Sofia: Institut po sotsiologiya.

Kezler, Dirk. 1996. "Potraga za dobrim drustvom." *Treci program Radio Beograda* 107–108, 111–115.

Kharkhordin, Oleg. 1994. "The Corporate Ethic, the Ethic of Samostoyatelnost and the Spirit of Capitalism: Reflections on Market-Building in Post-Soviet Russia." *International Sociology* 9 (4): 405–430.

Khmelko, Valeriy. 1984. *Sotsialnaia napravlennost' lichnosti.* Kiev: Politizdat.

Khmelko, Valeriy, and Andrew Wilson. 1998. "Regionalism and Ethnic and Linguistic Cleavages in Ukraine." In *Contemporary Ukraine: Dynamics of Post-Soviet Transition,* ed. Taras Kuzio, 61–80. New York: M. E. Sharpe.

Kin, Majk Forest. 2001. "Razumeti svet koji se menja." *Knjizevni glasnik* 2: 141.

Kirch, Aksel, ed. 1997. *The Integration of Non-Estonians into Estonian Society: History, Problems and Trend.* Tallinn: Estonian Academy Publishers.

Kirdina, Svetlana. 2000. *Institutsionaliye matritsi i razvitie Rossii.* Moscow: TEIS.

Kirienko, Victor V., ed. 1999. *Mentalitet vostochnyh slavjan: Istorija, nastojaschee, perspektivy.* Gomel: Gomel State Technical University.

Kirn, Andrej. 1994. "Znanost in druzba." *Teorija in praksa* 31: 438–441.

Klaus, Vaclav. 2000. Poznamky k Hayekove "nove knize." *Lidove noviny* (Praha) 29 April.

Klicius, Antanas. 2001. "Verslo raida: vingiai ir problemos." *Filosofija: Sociologija* 2: 26–34.

Klinar, Peter. 1993. "O beguncih v Sloveniji." *Teorija in praksa* 30: 75–84.

Kloskowska, Antonina. 1992. "Neighborhood Cultures: Some Aspects of Difficult Historical Neighborhoods." *International Sociology* 7 (1): 55–68.

Kluegel, James R., David S. Mason, and Bernd Wegener. 1999. "The Legitimation of Capitalism in the Post-Communist Transition: Public Opinion about Market Justice 1991–96." *European Sociological Review* 15 (3): 251–284.

Kohn, Melvin, Atsushi Maoi, Carrie Schoenbach, Carmi Schooler, and Kazimierz M. Slomczynski. 1990. "Position in the Class Structure and Psychological Functioning in the United States, Japan and Poland." *American Journal of Sociology* 95 (4): 964–1008.

Kohn, Melvin, Kazimierz M. Slomczynski, Krystyna Janicka, Valeri Khmelko, Bogdan W.Mach, Vladimir Paniotto, Wojciech Zaborowski, Roberto Gutierrez, and Cory Heyman. 1997. "Social Structure and Personality under Conditions of Radical Social Change." *American Sociological Review* 62 (4): 614–638.

Kohn, Melvin, Wojciech Zaborowski, Krystyna Janicka, Bogdan W. Mach, Valeriy Khmelko, Kazimierz M. Slomczynski, Cory Heyman, and Bruce Podobnik. 2000. "Complexity of Activities and Personality under Conditions of Radical Social Change: A Comparative Analysis of Poland and Ukraine." *Social Psychology Quarterly* 63 (3): 187–207.

Kojder, Andrzej, Elzbieta Lojko, Wieslaw Staskiewicz, and Anna Turska, eds. 1989–1993. *Elementy socjologii prawa.* 5 vols. Warsaw: Uniwersytet Warszawski.

Kolaric, Zinka. 1994. "Vloga humanitarnih neprofitnih-volonterskih organizacij v slovenskemsistemu blaginje v 90. letih." *Casopis za kritiko znanosti* 22: 143–150.

Kolarska-Bobinska, Lena. 1994. "Social Interests and Their Political Representation: Poland in Transition." *The British Journal of Sociology* 45 (1): 109–126.

Kolarska-Bobinska, Lena, Piotr Lukasiewicz, and Zbigniew W. Rykowski, eds. 1990. *Wyniki badan-wyniki wyborow 4 czerwca 1989.* Warsaw: Polskie Towarzystwo Socjologiczne.

Kollar, Miroslav, and Grigorij Meseznikov, eds. 2000. *Slovensko 2000: Suhrnna sprava o stave spolocnosti*. Bratislava: Instittut pre verejne otazky.

Kollo, Janos. 1992. "Munkaban es munka nelkul-a fordulat utan." *Szociologiai Szemle* 2 (4): 15–20.

Kolosi, Tamas. 1987. *Tagolt tarsadalom*. Budapest: Gondolat.

———. 2000. *A terhes babapiskota*. Budapest: Osiris.

Kolosi, Tamas, and Akos Rona-Tas. 1992. "Az utolsokbol leszek az elsok? A rendszerval-tas tarsadalmi hatasai Magyarorszagon." *Szociologiai Szemle* 2 (2): 3–26.

Kolosi, Tamas, Ivan Szelenyi, Szonja Szelenyi, and Bruce Western. 1991. "Politikai mezok a posztkommunista atmenet korszakaban: Partok es osztalyok a magyar politikaban (1989–1990)." *Szociologiai Szemle* 1 (1): 5–34.

Konecki, Krzysztof. 2000. *Studia z metodologii badan jakosciowych: Teoria ugrun-towana*. Warsaw: PWN.

Konopasek, Zdenek, ed. 2000. *Our Lives as Database: Doing Sociology of Ourselves*. Praha: Karolinum.

Konrad, Gyorgy, and Ivan Szelenyi. 1979a. *The Intellectuals on the Road to Class Power: A Sociological Study of the Role of the Intelligentsia in Socialism*. New York: Harcourt Brace Jovanovich.

———. 1979b. *The Intellectuals on the Road to Class Power*. Brighton: Harvester Press.

———. 1979c. *La marche au pouvoir des intellectuels: le cas des pays de l'est*. Paris: Edi-tions du Seuil.

———. 1989. *Az ertelmiseg utja az osztalyhatalomhoz*. Budapest: Gondolat.

Koroleva, Ilze, ed. 1997. *Invitation to Dialogue: Beyond Gender (In)Equality*. Riga: In-stitute of Philosophy and Sociology Latvian Academy of Sciences.

———, ed. 2001. *IT laikmets: jaunatne un socialas izmainas*. Riga: Institute of Philoso-phy and Sociology.

Koroleva, Ilze, and Ritma Rungule. 1997. "Old Education in New Circumstances." *Hu-manities and Social Sciences: Latvia* 4 (13)/1 (14): 213–236.

———. 2000. *Narkotiku lietosanas uzsaksanas motivacija jaunatnes vidu Rigas pilse-tas izklaides vietas*. Riga: Filozofijas un sociologijas instituts.

Koroleva, Ilze, Ritma Rungule, Sandra Sebreand, and Ilze Trapenciere. 1999. *Latvijas jaunatnes sociologiskais portrets*. Riga: Filozofijas un sociologijas institutes.

Korubin, Jovan. 1994. *Ziviot pesok-inteligenciata*. Kumanovo: Prosveta.

———. 1999. *Zbogum Intelektualci*. Skopje: Matica Makedonska.

Korzhov, Gennadiy. 1999. "Historical and Cultural Factors of Entrepreneurship Re-Emergence in Post-Socialist Ukraine." *Polish Sociological Review* 4: 503–532.

Kostenko, Nataliia. 1999. *Media v vyborach: mezhdu politikoi i kulturoi*. Kiev: NAS In-stitute of Sociology.

Kozek, Wieslawa, and Jolanta Kulpinska, eds. 1998. *Zbiorowe stosunki pracy w Polsce: Obraz zmian*. Warsaw: Scholar.

Kramberger, Anton, and Vasja Vehovar. 2000. "Regime Change and Elite Dynamics in Slovenia during the 1990s: What Can the Elite Reproduction Rates Tell Us?" *Druzboslovne razprave* 16 (Special Issue): 143–181.

Krasko, Nina. 1996. *Instytucjonalizacja socjologii w Polsce 1920–1970*. Warsaw: PWN.

Krasnodebski, Zdzislaw. 1998. Profesorowie i rolnicy. *Zycie* (Warsaw) 6 July: 11.

Kravchenko, Nikolai S. 1997a. *Sociologija*. Moscow: Academia.

———. 1997b. *Sociologija: Sbornik zadach*. Moscow: Academia.

————. 1997c. *Sociologija: Slovar'*. Moscow: Academia.

————. 1997d. *Sociologija: Hrestomatija*. Moscow: Academia.

Krikstopaitis, Juozas A. 1997. *Prievarta patyrusiu laikysena*. Vilnius: Pradai.

Krivy, Vladimir. 1999. "Elections Results 1998–1999." In *Slovakia 1998–1999*, ed. Grigorij Meseznikov, Michal Ivantysyn, and Thomas Nicholson. Bratislava: Instittut pre verejne otazky.

Krukauskiene, Eugenija, ed. 2000. *Europos keliu*. Vilnius: Lietuvos filosofijos ir sociologijos institutas.

Kruusvall, Juri. 1994. *Environmental and Social Influence on Human Activity*. Tartu: Tartu University Press.

————. 1998a. "Disturbances and Expectations Concerning State Ethnopolicy among Estonians and Non-Estonians." In *Pilsoniska apsina*, ed. Elmars Vebers, 272–283. Riga: IU Macibu apgabs.

————. 1998b. "Usaldus ja usaldamatus rahvussuhetes." In *Vene Kusimus ja Eesti* valikud, ed. Mati Heidmets, 29–76. Tartu: Tartu University.

Krymkowski, Daniel H. 1991. "The Process of Status Attainment among Men in Poland, the U.S. and West Germany." *American Sociological Review* 56 (1): 46–59.

Kryshtanovskaya, Olga. 1998. "Transformatsiya staroy nomenklatury v novuyu rossiyskuyu elitu." In *Transformatsiya socialnoy struktury i stratifikatsiya rossiyskogo obshchestva*, ed. Zinaoda Golenkova, 263–288. Moscow: Institute of Sociology.

Krzeminski, Ireneusz, ed. 1996. *Czy Polacy sa antysemitami? Wyniki badania sondazowego*. Warsaw: Oficyna Naukowa.

Kubiak, Hieronim, ed. 1997. *Partie polityczne w wielkim miescie: Szkice do portretu partii politycznych w Krakowie*. Krakow: Instytut Socjologii Uniwersytetu Jagiellonskiego.

Kubiak, Hieronim, and Jerzy Wiatr, eds. 2000. *Between Animosity and Utility: Political Parties and Their Matrix*. Warsaw: Scholar.

Kuhn, Thomas S. 1999. *Struktura Znanstvenih Revolucija*. Trans. Mirna Zelic. Zagreb: Jesenski i Turk.

Kultura i Spoleczenstwo. 1993. "Problemy badaczy w badaniach spoleczenstwa polskiego w dobie transformacji: Przeglad perspektyw badawczych." *Kultura i Spoleczenstwo* 37 (3): Special Issue.

————. 1994. "Przeobrazenia swiadomosci i struktury spolecznej." *Kultura i Spoleczenstwo* 38 (1): Special Issue.

————. 1995. "Biografia a tozsamosc narodowa." 1995. *Kultura i Spoleczenstwo* 39 (4): Special Issue.

————. 1998. "Bieda i cierpienie." *Kultura i Spoleczenstwo* 42 (2): Special Issue.

————. 1999. "Narodziny badan opinii publicznej w Polsce." *Kultura i Spoleczenstwo* 43 (4): Special Issue.

Kupferberg, Feiwel. 1996. "Strategic Learning: East Germany as a 'Mode Case' for Transformation Theory." *International Sociology* 11 (4): 457–480.

Kurcz, Zbigniew. 1995. *Mniejszosc niemiecka w Polsce*. Wroclaw: Wydawnictwo Uniwersytetu Wroclawskiego.

Kurczewski, Jacek, and Iwona Jakubowska-Branicka, eds. 1994. *Biznes i klasy srednie: Studia nad etosem*. Warsaw: Instytut Stosowanych Nauk Spolecznych Uniwersytetu Warszawskiego.

Kusa, Zuzana. 1996. "Komunikacia na strankach casopisu Sociologia." In *Problemove polia slovenskej sociologie*, ed. Zuzana Kusa, 17–23. Bratislava: SSS.

———. 1997. "Nechcena kontinuita?" In *O kontinuitu a modernu*, ed. Ludovit Turcan and Eva Laiferova, 155–160. Bratislava: Sociologicky ustav SAV.

Kutsar, Dagmar. 1995. *Transformation in Estonia as Reflected in Families: Insight into Social Stress and Poverty*. Tartu: Tartu University Press.

———, ed. 2000. *Children in Estonia*. Tallinn: United Nations Development Program.

Kutsar, Dagmar, and Avo Trumm. 1998. "Poverty as an Obstacle to the Realization of Human Rights." In *Human Rights in Estonia*, ed. Anu Narusk, 11–18. Tallinn: United Nations Development Programme.

Kutsenko, Olena. 2000. *Obschestvo nieravnykh. Klassovyi analiz nieravenstv v sovriemiennom obschestve: opyt zapadnykh sotsiologov*. Kharkov: Kharkov National University.

Kutuiev, Pavlo. 1999a. "Democracy, State and Development: The Case of Post-Leninist Ukraine." *Naukovi zapysky* 11: 4–12.

———. 1999b. "Ratsionalny kapitalism v Ukraini: mizh mifom ta realnistiu." *Sotsiologia: teoria, metody, marketing* 2: 5–20.

Kuzio, Taras, ed. 1998. *Contemporary Ukraine: Dynamics of Post-Soviet Transition*. New York: M.E. Sharpe.

Kuzmanovic, Bora. 1993. *Studentski protest '92*. Beograd: Univerziteta u Beogradu.

Kwasniewicz, Wladyslaw. 1998. "Wspolczesne realia uniwersyteckiego ksztalcenia socjologow." *Ruch Prawniczy, Ekonomiczny i Socjologiczny* 60 (3/4): 431–442.

Laaman, Ed. 1936. *Eestiuuhiskond: selle koostis, areng ja iseloom*. Tartu: Eesti Kirjanduse Selts.

Labath, Vladimir. 2001. *Rizikova mladez*. Praha: Sociologicke nakladatelstvi.

Ladanyi, Janos, and Ivan Szelenyi. 1995. "Egy posztkommunista 'New Deal,' eselyei I." *Kritika* 12 (1): 8–13.

———. 1996. "Egy posztkommunista 'New Deal,' eselyei II." *Kritika* 13 (1): 30–33.

Lagerspetz, Mikko. 1996. *Constructing Post-Communism: A Study in the Estonian Social Problems Discourse*. Turku: University of Turku.

———. 2001. "From 'Parallel Polis' to 'The Time of the Tribes': Post-Socialism, Social Self-Organization and Post-Modernity." *Journal of Communist Studies and Transition Politics* 17 (2): 1–18.

Lagerspetz, Mikko, Krista Loogma, and Pille Kaselo. 1998. "Waiting for the Citizen: The Views of Estonian Influential Groups on Social Problems." In *Journalists, Administrators and Business People on Social Problems: A Study around the Baltic Sea*, ed. Sari Hanhinen and Jukka Torronen, 33–58. Helsinki: Nordic Council for Alcohol and Drug Research.

Lagerspetz, Mikko, Rein Ruutsoo, and Erle Rikmann. 2000. "Olelemisest osalemiseni? Eesti kodanikualgatuse hetkeseis ja arenguvõimalused" (with an English summary, "From Vegetation to Participation? The Present and Future of Civic Initiative in Estonia"). *Akadeemia* 12 (2): 269–298.

Laiferova, Eva.1995. "70 rokov odboru sociologie na FF UK v Bratislave." In *Sociologia v meniacej sa spolocnosti*, ed. Eva Laiferova, 3–20. Bratislava: Katedra sociologie FF UK.

———. 1999. "Vyucba sociologie pre sociologov a nesociologov: Aktualne podnety a ich vplyv na obsah, metodiku a ciele pedagogickeho procesu." *Sociologia* 31 (5): 515–526.

Lakis, Juozas. 1995. "Ethnic Minorities in the Postcommunist Transformation in Lithuania." *International Sociology* 10 (2): 173–184.

Lakis, Peteris. 1997. "Mechanisms for Establishment of a Political Elite in Post-Communist Societies." *Humanities and Social Sciences: Latvia* 4 (13)/1 (14): 199–212.

Laky, Terez. 1992. "A privatizacio magyarorszagi sajatossagai es nehany erzekelheto tarsadalmi hatasa." *Szociologiai Szemle* 2 (1): 45–61.

Lapin, Nikolai. 2000. "Inversiya dominantnikh protsesov sotsio-kulturno transformatsii." In *Ezhegodnik ROS: Dinamika sotsialnikh teorii,* ed. Valery Mansurov, 56–72. Moscow: ROS.

Lauristin, Marju, and Peeter Vihalemm, eds. 1997. *Return to the Western World: Cultural and Political Perspectives on the Estonian Post-Communist Transition.* Tartu: Tartu University Press.

Lazic, Mladen, ed. 1994. *Razaranje drustva – Jugoslovensko drustvo u krizi devedesetih.* Beograd: Filip Visnjic.

———. 1996. "Delatni potencijal drustvenih grupa." *Sociologija* 38 (2): 259–288.

———. 2000. "Rekapitulacija." In *Racji hod,* ed. Mladen Lazic, 5–12. Beograd: Filip Visnjic.

Leifman, Hakan. 2000. "Studying Social Problems on the Basis of Official Statistics." In *Statistics on Alcohol, Drugs and Crime in the Baltic Sea Region,* ed. Hakan Leifman and Nina Edgren Henrichson, 7–16. Helsinki: Nordic Council for Alcohol and Drug Research.

Lengyel, Gyorgy. 1994. "A magyar gazdasagi vezetes professzinalizaciojanak ket hullama." *Szociologiai Szemle* 4 (3): 3–14.

Leonas, Petras. 1939. *Sociologijos paskaitos.* Kaunas: Vytauto Didziojo universitetas.

Lewenstein, Barbara. 1999. *Wspolnota spoleczna a uczestnictwo lokalne.* Warsaw: Instytut Stosowanych Nauk Spolecznych Uniwersytetu Warszawskiego.

Lewenstein, Barbara, and Wojciech Pawlik, eds. 1994. *A mialo byc tak pieknie … Polska scena publiczna lat dziewiecdziesiatych.* Warsaw: Instytut Stosowanych Nauk Spolecznych Uniwersytetu Warszawskiego.

Lietuva ir Sajudis. 1990. Vilnius: Filosofijos, sociologijos ir teises institutas.

Light, J.R. Donald, and Suzanne Keller. 1975. *Sociology.* New York: Alfred A. Knopf.

Litvan, Gyorgy, and Laszlo Szucs, eds. 1973. *A szociologia elso magyar muhelye: A Huszadik Szazad kore.* Budapest: Gondolat.

Loogma, Krista, and Erik Terk. 1999. *Scenarios for the Development of the Economic Structure and Their Impact on the Structure of Employment and the Nature of Work.* Tallinn: Estonian Institute for Futures Studies.

Lukasiewicz, Piotr. 1991. "Socjologia ograniczona." *Krytyka* 34/35: 47–50.

Lutynska, Krytyna. 1993. *Surveye w Polsce: Spojrzenie socjologiczno-antropologiczne.* Warsaw: IFiS PAN.

Macariev, Plamen. 1999. *Bulgaria: Facing Cultural Diversity.* Sofia: IRIS-ACCESS.

Mach, Bogdan W., Karl Ulrich Mayer, and Michal Pohoski. 1994. "Job Changes in the Federal Republic of Germany and Poland: A Longitudinal Assessment of the Impact of Welfare-Capitalist and State-Socialist Labour-Market Segmentation." *European Sociological Review* 10 (1): 1–28.

Machacek, Ladislav. 1996. *Obcianska participacia a mladez.* Bratislava: Sociologicky ustav SAV.

———. 2000. "Slovenska sociologicka spolocnost' pri SAV na prelome tisicrocia." *Sociologia* 34 (2): 197–205.

Machonin, Pavel. 1997. *Socialni transformace a modernizace.* Praha: Sociologicke nakladatelstvi.

Machonin, Pavel, and Jaroslav Krejci. 1996. *Czechoslovakia 1918–1989: Laboratory for Social Change.* Oxford: Macmillan Press.

Machonin, Pavel, and Milan Tucek. 1996. *Ceska spolecnost v transformaci.* Praha: Sociologicke nakladatelstvi.

Makarovic, Jan. 1994. "How the New Political Elite in Slovenia Understands Democracy." In *Small Societies in Transition: The Case of Slovenia,* ed. Frane Adam and Grega Tomc, 51–74. Ljubljana: Slovene Sociological Association.

Makeev, Serhii. 1989. *Sotsial'nyie pieriemieschienia v krupnom gorodie.* Kiev: Naukova dumka.

———, ed. 1999. *Podvizhost' struktury: sovriemiennyie processy sotsial'noi mobil'nosti.* Kiev: NAS Institute of Sociology.

Makeev, Sergij, and Nataliya Kharchenko. 1999. "The Differentiation of Income and Consumption in Ukraine: On the Path to Poverty." *International Journal of Sociology* 29 (3): 14–30.

Mali, Franc. 2000. "Obstacles in Developing University, Government and Industry Links: The Case of Slovenia." *Science Studies* 13: 31–50.

Malnar, Brina, and Niko Tos. 1995. "Projekt Slovensko javno mnenje-primer infrastrukturne podatkovne baze slovenske sociologije." In *Zbornik ob 30 letnici Slovenskega socioloskega drustva,* ed. Zinka Kolaric, 59–73. Ljubljana: Slovensko sociolosko drustvo.

Malysheva, Marina. 1999. *Between Peasants and Love Machines: 'Democratic' Perspectives for Russian Women and the Future of (Un-)Paid Women's Work.* Bonn: NRO Frauenforum.

Mandic, Srna. 1996. *Stanovanjska politika in razvoj.* Ljubljana: Institut za druzbene vede.

Mantarova, Anna. 2000. *Prestapnost i sotsialna transformatsiya.* Sofia: Institut po sotsiologiya.

Manterys, Aleksander. 2000. *Klasyczna idea definicji sytuacji.* Warsaw: Instytut Stosowanych Nauk Spolecznych Uniwersytetu Warszawskiego.

Mares, Petr. 1994. *Nezamestnanost jako socialni problem.* Praha: Sociologicke nakladatelstvi.

———. 1999. *Sociologie nerovnosti a chudoby.* Praha: Sociologicke nakladatelstvi.

Marianski, Janusz. 1994. *Etos pracy bezrobotnych.* Lublin: KUL.

Markowski, Radoslaw, ed. 1999. *Wybory parlamentarne 1997: System partyjny, postawy polityczne, zachowania wyborcze.* Warsaw: ISP PAN.

Marshall, Gordon. 1996. "Was Communism Good for Social Justice? A Comparative Analysis of the Two Germanies." *British Journal of Sociology* 47 (3): 397–420.

Marx, Karl. 2000. *Sotsiologia.* Mascow: Kanon Press.

Masaryk, Tomas Garrigue. 1995. *Spisy 11,12,13: Rusko a Evropa.* Praha: Ustav TGM.

———. 1998. *Spisy 1: Sebevrazda jako hromadny jev moderni osvety.* Praha: Ustav TGM.

———. 2000. *Spisy 8: Moderni clovek a nabozenstvi.* Praha: Ustav TGM.

———. 2001a. *Spisy 2: Pokus o konkretni logiku.* Praha: Ustav TGM.

———. 2001b. *Spisy 3: Zakladove konkretne logiky.* Praha: Ustav TGM.

Masiulis, Kestutis.1997. *Lietuvos elitas.* Vilnius: Pradai.

Maslova, Olga. 1995. "Kachestvennaya i kolichestvennaya sotsiologie: metodologia i metody." *Sotsiologia* 4 (5/6): 5–16.

Mateju, Petr, and Jiri Vecerník, eds. 1999. *Ten Years of Rebuilding Capitalism.* Prague: Academia.

Mateju, Petr and Klara Vlachova, eds. 1999. *Nerovnosti, spravedlnost a politika: Ceska republika 1991–97.* Praha: Sociologicke nakladatelstvi.

Matonyte, Irmina. 2001. *Posovietinio elito labirintai.* Vilnius: Knygiai.

Matousek, Oldrich.1993. *Rodina jako instituce a vztahova sit.* Praha: Sociologicke nakladatelstvi.

Matulionis, Arvydas. 2000. "Kulturos vertybiu vartojimo savitumas ir dinamika: Menininku socialine padetis." In *Kulturologija,* Vol. 6, ed. Arvydas Matulionis, 434–519. Vilnius: Gervele.

Melchior, Malgorzata. 1990. *Spoleczna tozsamosc jednostki.* Warsaw: Uniwersytet Warszawski.

Melnyk, Tetiana, ed. 1999. *Gendernyi analiz ukrains'koho suspil'stva.* Kiev: United Nations.

Mendras, Henri. 1997. *Elementy socjologii.* Trans. Andrzej Biernacki. Wroclaw: Siedmiorog.

Menshikov, Vladimir. 2001. "The Advent of Participation in Public Policy." In *LATVIA: Human Development Report 2000/2001,* ed. Talis Tisenkopfs, 75–104. Riga: United Nations Development Program.

Mihailescu, Ioan. 1999. *Familia in societatile europene.* Bucuresti: Editura Universitatii din Bucuresti.

Mihailov, Stoyan, and Nikolai Tilkidzhiev, eds. 1996. *Entziclopedichen retchnik po sotsiologiya.* Sofia: M&M.

Mihailovic, Srecko. 1999. *Dva ogleda o legitimitetu. Javno mnenje o legitimitetu trece Jugoslavije.* Beograd: Friedrich Ebert Stiftung

Miler, Hans-Peter. 1996. "Narusivac mira srednjeg dometa." *Treci program Radio Beograda* 107–108, 119–122.

Milic, Andjelka. 1996. "Women and Work in Former Yugoslavia and Their Present Situation." In *Family, Women and Employment in Central and Eastern Europe,* ed. Barbara Lobozinska, 237–244. Westport, Conn.: Greenwood.

Milic, Andjelka, and Ljiljana Cikaric. 1998. *Generacija u protestu.* Beograd: Univerziteta u Beogradu.

Mills, C. Wright. 1959. *The Sociological Imagination.* New York: Oxford University Press.

Mimica, Aljosa, ed. 1999. *Tekst i kontekst.* Beograd: Zavod za udzbenike i nastavna sredstva.

Mimica, Aljosa, and Vladimir Vuletic. 1998. "Gde se dede treci klasik? Analiza citiranosti Marksovih, Veberovih i Dirkemovih radova u casopisu." *Sociologija* 1959–1996. *Sociologija* 40 (1): 71–94.

Minev, Duhomir, ed. 2000. *Promeniyashtite se litsa na demokratziata: Ikonomitcheska, industrialna, politicheska.* Sofia: Fondatzia Perspektiva.

Minev, Duhomir, Georgi Fotev, and Ahthoni Vendov. 1996. *Balgarsksta ikonomika: Reformi, promeni I perspektivi.* Pernik: Poligraf.

Ministry of Statistics and Analysis. 2000. *Itogi Perepisi naselenija Respubliki Belarus 1999 goda: Naselenie Respubliki.* Minsk: Ministry of Statistics and Analysis.

Mircev, Dimitar. 1991. *Dramata na pluralizacijata: Politologija na krizata i sistemskite promeni*. Skopje: Magazin.

———. 1998. *Politickite govori na sovremieto*. Skopje: Misla.

Mircev, Dimitar, and Stojmen Mihajlovski. 1995. *Instituciite na izpornata demorkratija vo sovremenite politicki sistemi: Komparativna monografska analiza*. Skopje: Institut az sociloski i politicko pravni istrazuvanja.

Misztal, Barbara A. 1993. "Understanding Political Change in Eastern Europe: A Sociological Perspective." *Sociology* 27 (3): 451–470.

Misztal, Bronislaw. 1992. "Between the State and Solidarity: One Movement, Two Interpretations: The Orange Alternative Movement in Poland." *British Journal of Sociology* 43 (1): 55–78.

———. 2000. *Teoria socjologiczna a praktyka spoleczna*. Krakow: Universitas.

Mitev, Petar-Emil. 1995. "Balgarskoto obchtestvo: Balgarskata sotsiologiya, Balgarskata sotsiologicheska asotsiatsia." *Sotsioligicheski Problemi* 4:120–132.

———, ed. 1998. *The Bulgarian Transition: Challenges and Cognition*. Sofiya: LIK.

Mitev, Petar-Emil, Veronika Ivanova, and Vladimir Shubkin. 1998. "Katastroficheskoie soznaniie v Bolgarii i Rosii." *Sotsiologicheskiie islliedovaniia* 10.

Mitrikas, Alfonsas A. ed. 1999. *Vertybes permainu metais*. Vilnius: Lietuvos filosofijos ir sociologijos institutas.

Mladenovski, Gorge. 1995. "Kulturniot pluralizam: Pojava, konceptualni dilemi i prakticni implikacii." *Socioloska revija* 1.

———. 2000. *Antopologija (hrestomatija)*. Skopje: Filozofski Fakultet.

Mlcoch, Lubomir, Pavel Machonin, and Milan Sojka. 2000. *Ekonomicke a spolecenske promeny v ceske spolecnosti po roce 1989*. Praha: Karolinum.

Mlinar, Zdravko. 1995. *Avtonomija in povezovanje v prostoru*. Ljubljana: Institut za druzbene vede.

Molnar, Aleksandar. 1996. "O delanju drustvenih grupa." *Sociologija* 38 (2): 289–313.

———. 2000. "Totalitarna vlast i 'modernizacija.'" *Sociologija* 42 (1): 107–134.

Morawski, Witold. 1998. *Zmiana instytucjonalna: Spoleczenstwo, gospodarka, polityka*. Warsaw: PWN.

Motuzas, Remigijus, ed. 2000. *Tautines mazumos demokratineje valstybeje*. Vilnius: Tautiniu mazumu ir iseivijos departamentas.

Mouzelis, Nicos. 2000. *Sociologijska Teorija: Sto je Poslo Kkrivo?* Trans. Suzana Kovacevic. Zagreb: Jesenski I Turk.

Mozny, Ivo. 1991. *Proc tak snadno?* Praha: Sociologicke nakladatelstvi.

———. 1999. *Sociologie rodiny*. Praha: Sociologicke nakladatelstvi.

Mrksic, Danilo. 2000. "Restratifikacija i promene materijalnog standarda." In *Racji hod*, ed. Mladen Lazic, 237–292. Beograd: Filip Visnjic.

Mucha, Janusz, ed. 1999a. *Kultura dominujaca jako kultura obca*. Warsaw: Oficyna Naukowa.

———, ed. 1999b. *Spoleczenstwo polskie w perspektywie czlonkostwa w Unii Europejskiej*. Warsaw: IFiS PAN.

Mueller, Carol. 1997. "International Press Coverage of East German Protest Events, 1989." *American Sociological Review* 62 (5): 820–832.

———. 1999. "Escape from the GDR, 1961–89: Hybrid Exit Repertoires in a Disintegrating Leninist Regime." *American Journal of Sociology* 105 (3): 697–735.

Mueller, Klaus. 1995. "Vom Post-Kommunismus zur Postmodernitaet? Zur Erklaerung sozialen Wandels in Osteuropa." *Koelner Zeitschrift fuer Soziologie und Sozialpsychologie* 47 (1): 37–64.

Muench, Richard. 1991. "American and European Social Theory: Cultural Identities and Social Forms of Theory Production." *Sociological Perspectives* 34 (3): 313–335.

Musil, Jiri. 2001. "Gellner's Philosophy of History: Interpretations and Problems." *Czech Sociological Review* 9 (2): 153–172.

Narusk, Anu, ed. 1995. *Everyday Life and Radical Social Changes in Estonia.* Tallinn: Eesti Teaduste Akadeemia kirjastus.

———, ed. 1999. *Argielu Eestis 1990ndatel aastatel.* Tallinn: Tallinna Pedagoogikaulikooli Rahvusvaheliste ja Sotsiaaluuringute Instituut.

Narusk, Anu, and Leeni Hansson. 1999. *Estonian Families in the 1990s: Winners and Losers.* Tallinn: Estonian Academy Publishers.

Nemedi, Denes. 1985. *A nepi szociografia 1930–1938.* Budapest: Gondolat.

———. 1996. *Durkheim: Tudas es tarsadalom.* Budapest: Aron Kiado.

———. 2000. "A kritikai elmelet normativ bazisanak problemaja Habermasnal." In *Tarsadalomelmelet-elmelettortenet,* ed. Denes Nemedi, 171–208. Budapest: Uj Mandatum.

Nemirovsky, Valentin, and Dmitry Nevirko. 1998. *Teoreticheskaya sotsiologia: netraditsionnye podkhodi.* Mrasnoyarsk: Krasnoyarsky Gos. Un.

Nickolov, Lynben, Kolyo Koev, Deyan Deyanov, and Andrey Raichev. 1992. "The Round Table: Sociology in Bulgaria." *International Sociology* 7 (1): 99–114.

Niezgoda, Marian, ed. 1979. *Procesy uprzemyslowenia i urbanizaciji w spoleczenstwie socjalistycznym: Materialy seminarium Krakowsko-Skopijskiego.* Krakow: Uniwersytet Jagiellonski.

Nikolov, Stefan. 1999. *Blagotvoriyachtiyat sector.* Sofiya: RIK Letera.

Noelle, Elisabeth. 1993. *Massovye oprosy: Vvedenie v metodiku demoscopii.* N. Mansurov. Moscow: Progress.

Noelle-Noiman, Elisabeth. 1996. *Obschestvennoe mnenie: Otkrytie spirali molchanija.* Trans. L. Rybakova. Moscow: Progress-Academia.

Nohejl, Marek. 2001. *Lebenswelt a kazdodennost v sociologii Alfreda Schutze.* Praha: Sociologicke nakladatelstvi.

Novak, Mojca, Grega Tomc, and Frane Adam. 1993. *Procesi modernizacije in postsocialisticni razvoj.* Ljubljana: Institut za druzbene vede.

Novikova, Lidia G. 2001. *Religioznost' v Belarusi na rubezhe vekov.* Minsk: BTN Business Trade News-Inform.

Nowicka, Ewa, ed. 1990. *Swoi i obcy.* Warsaw: Instytut Socjologii Uniwersytet Warszawski.

Oberschall, Anthony. 1996. "The Great Transition: China, Hungary, and Sociology Exit Socialism into the Market." *American Journal of Sociology* 101 (4): 1028–1041.

Oksamytna, Svitlana. 1999. "Tendentsii miezhpokoliennoi mobil'nosti." In *Podvizhost' struktury: sovriemiennyje processy sotsial'noi mobil'nosti,* ed. Serhii Makieiev, 78–96. Kiev: NAS Institute of Sociology.

Ondrejkovic, Peter. 1997. *Socializacia mladeze ako vychodiskova kategoria sociologie vychovy a sociologie mladeze.* Bratislava: Veda.

———. 1999. *Socialna patologia.* Bratislava: Amos.

Opp, Karl-Dieter, and Christiane Gern. 1993. "Dissident Groups, Personal Networks, and the East German Revolution of 1989." *American Sociological Review* 58 (5): 659–680.

Oshavkov, Zhivko, ed. 1968. *Procesat na preodoliyavane na religiyata v Balgariya.* Sofia: Izdatelstvo na Balgarskata Akademiya na Naukite.

———, ed. 1976. *Sotsiologicheskata struktura na savremennoto balgarsko obshtestvo.* Sofia: Izdatelstvo na Balgarskata Akademiya na Naukite.

Osipov, Gennadiy. 1998. *Russiyskaja sociologicheskaja enciklopedija.* Moscow: Russian Academy of Sciences Institute for Social and Political Studies.

———. 2000a. *Sozialnoe mifotverchestvo i sozialnaya praktika.* Moscow: ISPI RAN

———, ed. 2000b. *Rossia v poiskakh strategii: obshchestvo i vlast.* Moscow: ISPI RAN.

Osovs'kyi, Volodymyr. 1999. "Stan gromads'koii dumky v Ukraiini: Case study." In *Ukrains'ke suspil'stvo: monitoryng sotsial'nykh zmin (1994–1999),* ed. Vorona Valerii and Anatolii Ruchka, 356–378. Kiev: NAS Institute of Sociology.

Osterberg, Dag. 1989. "Social Statistics, Social Research and Sociology." *Studies of Higher Education and Research* 4.

Paadam, Katrin. 2000. *Home-Creation Strategies of Women in Old Urban Residential Districts: Applying Qualitative Methods.* Tallinn: Tallinn Technical University.

Panina, Nataliia. 1998. *Tekhnologiia sotsiolohichnoho doslidzhennia.* Kiev: NAS Institute of Sociology.

Panina, Natalia, and Evgeniy Golovakha, eds. 1999. *Tendencies in the Development of Ukrainian Society (1994–1998): Sociological Indicators.* Kiev: NAS Institute of Sociology.

Paniotto, Volodymyr. 1999. "The Level of Anti-Semitism in Ukraine." *International Journal of Sociology* 29 (3): 66–75.

Pasiak, Jan. 1997. "K problematike interdisciplinarnosti v slovenskej sociologii I." Obdobie obnovy a renesancie sociologie na Slovensku. In *O kontinuitu a modernu,* ed. Ludovit Turcan and Eva Laiferova, 94–108. Bratislava: Sociologicky ustav SAV.

Patchkova, Petya. 1996. *Elitat v svetlinata na izborite.* Sofia: M&M.

Patrakova, Anzhela. 1999. "Sotsial'na otsinka jak metod sotsiolohichnoho doslidzhennia." *Naukovi zapysky* 11: 26–38.

Pecujlic, Miroslav, and Vladimir Milic. 1995. *Sociologija.* Beograd: By Authors.

Petroska, Blaga. 1994. *Semejstvoto vo Makedonija vo 20-ot vek.* Skopje: Zbornik na Filozofskiot Fakultet.

———. 1996. *Macedonian Ethnic Identity in Toronto.* Skopje: Faculty of Philosophy.

———. 1998. *Sociologija.* Skopje: Studenski zbor.

Petrusek, Miloslav. 1991. *Alternativni sociologie.* Praha: Klub osvobozeneho samizdatu.

———. 1993. *Teorie a metoda v moderni sociologii.* Praha: Vydavatelstvi Karolinum.

———. 1994. *Sociologicke skoly, smery, paradigmata.* Praha: Sociologicke nakladatelstvi.

———. 2000. "Poznamky ke Klausovym 'poznamkam.' *Lidove noviny* (Praha), 13 May 2000.

Pettai, Iris. 2000. "Tolerance between Estonians and Non-Estonians." In *Integration of Estonian Society: Monitoring 2000,* ed. Marju Lauristin and Raivo Vetik, 6–10. Tallinn: Insitute of International and Social Studies.

Pickvance, Kathy. 1997. "Social Movements in Hungary and Russia: The Case of Environmental Movements." *European Sociological Review* 13 (1): 35–54.

Piotrowski, Andrzej. 1998. *Lad interakcji: Studia z socjologii interpretatywnej.* Lodz: Wydawnictwo Uniwersytetu Lodzkiego.

Pohorila, Nataliya, ed. 1999–2000. "Social Problems in Post-Communist Ukraine: Special Issues." *International Journal of Sociology* 29 (3/4).

Pohorila, Nataliya, and Kazimierz M. Slomczynski. 2000. "Individual Income Gains and Losses in Ukraine, 1993–1996: A Test of the Human Capital and Mental Adjustment Hypothesis." *International Journal of Sociology* 29 (4): 54–76.

Pokol, Bela. 1990. "Professionelle Institutionensysteme-Reformulierungsvorschlaege zur Niklas Luhmanns Systemtypologie." *Zeitschrift fuer Soziologie* 19 (5): 329–344.

Poland and Hungary Actions for Reconstruction of Economy (PHARE). 1994. *A Science and Technology Strategy for Slovenia.* Ljubljana: Ministry for Science.

Polish Sociological Review. 2000. "Death of Classes in Poland?" *Polish Sociological Review* 2 (130): Special Issue.

Pommersbach, Joanna, and Jacek Wozniak. 1991. "The TransEuropean Mobility Scheme for University Students (TEMPUS): Some Considerations." *International Sociology* 6 (4): 473–480.

Popova, Iryna. 1998. *Sotsiologia: propedevtychnyi kurs.* Kiev: Tandem.

———. 2000. *Povsiednievnyie idieologii: kak oni zhivut, meniaiutsia i ischezaiut.* Kiev: NAS Institute of Sociology.

Potucek, Martin. 1995. *Socialni politika.* Praha: Sociologicke nakladatelstvi.

———, ed. 1999. *Ceska spolecnost na konci tisicileti.* Praha: Karolinum.

Pribytkova, Iryna, and Arstan Zholdasev. 2000. "Profile and Migration Intentions of Crimean Tatars Living in Uzbekistan." In *Sociology in Ukraine: Selected Works Published during 1990s,* ed. Evgeniy Golovakha, Natalia Panina, and Valeriy Vorona, 306–330. Kiev: NAS Institute of Sociology.

Purvaneckas, Andrius, and Giedre Purvaneckiene. 2001. *Moteris Lietuvos visuomeneje.* Vilnius: Danielius.

Pusic, Ljubinko. 1997. *Grad, drustvo, prostor: Sociologija grada.* Beograd: Zavod za udzbenike i nastavna sredstva.

Raciborski, Jacek, ed. 1991. *Wybory: Narodziny demokracji w krajach Europy Srodkowo-Wschodniej.* Warsaw: Uniwersytet Warszawski.

———. 1997. *Polskie wybory: Zachowania wyborcze spoleczenstwa polskiego 1989–1995.* Warsaw: Scholar.

Racz, Jozsef, and Zoltan Zetenyi. 1994. "Rock Concerts in Hungary in the 1980s." *International Sociology* 9 (1): 43–54.

Radaev, Vadim. 2000. "Return of the Crowds and Rationality of Action: A History of Russian 'Financial Bubbles' in the Mid-1990s." *European Societies* 2 (3): 271–294.

Radaev, Vadim, and Ovsey Shkaratan. 1992. "Etacratism: Power and Property: Evidence from the Soviet Experience." *International Sociology* 7 (3): 301–316.

———. 1996. *Social'naja stratifikacija.* Moscow: Aspect-Press.

Ray, Larry. 1997. "Post-Communist: Postmodernity or Modernity Revised." *British Journal of Sociology* 48 (4): 543–560.

Reich, Wilhelm. 1999. *Masovne Psihologija Fasizma.* Trans. Zarka Puhovski and Nedezca Cacinovic. Zagreb: Jesenski i Turk.

Rena-Tas, Akos. 1994. "The First Shall Be Last? Enterpreneurship and Communist Cadres in the Transition from Socialism." *American Journal of Sociology* 100 (1): 40–69.

Rener, Tanja, and Mirjan Ule, eds. 1998. *Youth in Slovenia*. Ljubljana: Ministry of Education and Sport.

Reszke, Irena. 1998. *Stereotypy prywatnych przedsiebiorcow w Polsce*. Warsaw: IFiS PAN.

Rifkin, Jeremy. 1999. *Biotehnolosko Stoljece*. Trans. Ljerka Pustisek. Zagreb: Jesenski i Turk.

Ritzer, George. 1997. *Suvremena Sociologijska Teorija*. Zagreb: Globus.

———. 1999. *Mekdonaldizacija Drustva*. Trans. Zrinka Paulic. Zagreb: Jesenski i Turk.

Rizman, Rudi. 1993. "The Sociological Dimension of Conflicts between Ethnonationalisms." In *Kleine Nationen und ethnische Minderheiten in Umbruch Europas*, ed. Silvo Devetak, Sergej Flere, and Gerhard Seewann, 304–308. Munich: Slavica Verlag.

Robert, Peter. 1991a. "Educational Transition in Hungary from the Postwar Period to the End of the 1980s." *European Sociological Review* 7 (3): 213–236.

———. 1991b. "Egyenlotlen eselyek az iskolai kepzesben." *Szociologiai Szemle* 1 (1): 59–85.

———. 1997. "Foglalkozasi osztalyszerkezet: elmeleti es modszertani problemak." *Szociologiai Szemle* 7 (2): 5–48.

———. 1998. "Occupational Class Structure: Theoretical and Methodological Problems." *Review of Sociology* 8 (Special Issue): 58–76.

Rohatiuk, Mykhailo. 1999. *Migratsii naselennia Ukrainy sa umov perekhodnoi ekonomiky: metodologia ta praktyka reguliuvannia*. Lviv: Svit.

Roller, Edeltraud. 1994. "Ideological Basis of the market Economy: Attitudes toward Distribution Principles and the Role of Government in Western and Eastern Germany." *European Sociological Review* 10 (2): 105–118.

Roter, Zdenko. 1992. "Premisljevanje o (katoliski) Sloveniji." *Teorija in praksa* 29: 627–636.

Rozenfeld, User D., ed. 1999. *Eetno-social'nye i konfessional'nye processy v sovremennom obschestve*. Grodno: Grodno State University.

Ruchka, Anatolii, and Volodymyr Tancher. 1992. *Ocherki istorii sotsiologicheskoi mysli*. Kiev: NAS Institute of Sociology.

Rungule, Ritma, Maruta Pranka, and Ilze Trapenciere. 1998. "Bright Sides of the Transition Overshadowed by New Social Problems." In *Public Opinion on Social Problems*, ed. Jacek Moskalewicz and Christoffer Tigerstedt, 43–67. Helsinki: Nordic Council for Alcohol and Drug Research.

Rus, Veljko, and Bostjan Zalar. 1996. "Neokorporativizem in drzava blaginje." In *Slovenska smer*, ed. Dimitrij Rupel, 125–154. Ljubljana: Cankarjeva zalozba.

———, eds. 1999. *Privatisation of Social Services*. Ljubljana: Slovenian Sociological Association.

Rutkevitch, Mikhail. 1982. *Stanovlenie sotsialnoy odnorodnosti*. Moscow: Polizdat.

Ruus, Viive-Riina, ed. 2000. *Konelev ja koneldav inimene: Eesti erinevate eluvaldkondade diskursus*. Tallinn: Tallinna Pedagoogikaulikooli kirjastus.

Rychard, Andrzej. 1993. *Reforms, Adaptation, and Breakthrough*. Warsaw: IFiS Publishers.

Saar, Ellu. 1997. "Transitions to Tertiary Education in Belarus and the Baltic Countries." *European Sociological Review* 13 (2): 139–158.

Saar, Ellu, Mikk Titma, and Paul Kenkmann. 1994. "Estonian Sociology: The Emergence of an Empirical Tradition." In *Eastern Europe in Transformation: The Impact on Sociology*, ed. Mike Forrest Keen and Janusz L. Mucha, 157–162. Westport, Conn.: Greenwood Press.

Sadar-Cernigoj, Nevenka, Istenic Majda, and Marina Trbanc. 1994. *Kvaliteta zivljenja*. Ljubljana: Institut za druzbene vede.

Sadowski, Andrzej. 1995. *Pogranicze polsko-bialoruskie: Tozsamosc mieszkancow*. Bialystok: TransHumana.

Sandu, Dumitru. 1996a. *Social Types in Post-Communist Tansition*. Paris: Editions Ant. N. Sakkoulas.

———. 1996b. *Sociologia tranzitiei: Valori si tipuri sociale in Roinania*. Bucuresti: Staff.

Sardar, Ziiuddin. 2001. *Thomas Kuhn i Ratovi Znanosti*. Trans. Ljerka Pustisek. Zagreb: Jesenki i Turk.

Saulauskas, Marius. 1998. "Postkomunistines revoliucijoszzelmenys: Is revoliucinio tarpsnio i postmodernia Lietuva?" *Sociologija* 2: 77–94.

Saulys, Kazimieras. 1920. *Sociologija*. Kaunas: Kazimiero Draugija.

Sawinski, Zbigniew, and Henryk Domanski. 1991a. "Dissensus in assessment of occupational prestige: The case of Poland." *European Sociological Review* 7 (3): 253–266.

———. 1991b. "Stability of Prestige Hierarchies in the Face of Social Changes: Poland 1958–1987." *International Sociology* 6 (2): 227–242.

Schenk, Juraj. 1993. *Samoorganizacia socialnych systemov*. Bratislava: Iris.

Schienstock, Gerd, and Franz Traxler. 1993. "Von der stalinistischen zur marktvermittelten Konvergenz? Zur Transformation der Struktur und Politik der Gewerkschaften in Osteuropa." *Koelner Zeitschrift fuer Soziologie und Sozialpsychologie* 45 (3): 484–506.

Schuman, Howard, and Amy D. Corning. 2000. "Collective Knowledge of Public Events: The Soviet Era from the Great Purge to Glasnost." *American Journal of Sociology* 105 (4): 913–956.

Seduikiene, Jurate, ed. 1999. *Violence against Women in Lithuania*. Vilnius: Danielius.

Sekulic, Dusko, Garth Massey, and Randy Hodson. 1994. "Failed Sources of a Common Identity in the Former Yugoslavia." *American Sociological Review* 59 (1): 83–97.

Semenova, Victoria. 1996. *Sudby ludey: Rossia 20 vek*. Moscow: Institute of Sociology.

Senet, Ricard. 1996. "Nesto je trulo u gradu." *Treci program Radio Beograda* 107–108, 127–134.

Shavel, Sergei A. 1996. *Tendencii izmenenij v social'noi structure Belarusi*. Minsk: National Academy of Sciences (NAS) Institute of Sociology.

Shavel, Sergei A., Anatoly V. Rubanov, and Rosa A. Smirnova. 1998. *Social'naja stratifikacija, mobil'nost', identifikacija*. Minsk: NAS Institute of Sociology.

Shavel, Sergei A., and Rosa A. Smirnova. 1998. *Social'naja reabilitacija naselenija, postradavshego ot Chernobyl'skoi katastrofy*. Minsk: NAS Institute of Sociology.

Shlapentokh, Vladimir, Vladimir Shubkin, and Vladimir Yadov. 1999. *Katastroficheskoie soznaniie v sovriemiennom mirie*. Moscow: Assotsiatsiia Nauchnykh Fondov.

Shul'ha, Mykola, ed. 1999. *Ukrain'ske suspil'stvo na porozi tret'oho tysiacholittia*. Kiev: NAS Institute of Sociology.

———, ed. 2001. *Problemy rozvytku sotsiologichnoi teorii: materialy Pershoi Vseukrainskoi Konferencii*. Kiev: NAS Institute of Sociology.

Shul'ha, Mykola, Olexandr Potiekhin, Nataliia Boiko, Olena Parakhons'ka, and Tetiana Shul'ha. 1998. *Pravliacha elita suchasnoii Ukraiiny*. Kiev: Ukrainian Center for Peace, Conversion and Conflict Resolution Studies.

Siauliu miesto socialine raida. 1980. Vilnius: Filosofijos, sociologijos ir teises institutas.

Sidorenko-Stevenson, Svetlana. 1996. "Moskovskie bezdomnie." *Chelovek* 2: 116–125.

Siemaszko, Andrzej, ed. 2000. *Crime and Law Enforcement in Poland on the Threshold of the 21st Century*. Warsaw: Oficyna Naukowa.

Siemienska, Renata. 1997. *Plec a wybory: Od wyborow parlamentarnych do wyborow prezydenckich*. Warsaw: Instytut Studiow Spolecznych Uniwersytet Warszawski.

———. 2000. *Nie moga, nie chca, czy nie potrafia? O postawach i uczestnictwie politycznym kobiet w Polsce*. Warsaw: Scholar.

Sik, Endre. 1999a. " 'Emberpiac' a Moszkva taren." *Szociologiai Szemle* 9 (1): 97–119.

———. 1999b. " 'Slave Market' in Moscow Square." *Review of Sociology* 9 (Special Issue): 115–129.

Sikorska, Joanna. 1998. *Konsumpcja: Warunki, zroznicowania, strategie*. Warsaw: IFiS PAN.

Silver, Brian D., and Mikk Titma. 1996. "Estonia on the Eve of Independence." *International Journal of Sociology* 26 (1): 7–19.

Sim, Stuart. 2001. *Derida i Kraj Povijesti*. Trans. Neven Duzenea. Zagreb: Jesenski i Turk.

Simonyi, Agnes. 1995. "Munka nelkul." *Szociologiai Szemle* 5 (1): 55–70.

Skopljanac-Brunner, Nena, Stjepan Gredelj, Alija Hodzic, and Branimir Kristofic, eds. 2000. *Media and War*. Zagreb: Centre for Transition and Civil Society Research.

Skotnicka-Illasiewicz, Elzbieta. 1997. *Powrot czy droga w nieznane: Europejskie dylematy Polakow*. Warsaw: Centrum Europejskie Uniwersytetu Warszawskiego i Instytut Kultury.

Skultans, Vieda. 1997. "Theorizing Latvian Lives: The Quest for Identity." *Journal of the Royal Anthropological Institute* 3 (4): 761–780.

Slomczynski, Kazimierz M., Krystyna Janicka, Bogdan Mach, and Wojciech Zaborowski. 1996. *Struktura spoleczna a osobowosc: Psychologiczne funkcjonowanie jednostki w warunkach zmiany spllecznej*. Warsaw: IFiS PAN.

———. 1999. *Mental Adjustment to the Post-Communist System in Poland*. Warsaw: IFiS Publishers.

Smelser, Neil. 1988. *Sociology*. New Jersey: Prentice Hall.

———. 1994. *Sociologija*. Trans. Vladimir Yadov. Moscow: Fenix.

Smrke, Marjan. 1996. *Religija in politika: Spremembe v dezelah prehoda*. Ljubljana: Znanstveno in publicisticno sredisce.

Sokhan', Lidiia, and Vsevolod Tykhonovych. 1980. *Obraz zhyzni: tieorieticheskiie i mietodologichieskiie probliemy sotsial'no-psichologicheskogo issliedovania*. Kiev: Naukova dumka.

Sokolova, Galina N. 1994. *Ekonomicheskoe myshlenie: Real'nost' i perspektivy.* Minsk: Navuka i Technica.

———. 1998a. *Ekonomicheskaja sociologija.* Minsk: Vysheishaja shkola.

———. 1998b. *Social'nye mehanizmy kontrolja rynka truda.* Minsk: Technologiya.

Sokolova Galina N., and Oleg V. Kobyak. 2000. *Ekonomicheskaja sociologija: Hrestomatija.* Minsk: Belaruskaya Navuka.

Sokolova, Galina N., Oleg V. Kobyak, and Alexandra B. Alexandrova. 2000. *Ekonomicheskaja sociologija: Praktikum.* Minsk: Belaruskaya Navuka.

Sopoci, Jan, and Bohumil Buzik. 1999. *Teorie socialnej stratifikacie a mobility.* Bratislava: FiF Univerzita Komenskeho.

Sorensen, Annemarie, and Heike Trappe. 1995. "The Persistence of Gender Inequality in Earnings in the German Democratic Republic." *American Sociological Review* 60 (3): 398–406.

Sozanski, Tadeusz, Jacek Szmatka, and Marian Kempny, eds. 1993. *Struktura, wymiana, wladza: Szkice z socjologii teoretycznej.* Warsaw: IFiS PAN.

Splichal, Slavko, and Franc Mali. 1999. "Objektivnost ali arbitrarnost?" *Teorija in praksa* 36: 893–912.

Srubar, Ilja. 1991. "War der reale Sozialismus modern? Versuch einer strukturellen Bestimmung." *Koelner Zeitschrift fuer Soziologie und Sozialpsychologie* 43 (3): 415–432.

———. 1994. "Variants of the Transformation Process in Central Europe: A Comparative Assessment." *Zeitschrift fuer Soziologie* 23 (3): 198–221.

Staniszkis, Jadwiga. 1991. *The Dynamics of Breakthrough in Eastern Europe.* Berkeley: University of California Press.

Stankuniene, Vlada, ed. 1997. *Seima ir gimstamumas Lietuvoje.* Vilnius: Lietuvos filosofijos ir sociologijos institutas.

Stanojevic, Miro. 1996. *Socialno partnerstvo: Modeli industrijskih odnosov ob koncu 20. stoletja.* Ljubljana: Enotnost.

Stark, David. 1996. "Recombinant Property in East European Capitalism." *American Journal of Sociology* 101 (4): 993–1027.

Stasiak, Andrzej, and Wlodzimierz Zglinski, eds. 1995. *Problemy polsko-bialoruskiej wspolpracy przygranicznej.* Warszawa-Minsk: Polski Biuletyn No. 8.

Stebe, Janez. 1997. "Zakaj Slovenci potrebujemo svoj arhiv druzboslovnih podatkov?" *Teorija in praksa* 34: 609–631.

Stefanov, Ivan. 1996. "Novoto litse na sotsiologiyata." *Sotsioligicheski Problemi* 4: 121–129.

Stegnii, Olexandr, and Mykola Churilov. 1998. *Regionalizm v Ukraini jak objekt sotsial'nogo doslidzhennia.* Kiev:Sotsis-Gallup.

Stepanov, Evgeniy. 1996. *Konfliktologia perekhodnogo perioda: Metodologicheskiye, tereticheskiye, rekhnologicheskiye problemi.* Moscow: Institute of Sociology.

Stepin, Vyacheslav. 2000. *Teoreticheskoye znaniye: struktura istoricheskoy evolutsii.* Moscow: Progress-Traditsia.

Stojonovski, Nelko. 1998. *Nalcijeto na trnazicijata: Porast na socijalnata patologija.* Prilep: Ekonomski Fakultet.

Strompl, Judit. 2000. "The Transition in Estonian Society and Its Impact on a Girl's Reformatory School." *European Journal of Social Work* 3 (1): 29–41.

Studia Socjologiczne. 1998. Untitled. *Studia Socjologiczne* 3: Special Issue.

———. 2000. "Teoria wyboru spolecznego." *Studia Socjologiczne* 1/2: Special Issue.

Subrt, Jiri. 2001. *Postavy a problemy soudobe teoreticke sociologie.* Praha: Nakladatel-stvi ISV.

Sulce, Gerhard. 1996. "Sociologija se mora definitivno odvojiti od prirodnih nauka." *Treci program Radio Beograda* 107–108, 123–127.

Sulek, Antoni. 1990. *W terenie, w archiwum i w laboratorium: Studia nad warsztatem socjologa.* Warsaw: Instytut Socjologii Uniwersytet Warszawski.

Svetlik, Ivan. 1996. "Quality of Working Life." *Druzboslovne razprave* 12: 15–27.

Svetlik, Ivan, and Adigun Isac, eds. 2000. *Managing Cultural Diversity: Implications for the EU Integration.* Ljubljana: Institute for Social Sciences.

Szabo, Mate. 1998. *Tarsadalmi mozgalmak es politikai tiltakozas.* Budapest: Villanyi uti Konyvek Kiado.

Szacki, Jerzy. 1981. *Historia mysli socjologicznej.* Warsaw: PWN.

———, ed. 1995. *Sto lat socjologii polskiej: Od Supinskiego do Szczepanskiego.* Warsaw: PWN.

Szakolczai, Arpad, and Laszlo Fustos. 1998. "Value Systems in Axial Moments: A Comparative Analysis of 24 Countries." *European Sociological Review* 14 (3): 211–230.

Szalai, Erzsebet. 1994. *Utelagazas: Hatalom es ertelmiseg az allamszocializmus utan.* Budapest-Szombathely: Pesti Szalon-Savaria University Press.

———. 1996. *Az elitek atvaltozasa.* Budapest: Cserepfalvi Kiado.

———. 1999. *Oroszlanok es globalizacio.* Budapest: Magyar Tudományos Akademia Politikatudomanyi Intezet.

Szczepanski, Marek, ed. 1997. *Ethnic Minorities and Ethnic Majority.* Katowice: Wydawnictwo Uniwersytetu Slaskiego.

Szelenyi, Ivan. 1988. *Socialist Entrepreneurs: Embourgeoisement in Rural Hungary.* Madison: University of Wisconsin.

———. 1995. *The Rise of Managerialism: The New Class after the Fall of Communism.* Discussion Paper No. 16. Budapest: Collegium Budapest.

Szelenyi, Ivan, and Szonja Szelenyi. 1991. "Osztalyok es partok a posztkommunista atmenetben." *Magyar Tudomany* 12: 1415–1428.

Szelenyi, Ivan, Don Treiman, and Edmund Wnuk-Lipinski, eds. 1995. *Elity w Polsce, w Rosji i na Wegrzech: Wymiana czy reprodukcja.* Warsaw: ISP PAN.

Szelenyi, Szonja, and Karen Ascheffenburg. 1993. "Volt-e a szocialista reformnak eredmenye? Osztalykulonbsegek az iskolai vegzettsegben Magyarorszagon." *Szociologiai Szemle* 3 (2): 71–91.

Szelenyi, Szonja, Ivan Szelenyi, and Winifred R. Poster. 1996. "Interests and Symbols in Post-Communist Political Culture: The Case of Hungary." *American Sociological Review* 61 (3): 466–477.

Szomolanyi, Sona. 1990. "Historia zrodu a formovania sociologickeho pracoviska SAV." *Sociologia* 22 (3): 367–382.

———. 1999. *Klukata cesta Slovenska k demokracii.* Bratislava: Stimul.

Sztompka, Piotr. 1990. "Agency and Revolution." *International Sociology* 5 (2): 129–144.

———. 1993. "Civilizational Incompetence: The Trap of Post-Communist Societies." *Zeitschrift fuer Soziologie* 22 (2): 85–95.

———. 1994. *The Sociology of Social Change.* Oxford: Blackwell.

———. 1996a. *Sociologija social'nyh izmeneniy.* Trans. Vladimir Yadov. Moscow: Aspekt Press.

————. 1996b. "Trust and Emerging Democracy: Lessons from Poland." *International Sociology* 11 (1): 37–62.

————, ed. 1999. *Imponderabilia wielkiej zmiany: Mentalnosc, wartosci i wiezi spoleczne czasow transformacji.* Warszawa-Kraków: PWN.

Szydlik, Marc. 1994. "Incomes in a Planned and a Market Economy: The Case of the German Democratic Republic and the 'Former' Federal Republic of Germany." *European Sociological Review* 10 (3): 199–218.

Tabuna, Ausma. 1997. "Migration in Latvia and the Attitude of Residents toward Immigrants." *Humanities and Social Sciences: Latvia* 4(13)/1(14): 135–147.

Tabuns, Aivars. 1997. "Sociology in Latvia: Yesterday, Today and Tomorrow." *Humanities and Social Sciences: Latvia* 4(13)/1(14): 7–63.

————. 1998a. "Transformation Risks: The Experience of Disintegrated Societies." In *Central and Eastern Europe Continuing Transformation,* ed. Nikolai Genov, 8–103. Paris: UNESCO-MOST.

————. 1998b. "Social Sciences and the Challenge of Transition: Latvia." In *Compendium of National Reports* (Provisional Version), 83–207. Strausburg: Council of Europe.

————, ed. 1998c. *Sabiedribas parmainas Latvija.* Riga: Institute of Philosophy and Sociology, Baltic Studies Centre.

————, ed. 2001. *National, State and Regime Identity in Latvia.* Riga: Baltic Studies Centre.

Tabuns, Aivars, and Vanaga Sanita. 1999. "Labor Market in Latvia: Employment and Unemployment." In *Unemployment Risks and Reactions,* ed. Nikolai Genov, 230–252. Paris: Friedrich Ebert Stiftung.

Tabuns, Aivars, and Ausma Tabuna. 1999. "Estranged Europeans: Sociological Investigation of Latvian Society." *Humanities and Social Sciences: Latvia* 1 (22): 4–35.

————. 2000. "Globalization and Development of Democracy in Latvia." *Annales of the European Academy of Sciences and Arts* 28 (9): 58–78.

Tabuns, Aivars, and Talis Tisenkopfs. 2001. "Attitudes towards European Integration." In *National, State and Regime Identity in Latvia,* ed. Aivars Tabuns, 201–227. Riga: Baltic Studies Centre.

Taljunaite, Meilute, ed. 1995. *Lithuanian Society in Social Transition.* Vilnius: Institute of Philosophy, Sociology, and Law.

————, ed. 1999. *Socialinis strukturinimasis ir jo pazinimas.* Vilnius: Lietuvos filosofijos ir sociologijos institutas.

Tamas, Pal. 1994. "A sundiszno es a surolokefe: Szociologia es tarsadalmi gyakorlat az uj Kelet-Europaban." In *XXX: 1963-ban alakult meg a Szociologiai Kutatocsoport,* ed. Istvan Kemeny and Laszlo Gabor, 327–348. Budapest: Magyar Tudomanyos Akademia Szociologiai Intezete.

Tarasov, Vladimir S. 1999. *Gosudarstvo I ekonomicheskoe razvitie obschestva.* Minsk: Belaruski knigazbor.

Tarkowska, Elzbieta, ed. 2000. *Zrozumiec biednego: O dawnej i obecnej biedzie w Polsce.* Warsaw: IFiS PAN.

Taseva, Marija. 1997. *Etnickite grupi vo Makedonija.* Vol. 1. Skopje: Filozofski Fakultet.

————. 1998. *Etnicikite grupi vo Makedonija.* Vol. 2. Skopje: Filozofski Fakultet.

————. 1999. *Socioloski teorii.* Skopje: Universitet Sv. Kiril i Metodij.

Tchikalova, Irina R. 2000. *Partii I vlast' v SShA i Velikobritanii: Gendernaja politika v 1970–1990-e gody.* Minsk: Tesey.

Tikhonova, Natalia. 1999. *Faktori sotsialnoi stratifikatsii v usloviakh perekhoda k rynochnoi ekonomikie.* Moscow: ROSSPAN.

Tilkidjiev, Nikolai, ed. 1998. *The Middle Class as a Precognition of a Sustainable Society.* Sofia: LIK.

Tisenkopfs, Talis. 1993. "Perceptions of Ethnicity in Latvian Childhood Memories." *Childhood: A Global Journal of Child Research* 1: 110–118.

———. 1995a. "Youth in Latvia: Identities and Mobility in a Transitional Society." In *Values and Post-Soviet Youth: The Problem of Transition,* ed. Luigi Tomasi, 116–140. Milano: Franco Angeli.

———. 1995b. "Search for the Center in a Peripheral Society: A Case Study of Youth Identities in Latvia." *Nordic Journal of Youth Research* 3 (3): 2–19.

———. 1997. "Young People and New Capitalism." *Humanities and Social Sciences: Latvia.* 4 (13)/1 (14): 167–198.

———, ed. 1998a. *Latvia Human Development Report 1998: The Role of the Individual, the State, and the Private Sector in Human Development.* Riga: United Nations Development Program.

———. 1998b. "Post-Collectivist Farmers as Social, Economic, and Political Group." In *Actors on the Changing European Countryside,* ed. Leo Granberg and Imre Kovach, 131–143. Budapest: Hungarian Academy of Sciences.

———. 1999a. "Rurality as Creative Field: Towards an Integrated Rural Development." *Sociologia Ruralis* 3 (39): 411–430.

———. 1999b. "Constructed Countryside: Postsocialist and Late Modern Mixture in Rural Change." *Humanities and Social Sciences: Latvia* 1 (22): 72–111.

———, ed. 1999c. *Latvia Human Development Report 1999: Globalization and Human Development in Latvia.* Riga: United Nations Development Program.

———. 2001a. "Globalization and Peripheral Identity." In *New Horizons in Sociological Theory and Research,* ed.. Luigi Tomasi, 221–255. New York: Ashgate.

———, ed. 2001b. *Latvia Human Development Report 2000/2001: Public Policy Process in Latvia.* Riga: United Nations Development Program.

Titarenko, Larissa G. 1998. *Gendernaja sociologija.* Minsk: Belarusian State University.

Titkow, Anna, and Henryk Domanski, eds. 1995. *Co to znaczy byc kobieta w Polsce.* Warsaw: IFiS PAN.

Titma, Mikk, ed. 1997. *Social'noe rassloenie vozrastnoi kogorty.* Moscow: NAS Institute of Sociology.

———, ed. 1999. *Kolmekumneaastaste polvkonna sotsiaalne portree* (with an English summary, Social Portrait of a Generation in Their Thirties). Tartu-Tallinn: Eesti Teaduste Akadeemia kirjastus.

Titma, Mikk, and Ellu Saar. 1995. "Regional Differences in Soviet Secondary Education." *European Sociological Review* 11 (1): 37–58.

Todorova, Elka. 1999. *Realnata pomosht.* Varna: Varnenski Svoboden Universitet Tshernoriyets Hrabar.

Toka, Gabor, and Jaap Dronkers. 1996. "Sibling Resemblance in Education Attainment, Occupational Prestige and Wealth in Hungary during the Communist Regime." *European Sociological Review* 12 (3): 251–270.

Tomka, Miklos. 1998. "Coping with Persecution: Religious Change in Communism and in Post-Communist Reconstruction in Central Europe." *International Sociology* 13 (2): 229–248.

Tonovski, Gorgi. 2000. *Sociologija.* Skopje: Fakultet za turizam i ugostitelstvo Ohrid.

Tos, Niko, ed. 1999. *Vrednote v prehodu: Slovensko javno mnenje 1990–1998.* Ljubljana: Fakulteta za druzbene vede.

Toschenko, Jan, ed. 1998. "Belarusi: Vremja nadezhd." *Sotsiologicheskiye Issledovaniya* 9 (Special Issue).

Trajkovski, Ilo. 2000. *Sociologijata: Sto e kako se praktikuva.* Skopje: Matica Makedonska.

Trapenciere, Ilze, Maija Asmane, and Janina Krutskih. 1994. "Three Decades of Sociology in Latvia." In *Eastern Europe in Transition: The Impact on Sociology,* ed. Mike Forrest Keen and Janusz L. Mucha, 145–148. Westport, Conn.: Greenwood Press.

Trapenciere, Ilze, Ritma Rungule, Maruta Pranka, Tana Lace, and Nora Dudwick. 2000. *Listening to the Poor: Social Assessment of Poverty in Latvia.* Riga: Ministry of Welfare of the Republic of Latvia and United Nations Development Program.

Trappe, Heike, and Rachel A. Rosenfeld. 1998. "A Comparison of Job Shifting Patterns in the Former East Germany and the Former West Germany." *European Sociological Review* 14 (4): 343–368.

Turcan, Ludovit. 2000. "The Circumstances of the Development of Sociology in Central European Countries: Slovak Sociology in the 20th Century." *Slovak Sociological Review* 32 (6): 507–521.

Turcan, Ludovit, and Eva Laiferova. 1997. "Kontinuita a modernizacia v sociologii na Slovensku v 20.storoci." In *O kontinuitu a modernu,* ed. Ludovit Turcan and Eva Laiferova, 7–19. Bratislava: Sociologicky ustav SAV.

Turner, Jonathan H. 1985. *Struktura teorii socjologicznej.* Trans. Jacek Szmatka. Warsaw: PWN.

———. 1998. *Socjologia: Koncepcje i ich zastosowanie.* Trans. Ewa Rozalska. Poznan: Zysk i Ska.

Turska, Anna, Elzbieta Lojko, Zbigniew Cywinski and Andrzej Kojder. 1999. *Spoleczne wizerunki prawa.* Warsaw: Uniwersytet Warszawski.

Turza, Karel. 1992. "Drustvo ubijaju, zar ne?" *Socioloski pregled* 26: 163–165.

———. 1996a. *Cemu jos sociologija?* Beograd: Gutenbergova galaksija.

———. 1996b. "Cemu jos sociologija?" *Treci program Radio Beograda* 107–108, 103–105.

———. 1996c. *Modernost na biciklu.* Beograd: Akademia nova.

———. 1998. *Luis Mamford: Jedna kritika modernosti.* Beograd: Zavod za udzbenike i nastavna sredstva.

Ule, Mirjam, and Vlado Miheljak. 1995. *Prihodnost mladine.* Ljubljana: Drzavna zalozba Slovenije.

Uzdila, Juozas V. 2001. *Lietuviu seimotyra.* Vilnius: Vilniaus Pedagoginis universitetas.

Valantiejus, Algimantas. 1999. "Teoriniu prielaidu ir savoku sistema Jeffery Alexanderio sociologijoje." *Sociologija* 1 (3): 40–56.

———. 2000. "Vytauto Kavolio kulturos sociologijos metmenys." In *Vytautas Kavolis: Asmuo ir idejos,* ed. Rita Kavoliene and Darius Kuolys, 139–162. Vilnius: Baltos lankos.

Valic-Nedeljkovic, Dubravka. 1997. *Rikoset reci. Jezicka analiza radijskih izvestaja sa ratista.* Beograd: Mediji.

Van Duin, Peter, and Zuzana Polackova. 2000. "Democratic Renewal and the Hungarian Minority Question in Slovakia: From Populism to Ethnic Democracy?" *European Societies* 2 (3): 335–360.

Van Eijck, Koen, and Paul M. De Graaf. 1995. "The Effects of Family Structure on the Educational Attainment of Siblings in Hungary." *European Sociological Review* 11 (3): 273–292.

Vebers, Elmars. 1996. "Ethnic Minorities in Latvia in the 1990s." *Humanities and Social Sciences: Latvia* 3 (12): 4–28.

———, ed. 1998. *Pilsoniska apzina*. Riga: Institute of Philosophy and Sociology Ethnic Studies Center.

———, ed. 2000. *Integracija un etnopolitika*. Riga: Institute of Philosophy and Sociology.

Vecernik, Jiri. 1991. "Earnings Distribution in Czechoslovakia: Inter-temporal Changes and International Comparison." *European Sociological Review* 7 (3): 237–252.

———. 1998. "Obcan a trzni ekonomika." Praha: Nakladatelstvi Lidove noviny.

Vecernik, Jiri, and Petr Mateju, eds. 1998. *Zprava o vyvoji ceske spolecnosti 1989–1998*. Praha: Academia.

Vedres, Balazs. 1997. " 'Okonokrata' menedzser-elit-az atalakulas nyertesei?" *Szociologiai Szemle* 7 (1): 111–131.

Vejvoda, Ivan, and Mary Kaldor, eds. 1999. *Democratization in East and Central Europe*. London: Pinter Cassell Academic Publishers.

Vetik, Raivo. 1999. *Inter-Ethnic Relations in Estonia, 1988–1998*. Tampere: Acta Universitatis Tamperensis.

Vihalemm, Peeter. 2001. "Development of Media Research in Estonia." *Nordicom Information* 23 (2): 63–76.

Vihalemm, Triin. 1999. *Formation of Collective Identity among Russophone Population in Estonia*. Tartu: Tartu University Press.

Vladimirov, Jeliu, Ivan Kazarski, Todor Todorov, and Momchil Badzakov. 1998. *Balgariya v kragovete na anomiyata*. Sofiya: Sofiiski novini.

Voelker, Beate, and Hank Flap. 1997. "The Comrades' Belief: Intended and Unintended Consequences of Communism for Neighborhood Relations in the Former GDR." *European Sociological Review* 13 (3): 241–266.

Volovych, Volodymyr. 1998. "Sotsiologichna osvita v Ukrajini." *Sotsiologia: teoria, metody, marketyng* 1/2: 202–209.

Volovych, Volodymyr, and Valentyn Tarasenko, eds. 2000. *Sotsiologia: korotkyi entsyklopedychnyi slovnyk*. Kiev: Ukrains'kyi centr dukhovnoii kul'tury.

Volovych, Volodymyr, Volodymyr Yevtukh, Volodymyr Popovych, Vasyl Kousherec, and Kostiantyn Korzh. 2000. "Transit Migration in Ukraine." In *Sociology in Ukraine*, ed. Golovakha Evgeniy, Natalia Panina, and Valeriy Vorona, 207–243. Kiev: NAS Institute of Sociology.

Vooglaid, Ulo. 1995. "Noukogude Eesti sotsioloogia algus ja lopp: Intervjuu Sirje Kinile." *Looming* 1: 115–122.

Voormann, Rein. 1995. "Gender Segregation in the Estonian Labour Market: Stability, Not Change." In *Growing up in Europe*, ed. Lynne Chisholm, Peter Buchner, Heinz-Hermann Kruger, and Manuela du Bois-Remonds, 153–160. New York: De Gruyter.

Vorona, Valerii, Volodymyr Durdynets, and Yurii Saienko, eds. 2000. *Post-Chernobyl'skii sotsium: 15 rokiv po avarii*. Kiev: Stylos.

Vorona, Valerii, Yevgenii Holovakha, and Nataliia Panina. 1999. "Gromads'ka dumka ta masovi nastroii u Rosii ta v Ukraini: pered i pislia serpnevoho finansovogo kryzysu." *Sotsiologia: teoria, metody, marketyng* 1: 122–130.

Vorona, Valerii, and Anatolii Ruchka, eds. 1999. *Ukraiins'ke suspil'stvo: monitoryng sotsial'nykh zmin (1994–1999)*. Kiev: NAS Institute of Sociology.

Vosyliute, Anele, ed. 1996–2000. *Is Lietuvos sociologijos istorijos,* 3 vols. Vilnius: Lietuvos filosofijos ir sociologijos institutas.

———, ed. 1998. *Socialines grupes: Raiska ir ypatumai.* Vilnius: Lietuvos filosofijos ir sociologijos institutas.

———, ed. 1999. *Moterys: Tapatumo paieskos.* Vilnius: Lietuvos filosofijos ir sociologijos institutas.

———. 2001a. "Consumer's Society: Feminist Dimension." *Filosofija: Sociologija* 4: 44–53.

———. ed. 2001b. *Sociologija amziu sanduroje.* Vilnius: Lietuvos Karo akademija.

Vujovic, Sreten. 1997. *Grad u senci rata.* Beograd: Prometej, Novi Sad i Institut za socioloska istrazivanja Filozofskog fakulteta u Beogradu.

Warsaw Business Journal. 2000. "Market Research Companies: Ranked by 1999 Revenue from Market Research." *Warsaw Business Journal* 8 (14): 16–18.

Warzywoda-Kruszynska, Wielislawa, and Jolanta Grotowska-Leder. 1998. *Wielkomiejska bieda w okresie transformacji (zasilkobiorcy pomocy spolecznej).* Lodz: Instytut Socjologii Uniwersytetu Lodzkiego.

Wasilewski, Jacek, and Wlodzimierz Wesolowski, eds. 1992. *Poczatki parlamentarnej elity: Poslowie Sejmu kontraktowego.* Warsaw: IFiS PAN.

Wats, Larry. 1993. *Relatii interetnice in Romania: Diagnoza sociologica si evaluarea tendintelor.* Bucuresti: Project on Ethnic Relations.

Watson, Peggy. 1993. "Eastern Europe's Silent Revolution: Gender." *Sociology* 27 (3): 471–487.

Weinberg, Elizabeth A. 1992. "Perestroika and Soviet Sociology." *British Journal of Sociology* 43 (1): 1–10.

Weitman, Sasha. 1992. "Thinking the Revolutions of 1989." *British Journal of Sociology* 43 (1): 11–24.

Wessely, Anna. 1996. "The Cognitive Chance of Central European Sociology." *Replika* (Special Issue): 11–19.

Wnuk-Lipinski, Edmund. 1996. *Demokratyczna rekonstrukcja: Z socjologii radykalnej zmiany spolecznej.* Warsaw: PWN.

Wodz, Kazimiera, ed. 1993. *W kregu ubostwa: Proba analizy psychospolecznych aspektow zjawiska.* Katowice: Slask.

World Bank. 1997. *World Development Report.* Oxford: Oxford University Press.

Wright, Eric. 2001. *Lacan i Postfeminizam.* Trans. Ljerka Pustisek. Zagreb: Jesenski i Turk.

Wyka, Anna. 1993. *Badacz spoleczny wobec doswiadczenia.* Warsaw: IFiS PAN.

Yadov, Vladimir, ed. 1967. *Chelovek i ego rabota.* Moscow: Nauka.

Yadov, Vladimir. 1987. *Sotsiologicheskie issledovania: metodologia, programma, metody.* Moscow: Nauka.

Yadov, Vladimir A., and Victoriya V. Semenova. 1998. *Strategija sociologicheskogo issledovanija.* Moscow: Universitet.

Yakuba, Olena. 1996. *Sociologia: uchebnoe posobie dla studentov.* Kharkov: Konstanta.

Yakuba, Olena, Ol'ha Kutsenko, Larysa Khyzhniak, Mykhailo Beznosov, and Iryna Yevdokimova. 1997. *Izmienieniie sotsial'no- klassovoi struktury obschestva v usloviach yego transformatsii.* Kharkov: Osnova.

Yakubovich, Valery, and Irina Kozina. 2000. "The Changing Significance of Ties: An Exploration of the Hiring Channels in the Russian Transitional Labor Market." *International Sociology* 15 (3): 479–500.

Yanitsky, Oleg. 1999. "The Environmental Movement in a Hostile Context: The Case of Russia." *International Sociology* 14 (2): 157–172.

Yevtukh, Volodymyr. 1997. *Etnopolityka v Ukraini: pravnychyi ta kul'turolohichnyi aspekty*. Kiev: NAS Institute of Sociology.

Zakharchenko, Mark, and Oleksandr Pohorilyi. 1993. *Istoriia sotsiolohii: vid antychnosti do pochatku XX stolittia*. Kiev: Lybid.

Zakharieva, Mariyana. 1996. *Inovatsiyata v obrazovanieto*. Sofia: Natsionalno i globalno razvitie.

Zamfir, Catalin, ed. 1999. *Politici sociale in Romania: 1990–1998*. Bucuresti: Expert.

Zamfir, Elena, and Catalin Zamfir, eds. 1993. *Tiganii intre ignorare si ingrijorare*. Bucuresti: Alternative

———, eds. 1995. *Politici sociale: Romania in context European*. Bucuresti: Alternative.

Zamfir, Elena, and Marian Preda, eds. 2000. *Strategii antisaracie si dezvoltare comunitara*. Bucuresti: Expert.

Zarina, Inna. 1995. "Actual and Desired Family Models in Latvia." *Humanities and Social Sciences: Latvia* 2 (7): 48–61.

Zaslavskaya, Tatyana, and Rozalina Ryvkina. 1991. *Sotsiologia ekonomicheskoi zhizni*. Novosibirsk: Nauka.

Zepa, Brigita. 1997. "State, Regime Identity, and Citizenship." *Humanities and Social Sciences: Latvia* 4 (13)/1 (14): 81–102.

———. 1998. "Latvia and Europe: Competing or Congruous Identities: Which identity for which Europe?" In *Belarussian, Estonian, Latvian, and Russian Post–Cold War Identities in Europe*, ed. Antje Herrberg, 37–51. Aalborg: Aalborg University Press.

———, ed. 1999a. *Conditions of Enhancement of Civic Participation*. Riga: Baltic Data House.

———. 1999b. "Conditions which Facilitate and Impede Political Participation: Latvia in Comparison with Norway." *Humanities and Social Science: Latvia* 1 (22): 36–49.

Zepa, Brigita, and Aija Zobena. 1996. *Cilveks un dzive sociologijas skatijuma*. Riga: Latvijas universitate.

Zherebkina, Iryna, ed. 1999. *Femina post-sovietica: ukrainskiie zhenschiny v pieriekhodnyi pieriod*. Kharkov: Kharkov Center of Gender Studies.

Zielinski, Florian. 1994. "The Rise and Fall of Governmental Patronage of Art: A Sociologist's Case Study of the Polish Poster between 1945–90." *International Sociology* 9 (1): 29–41.

Ziliukaite, Ruta. 2000. "Religiniu vertybiu kaita Lietuvoje 1990–1999." In *Kulturologija*. Vol. 6, ed. Arvadas Matulionis, 213–251. Vilnius: Gervele.

Ziolkowski, Marek, Barbara Pawlowska, and Rafal Drozdowski. 1994. *Jednostka wobec wladzy*. Poznan: Nakom.

Zirnite, Mara, ed. 2001. *Spogulis: Latvijas mutvardu vesture*. Riga: Latvijas Universitates Filozofijas un sociologijas instituts.

Zivkovic, Jovan, and Djokica Jovanovic, eds. 1997. *Ka sociologiji*. Pristina: Univerzitet u Pristini.

Zlobina, Olena, and Vsevolod Tychonovych. 2001. *Suspil'na kryza i zhytt'ievi stratehii osobystosti*. Kiev: Stylos.

Zlotnikov, Anatoly G., ed. 1993. *Mezhdunarodnye otnoshenoja v Vostochno-Polesskom regione Belarusi*. Gomel: Radzimichy.

———. 1994. *Sovremennaja social'no-ekonomicheskaja situacija v Gomelskom regione v zerkale post-Chernobyl'skih problem*. Gomel: Radzimichy.

Zlotnikov, Anatoly G., Ludmila M. Zlotnikova, and Anatoly P. Kasyanenko. 1991. *Zhitely Gomelja v extremal'nyh uslovijah: Socio-psihiligicheskij klimat goroda*. Gomel: Radzimichy.

Znebejanek, Frantisek. 1997. *Socialni hnuti*. Praha: Sociologicke nakladatelstvi.

Zunic, Dragan. 1995. *Sociologija umetnosti*. Nis: Univerzitet u Nisu.

Zybertowicz, Andrzej. 1995. *Przemoc i poznanie: Studium z nie-klasycznej socjologii wiedzy*. Torun: Uniwersytet Mikolaja Kopernika.

Index

Abraham, Dorel, 134
Academic, 40 n.1
Academy of Sciences: Belarus, 19, 22, 24, 26; Bulgaria, 29, 33, 40 n.1; Czech Republic, 40 n.1, 51, 53, 54, 55, 56, 59 n.1; Estonia, 64, 65, 68; Hungary, 74, 85; Latvia, 88–89, 93; Lithuania, 98, 100; Poland, 29, 119, 121, 124, 128–29; Romania, 134, 136, 138; Russia, 143–44; Slovakia, 154, 160, 162; Ukraine, 175, 176, 177, 179, 183, 185
Accreditation, 88, 121, 159, 163
Action research, 111
Actually existing socialism, 109
Adam Mickiewicz University, 121
Adamik, Maria, 13
Adamski, Wladyslaw, 127
Adorno, Theodor, 178
Agrarian proletariat, 81
Akadeemia, 66
Akhiezer, Alexander, 151
Alan, Josef, 51, 60 n.3
Albania, 6
Albanians, 6
Alexander, Jeffrey, 180
Alexandru Ioan Cuza University, 134, 135
Altai University, 143

American Journal of Sociology, 14, 128, 178
American Sociological Review, 14, 128, 178
American sociology, 17
Andorka, Rudolf, 13, 79
Angelusz, Robert, 80, 84
Anglia Polytechnic University, 137
Annales, 168
Anomie, 37, 180
Ante, Markovic, 187
Anthropos, 169
Antimodernity, 188
Archiva Pentru Stiinta si Reforma Sociala, 134
Archive of Polish Sociology, 127
Arendt, Hannah, 51, 178
Aristej, 168
Aron, Raymond, 51, 56
Arsov, Boris, 108
Aschaffenburg, Karen, 80
Astra, Lina, 102
Aula, 77
Austro-Hungarian Empire, 137

Babes Bolyai University, 134, 135
Babosov, Eugeny, 19, 20
Badescu, Illie, 134
Bagdonavicius, Vaclovas, 97

Balakirieva, Olha, 176
Balaton, 76
Balazas, Vedres, 83
Balkan nations, 6, 11, 33, 110
Baltic Data House (BDH), 90, 92, 93
Baltic Media Facts, 90
Baltic Media Facts Gallup, 67
Baltic States, 3, 16, 88, 90
Baltijos tyrimai, 100
Bashkirova, Elena, 13
Baudrillard, Jean, 89
Bauman, Zygmunt, 56, 101, 122
Belarus, 2, 3, 4
Belarusian sociology: areas of sociologi-
   cal research 20–23; Center for
   Concrete Sociological Research, 19,
   20; under Communist influence, 19,
   20; funding and finances, 26–27;
   international contacts and collabo-
   ration, 25–26; journals, 21; method-
   ology, 23; research institutes in
   Minsk, 21, 22; role and relation to
   policy makers, 27; teaching of soci-
   ology, 23–25; types of research
   centers, 25
Belarusian State University (BSU), 19,
   20, 23, 24, 25, 26, 27 n.1
Belgrade University, 107, 113, 193
Bell, Daniel, 51, 56, 178
Belohradsky, Vaclav, 58, 59
Berger, Peter, 101, 120
Bernoulli, Jacob, 39
Bertalan, Laszlo, 79
Bielienok, Olexii, 185
BIOGRAF, 162
Biographic methods, 23, 111, 122, 124
Biographic sociology, 57–58, 150
Blaha, Inocenc A., 60 n.3
Bogardus scale, 183
Bolsheviks, 142
Bonjean, Charles M., 101
Bosnia and Herzogovina, 5, 187
Bourdieu, Pierre, 56, 78, 101, 122, 133,
   145, 178
Bourgeois science, 8, 9, 29, 181
Brain drain, 100
British Journal of Sociology, 14, 128, 178
British Sociological Association, 33

Broom, Dorothy, 101
Broom, Leonard, 101
Brzezinski, Zbigniew, 38
Bucharest school of sociology, 134
Bucharest University, 32
Bulgaria, 107; EU membership, 7, 8
Bulgarian *Human Development Reports*,
   36
Bulgarian Scientific-Sociological Association, 29
Bulgarian Sociological Association, 33,
   35
Bulgarian sociology, 9, 49; areas of
   research, 30; under Communist
   influence, 10, 29, 30, 39; funding
   and finances, 32, 34; Global and
   Regional Development, 36–37;
   identity crisis, 39; institutional
   heritage and developments, 32–34;
   international collaboration and
   contacts, 29, 32, 36; methodology,
   30, 35–36; post-Communist discourse, 31; publications, 33–34;
   relations among private and public
   institutes, 35; research centers,
   33–36; role and relation to policy
   makers, 30, 38–39; teaching of
   sociology, 31–32; and transformation, 38–39
Buslov, Konstantin, 19

Caldarovic, Ognjen, 18
Calitatea vietii, 134
Canada, 110
Capitalism, theories of, 146–47
Cardinal Stefan Wyszynski University,
   160
Case study, 23, 111
Case Western Reserve University, 137
Casopis za Kritiko Znanosti, 169
Cassandra, 39
Catholic Church, 103
Catholic sociology, 9
Catholic University of Lublin, 121
Ceausescu, Nicolai, 11
Central and Eastern Europe: history of
   1–8; transformation, 2, 3; visa
   requirements, 8

Central and Eastern European Barometer, 95

Central European University, 119, 121, 128–29, 177

Centrum pre Vyskum Rodiny, 156

Chalakov, Ivan, 40 n.1

Chalupny, Emanuel, 60 n.3

Changes in the Social Structure in Macedonia, 110

Charles University, 53, 54

Chechen problem, 151

Chechnya, 4

Chernobyl catastrophe, 22, 26, 27, 183, 184

Chernovolenko, Vilen, 176

Chernysh, Mikhail, 148

Chernysh, Nataliia, 177

Chicago school of sociology, 133

Chisinau State University, 137

Chuo University, 160

Churilov, Mykola, 176

Civil society, 3, 47, 68–69, 102, 114, 118, 125–26

Class, 80, 83–84, 124–25, 147–48

Climate for sociology, 1

CNN, 39

Code of ethics, 94

Cold War, 17

Collegium Civitas, 120

Collins, Randall, 180

Colonization of Eastern European sociology, 78

Comenius University, 153, 157, 158, 160

Commercial research, in Belarus, 19, 25; in Bulgaria, 34–35

Communism, 148

Communist order of life, 189

Communist Party: Belarus, 19, 20, 23; Czech Republic, 49–50, 51, 52, 59–60 n.1; former Czechoslovakia, 155; influence on sociology, 9, 10, 12, 142; Latvia, 87; Lithuania, 98; Party sociologists, 11; Poland, 117, 118; Romania, 134; Russia, 143–44; Slovakia, 154, 155, 161; Soviet Union, 141–42, Ukraine, 175, 179

Computer technology, 76, 177, 178

Comte, Auguste, 97

Concrete sociology, 10, 19

Conflict perspective, 58

Consolidation of democracy, 38

Constantinescu, Miron, 133–34

Contemporary Ukraine: Dynamics of Post-Soviet Transition, 184

Cornell University, 26

Coser, Lewis, 178

Council of International Programs, 138

Council of Mutual Economic Aid (COMECON), 4

Critique of bourgeois sociology, 145–46

Croatia, 3, 5, 14, 187

Croatian International Center for Universities, 42

Croatian Sociological Association, 45, 46

Croatian sociology, 9, 41; areas of research, 44–45; under Communist influence, 11, 41, 42; decommunization, 41; disciplinary identity, 46–47; funding and finances, 42, 44, 45, 47; international collaboration and contacts, 42; journals and publishing houses, 45–46; paradigmatic differentiation, 57; professionalization, 41; research centers and institutes, 43–44; role and relation to policy making, 45, 46–47; teaching of sociology, 41, 42–43

Croats, 5

Csepeli, Gyorgy, 13, 78, 85

Csite, Andras, 81

Csontos, Laszlo, 79

Cultural capital, 80

Cultural pluralism, 112

Cultural Pluralism and Social Organization, 112

Current Contents, 119

Cyprus, 7

Cyril and Methodius University, 114

Czech region, 3

Czech Republic, 14, 154; EU membership, 7; and NATO, 7

Czech Sociological Review, 55, 162

Czech Sociological Society, 51, 60 n.1

Czech sociology: areas of research, 53, 54–55, 58; under Communism, 9, 11, 49–51, 57; decommunization, 52, 53; exiled sociologists, 59; funding and finances, 56; institutional changes, 53, 57; international collaboration and contacts, 54, 56; journals and publishing houses, 54–55; methodology, 57–58; Prague centrism, 56; relation with economists, 52–53; research centers and institutes, 56; role and relation to policy makers, 52, 56; teaching of sociology, 56
Czechoslovak Sociological Society, 49–50, 59 n.1
Czechoslovak sociology, 54
Czechoslovakia, 2, 3, 73; division of, 4, 7, 50, 154, 156–57; EU membership, 7

Dahrendorf list, 51
Dahrendorf, Ralf, 51, 196 n.6
Darwin, Charles, 97
Data standardization, 94, 95
Davidov, Yurij, 145–47
Davidyuk, Georgy, 19
Davydov, Jurij Nikolajevitch, 51
Dayton Agreement, 5
Decommunization, 3; in Belarus, 20, 24; Czech republic, 52; Latvia, 87; Poland, 118–19; Romania, 130; Slovakia, 155–56
Deiyanova, Liliyana, 31
De-Marxization, 189–91
De-Stalinization, 10
Dettling, Wanfried, 196 n.6
Devolution, 2, 37
Dialogue of the deaf, 174
Dimitrov, Georgi, 30, 40 n.1
Discourse analysis, 23
Dissidents, 54, 100
Djindjic, Zoran, 6
Doktor, Tadeusz, 126
Domanski, Henryk, 125, 130
Donchenko, Olena, 182
Donetsk coal mining industry, 181
Drustvena Istrazivanja, 46

Druzboslovene razprave, 169
Dubska, Irena, 50
Dudek, Antoni, 118
Durkheim and Contemporary Sociology, 112
Durkheim, Emile, 56, 78, 112, 133, 180, 190

East European and Slavonic Review, 18 n.1
East European Constitutional Review, 18 n.1
East European Politics and Societies, 18 n.1
East European Quarterly, 18 n.1
East German Politburo, 12
East German sociology, 9
Economic Life in Macedonia in the 19th Century, 108
Economic Tendencies in Belarus, 22
Eisenstadt, Samuel, 145
Elias, Norbert, 178
Elsukov, Albert, 24
ELTE (Eotvos Lorand) University, 74, 75, 77
Embourgeoisement, 150
EMOR Ltd., 63, 67, 72 n.3
Empirism, 70, 71, 157
Encyclopedia Socjologii, 119
Entrepreneurs, in Hungary, 82, 83, 84; Lithuania, 103; Ukraine, 182
Entziclopedichen retchnik po sotsiologiya, 33–34
ES Turuuingute AS, 63, 72 n.2, n.3
Esely, 76
Estonia, 2, 4, 17, 63; EU membership, 7
Estonian Association of Sociologists, 66, 71 n.1
Estonian sociology, 9, 61; areas of research, 67–69, 71; under Communism, 61, 62–63; funding and finances, 64, 67, 69; institutional structures, 62–66, 71; international collaboration and contacts, 25, 65, 67, 68, 72 n.3; journals and publishing houses, 65–66; methodology, 63, 68, 70; research centers and institutes, 63–64; role and relation

to policy makers, 69–71; teaching of
    sociology, 62, 64–65
Ethnic cleansing, 6
Ethnic conflicts, 136–37
Ethnic identity, 31
Ethnic particularism, 112
Ethnic Russians, 2
Ethnicity, 2, 3, 5, 10, 12; in Belarus,
    22–23; Estonia, 69; Hungarian, 82,
    84–85; Latvia, 92–93; Macedonia,
    110; Poland, 126–27; Romania,
    136–37; Ukraine, 183; Yugoslavia,
    188, 191, 194
Ethnonationalism, 194
Euro, 6
European Barometer, 21, 35
European Consortium of Sociological
    Research, 85
European Credit Transfer System, 158,
    167
European Economic Community, 7. *See
    also* European Union
European Journal of Communication, 26
European Societies, 15, 128
European Sociological Association
    (ESA), participation of CEE sociolo-
    gists, 12, 13–14, 15, 42, 85, 102,
    128, 172
European Sociological Association
    of Marketing and Research
    (ESOMAR), 179
European Sociological Review, 15, 128
European sociology, 17
European Union, 2, 3, 5, 8, 43; accession
    and entry of CEE nations, 7, 52,
    103, 127, 136, 138; support of re-
    search in CEE, 26, 36, 88, 104, 160
Evry University, 113
Evtimov, Ivan, 40 n.1
Experts, 38–39, 120

Face-to-face interviews, 35
Falsified Marxism, 142
Faltan, Lubomir, 162
Federal Republic of Yugoslavia, 189–90,
    191, 192–93, 195
Feher, Ferenc, 73
Ferge, Zsuzsa, 79

Fibich, Jindrich, 50
Fifth Framework Program, 88
Filosofijia: Sociologija, 100
Filosofska i sotsiologichna dumka, 176,
    178, 180, 185
Finland, 65
Finnish Gallup Media, 90
Focus groups, 23, 30, 34, 122
Forbidden topics, 21, 30, 69, 117, 148
Ford Foundation, 143
Foreign foundations, 26, 34, 110, 119,
    129
Foucault, Michel, 89
Francophone sociology, 108, 111–12
Frey, Maria, 82
Friedman, Georges, 133
Friedrich Ebert Foundation, 34, 119,
    196 n.8
Friedrich Naumann Foundation, 34
Fulbright, 26

Gaidys, Vladas, 100
Gaizutis, Algirdas, 103
Gajdos, Peter, 162
Gallup Finlandia, 63
Gallup International, 21, 33, 72 n.3, 74,
    176, 179
Gallup International Balkan British
    Social Surveys, 34
Gazso, Ferenc, 81
Gender studies: in Belarus, 23, 24; Czech
    Republic, 53; Lithuania, 104; Mace-
    donia, 110; Poland, 121, 126; Russia,
    149; Soviet Union, 149; Ukraine,
    183
General Social Survey, 123, 184
Genov, Nikolai, 38, 40 n.1
Genova, Jelka, 40 n.1
Georgievski, Petre, 109
German Democratic Republic, 9, 73;
    sociology in, 12. *See also* East Ger-
    man sociology
German Marshall Fund, 34
Germany, 4
Gesellschaft fur Konsumforschung
    (GfK), 34, 72 n.3, 159
Giddens, Anthony, 56, 59, 89, 101, 145,
    178, 192

Glasnost, 18 n.1
Globalization, 34, 130
Goethe Institute, 56
Goethe University, 32
Goffman, Erving, 89
Goldthorpe, John, 80, 178
Golod, Sergej, 144
Golovakha, Yevhenii, 181, 182
Gorbachev, Mikhail, 4, 141
Gorbachyk, Andrii, 181
Gordon, Leonid, 141, 148, 150
Gray economy, 111
Greece, 5, 107
Grey zone, 50, 60 n.2, n.3
Grigas, Romualadas, 102
Grodno State University, 23
Grounded theory, 111, 122
Group for Transforming European Stud-
    ies, 26
Grushin, Boris, 141
Gusti, Dimitrie, 134–35

Habermas, Jurgen, 78, 145, 178, 180
Hadzhiyski, Ivan, 29
Halas, Elzbieta, 14, 128
Hankiss, Elmer, 83
Harcsa, Istvan, 81
Havas, Gabor, 84
Havel, Vaclav, 52, 60 n.2
Heller, Agnes, 73
Hirner, Alexander, 153
Historical materialism, 8, 9, 97, 101, 180
Historikerstreit, 190
History of Theoretical Sociology,
    145–46
History of Western Thought, The, 51
Hodza, Milan, 153
Hogheschool Sittard, 137
Holocaust, 126
Hulakova, Marie, 51
Humanistic Marxism, 45
Humanities and Social Sciences, 65
Humanities and Social Sciences: Latvia,
    93
Hungarian Broadcasting Company, 84
Hungarian Household Panel Survey, 79
Hungarian Sociological Association, 74,
    76, 85

Hungarian sociology, 16, 73; areas of
    research, 77, 79–85; under Commu-
    nism, 8, 10, 73, 78; decommuniza-
    tion, 74; funding and finances,
    75–76; institutional environment,
    73, 74; international collaboration
    and contacts, 76, 85–86; journals
    and publishing houses, 76–77;
    research institutes and centers, 7;
    role in society, 86; teaching of soci-
    ology, 74; theoretical approaches,
    77–79
Hungarians, 3, 82, 136
Hungary, 3, 4, 8, 14; EU membership, 7;
    and NATO, 7; transformation, 73
Huntington, Samuel, 67
Hyperinflation, 192–93
Hyperion University, 135

IDENTITY, 162
Ilic, Vladimir, 190–91
Illner, Michal, 53
In-depth interviews, 34
Inequality, 10
Informal labor market, 82
Ingelhart, 67
Inoi Vzgljad, 23
Institut pre Verejne Otazky, 156
Institutional duality, 74
Intellectuals, role of, 31, 83
Intelligentsia in socialist society, 10, 110,
    147–49. See also Intellectuals, role
    of
International Code of Marketing and
    Social Research Practice, 64
International Journal of Sociology, 185
International Monetary Fund, 138
International research machine, 86
International Social Science Council, 36,
    37
International Social Survey, 92, 95, 123,
    161
International Sociological Association
    (ISA): Executive Committee,
    12–13, 196 n.7; participation of
    CEE sociologists, 12–13, 15, 42, 66,
    85, 102, 128, 145, 161, 162, 172,
    196 n.7

International Sociology, 15, 128
Internet, 32, 63, 123, 159, 177, 178
Interrupted embourgeoisement, 80
Interuniversity Center for Postgraduate
    Studies, 42
Iosifov, Asen, 40 n.1
Italy, 6
Ivo Pilar, 44, 46
Izbor, 33
Iztok-Iztok, 33

Jagiellonian University, 25, 109, 113, 121
Jakubowska-Branicka, Iwona, 125
Jambrek, Perter, 172
Jasenski and Turk, 46
Jerabek, Hynek, 58
Jews, 126–27, 136–37
Jodl, Miloslav, 50
Jogan, Maca, 13, 172
Joosing, Marje, 72 n.1
Jowitt, Ken, 180
Juozeliuniene, Irena, 102

Kabele, Josef, 59
Kaesler, Dirk, 196 n.6
Katinaite, Palmyra, 97
Kaunas Politechnical Institute, 98
Kaunas Technological University, 100,
    101
Kaunas Theological Seminary, 97
Kavolis, Vytautas, 103
Keen, Mike, 196 n.8
Keller, Jan, 55
Kemeny, Istvan, 84
Kempny, Marian, 126
Kenkmann, Paul, 64
Kertesi, Gabor, 84
Khmelko, Valeriy, 176, 181
Khruschev, Nikita, 19
Khrushchev's thaw, 10, 179
King Boduen Fund, 34
Kirdina, Svetlana, 151
Kivirahk, Juhan, 72 n.1
Klaipeda University, 100
Klaus, Vaclav, 52, 53, 60 n.2
Kleptocratic private property, 188
Klicus, Antanas, 103
Klofac, Jaroslav, 50

*Koelner Zeitschrift fuer Soziologie und
    Sozialpsychologie*, 14
Koev, Kolio, 40 n.1
Kohn, Melvin, 184
Kojder, Andrzej, 130
Kolarska-Bobinska, Lena, 14
Kollo, Janos, 81
Kolosi, Tamas, 80, 83
Konapasek, Zdenek, 58
Konrad Adenauer Foundation, 34
Konrad, Gyorgy, 10, 83
Korzhov, Gennadiy, 182
Kostunica, Vojislav, 6
Kovach, Imre, 81
Kovalevskji, Maxim, 97
Krakow-Skopje Seminars, 109, 110
Krasko, Nina, 127
Krasnodebski, Zdzislaw, 118
Krauze, Tadeusz, 185
Kreidl, Martin, 55
Krejci, Jaroslav, 50, 59
Krikstopaitis, Juozas Algimantas, 102
Kritika I Humanizam, 33
Krivy, Vladimir, 162
Kroeber, Alfred, 133
Kruusvall, Juri, 64, 72 n.1
Kryshtanovskaya, Olga, 149
Krzeminski, Ireneusz, 118
Kuhn, Thomas, 180
Kuljic, Todor, 191
Kulpinska, Jolanta, 128
Kultura I Spoleczenstwo, 123, 125
Kurczewski, Jacek, 125
Kusa, Aua, 162
Kusa, Zuzana, 162
Kutsar, Dagmar, 68
Kutuiev, Pavlo, 180
Kuvacic, Ivan, 13
Kuzmickas, Bronislovas, 102
Kwasniewicz, Wladyslaw, 13, 109, 128,
    130

Laaman, Eduard, 62
Ladanyi, Janos, 84
Lagerspetz, Mikko, 18, 64, 67
Laky, Terez, 82
Lamser, Vaclav, 50
Lapin, Nikolai, 151

Late Totalitarianism, 50
Latvia, 2, 4, 17; EU membership, 7, 8
Latvian Council of Sciences, 87–88, 90, 91, 92
Latvian Human Development Report, 92
Latvian Social Science Data Archive, 95
Latvian sociology, 9; areas of research, 90–93; decommunization, 87, 88; development of profession, 93–94; funding and finances, 87–88, 90, 95; institutional environment, 89–90, 93; international collaboration and contacts, 25, 88, 89, 90–91, 92, 93–94, 95, 96; journals, 93; relationship between academic and private research centers, 89–90; role and relation to policy makers, 96; teaching of sociology, 89–90, 95
Latvijas ZA Vestis, 93
Lazarsfeld, Paul, 133
Lazic, Mladen, 190
Lebenswelt, 187
Lengyel, Gyorgy, 14, 85
LEONARDO, 138
Levi-Strauss, Claude, 133
Lewenstein, Barbara, 126
Liberalism, 154
Life histories, 30
Limited sociology, 117
Lithuania, 4, 17; postsocialist, 98–99
Lithuanian Sociological Society, 100, 101–2
Lithuanian sociology, 9, 97; areas of research, 98, 99, 102–4; under Communism, 97–98, 103; decommunization, 98; funding and finances, 101, 102; institutional development and identity, 99–102; international collaboration and contacts, 25, 100, 101, 102, 104–5; journals, 100; language of scholarship, 17; methodology, 104; role and relation to policy makers, 99–100, 105; teaching of sociology, 100–101
Loewenstein, Bedrich, 50
London School of Economics, 62
Luaristin, Marju, 67

Luc, 108
Luhmann, Niklas, 178
Lukashenko, Alexander, 2
Lukasiewicz, Piotr, 117
Lund University, 137
Lustration law, 52
Luzny, Dusan, 55

Macarthur Foundation, 34
Macedonia, 5, 107
Macedonian Sociology, 107–8; areas of research, 109–11; under Communism, 108–9; institutionalization, 108, 114; international collaboration and contacts, 109, 110; methodology, 109, 110, 113, 114–15; teaching of sociology, 108, 109, 112, 113–14
Macha, Karel, 50
Machacek, Ladislav, 162
Machonin, Pavel, 50, 57, 58, 59
Madgarearu, Virgil, 134
Majerova, Vera, 57
Makieiev, Serhii, 176
Mali, Franc, 18
Malinowski, Bronislaw, 133
Malysheva, Marina, 149
Manaev, Oleg, 26
Management of Social Transformation (MOST) project, 37, 95
Managerial capitalism, 83
Mannheim, Karl, 178
Mansurov, Valery, 149
Market economy, 2, 3, 7, 52, 58
Market research: Croatia, 45; Estonia, 63–64, 71; Hungary, 74; Latvia, 90; Lithuania, 100; Romania, 134, 135; 144; Ukraine, 176, 179, 181
Marksisticka misao, 189
Marksizam u svetu, 189
Markus, Gyorgy, 73
Marx, Karl, 87, 97, 111, 146–47, 190
Marximusstreit, 189
Marxism, 23, 34, 44, 45, 66, 87, 109; in Macedonia, 111–12; Poland, 117, 118, 121–22, 123, 129; Romania, 133–34; Soviet-style, 141, 144; Yugoslavia, 189–91

Marxism-Leninism, 8, 9, 10, 11–12; Belarus, 19, 20, 24; Czech Republic, 52; departments of Marxist-Leninist sociology, 53; Estonia, 61; Russia, 143

Marxist theory, 146–47; Orthodox Marxism, 145; Orthodox Marxists, 111

Masaryk Czech Sociological Society, 57

Masaryk, Tomas G., 55

Masaryk University, 53

Masiulis, Kestutis, 104

Maslova, Olga, 150

Mateju, Petr, 57, 59

Matonyte, Irmina, 104

Matulionis, Arvydas, 103

Mauss, Marcel, 56

Max Weber and the Understanding of the Contemporary World, 112

Melchior, Malgorzata, 127

Merton, Robert, 133, 180

Metodicky vyskumny kabinet, 159

Migracijske Teme, 46

Mills, C. Wright, 196 n.9

Milosevic, Slobodan, 6, 188, 189, 194

Mimica, Aljosa, 190

Minev, Duhomir, 37

Mitev, Petar-Emil, 30, 38, 40 n.1

Mlcoch, Lubomir, 59

Mlinar, Zdravko, 172

Moldova, 2, 4

Molnar, Aleksandar, 190–91

Montenegro, 5, 6, 189, 194, 195

Moscow State University, 142

Mozny, Ivo, 54

Mucha, Janusz L., 13, 128, 130 n.1

Mueller, Hans-Peter, 196 n.6

Munch, Richard, 180

Musil, Jiri, 14, 53

Narusk, Anu, 68

National Foundation for Scientific Research (OTKA), 76, 77

National identity, 3, 92–93

National Institutes of Health (NIH), 184

Nationalism, 92–93, 136

Nationality, in Hungary, 84–85

NATO, 3, 112; and Kosovo, 6, 195 n.1; Partnership for Peace, 7; and post-Communist countries, 7, 34

Nehnevajsa, Jiri, 59

Nelkin, Dorothy, 38

Neo-Bolshevist school, 191

Neo-Marxism, 52

New Bulgarian University, 32

New class theory, 80

New Democracy Barometer Projects, 184

NGOs, 33, 34, 110, 138, 196 n.8

Nicholas Copernicus University, 121, 127, 160

Nikolov, Lyuben, 31

Nomenclature, 37, 80, 148, 149

Nomos, 126

Normalization, 11, 50–51, 52, 60 n.3, 153, 154

Nostrification, 87, 88, 98

Nova revija, 169

Novak, Mojca, 13, 172

Nowak, Leszek, 118

Nowicka, Ewa, 127

Obrabotka Sotsiologicheskikh Anket, 181

Obrebski, Jozef, 107

Open society, 102

Open Society Foundation (Fund), 34, 196 n.8

Open-ended interviews, 30, 68

Orkeny, Antal, 85

Oshavkov, Zhivko, 29

Osipov, Gennadij, 143–44, 151

Osiris, 77

Osterberg, Dag, 70

Paadam, Katrin, 13

Palacky University, 53

Panina, Nataliia, 177, 181

Paniotto, Volodymyr, 176

Parsons, Talcott, 178

Partisan expertise, 174

Passeron, Jean Claude, 133

Paths of a Generation, 95

Patras University, 137

Paul Lazarsfeld Society of Vienna, 184

Pavelson, Marje, 65

Pedagogical University of Tallinn, 64, 66, 68, 72 n.2

Perestroika, 18 n.1, 49, 63, 143, 145, 147, 182

Petrusek, Miloslav, 51, 54, 58, 60 n.3

Philadelphia Institute for Scientific Information, 119, 169

Philadelphia list, 119

Platt, Jennifer, 196 n.7

Plovdiv University, 32

Pohorila, Nataliya, 182

Polackova, Zuzana, 15

Poland, 4, 8, 14, 16, 17, 117–18; and NATO, 7

Poland and Hungary Assistance for Reconstruction of the Economy (PHARE), 34, 138, 159, 160

Polemos, 46

Polish General Social Survey, 123

Polish Sociological Association, 122, 127, 129

Polish Sociological Review, The, 119, 125

Polish sociology, 49, 117, 179; areas of research, 123–28, 129–30; under Communism, 8, 10, 117, 121; congresses, 127–28; decommunization, 118–19, 129; funding and finances, 119, 129, 130; and independence, 16, 119, 129–30; influence in CEE, 11, 25, 26, 54, 94, 109, 153; international collaboration and contacts, 119, 120, 121, 128–29; journals and publishing houses, 119; methodology, 122, 123; research institutes and centers, 121–22, 129; role and relation to policy makers, 119–20, 130; teaching of sociology, 119–21, 128–29

Politburo, 142

Political capitalism, 80

Political elite, 2, 3

Political Thought, 176

Politicization of sociologists, 38–39

Politologichni chytannia, 176

Polytechnic University (Romania), 134

Popova, Iryna, 177, 180

Positivism, 23, 61, 104, 111

Post-Chornobylskyi Sotcium: 15 rokiv pisla avarii, 183

Post-Communist era, 1, 2, 3; civil society in, 3; in Yugoslav Federation, 6

Postmodern society, 58

Postmodernism, 58, 122

Post-socialist society, 68, 69

Post-Soviet republics, 3

Posttotalitarian sociology, 30, 39

Potucek, Martin, 13, 59

Prague Spring of 1968, 11, 50–51, 52, 59

Praxis School, 43, 45

Prikladnaja sociologija, 20

Primary accumulation of wealth, 146–47

Private research companies, 25. *See also* Commercial research

Privatization, 37, 45, 47, 53; in Hungary, 81, 82; Poland, 124; voucher privatization, 52

Problem of language, 100, 104–5; Belarus, 21, 22; Estonia, 65; Latvia, 89, 94; Lithuanian, 101; Slovakia, 159; Slovenia, 169, 171; Yugoslavia, 193

Protestant ethic, 146

Przeglad Religioznawczy, 126

Public Institute for Sociological Research, 19

Public opinion polling, 16, 34; Croatia, 44, 45; Czech Republic, 57; Estonia, 63–64, 71; Latvia, 90, 92; Lithuania, 100; Poland, 121–22; 135–36; Slovenia, 171; Ukraine, 176, 179

Public opinion research: Hungary, 74; Slovakia, 159; Ukraine, 181

Public sphere, 78

Pure capitalism, 60 n.2

Qualitative methods: Belarus, 23; Bulgaria, 30; Czech republic, 57–58; Estonia, 68; Latvia, 95; Macedonia, 110, 111–12, 113; Poland, 122, 123; Russia, 144–45, 150

Qualitative quantitative debate, 58

Quantitative methods, 58; Estonia, 70; Hungary, 82; Macedonia, 110, 111–12, 113; Poland, 123; Russia, 145

Race, 10
Radaev, Vadim, 14, 15
Radcliffe-Brown, Alfred Reginald, 133
Raichev, Andrei, 40 n.1
Rannik, Erkki, 72 n.1
Rational choice theory, 79, 122
Real socialism, 54
Rehak, Jan, 58
Rehakova, Blanka, 58
Rene Descartes University, 160
Report on the Development of Czech Society 1989–98, 59
Retooled sociologists, 43
Revista de cercetari sociale, 134
Revista Romana de Sociologie, 134
Revue Francaise de Sociologie, 15
Riigikogu Toimetised, 66
Risk society, 171
Ritzer, George, 46, 58
Rivija za Sociologiju, 46
Road of Intellectuals to Class Power, The, 83, 86 n.3
Robert, Peter, 18, 80
Roma (Gypsy) ethnicity, 79, 81, 84, 136–37
Romania, 3, 8; EU membership, 7
Romanian sociology, 16, 136; areas of research, 136–37; under Communism, 8, 11, 133–34; decommunization, 133; funding and finances, 135, 137–38; international collaboration and contacts, 137–38; journals, 134; methodology, 133; research centers and institutes, 134; role and relation to policy makers, 136, 138–39; teaching of sociology, 134–35
Rona-Tas, Akos, 80
Rotman, David, 20
Rudolf Andorka Social Science Society, 74–75, 76
Russia, 2, 3, 4, 14, 142; and NATO, 7
Russian capitalism, 146–47
Russian Federation, 2, 4
Russian social sciences, 145
Russian society, 142, 146, 149
Russian Sociological Association, 141

Russian sociology, 8, 16, 49; areas of research, 148–50, 182; under Communism, 8, 10, 141, 145, 150; decommunization, 145; institutional change, 142–45, 151; international collaboration and contacts, 25, 54, 94, 144, 145; methodology, 144, 150, 151; role and relation to policy makers, 151; teaching of sociology, 143; theoretical evolution, 145–48, 151
Rychtarik, Karel, 51

Saar, Andrus, 71 n.1
Saar Poll Ltd., 63, 72 n.2, n.3
Saienko, Jurii, 183
Sajudis, 4, 99
Salda project, 56
Samizdat, 51
Schenk, Juraj, 162
Schulze, Gerhard, 196 n.6
Scientific Communism, 9; Belarus, 19, 24; Lithuania, 100–101; Russia, 143
Second economy, 80
Semenova, Victoria, 150
Sennett, Richard, 196 n.6
Serbia, 5, 107, 189, 194, 195
Serbian population, 6
Serbs, 3, 5, 6, 188, 191
Shkaratan, Ovsej, 148
Shlapentokh, Vladimir, 184
Sik, Endre, 82
Sik, Oto, 52
Siklova, Jirina, 50
Silesian University, 121, 124
Simmel, Georg, 56, 178
Simonyi, Agnes, 82
Simulacrum, 188
Slavic University, 32
Slomczynski, Kazimierz M., 182
Slovak Sociological Association, 154. *See also* Slovak Sociological Society
Slovak Sociological Review, The, 157, 162
Slovak Sociological Society, 50, 161–62. *See also* Slovak Sociological Association

Slovak sociology, 60 n.3, 153; areas of research, 159–61; under Communism, 9, 11, 153–54, 155; funding and finances, 156; institutional changes, 156, 163; international collaboration and contacts, 54, 153–54, 156, 158, 160, 162; professional organization, 161–62; teaching of sociology, 157–59, 163

Slovakia, 3, 50, 153; EU membership 7, 8; and NATO, 7; transformation after 1989, 154–55

Slovar' prikladnoi sociolgii, 20

Slovenia, 3, 14, 169, 187; sovereignty, 4–5

Slovenian Sociological Association, 169

Slovenian sociology, 9, 165; areas of research, 169–72; under Communism, 165; funding and finances, 165, 173; institutional changes, 165, 167, international collaboration and contact, 167, 172; journals and publishing houses, 168–69; role and relation to policy makers, 169–70, 173–74; teaching of sociology, 166–68

Smelser, Neil, 101, 178

Smith, Anthony D., 89

Social constructionism, 59, 66

Social Costs of Transformation Project, 79

Social differentiation, 148

Social engineering, 53, 70

Social experience, 58

Social homogeneity, 31, 148

Social inequality: Belarus, 21; Czech Republic, 54; Hungary, 80–81

Social interactionism, 66

Social movements, 10

Social noe rassloenie vozrastnoi kogorty, 25

Social optics, 84

Social statistics, 70

Social structure and transformation, 79–81

Socialines informacijos centras, 100

Socialism, 30, 83, 84, 148

Socialism with a human face, 142

Socialist economy, 3

Socialist Federative Republic of Yugoslavia (SFRY), 107, 108, 109, 187, 189

Socialist society, 147–48

Socijalna Ekologija, 46

Sociocide, 188, 192, 195 n.1

Sociologia, 157

Sociological Society of Montenegro, 196 n.7

Sociological Society of Serbia, 196 n.7

Sociological theory, 20, 59; Estonia, 64, 65, 66, 70, 71; Hungary, 77–79; Latvia, 91, 94–95; Macedonia, 109, 111–12; Poland, 122–23; Romania, 133; Russia, 145–48; Slovakia, 155–56, 157; Slovenia, 169; Ukraine, 180–81; Yugoslavia, 189–91

Sociologicke nakladatestvi (SLON), 55

Sociologicky Casopis, 51, 54, 55

Sociologicky Obzor, 51

Sociologicky sbornik, 153

Sociologicky spravodaj, 162

Sociologicky zapisnik, 162

Sociologie Ramaneasca, 134

Sociologija, 21, 100, 112, 190–91, 197 n.9

Sociologija Sela, 46

Sociologization (of other disciplines), 10

Sociology, 14

Sociology in Central and Eastern Europe, 1, 8–12; common historical influences, 17; division of labor, 15–16; empirical and applied focus, 10, 11, 12; positivistic character, 12; private and for-profit research centers, 16; problem of language, 17; problem of resources, 16; publication in major Western journals, 14–16; relative position in international context, 12–16; restricted topics, 10, 11, 12; strategies for survival, 9–10

Sociology in Ukraine: Selected Works Published during the 1990s, 181

Sociology of religion, 12

Sociology of the environment, 10

Sociology of youth, 68
Socioloski pregled, 197 n.9
Socrates Program, 32, 137, 139 n.2
Sofia University, 31, 32, 33
Sokhan, Lidia, 176
Sombart, Werner, 62, 146
Sorokin, Pitirim, 97, 148
Soros Foundation, 69, 76, 88, 89, 102, 113, 119, 143
Sotsialna polityka i sotsialna robota, 176
Sotsiologia: teoria, metody, marketing, 176, 178
Sotsiologicheski Pregleg, 33
Sotsiologicheskiye Issledovaniya, 25
Southeastern European University (aka van der Stoel University), 114
South-West University, 32
Sova-Harris (aka Sova-5), 34
Soviet Communist doctrine, 97
Soviet social science, 142
Soviet Sociological Association, 176; Baltic Branch, 12
Soviet sociology, 8, 23, 68, 141–42
Soviet totalitarian society, 142
Soviet Union, 2, 16, 49, 63, 73; putsch, 4, 7, 142
Spencer, Herbert, 97
Spezkhran, 145
Spiru Haret University, 135
Srubar, Ilja, 59
Stalin, Joseph, 41, 142
Stalinist period, 117
Stalinization, 8
Staniszkis, Jadwiga, 131 n.2
Stankuniene, Vlada, 104
Statistical Packages for the Social Sciences, 123
Stefanek, Anton, 60 n. 3, 153
Stefanov, Ivan, 30
Stepin, Vyacheslav, 151
Stevenson, Svetlana, 150
Stratification, 12; Belarus, 21; Czech Republic, 58; Hungary, 80; Russia, 147–48
Stray Path Not Accepted, A, 142
Strmiska, Zdenek, 50
Structural functionalism, 11, 112

Studentska Zalozba Cf, 168
Studia Humanitatis, 168
Studia Socjologiczne, 119, 178
Suchy, Cestmir, 54
Sulek, Antoni, 130
Svitak, Ivan, 50
Symbolic analytic capital, 104
Symbolic interactionism, 12
Szacki, Jerzy, 51, 118, 127
Szalai, Erzsebet, 84
Szazadveg, 76
Szelinyi, Ivan, 10, 13, 73, 80, 81, 83, 84
Szociologiai Szemle, 76, 77–85
Szomolanyi, Sona, 154
Szonda-Ipsos, 74
Sztompka, Piotr, 13, 128, 131 n.2

Taljunaite, Meilute, 103
Tamas, Pal, 39, 78
Tarasenko, Valentyn, 177
Tarde, Gabriel, 178
Tardos, Robert, 80
TARKI, 79, 85
Tarsadalomkutatas, 76
Tarsadalomkutatasi Intezet (TARKI), 74
Taseva, Marija, 110
Taylor Nelson Sofres, 90
Technical University of Tallinn, 65
Tendencies in the Development of Ukrainian Society 1994–1998, 181
Teorija in Praksa, 169
Thatcher, Margaret, 52
Theory of communicative action, 78
Thessaloniki University, 137
Third way, 60 n.2, 109
Third Yugoslavia, 188
Tiffin University, 137–38
Tikhonova, Natalya, 148
Tisenkopfs, Talis, 92
Titma, Mikk, 64, 67
Tocqueville, Alexis, 51
Tonisson, Ilmar, 62
Tooding, Liina-Mai, 64, 72 n.2
Touraine, Alain, 192
Trames: A Journal of the Humanities and Social Sciences, 65–66

Trans European Mobility Program for University Students (TEMPUS), 26, 113, 137–38, 139 n.1, 160
Transformation of the transformation, 37
Transition and Reconstruction of Societies, 112
Transparency International, 124
Treci program Radio Beograda, 196 n.6
Trnava, University, 157, 158
Tucek, Milan, 58
Tureikyte, Danute, 100
Turner, Jonathan, 120, 180
Turza, Karel, 18

Uj Mandatum, 77
Ukraina: aspecty pratsi, 176
Ukraine, 2, 3, 4, 8, 175
Ukrainian Sociological Association, 176, 178, 185
Ukrainian Sociological Review 1998–1999, 176
Ukrainian sociology, 175; areas of research, 181–83; under Communist influence, 175–76; decade of firsts, 185; funding and finances, 178–79, 184; institutional development, 176–79, 181; international collaboration and contacts, 25, 177, 178, 179, 180, 184–85; journals, 176, 178; methodology, 181; teaching of sociology, 177–78
Ukrainske suspilstvo: monitiryng 1994–1998, 182
Ukrainske suspilstvo na porozi: tretjogo tysiacholittia, 181
Ukrainsky ogliadach, 178
Umea University, 137
UNESCO, 36, 95, 160, 162
Union of Democratic Forces, 38
Union of Scientists of Bulgaria, 34
United Nations, 4, 5, 6, 179; Children's Fund, 138; Security Council, 5
United Nations Development Program, 34, 36, 90
United Nations Human Development National Reports, 66

United States Agency for International Development, 34, 138, 179
United States Information Agency, 21
University for National and Global Economy, 31, 32
University of Agriculture (Latvia), 88
University of Arizona, 113
University of Barcelona, 137
University of Belgrade, 193
University of Bialystok, 26
University of Bucharest, 134, 135, 136
University of Debrecen, 74
University of Dnipropetrovsk, 177
University of Godollo, 74
University of Kaunas, 97
University of Kharkov, 177
University of Kiev, 177
University of Latvia, 88, 89
University of Lincolnshire and Humberside, 26
University of Ljubljana, 166
University of Lodz, 121
University of Lund, 32
University of Lutsk, 177
University of Lviv, 177
University of Malaga, 26
University of Maribor, 167
University of Matej Bel, 157
University of Michigan, 144
University of Miskolc, 74
University of Nanterre, 26
University of Odessa, 177
University of Osijek, 42
University of Paris III, 26
University of Pavol Jozef Safarik, 157
University of Pecs, 74
University of Pristina, 191
University of Provance, 26
University of Rijeka, 42, 43
University of Skopje, 108
University of Split, 42, 43
University of St. Petersburg, 143
University of Stendal, 26
University of Szeged, 74
University of Tartu, 62, 63, 64, 67, 68, 72 n.1
University of Wroclaw, 121

University of Zagreb, 42, 43, 46
Urbicide, 195 n.3
Uzdila, Juozas V., 104

Value-free sociology, 58
Vander Zanden, James W., 178
Vavrousek, Josef, 60 n.2, n.3
Veblen, Thorstein, 56
Vecerka, Kazimir, 57
Velvet revolution, 52, 57
Vendov, Ahthoni, 37
Versailles Treaty, 107
Vetik, Raivo, 67, 72 n.1
Vienna Centre for Research and Documentation, 36
Vihalemm, Peeter, 67, 72 n.1
Vikerkaar, 66
Vilmorus, 100
Vilnius Pedagogical University, 100, 101
Vilnius University, 98, 100, 101
Vlachova, Klara, 55
Volkov, Vadim, 14
Volovych, Volodymyr, 177
Von Hayek, Friedrich, 53
Voormann, Rein, 72 n.1
Voronkov, Victor, 14
Vujovic, Sreten 195 n.3
Vuletic, Vladimir, 190
Vytautas Magnus University, 100, 101

Wallerstein, Immanuel, 145
War: in Kosovo, 6; in Yugoslavia, 4–7
Warsaw Pact, 3, 7, 50
Warsaw School for Social Psychology, 120
Warsaw University, 121, 123, 162
Weber, Max, 62, 78, 112, 133, 145, 146, 149, 190
Weberian thesis, 194
Welfare state, 52
Wesolowski, Wlodzimierz, 128
Wessely, Anna, 78
Western science networks, 86
Western sociology, 17, 89, 130, 151, 154, 178, 180
Wiez, 126

Winclawski, Wlodzimierz, 127
World Bank, 90, 138, 179
World Congresses of Sociology, 12, 13, 29, 128, 145
World Development Report, 182
World Sociology, 104, 177
World Values Survey, 95
World War II, 3, 8, 97, 107, 108, 117, 137, 165
Woroniecka, Grazyna, 126

Yadov, Vladimir, 13, 141, 143, 148
Yakuba, Olena, 177, 182
Yaskevich, Sergei, 23
Yeltsin, Boris, 4
Yevtukh, Volodymyr, 183
Yugoslav Federation, 2, 5, 6
Yugoslav Sociological Association, 11, 190, 196 n.7, 197 n.9
Yugoslav sociology, 9, 107–8, 187; areas of research, 194; under Communism, 1, 189; decommunization and de-Marxization, 189–91; funding and finances, 191–93; international contacts and collaboration, 192; journals and publishing houses, 188–89; role in society, 195; teaching of sociology, 191–92
Yugoslavia, 2, 3, 5, 187–88, 195 n.2; UN sanctions, 5, 6, 196 n.7; war, 4–7, 137

Zagreb University, 113
Zamfir Catalin, 134
Zaslavskaya, Tatyana, 141, 148
Zdenek Suda, 59
Zdravomyslov, Andrej, 141
Zdravomyslova, Elena, 13, 14
Zeman, Milos, 60 n.2
Zerkalo, 21
Zietschrift fuer Soziologie, 14
Znaniecki, Florian, 180
Znanstveno in Publicisticno Sredisce, 168
Zycie, 118

About the Editors and Contributors

EDITORS

MIKE FORREST KEEN (mkeen@iusb.edu) is Professor of Sociology at Indiana University South Bend. His most recent book is *Stalking the Sociological Imagination: J. Edgar Hoover's FBI Surveillance of American Sociology.* He has served as Chair of the American Sociological Association's section on the History of Sociology.

JANUSZ L. MUCHA (janusz.mucha@umk.pl) is Professor of Sociology and Head of the Cultural Studies Section of the Institute of Sociology at Nicolaus Copernicus University in Torun, Poland, and Professor at the Warsaw School for Social Psychology. His most recent book is *Dominant Culture as a Foreign Culture.*

CONTRIBUTORS

ILIE BADESCU (badescu@pcnet.ro) is Professor of the Faculty of Sociology and Social Work, and Chair of the Department of Sociology at the University of Bucharest. He has served as Chair of the Romanian Sociological Association. His latest book is *System of Noological Sociology.*

RADU BALTASIU (rtb@pcnet.ro) is Lecturer at the Faculty of Sociology and Social Work at the University of Bucharest. He is also working with the Romanian Ministry of Education. His last book, written with Ilie Badescu and Dan Dungaciu, is *History of Sociology.*

BOHUMIL BUZIK (su103@klemens.savba.sk) is Research Fellow at the Sociological Institute of the Slovak Academy of Sciences, and Scientific Secretary of the Slovak Sociological Association. He is the coauthor of two books, *Basic Sociology*, and *Theories of Social Stratification and Mobility*.

OGNJEN CALDAROVIC (ocaldaro@ffzg.hr) is Professor of Sociology at Zagreb University, Croatia. His most recent book is *How to Live with Technical Risks?*

MIKHAIL CHERNYSH (mfche@online.ru) is Senior Researcher at the Russian Academy of Sciences and Head of Research of its Institute of Sociology. Since 1991, he has been Principle Investigator for the project "Social Mobility and its Consequences in a Changing Society."

VYARA GANCHEVA (ganchevav@hotmail.com) is Associate Professor of the Institute of Sociology of the Bulgarian Academy of Sciences, and Lecturer at the Faculty of Journalism and Mass Communication at Sofia University. Her most recent article is "Social Sciences in a Changing Environment." She is a member of the Bulgarian Sociological Association and of the Union of Scientists in Bulgaria.

PETRE GEORGIEVSKI (petgeorg@ukim.edu.mk) is Professor of Sociological Methodology and Sociology of Education, and Chairperson of the Institute of Sociology of the Faculty of Philosophy at Cyril and Methodius University in Skopje, Macedonia. His most recent book is *Sociology of Education: Sociological Methodology and Methodological Approach in the Work of J. Obrembski and B. Arsov.*

MILEVA GUROVSKA (Milevag@soros.org.mk) is Associate Professor of the Institute of Sociology of the Faculty of Philosophy at Cyril and Methodius University. Her most recent book is *Sociology of Women's Work*. She is also a member of the *Assotiation Internationale des Sociologistes de Langues Francais* (AISLF).

MIKKO LAGERSPETZ (mikko@ehi.ee) is Professor of Sociology at the Estonian Institute of Humanities in Tallinn, President of the Estonian Association of Sociologists, and Docent at the University of Turku. His recent publications include "From 'Parallel *Polis*' to 'The Time of the Tribes:' Post-Socialism, Social Self-Organization and Post-Modernity," and "Consolidation as Hegemonization: The Case of Estonia."

EVA LAIFEROVA (eva.laiferova@fphil.uniba.sk) is an Assistant Lecturer and the Chairperson of the Department of Sociology at Comenius University in Bratislava, Slovak Republic. Her most recent article is "Reflections of Nationalism in Slovak Christian Sociology until 1948." She was a member of the Executive Committee of the Slovak Sociological Association for several years.

FRANC MALI (franc.mali@uni-lj.si) is Assistant Professor of Sociology of Science at the University of Ljubljana, Slovenia. He recently published, "Obstacles in Developing University, Government and Industry Links: The Case of Slovenia." He is a member of the Coordinating Committee of the Sociology of Science and Technology Research Network (SSTNET) of the European Sociological Association.

VALERY MANSUROV (mansurov@isras.ru) is Professor of Sociology, Head of the Survey Research Center of the Institute of Sociology of the Russian Academy of Sciences, Chairperson of a Chair of Applied Sociology at the State University of Humanitarian Sciences, and Visiting Professor of De-Montfort University. His most recent publications are *Russian Sociology Today,* and *Russia Today: A Sociological Outlook.* He has also served as President of the Russian Society of Sociologists.

DENES NEMEDI (nem9096@ella.hu) is Professor at the Institute of Sociology at Eotvos University in Budapest, Hungary. He is interested in the history and theory of sociology and public discourse analysis. He has published on German critical theory, French classical sociology, and discursive practices in the Hungarian public sphere.

MILOSLAV PETRUSEK (Mpetrusek@seznam.cz) is Professor of Sociology of the Faculty of Social Sciences at Charles University in Prague, and a Fellow of the Russian Academy of Social Sciences. He has served as both Vice-Chairman and Chairman of the Czech Masaryk Sociological Association. He is the author of several books including *Teorie a metoda v moderni sociologii.*

IRIS PETTAI (iris.pettai@neti.ee) is the Head of the Department of Sociological Studies of the Estonian Institute for Open Society Research. Her current research projects are social stratification, social mobility, development of ethnic relations in Estonia, financial behavior of the population, and adjustment to a market economy. She is a member of the Estonian Association of Sociologists.

NATALIYA POHORILA (pohorila@ukma.kiev.ua) is Associate Professor in the Department of Sociology at the National University Kyiv Mohyla Academy, and Research Assistant for the Kiev International Institute of Sociology. She recently served as Guest Editor for two special issues of the *International Journal of Sociology* entitled "Social Problems in Post-Communist Ukraine."

PETER ROBERT (robert@tarki.hu) is Associate Professor at the Department of Sociology at the ELTE University, Budapest. He is also a Senior Researcher at the Social Research Center (TARKI). He has published in *European Sociological Review, International Review of Sociology, Hungarian Review of Sociology,* and the *Hungarian Statistical Review.*

WANDA RUSETSKAYA is Professor of Sociology and the Head of the Department of Sociology of Culture at the Institute of Sociology of the National Academy of Science of Belarus. Her most recent article is "Specifica Identyfikacji Etniczno-Narodowosciowej Mieszkancow Pogranicza Bialorusko-Polskiego" (with Lilia P. Kunowska).

AIVARS TABUNS (atabuns@lza.lv) is Associate Professor of Sociology and Chairperson of the Faculty of Social Science at the University of Latvia. He is a Corresponding Member of the Latvian Academy of Sciences, and Member of the UNESCO Latvian National Commission. His most recent book is *National, State and Regime Identities in Latvia.*

OLGA TERESCHENKO (Olga@teresch.belpak.minsk.by) is Associate Professor of Sociology and Chairperson of the Department of Social Communication at Belarusian State University. Her most recent article is "Social Differentiation of the Young Generation in Post-Soviet Belarus."

KAREL TURZA (radiobg3@rts.co.yu) is Editor-in-chief of the Third Program of Radio Belgrade and President of the Yugoslav Sociological Association. He is author of *Who Needs Sociology?: Modernity on a Bicycle,* and *Lewis Mumford: A Critique of Modernity.*

ANELE VOSYLIUTE (vosylan@ktl.mii.lt) is Senior Social Researcher at the Lithuanian Institute of Philosophy and Sociology. Her most recent articles are "Analysis of the Problems of the Development of Sociology," and "Women and Consumption."